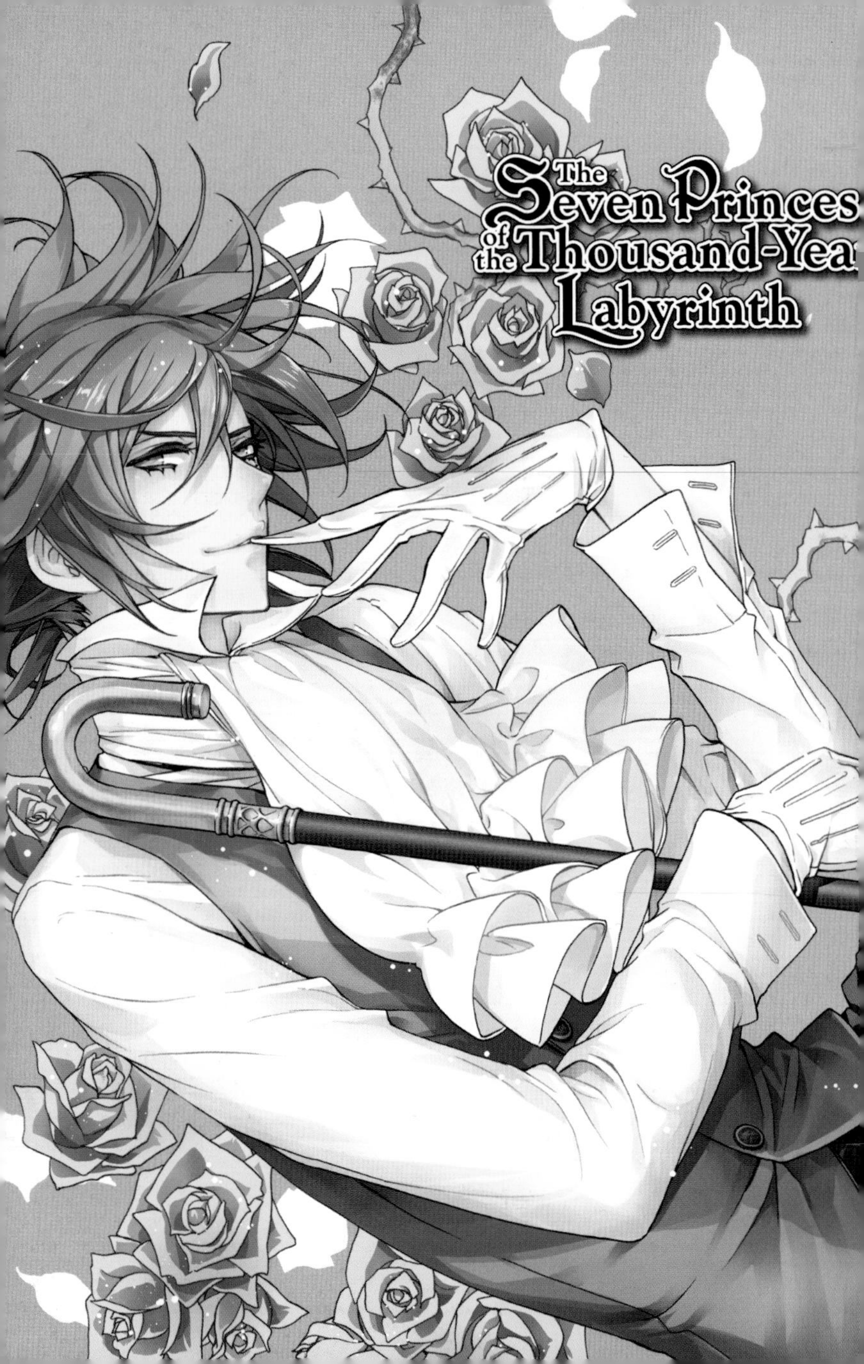
The Seven Princes of the Thousand-Yea
Labyrinth

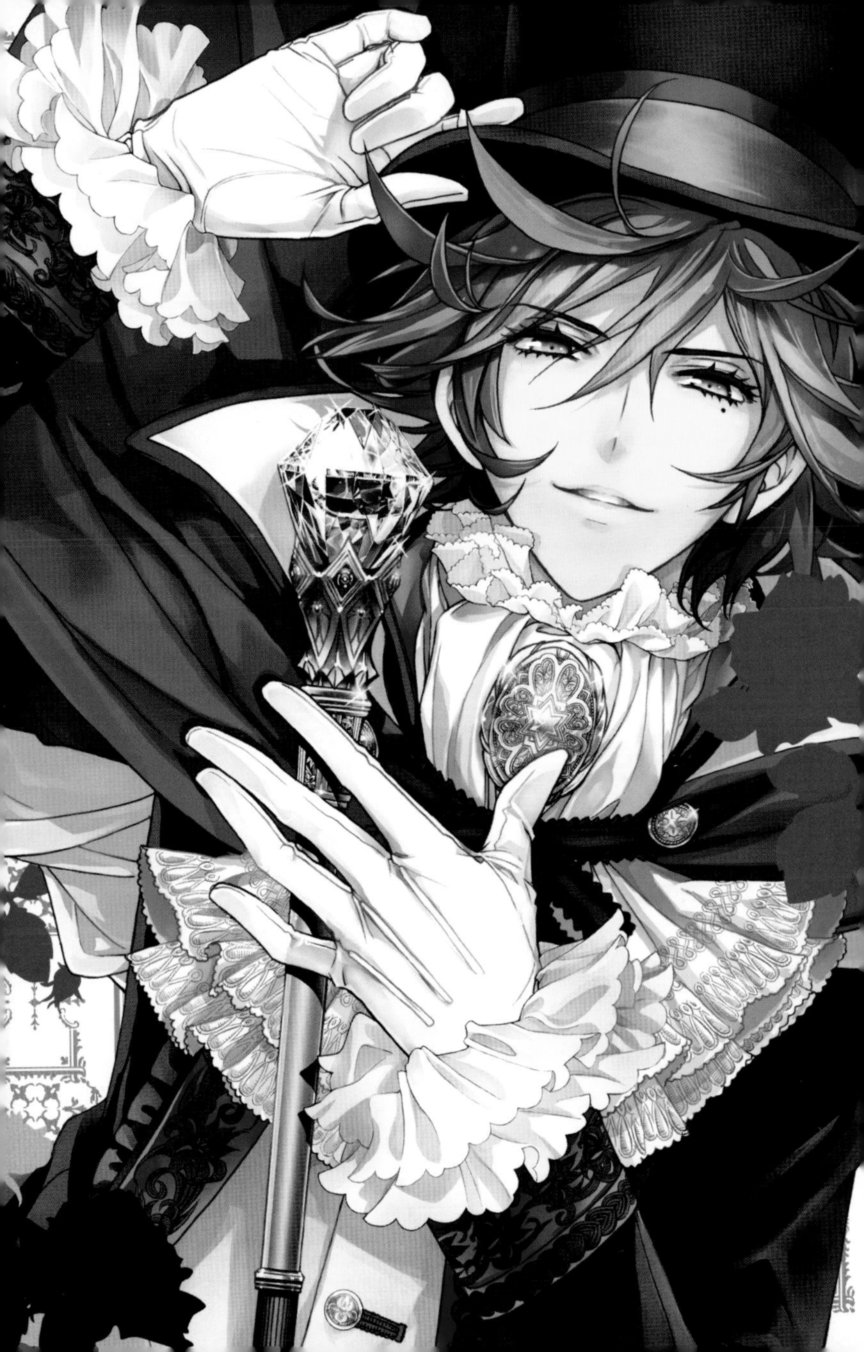

The Seven Princes of the Thousand-Year Labyrinth

Volume 3

Presented by
Atori Haruno
and
Aikawa Yu

SEVEN SEAS ENTERTAINMENT PRESENTS

The Seven Princes of the Thousand-Year Labyrinth

story and art by **ATORI HARUNO** and **AIKAWA YU** volume 3

TRANSLATION
Beni Axia Conrad

ADAPTATION
Ysabet MacFarlane

LETTERING AND RETOUCH
CK Russell

LOGO DESIGN
Courtney Williams

COVER DESIGN
Nicky Lim

PROOFREADER
Shanti Whitesides
Danielle King

ASSISTANT EDITOR
Jenn Grunigen

PRODUCTION MANAGER
Lissa Pattillo

EDITOR-IN-CHIEF
Adam Arnold

PUBLISHER
Jason DeAngelis

First published in Japan in 2015 by ICHIJINSHA Inc., Tokyo.
English translation rights arranged with ICHIJINSHA Inc., Tokyo, Japan.

ISBN: 978-1-626925-06-9

Printed in Canada

First Printing: July 2017

10 9 8 7 6 5 4 3 2 1

FOLLOW US ONLINE: ***www.gomanga.com***

READING DIRECTIONS

This book reads from ***right to left***, Japanese style. If this is your first time reading manga, you start reading from the top right panel on each page and take it from there. If you get lost, just follow the numbered diagram here. It may seem backwards at first, but you'll get the hang of it! Have fun!!

1
2
3
4
5
6
7
8
9

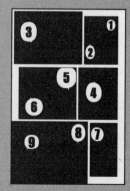

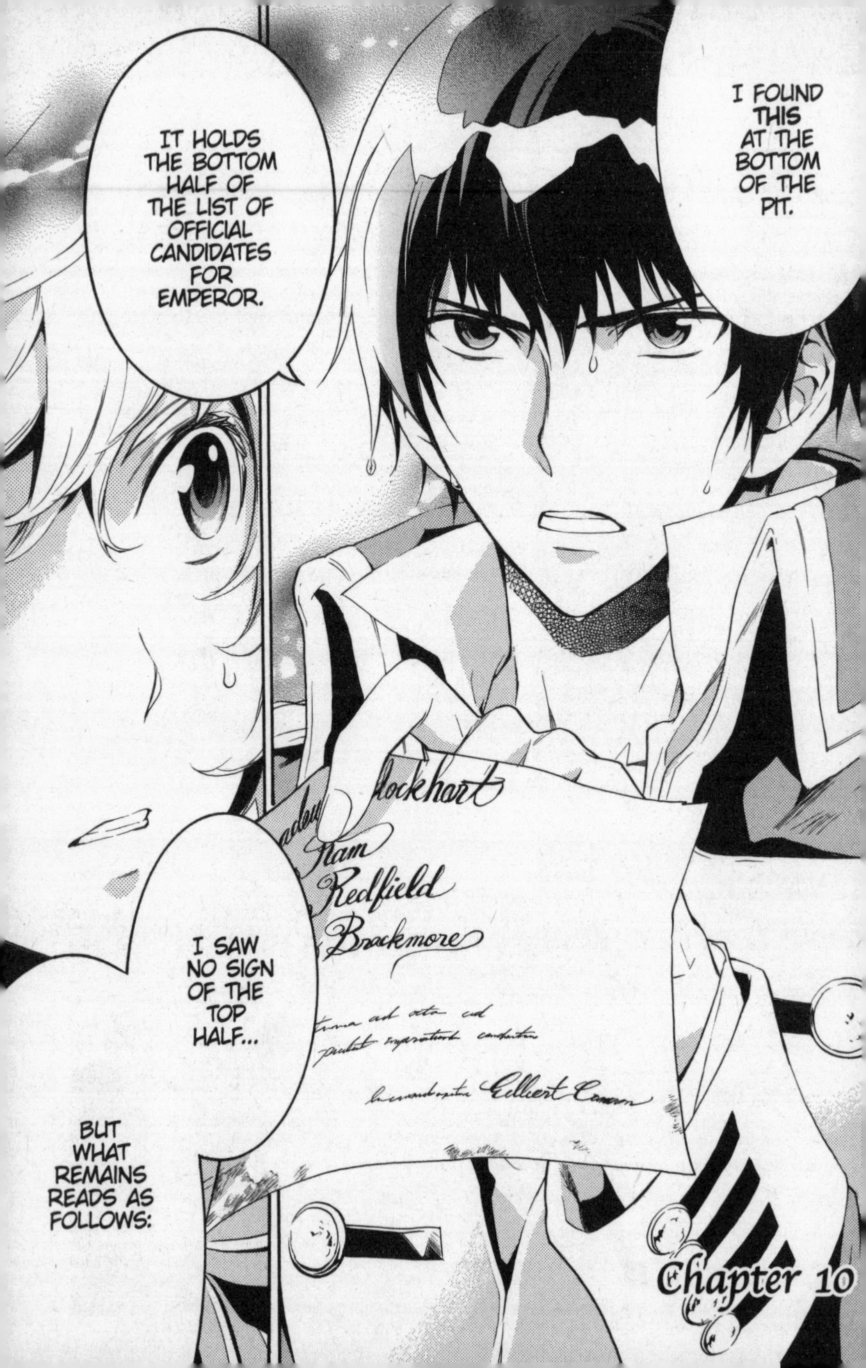
I FOUND THIS AT THE BOTTOM OF THE PIT.
IT HOLDS THE BOTTOM HALF OF THE LIST OF OFFICIAL CANDIDATES FOR EMPEROR.
Redfield
Brackmore
I SAW NO SIGN OF THE TOP HALF...
BUT WHAT REMAINS READS AS FOLLOWS:
Chapter 10

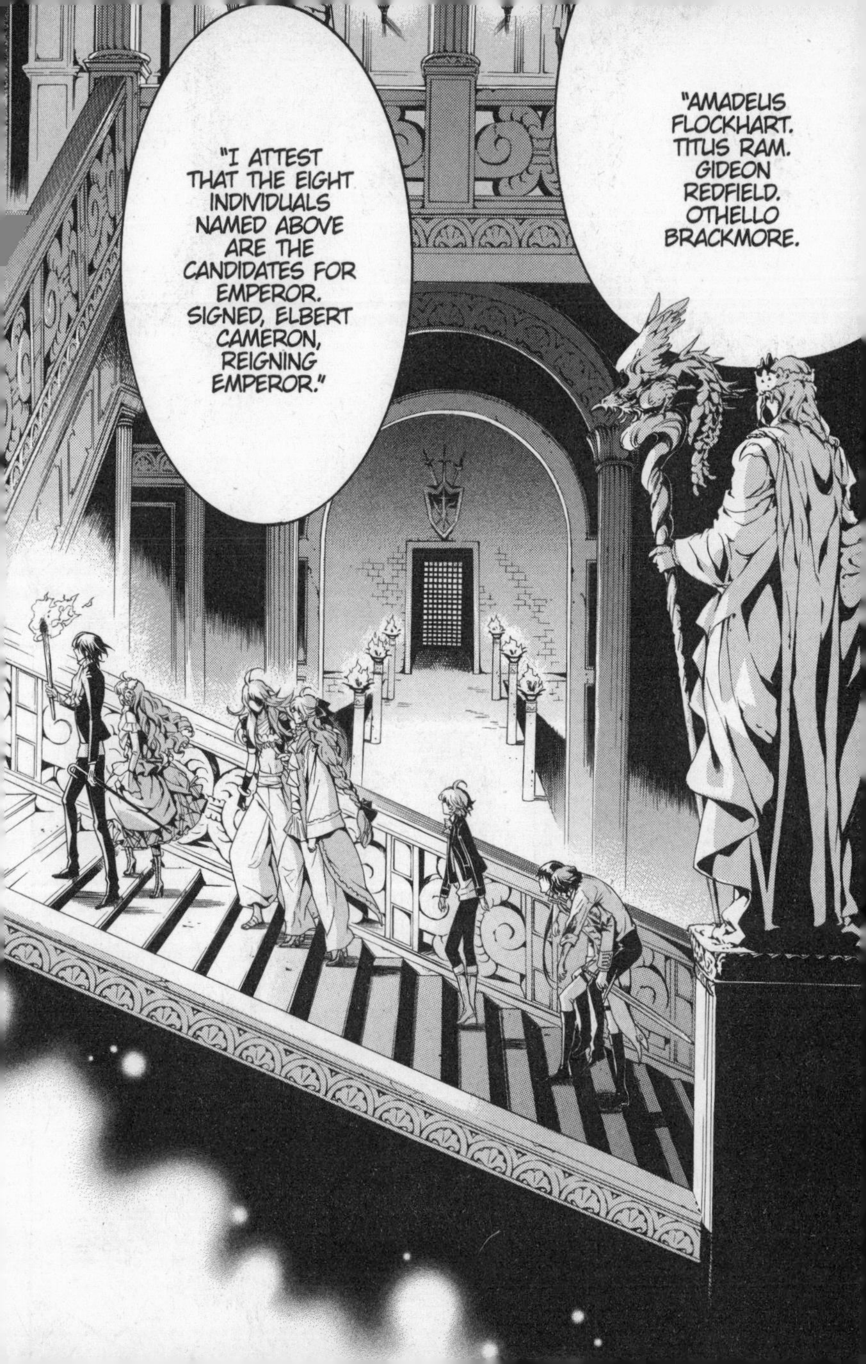
"AMADEUS FLOCKHART. TITUS RAM. GIDEON REDFIELD. OTHELLO BRACKMORE.
"I ATTEST THAT THE EIGHT INDIVIDUALS NAMED ABOVE ARE THE CANDIDATES FOR EMPEROR. SIGNED, ELBERT CAMERON, REIGNING EMPEROR."

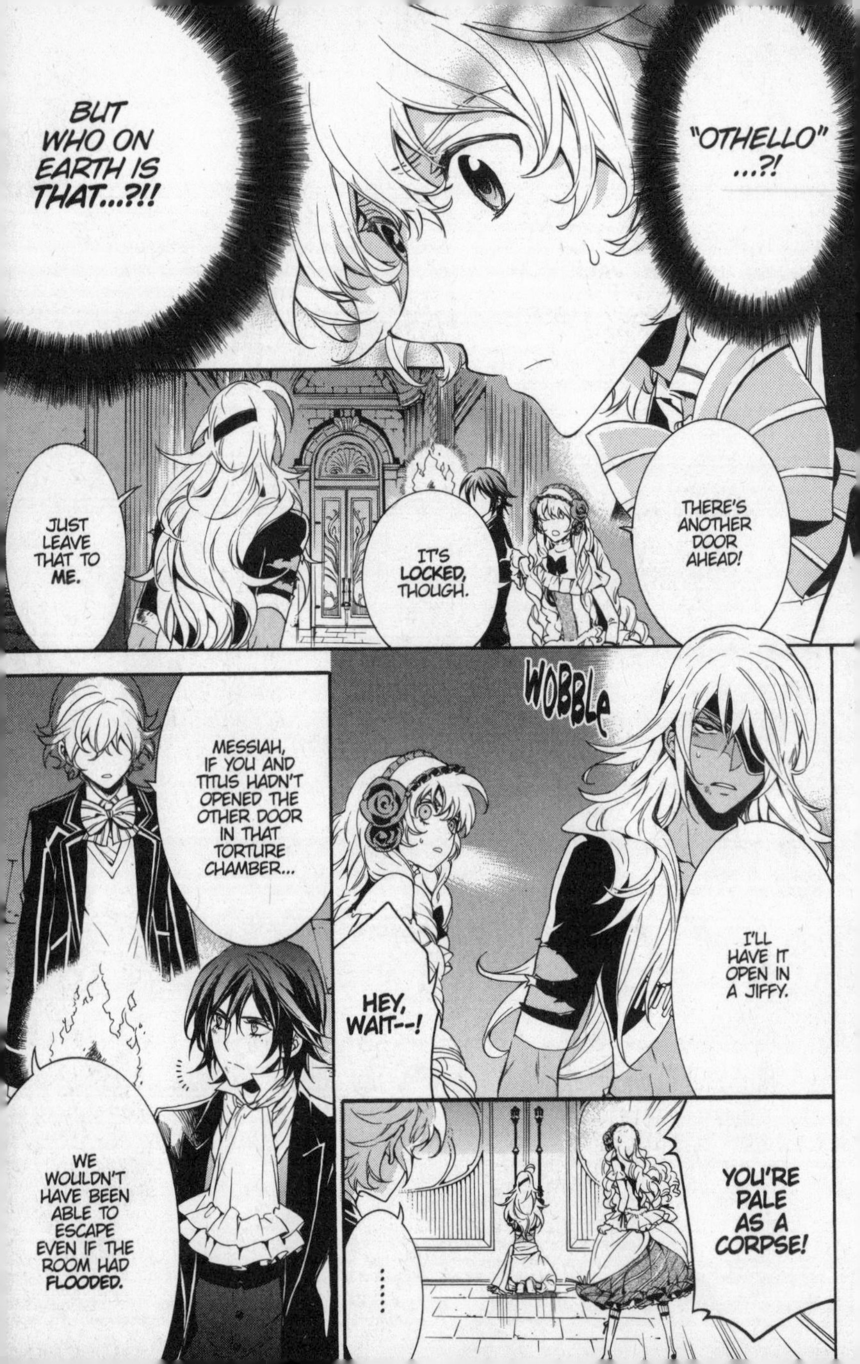
"OTHELLO" ...?!
BUT WHO ON EARTH IS THAT...?!!
THERE'S ANOTHER DOOR AHEAD!
IT'S LOCKED, THOUGH.
JUST LEAVE THAT TO ME.
WOBBLE
I'LL HAVE IT OPEN IN A JIFFY.
HEY, WAIT--!
YOU'RE PALE AS A CORPSE!
......
MESSIAH, IF YOU AND TITUS HADN'T OPENED THE OTHER DOOR IN THAT TORTURE CHAMBER...
WE WOULDN'T HAVE BEEN ABLE TO ESCAPE EVEN IF THE ROOM HAD FLOODED.

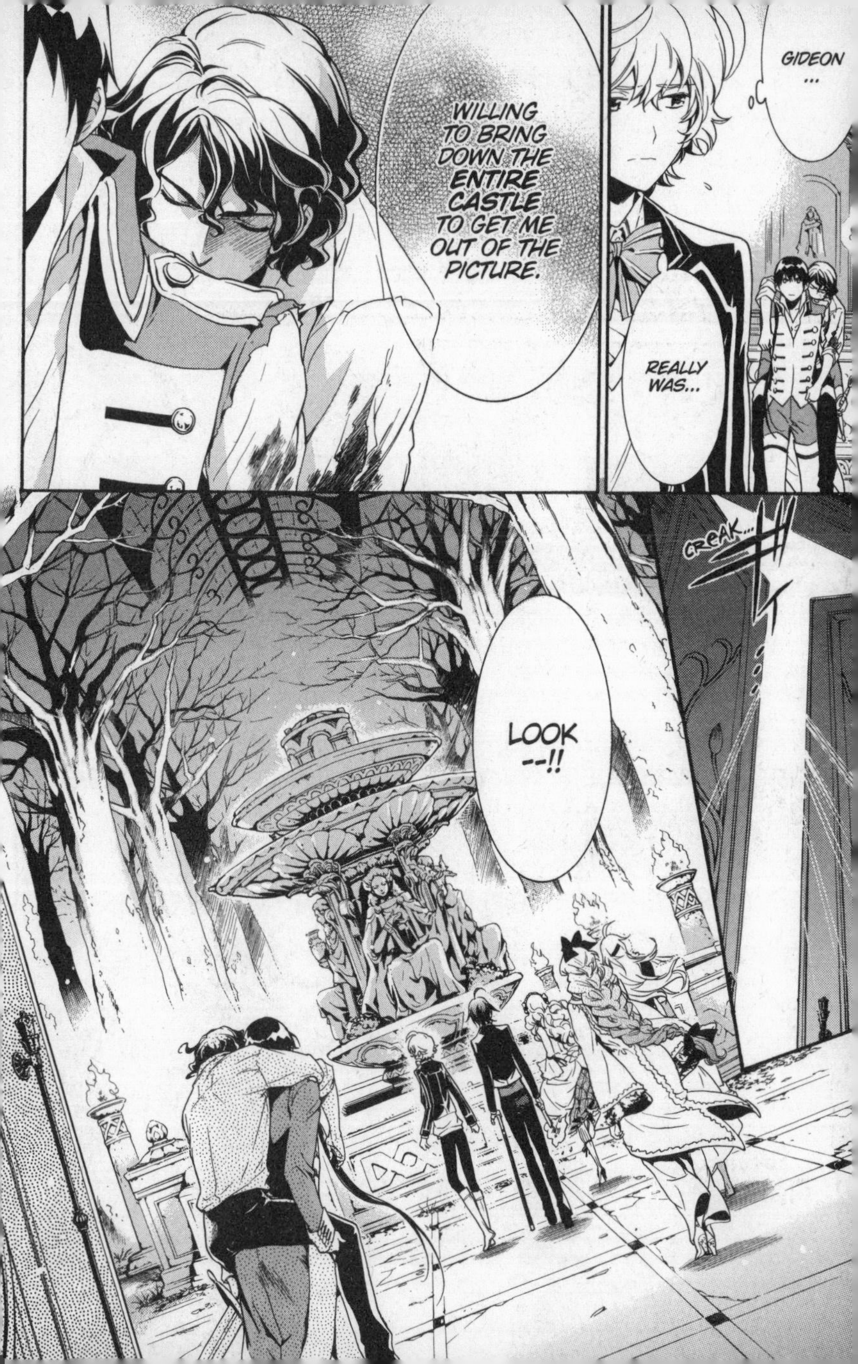
GIDEON ...
REALLY WAS...
WILLING TO BRING DOWN THE ENTIRE CASTLE TO GET ME OUT OF THE PICTURE.
CREAK...
LOOK --!!

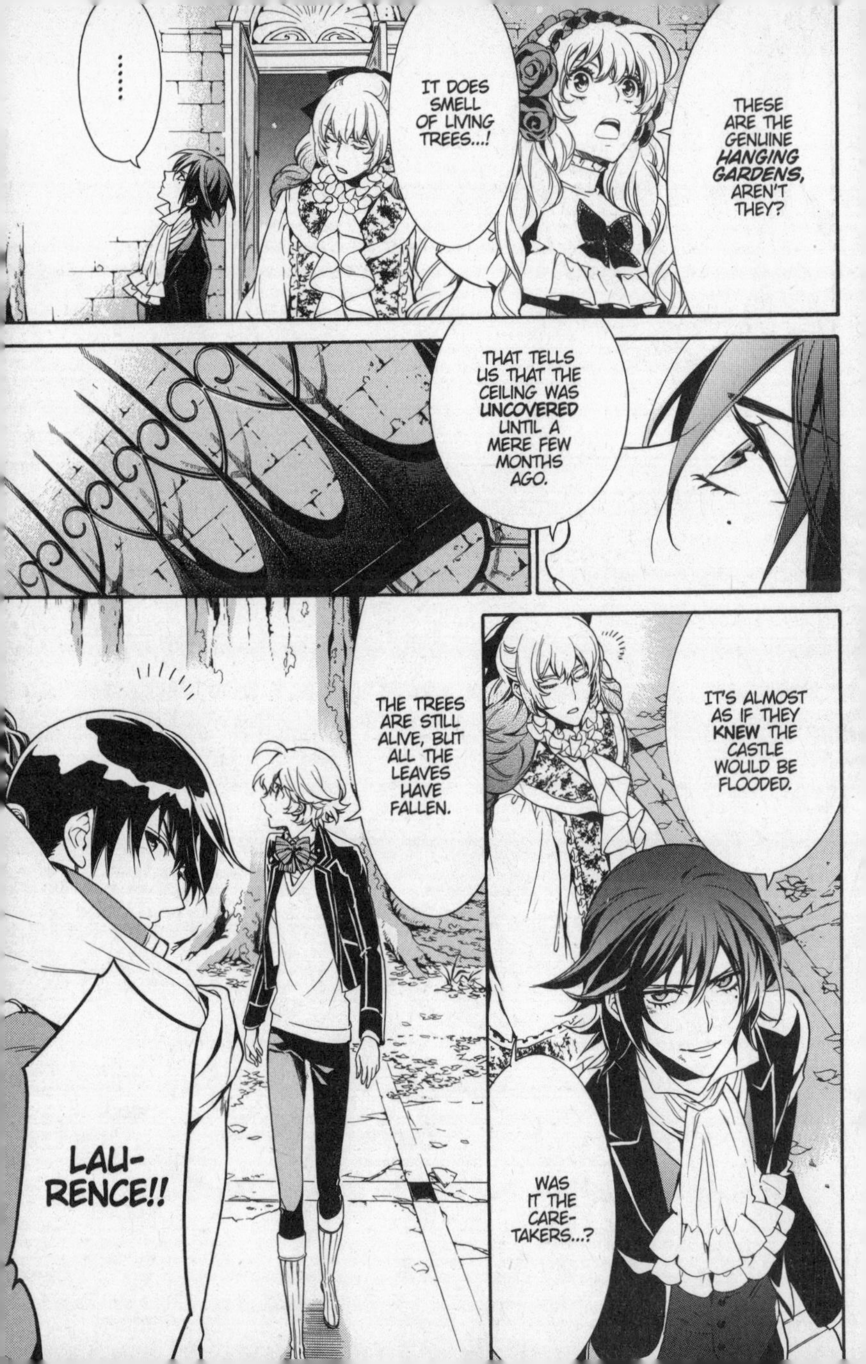
THESE ARE THE GENUINE *HANGING GARDENS*, AREN'T THEY?
IT DOES SMELL OF LIVING TREES...!
......
THAT TELLS US THAT THE CEILING WAS **UNCOVERED** UNTIL A MERE FEW MONTHS AGO.
IT'S ALMOST AS IF THEY **KNEW** THE CASTLE WOULD BE FLOODED.
WAS IT THE CARE-TAKERS...?
THE TREES ARE STILL ALIVE, BUT ALL THE LEAVES HAVE FALLEN.
LAU-RENCE!!

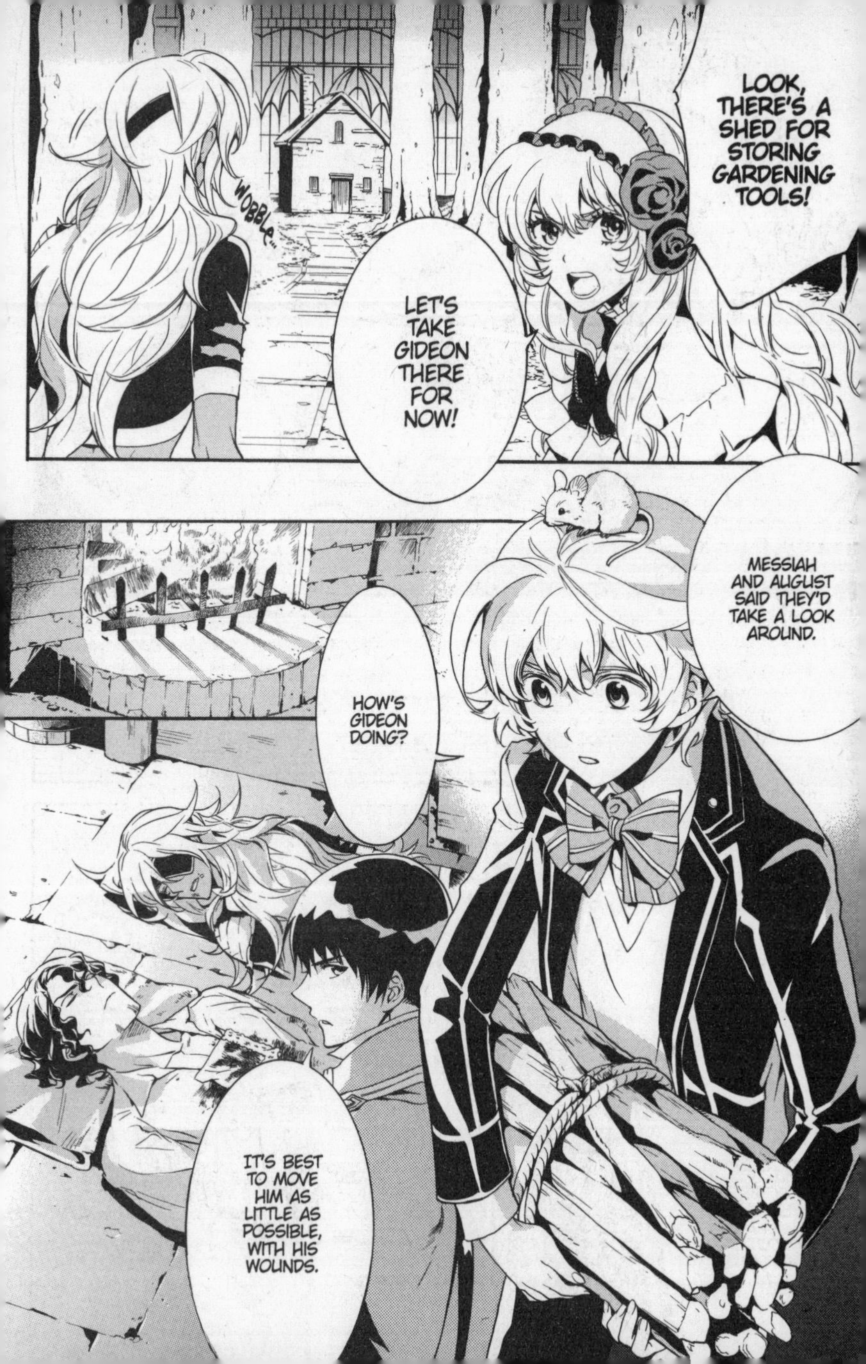
LOOK, THERE'S A SHED FOR STORING GARDENING TOOLS!
LET'S TAKE GIDEON THERE FOR NOW!
WOBBLE...
MESSIAH AND AUGUST SAID THEY'D TAKE A LOOK AROUND.
HOW'S GIDEON DOING?
IT'S BEST TO MOVE HIM AS LITTLE AS POSSIBLE, WITH HIS WOUNDS.

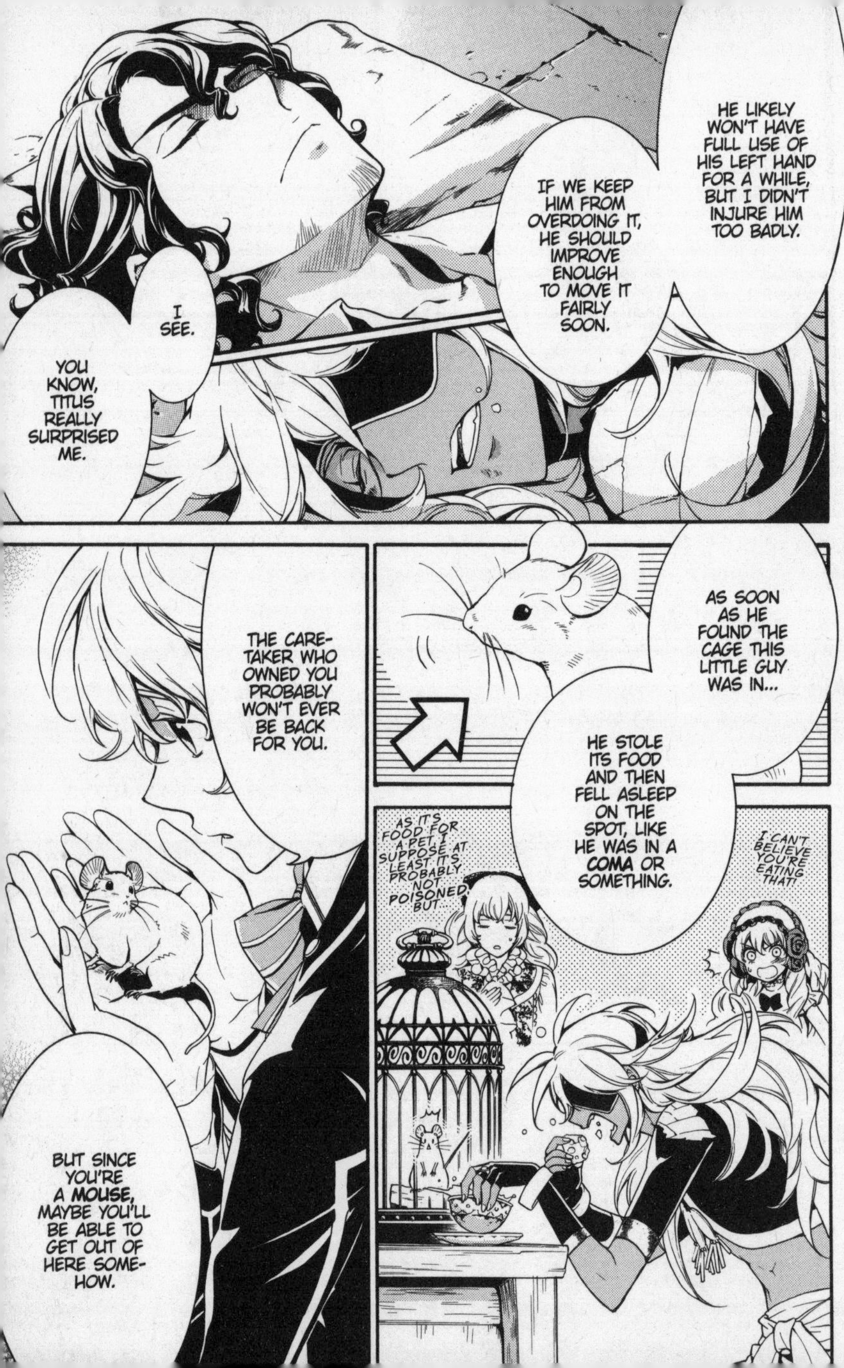
HE LIKELY WON'T HAVE FULL USE OF HIS LEFT HAND FOR A WHILE, BUT I DIDN'T INJURE HIM TOO BADLY.
IF WE KEEP HIM FROM OVERDOING IT, HE SHOULD IMPROVE ENOUGH TO MOVE IT FAIRLY SOON.
I SEE.
YOU KNOW, TITUS REALLY SURPRISED ME.
AS SOON AS HE FOUND THE CAGE THIS LITTLE GUY WAS IN...
HE STOLE ITS FOOD AND THEN FELL ASLEEP ON THE SPOT, LIKE HE WAS IN A **COMA** OR SOMETHING.
I CAN'T BELIEVE YOU'RE EATING THAT!
AS IT'S FOOD FOR A PET, I SUPPOSE AT LEAST IT'S PROBABLY NOT POISONED, BUT...
THE CARE-TAKER WHO OWNED YOU PROBABLY WON'T EVER BE BACK FOR YOU.
BUT SINCE YOU'RE A **MOUSE**, MAYBE YOU'LL BE ABLE TO GET OUT OF HERE SOME-HOW.

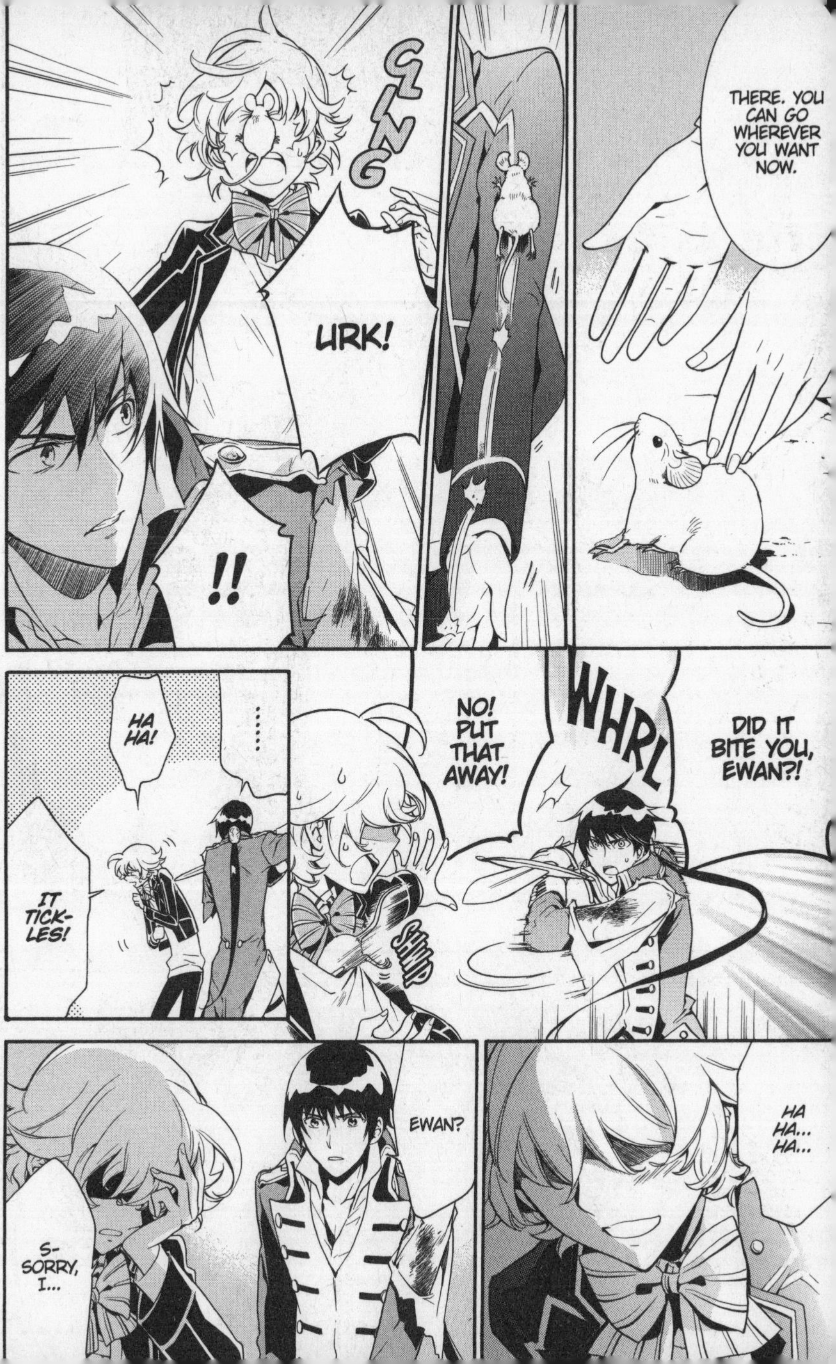
THERE. YOU CAN GO WHEREVER YOU WANT NOW.
GLING
URK!
!!
DID IT BITE YOU, EWAN?!
WHRL
NO! PUT THAT AWAY!
SHWIP
......
HA HA!
IT TICK-LES!
HA HA... HA...
EWAN?
S-SORRY, I...

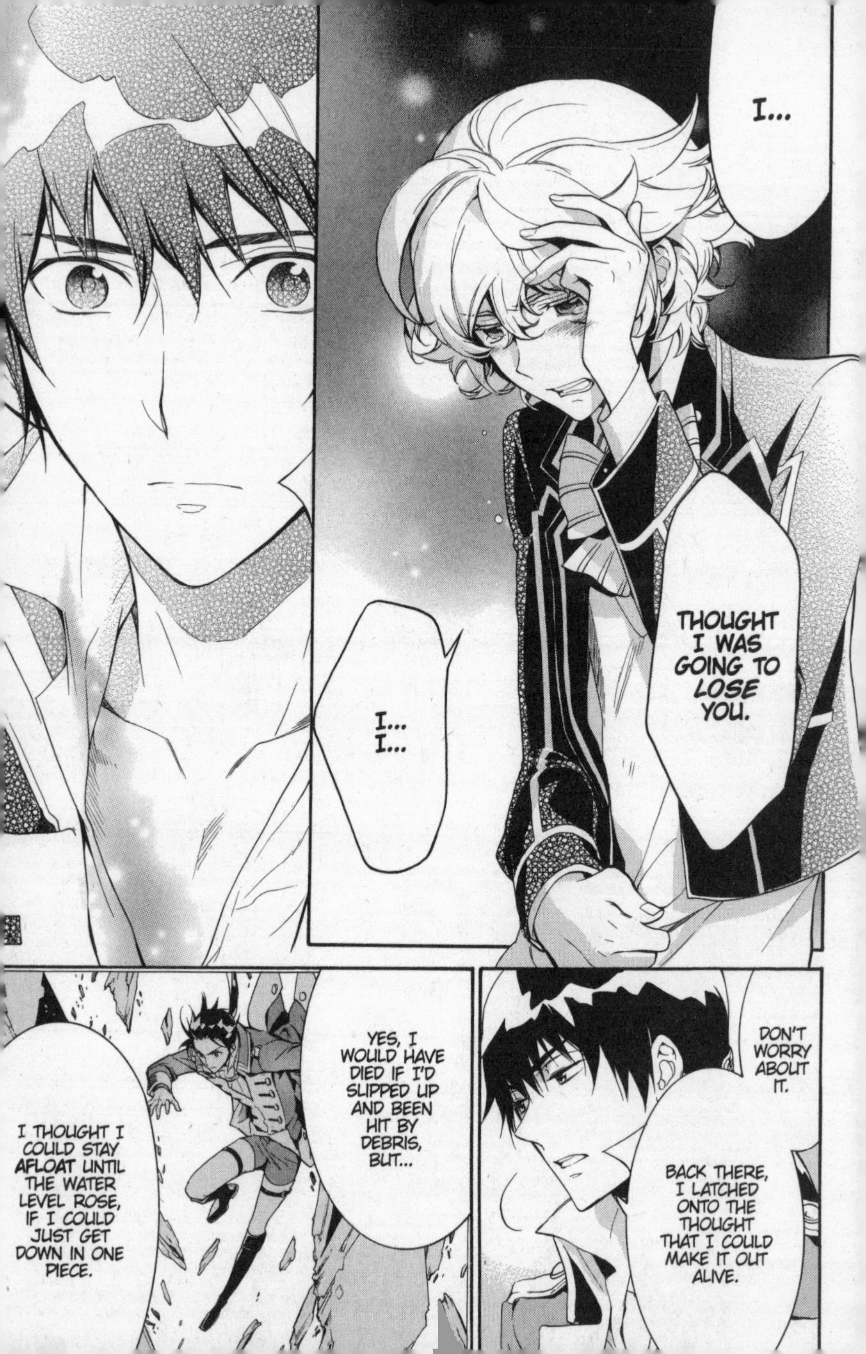
I...
THOUGHT I WAS GOING TO LOSE YOU.
I... I...
DON'T WORRY ABOUT IT.
BACK THERE, I LATCHED ONTO THE THOUGHT THAT I COULD MAKE IT OUT ALIVE.
YES, I WOULD HAVE DIED IF I'D SLIPPED UP AND BEEN HIT BY DEBRIS, BUT...
I THOUGHT I COULD STAY AFLOAT UNTIL THE WATER LEVEL ROSE, IF I COULD JUST GET DOWN IN ONE PIECE.

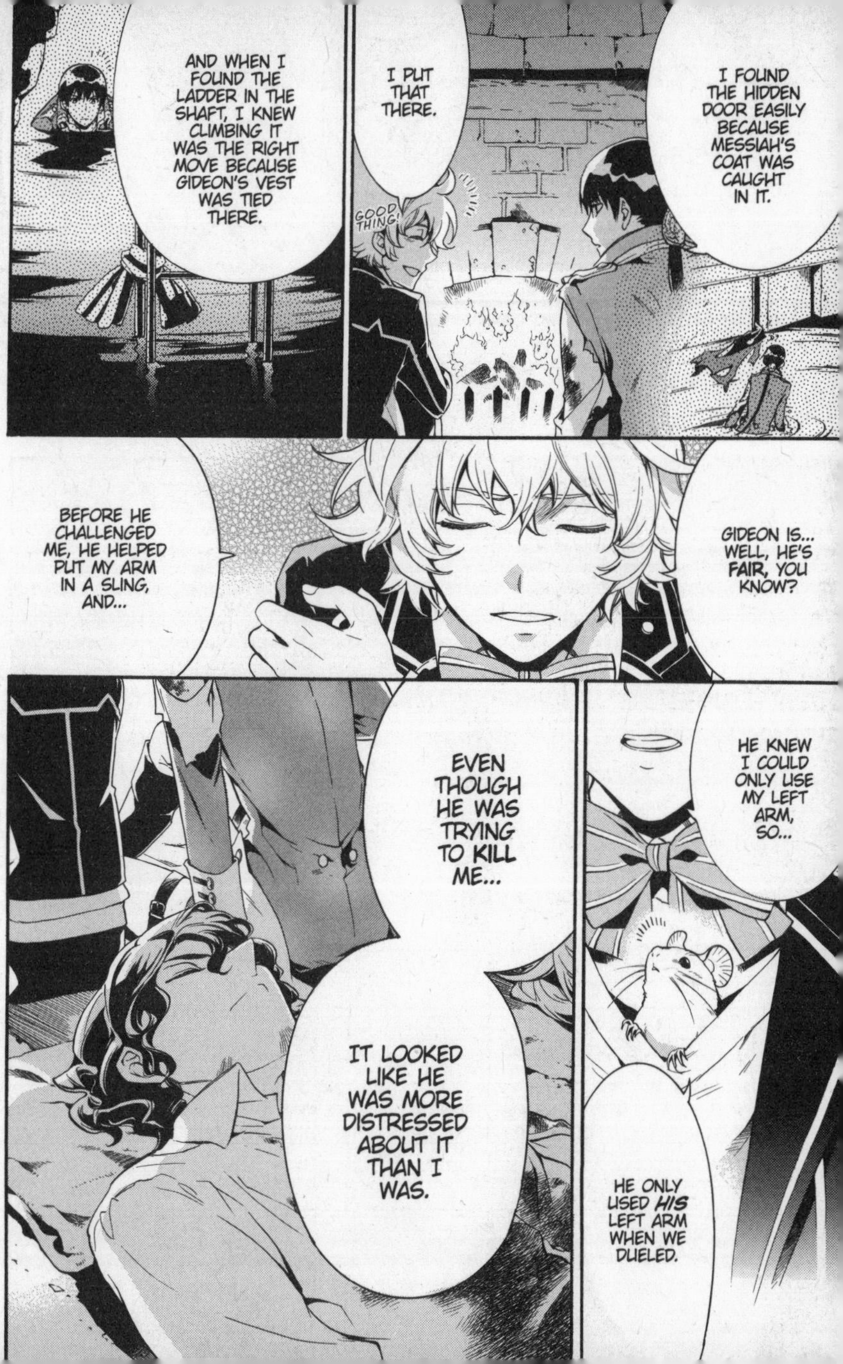
I FOUND THE HIDDEN DOOR EASILY BECAUSE MESSIAH'S COAT WAS CAUGHT IN IT.
I PUT THAT THERE.
GOOD THING!
AND WHEN I FOUND THE LADDER IN THE SHAFT, I KNEW CLIMBING IT WAS THE RIGHT MOVE BECAUSE GIDEON'S VEST WAS TIED THERE.
GIDEON IS... WELL, HE'S **FAIR**, YOU KNOW?
BEFORE HE CHALLENGED ME, HE HELPED PUT MY ARM IN A SLING, AND...
HE KNEW I COULD ONLY USE MY LEFT ARM, SO...
HE ONLY USED ***HIS*** LEFT ARM WHEN WE DUELED.
EVEN THOUGH HE WAS TRYING TO **KILL** ME...
IT LOOKED LIKE HE WAS MORE DISTRESSED ABOUT IT THAN I WAS.

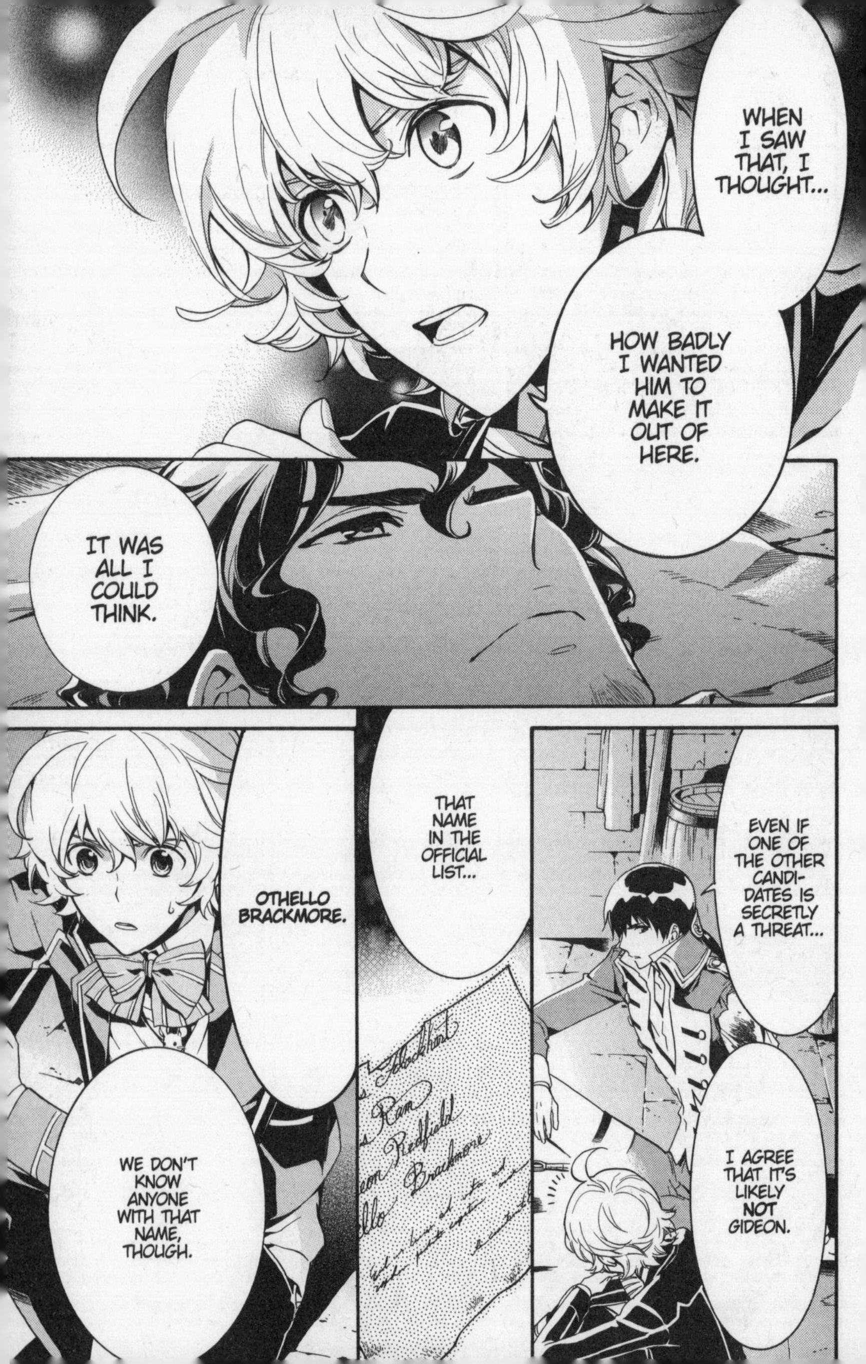
WHEN I SAW THAT, I THOUGHT...
HOW BADLY I WANTED HIM TO MAKE IT OUT OF HERE.
IT WAS ALL I COULD THINK.
EVEN IF ONE OF THE OTHER CANDIDATES IS SECRETLY A THREAT...
I AGREE THAT IT'S LIKELY NOT GIDEON.
THAT NAME IN THE OFFICIAL LIST...
OTHELLO BRACKMORE.
WE DON'T KNOW ANYONE WITH THAT NAME, THOUGH.

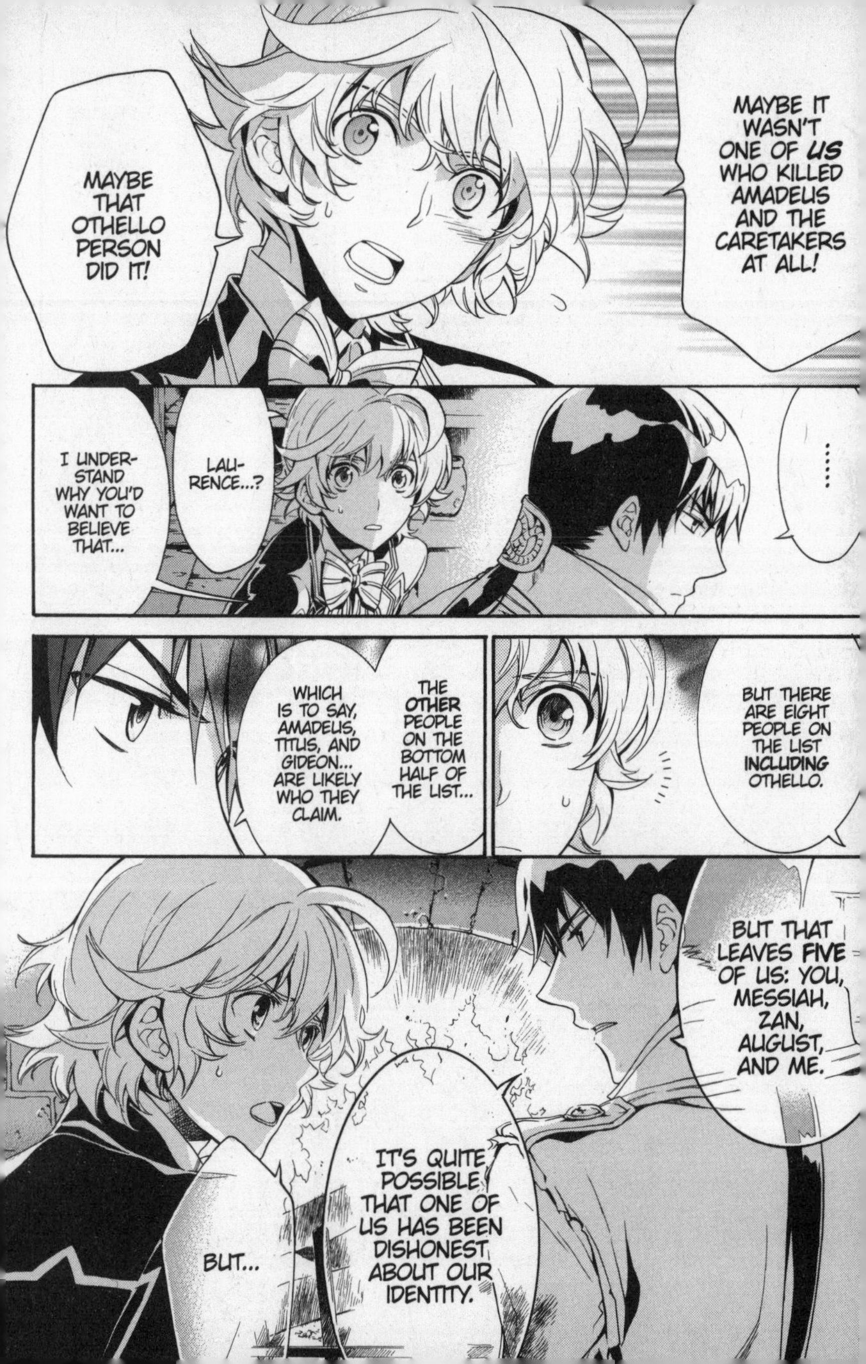

MAYBE IT WASN'T ONE OF US WHO KILLED AMADEUS AND THE CARETAKERS AT ALL!
MAYBE THAT OTHELLO PERSON DID IT!
......
LAURENCE...?
I UNDERSTAND WHY YOU'D WANT TO BELIEVE THAT...
BUT THERE ARE EIGHT PEOPLE ON THE LIST INCLUDING OTHELLO.
THE OTHER PEOPLE ON THE BOTTOM HALF OF THE LIST...
WHICH IS TO SAY, AMADEUS, TITUS, AND GIDEON... ARE LIKELY WHO THEY CLAIM.
BUT THAT LEAVES FIVE OF US: YOU, MESSIAH, ZAN, AUGUST, AND ME.
IT'S QUITE POSSIBLE THAT ONE OF US HAS BEEN DISHONEST ABOUT OUR IDENTITY.
BUT...

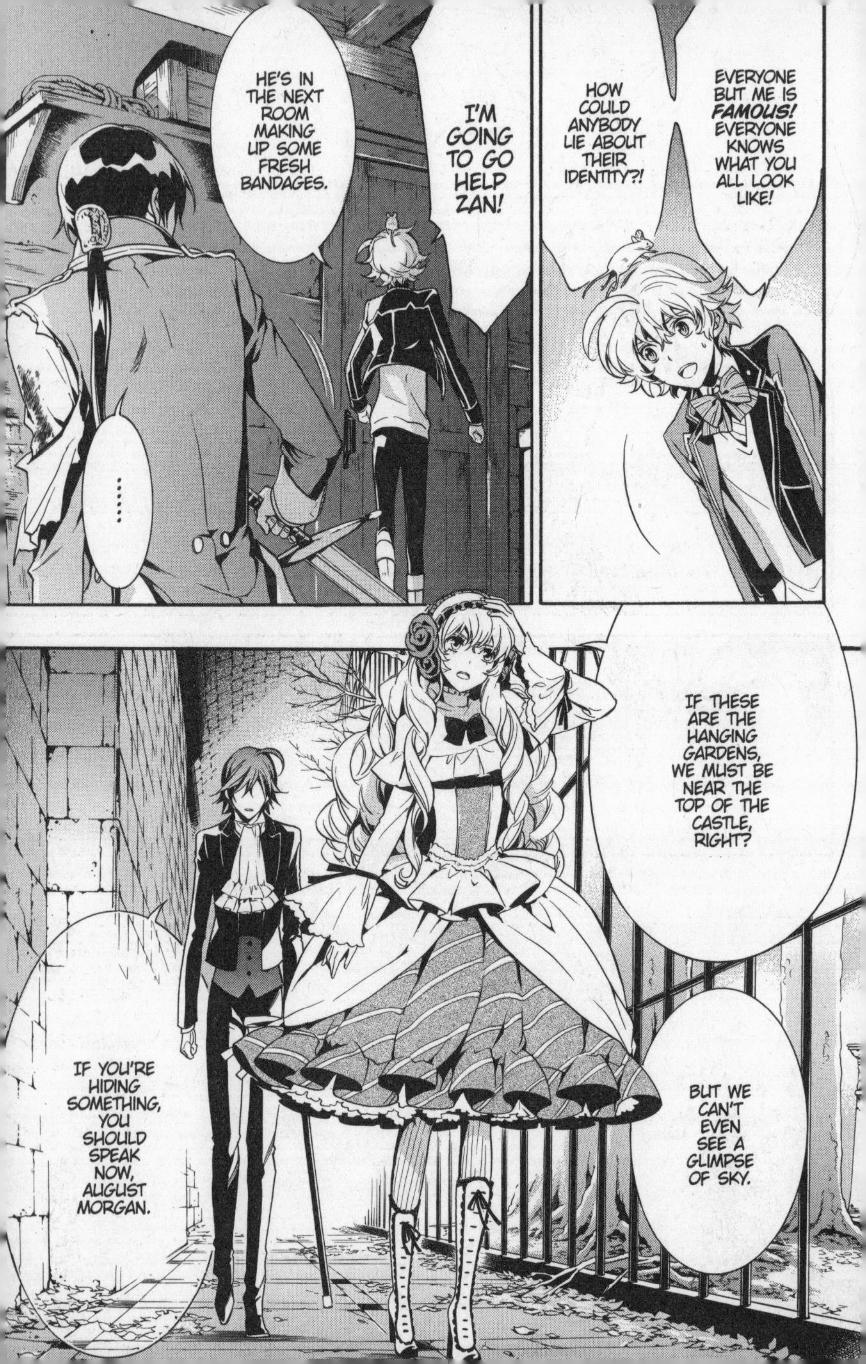
EVERYONE BUT ME IS *FAMOUS!* EVERYONE KNOWS WHAT YOU ALL LOOK LIKE!
HOW COULD ANYBODY LIE ABOUT THEIR IDENTITY?!
I'M GOING TO GO HELP ZAN!
HE'S IN THE NEXT ROOM MAKING UP SOME FRESH BANDAGES.
......
IF THESE ARE THE HANGING GARDENS, WE MUST BE NEAR THE TOP OF THE CASTLE, RIGHT?
BUT WE CAN'T EVEN SEE A GLIMPSE OF SKY.
IF YOU'RE HIDING SOMETHING, YOU SHOULD SPEAK NOW, AUGUST MORGAN.

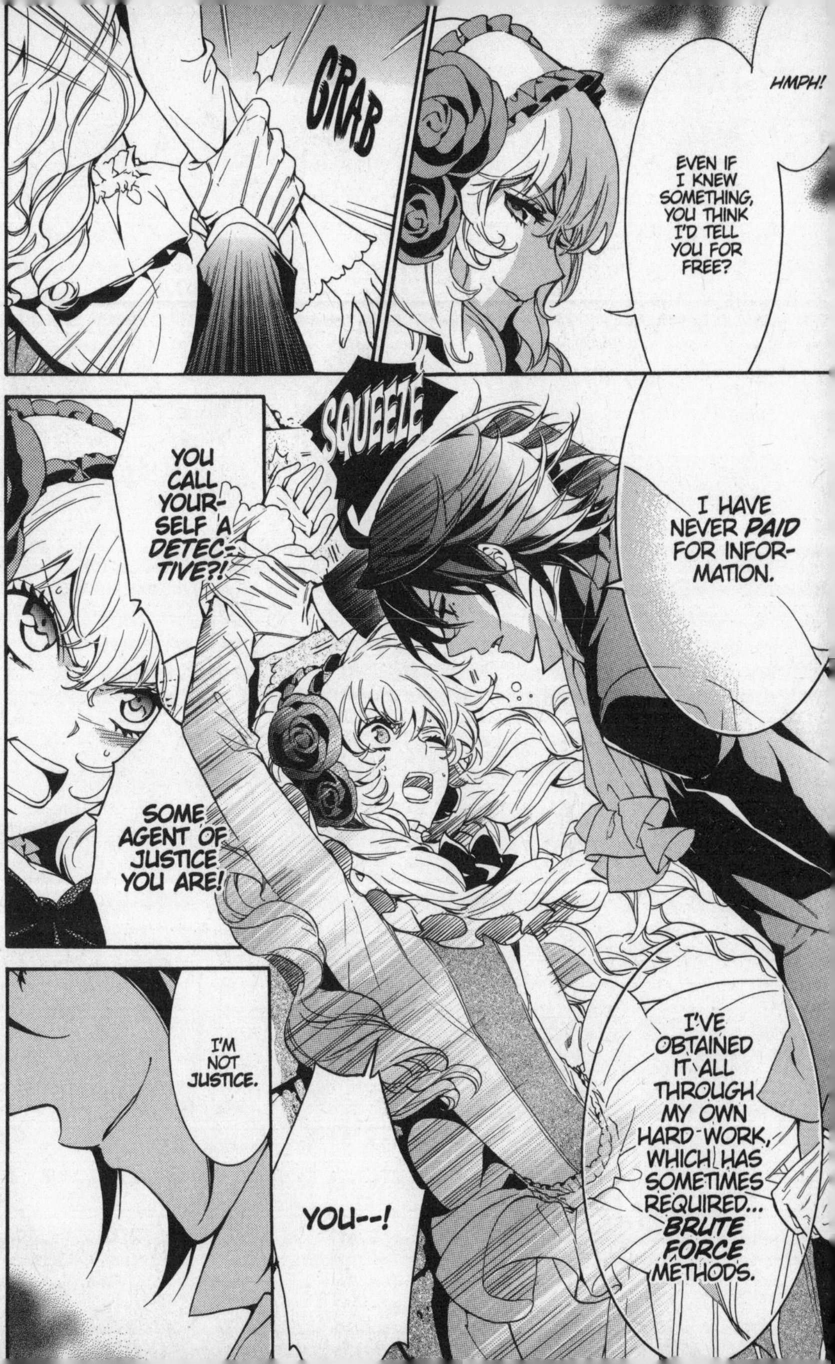
HMPH!
EVEN IF I KNEW SOMETHING, YOU THINK I'D TELL YOU FOR FREE?
GRAB
SQUEEZE
I HAVE NEVER *PAID* FOR INFORMATION.
I'VE OBTAINED IT ALL THROUGH MY OWN HARD WORK, WHICH HAS SOMETIMES REQUIRED... ***BRUTE FORCE*** METHODS.
YOU--!
YOU CALL YOURSELF A DETECTIVE?!
SOME AGENT OF JUSTICE YOU ARE!
I'M NOT JUSTICE.

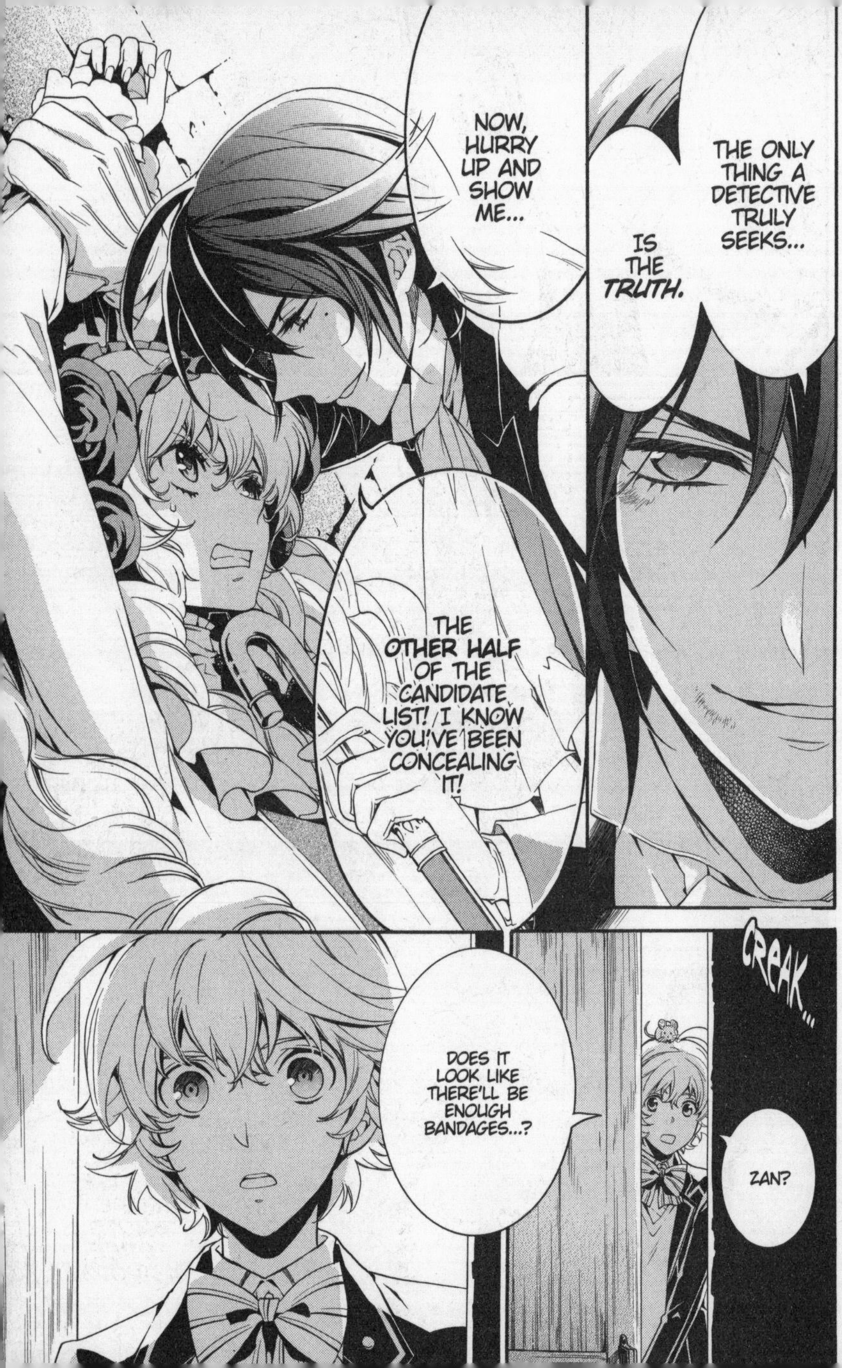
THE ONLY THING A DETECTIVE TRULY SEEKS...
IS THE TRUTH.
NOW, HURRY UP AND SHOW ME...
THE OTHER HALF OF THE CANDIDATE LIST! I KNOW YOU'VE BEEN CONCEALING IT!
CREAK...
ZAN?
DOES IT LOOK LIKE THERE'LL BE ENOUGH BANDAGES...?

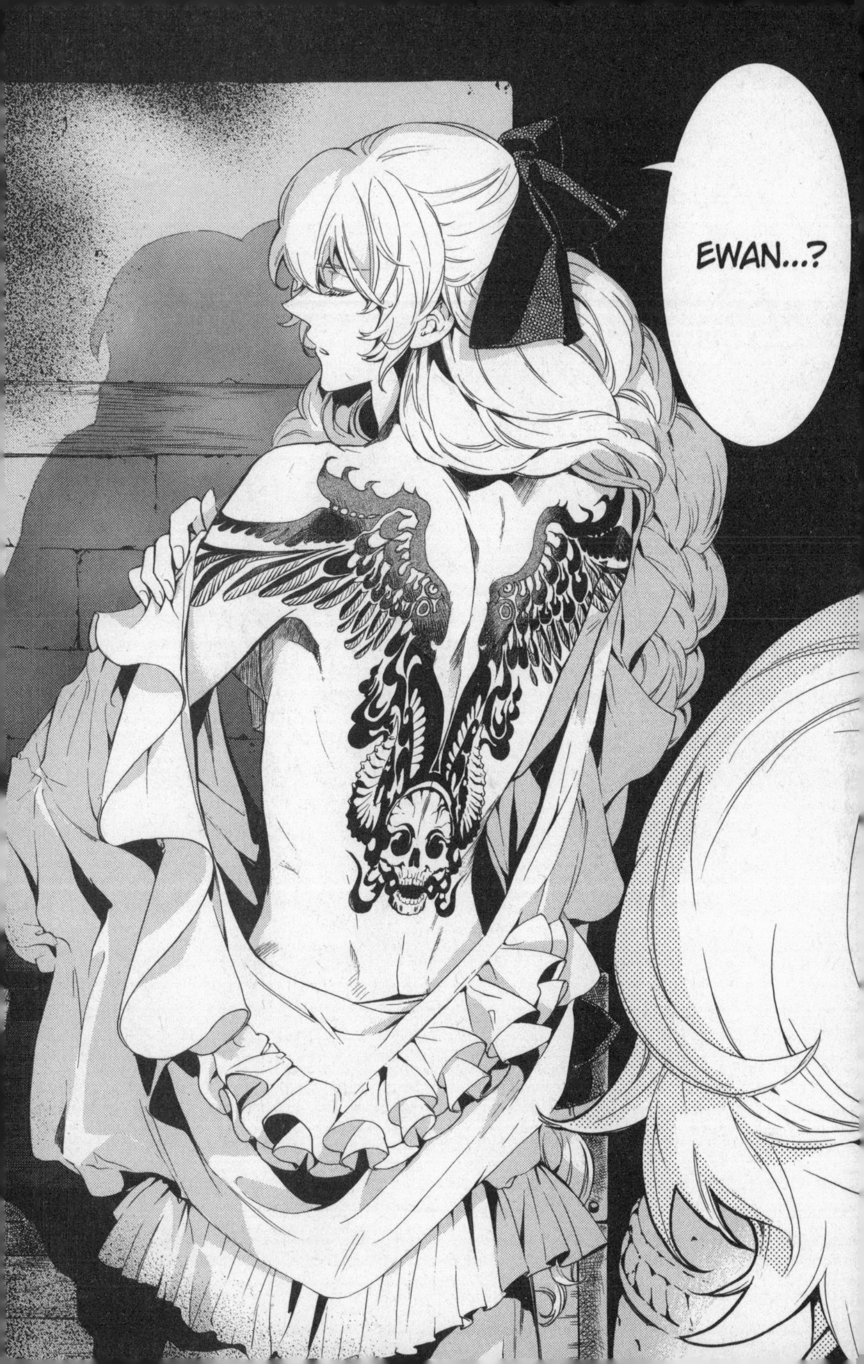
EWAN...?

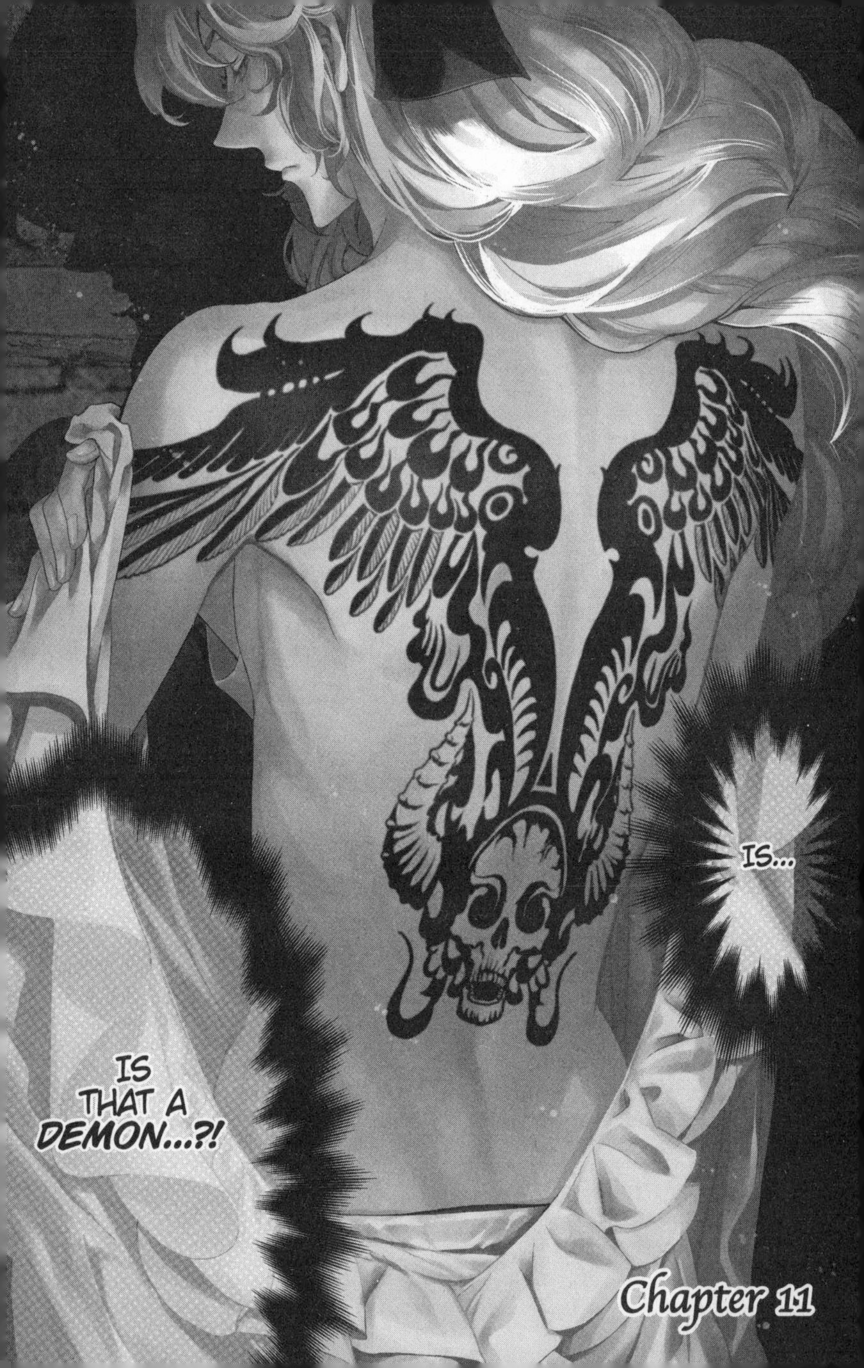
IS...
IS THAT A DEMON...?!
Chapter 11

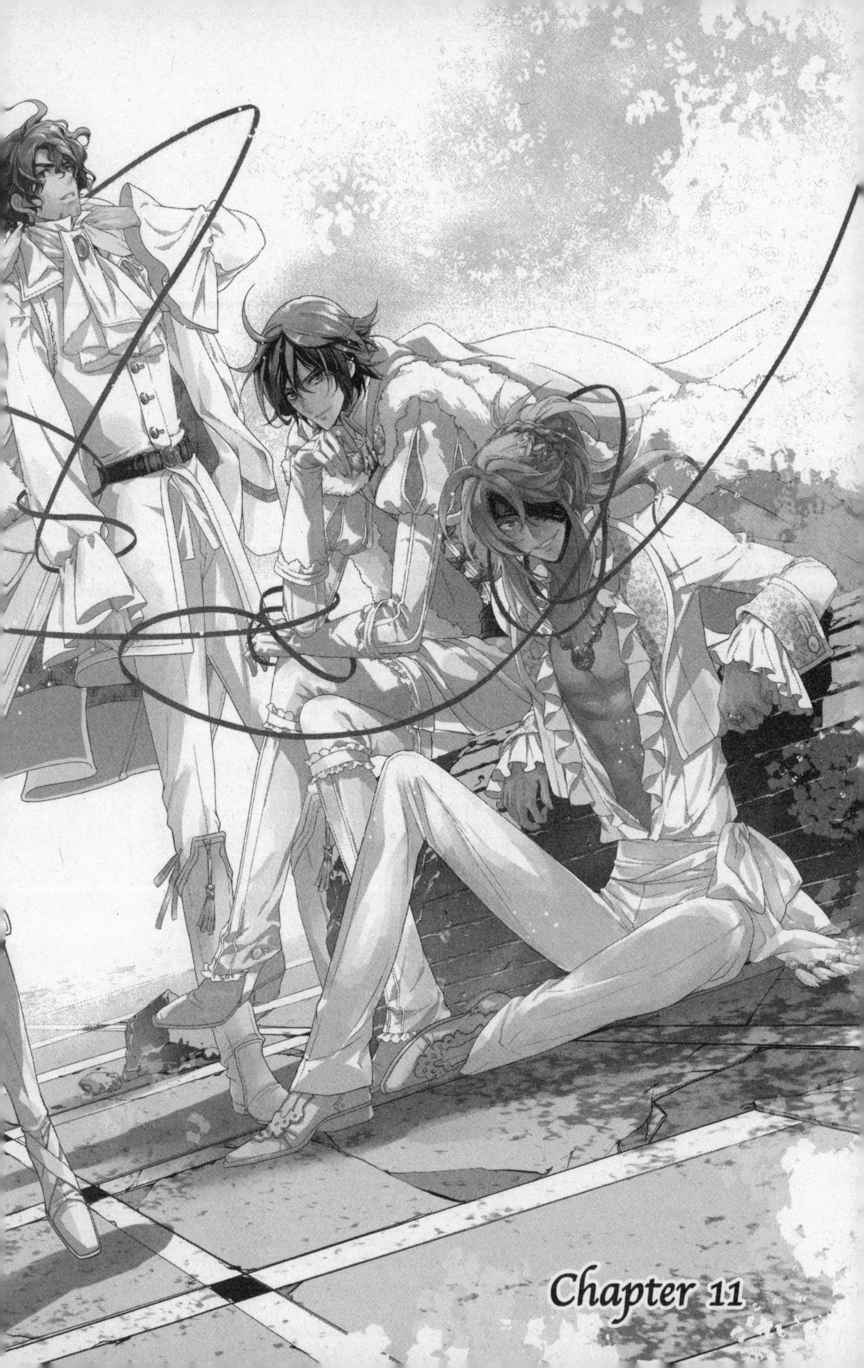

Chapter 11

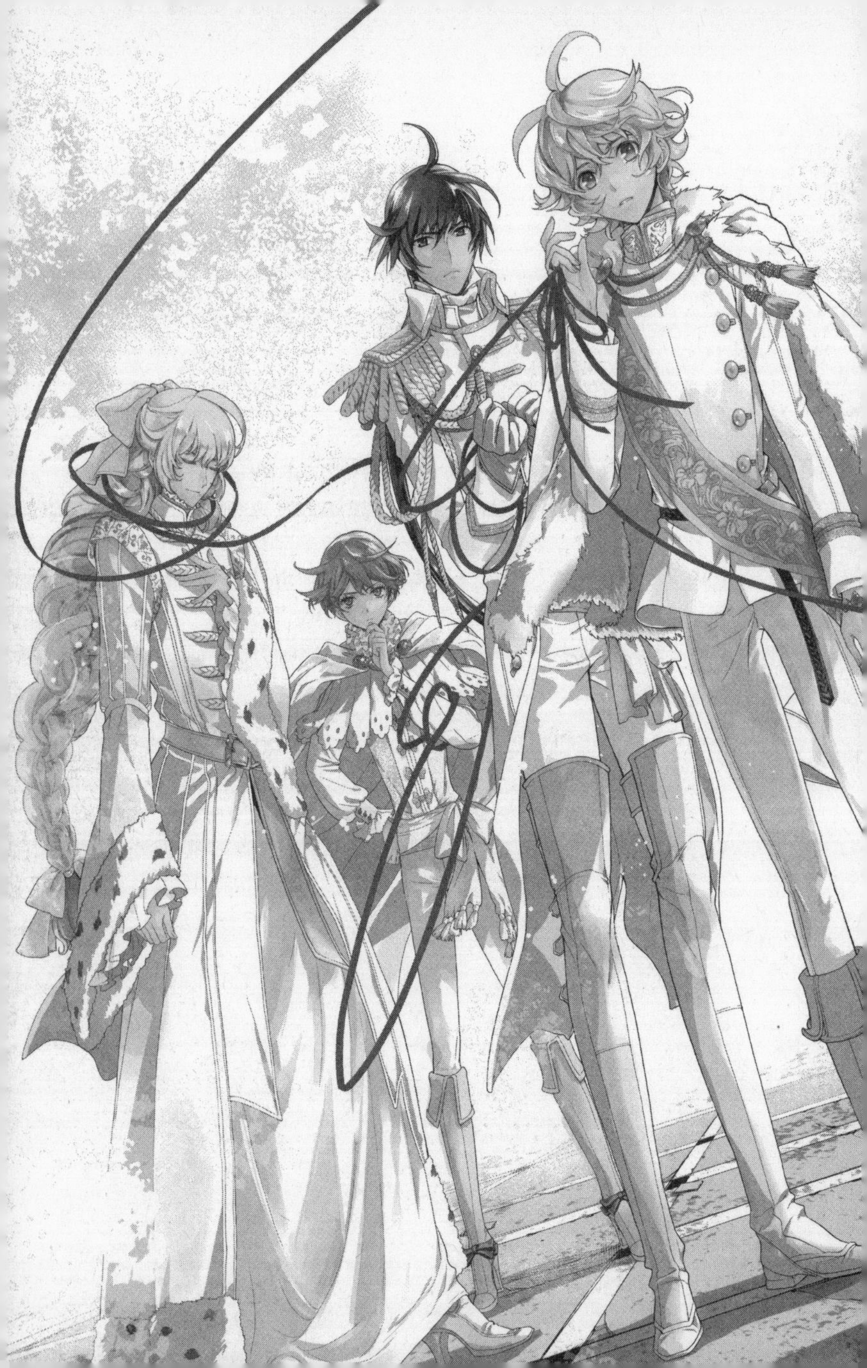

The Seven Princes of the Thousand-Year Labyrinth

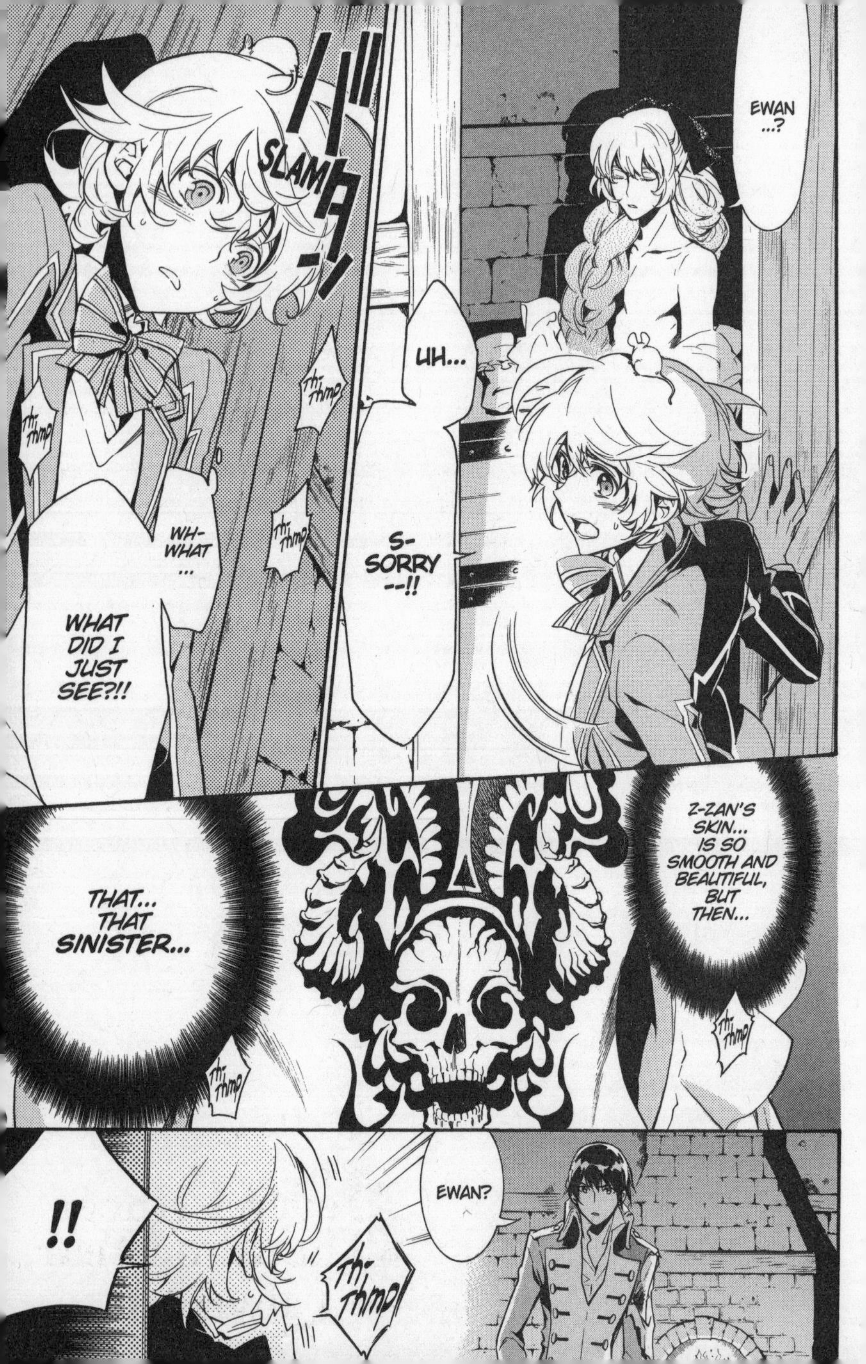
EWAN ...?
UH...
S-SORRY --!!
SLAM
thi-thimp
thi-thimp
WH-WHAT ...
thi-thimp
WHAT DID I JUST SEE?!!
Z-ZAN'S SKIN... IS SO SMOOTH AND BEAUTIFUL, BUT THEN...
thi-thimp
THAT... THAT SINISTER...
thi-thimp
EWAN?
!!
thi-thimp

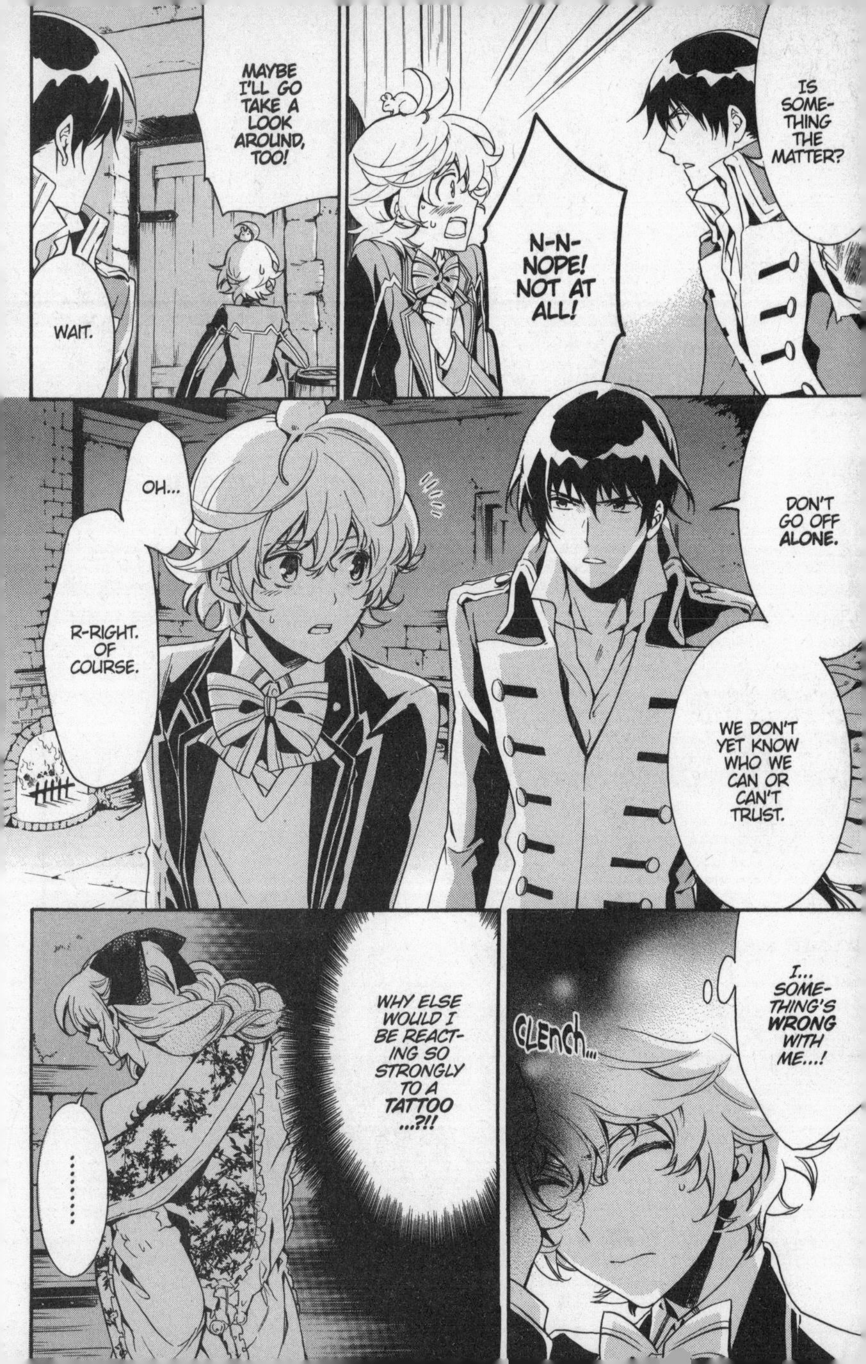
IS SOMETHING THE MATTER?
N-N-NOPE! NOT AT ALL!
MAYBE I'LL GO TAKE A LOOK AROUND, TOO!
WAIT.
DON'T GO OFF ALONE.
WE DON'T YET KNOW WHO WE CAN OR CAN'T TRUST.
OH...
R-RIGHT. OF COURSE.
I... SOMETHING'S WRONG WITH ME...!
CLENCH...
WHY ELSE WOULD I BE REACTING SO STRONGLY TO A TATTOO ...?!!
....

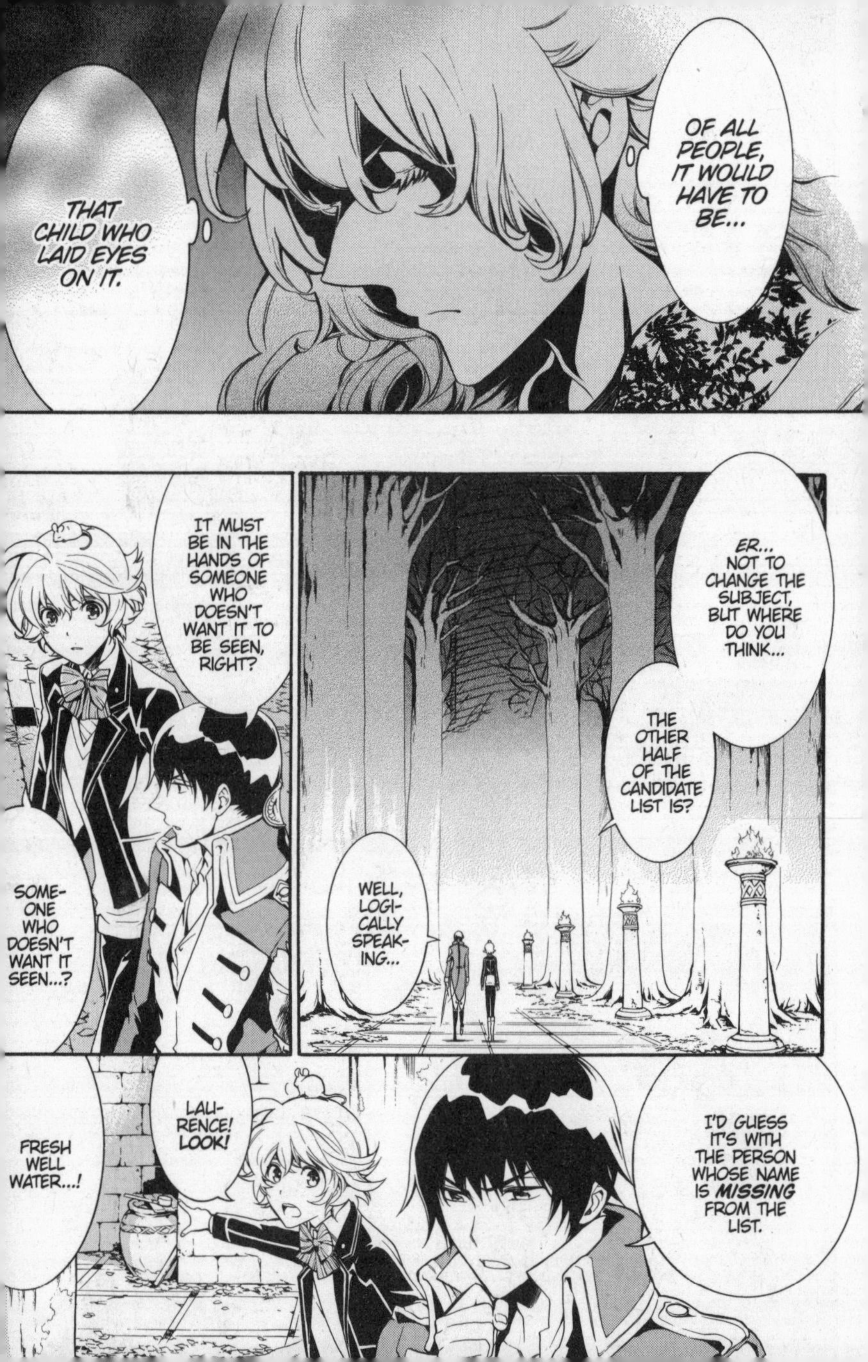
OF ALL PEOPLE, IT WOULD HAVE TO BE...
THAT CHILD WHO LAID EYES ON IT.
ER... NOT TO CHANGE THE SUBJECT, BUT WHERE DO YOU THINK...
THE OTHER HALF OF THE CANDIDATE LIST IS?
WELL, LOGICALLY SPEAKING...
IT MUST BE IN THE HANDS OF SOMEONE WHO DOESN'T WANT IT TO BE SEEN, RIGHT?
SOMEONE WHO DOESN'T WANT IT SEEN...?
I'D GUESS IT'S WITH THE PERSON WHOSE NAME IS *MISSING* FROM THE LIST.
LAURENCE! LOOK!
FRESH WELL WATER...!

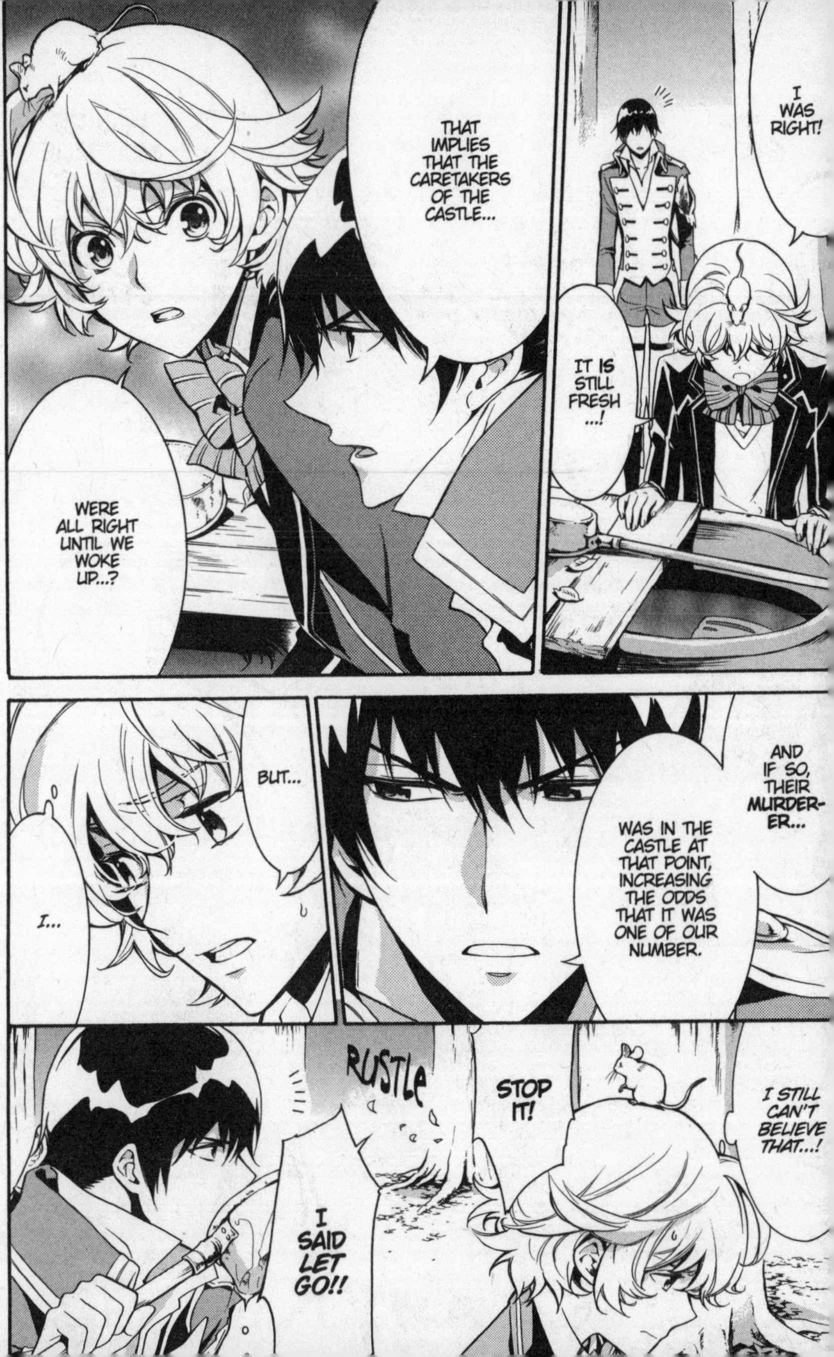
I WAS RIGHT!
IT IS STILL FRESH ...!
THAT IMPLIES THAT THE CARETAKERS OF THE CASTLE...
WERE ALL RIGHT UNTIL WE WOKE UP...?
AND IF SO, THEIR MURDERER...
WAS IN THE CASTLE AT THAT POINT, INCREASING THE ODDS THAT IT WAS ONE OF OUR NUMBER.
BUT...
I...
I STILL CAN'T BELIEVE THAT...!
STOP IT!
RUSTLE
I SAID LET GO!!

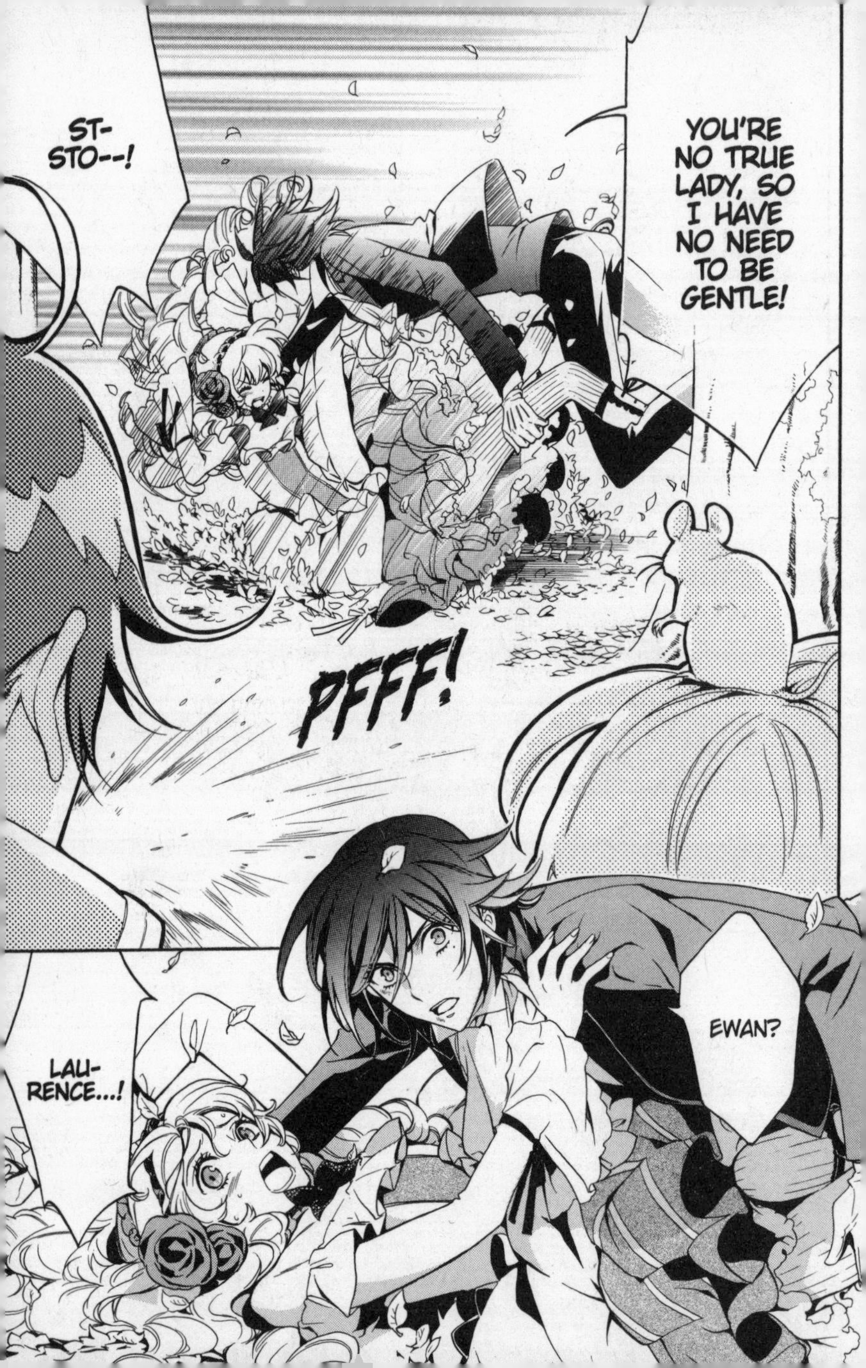
YOU'RE NO TRUE LADY, SO I HAVE NO NEED TO BE GENTLE!
ST-STO--!
PFFF!
EWAN?
LAU-RENCE...!

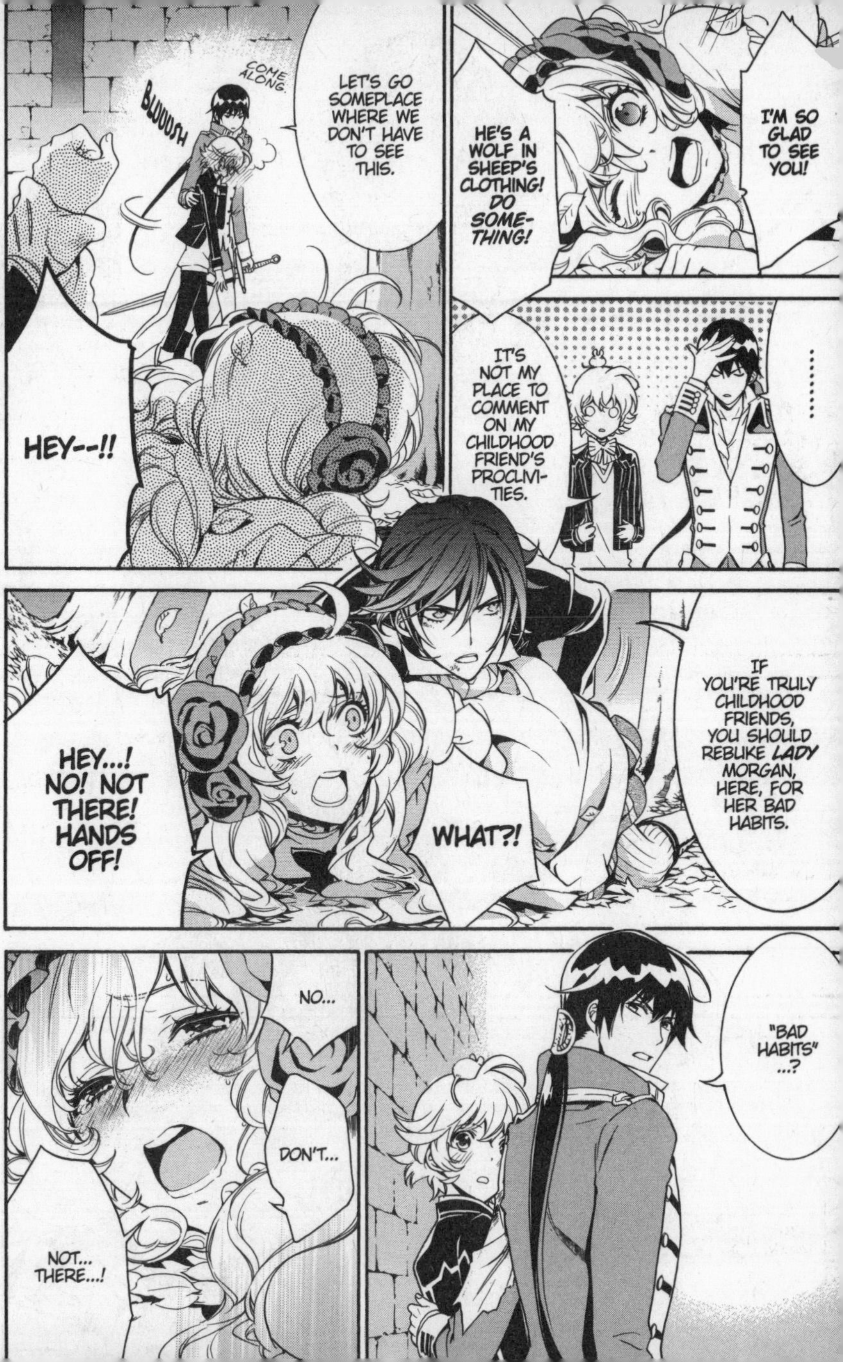
I'M SO GLAD TO SEE YOU!
HE'S A WOLF IN SHEEP'S CLOTHING! DO SOMETHING!
......
IT'S NOT MY PLACE TO COMMENT ON MY CHILDHOOD FRIEND'S PROCLIVITIES.
LET'S GO SOMEPLACE WHERE WE DON'T HAVE TO SEE THIS.
COME ALONG.
BLUUUSH
HEY--!!
IF YOU'RE TRULY CHILDHOOD FRIENDS, YOU SHOULD REBUKE LADY MORGAN, HERE, FOR HER BAD HABITS.
WHAT?!
HEY...! NO! NOT THERE! HANDS OFF!
"BAD HABITS" ...?
NO...
DON'T...
NOT... THERE...!

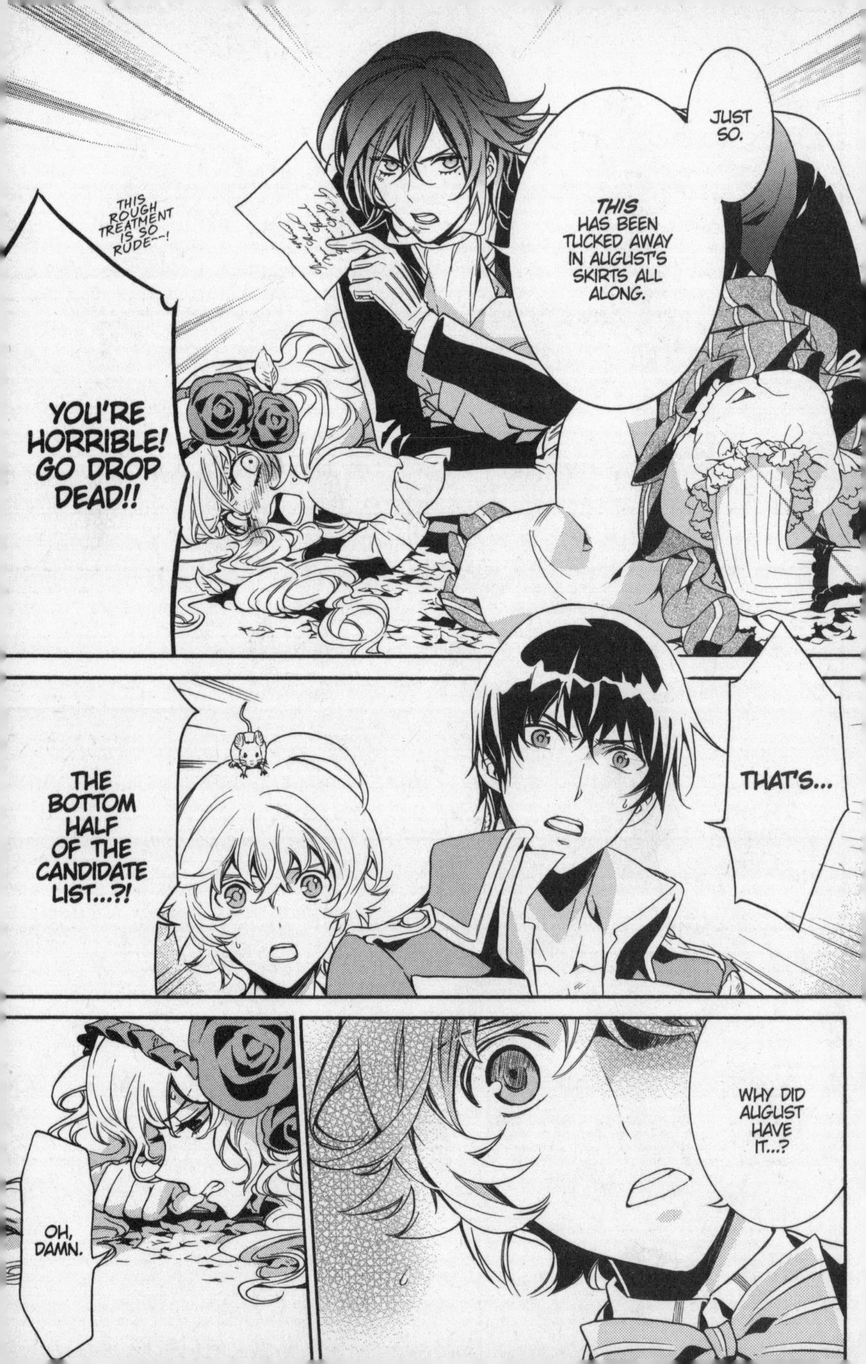
JUST SO.
THIS HAS BEEN TUCKED AWAY IN AUGUST'S SKIRTS ALL ALONG.
THIS ROUGH TREATMENT IS SO RUDE--!
YOU'RE HORRIBLE! GO DROP DEAD!!
THAT'S...
THE BOTTOM HALF OF THE CANDIDATE LIST...?!
WHY DID AUGUST HAVE IT...?
OH, DAMN.

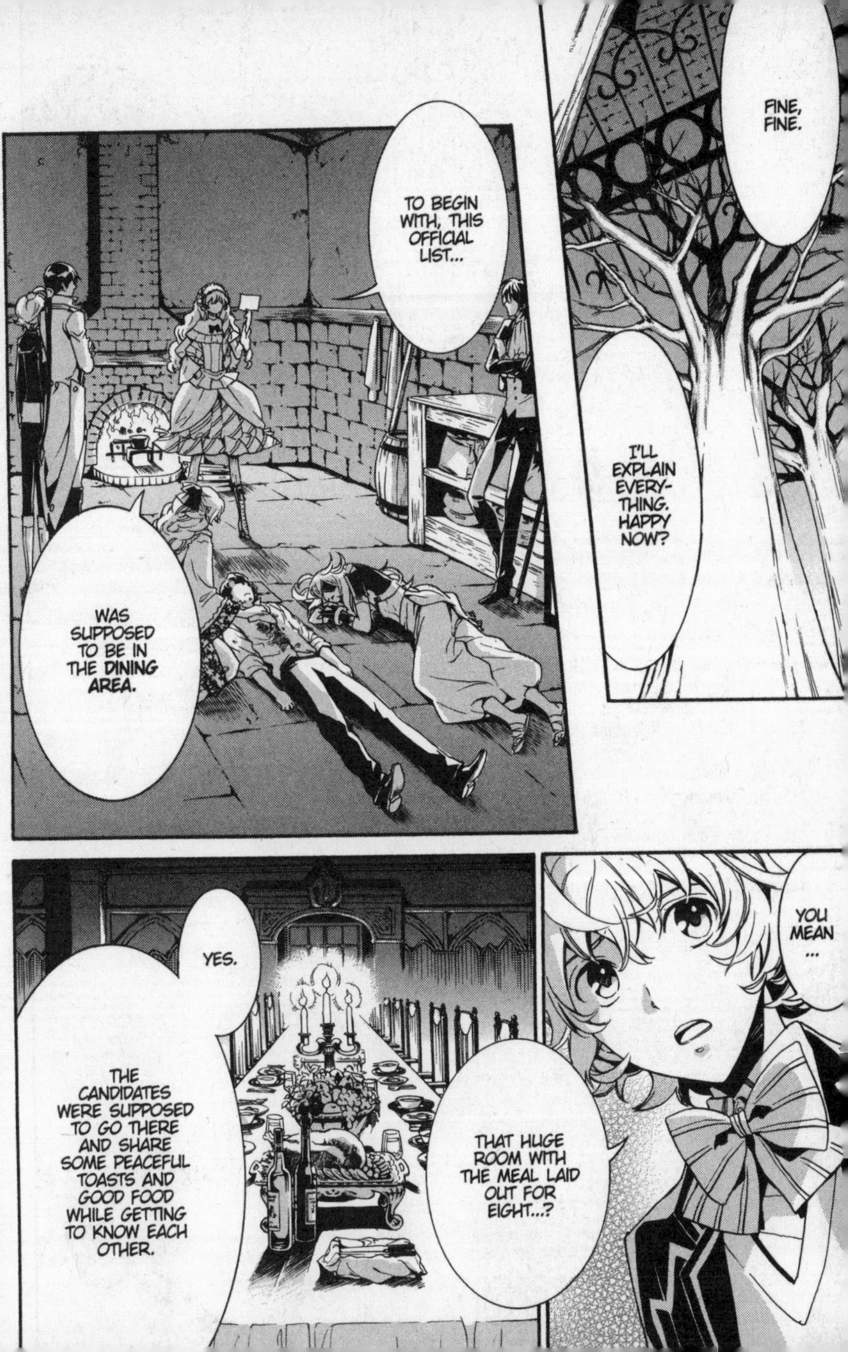
FINE, FINE.
I'LL EXPLAIN EVERY-THING. HAPPY NOW?
TO BEGIN WITH, THIS OFFICIAL LIST...
WAS SUPPOSED TO BE IN THE DINING AREA.
YOU MEAN ...
THAT HUGE ROOM WITH THE MEAL LAID OUT FOR EIGHT...?
YES.
THE CANDIDATES WERE SUPPOSED TO GO THERE AND SHARE SOME PEACEFUL TOASTS AND GOOD FOOD WHILE GETTING TO KNOW EACH OTHER.

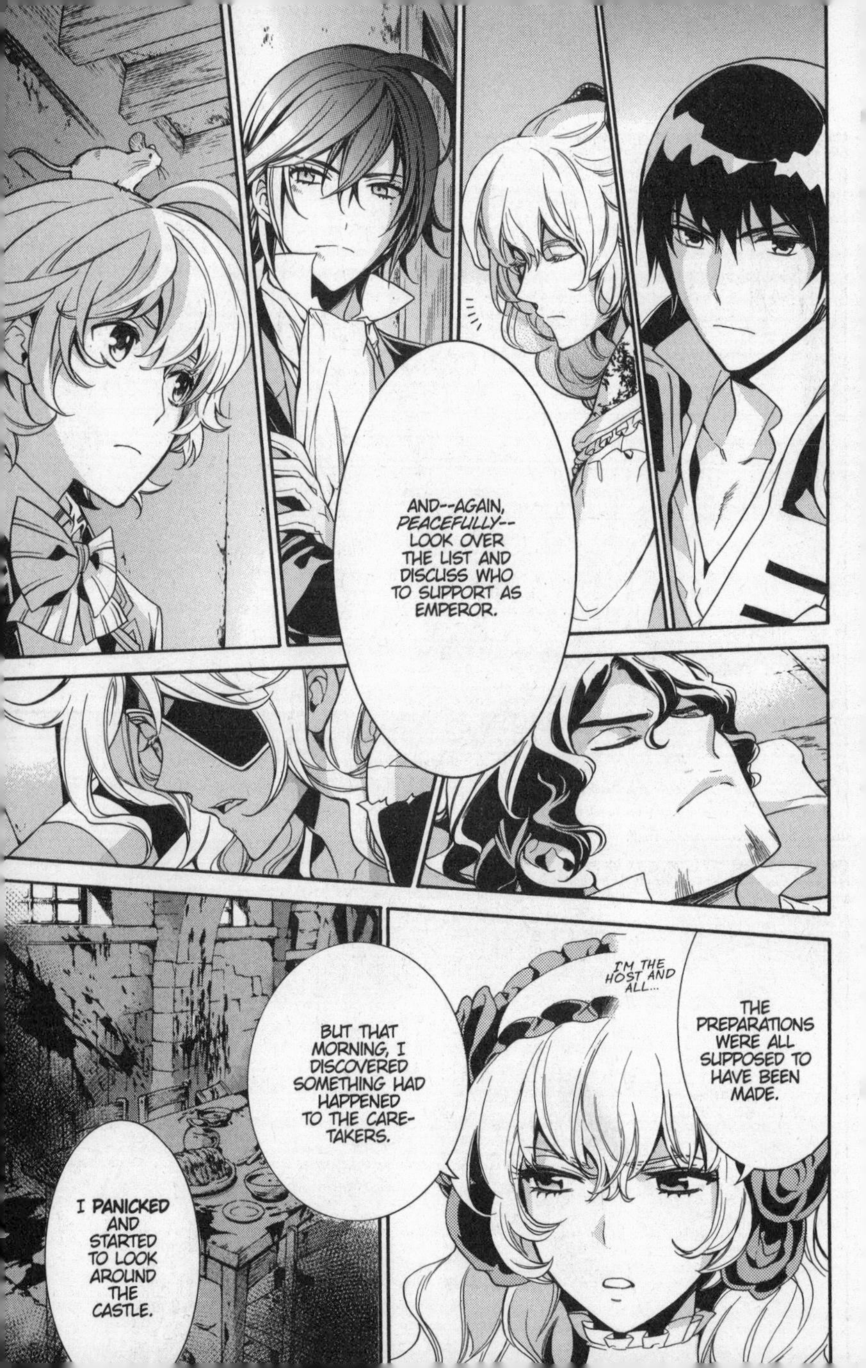
AND--AGAIN, *PEACEFULLY*--LOOK OVER THE LIST AND DISCUSS WHO TO SUPPORT AS EMPEROR.
THE PREPARATIONS WERE ALL SUPPOSED TO HAVE BEEN MADE.
I'M THE HOST AND ALL...
BUT THAT MORNING, I DISCOVERED SOMETHING HAD HAPPENED TO THE CARE-TAKERS.
I PANICKED AND STARTED TO LOOK AROUND THE CASTLE.

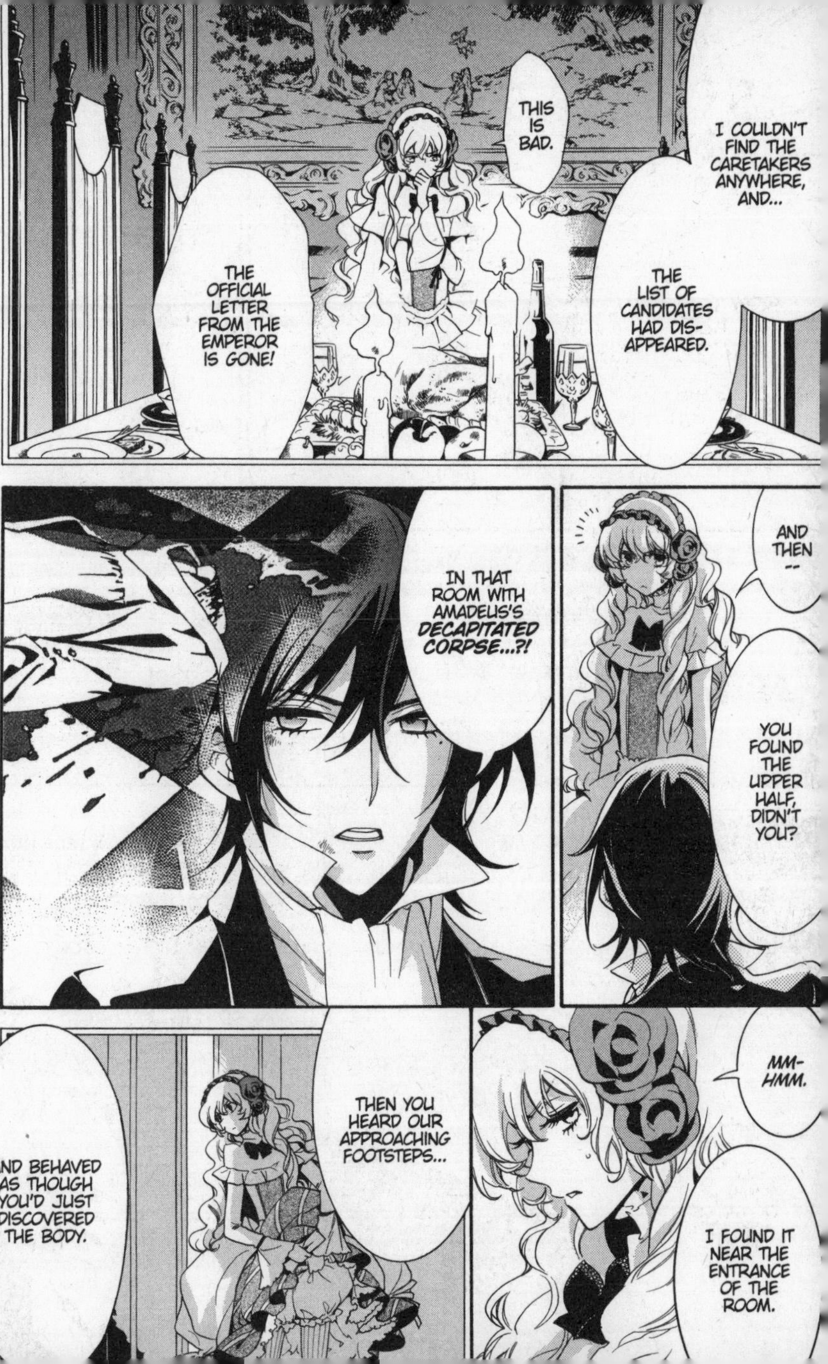
I COULDN'T FIND THE CARETAKERS ANYWHERE, AND...
THE LIST OF CANDIDATES HAD DIS-APPEARED.
THIS IS BAD.
THE OFFICIAL LETTER FROM THE EMPEROR IS GONE!
AND THEN --
YOU FOUND THE UPPER HALF, DIDN'T YOU?
IN THAT ROOM WITH AMADEUS'S *DECAPITATED CORPSE*...?!
MM-HMM.
I FOUND IT NEAR THE ENTRANCE OF THE ROOM.
THEN YOU HEARD OUR APPROACHING FOOTSTEPS...
AND BEHAVED AS THOUGH YOU'D JUST DISCOVERED THE BODY.

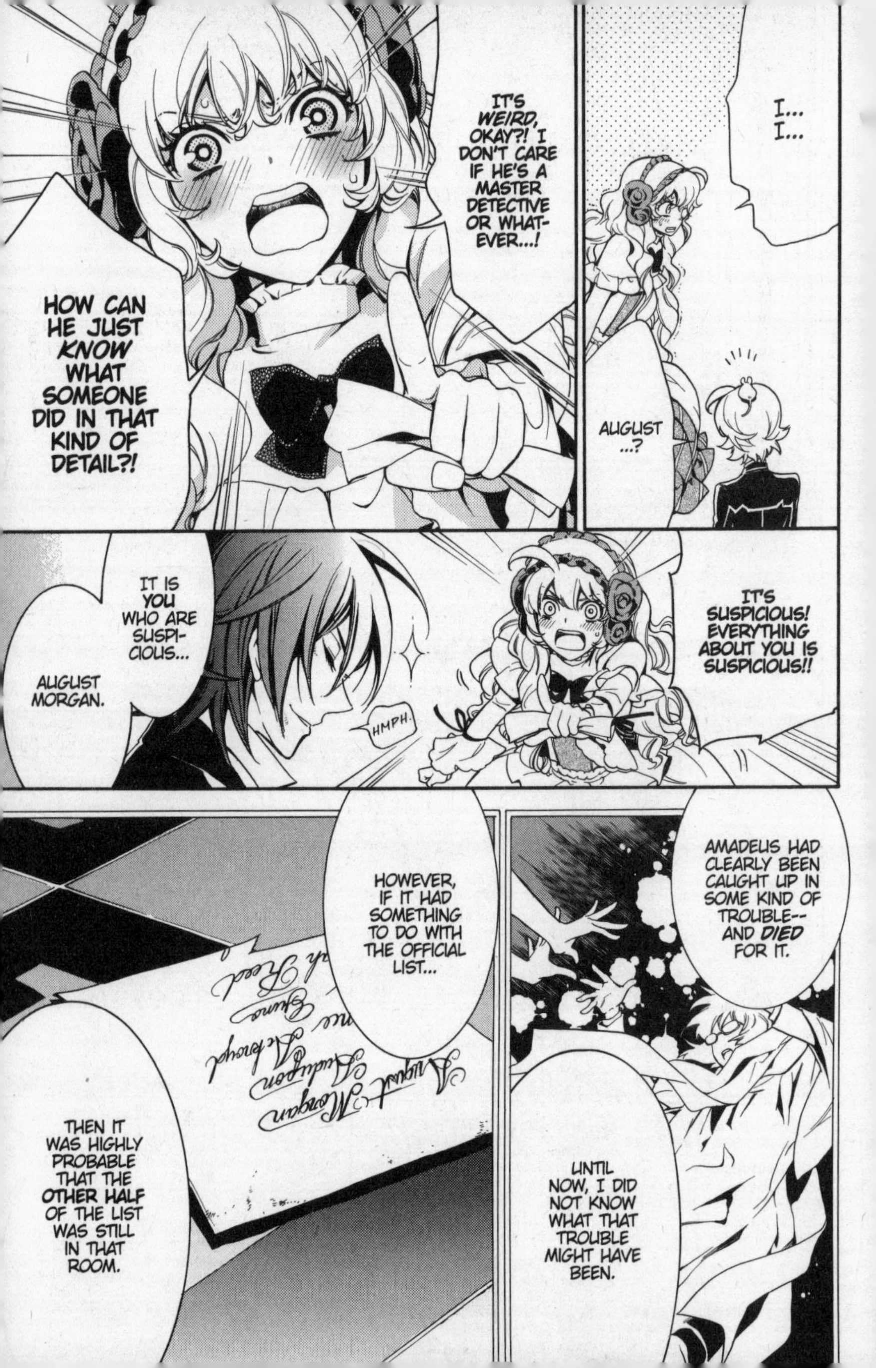
I...
I...
AUGUST ...?
IT'S *WEIRD*, OKAY?! I DON'T CARE IF HE'S A MASTER DETECTIVE OR WHAT-EVER...!
HOW CAN HE JUST *KNOW* WHAT SOMEONE DID IN THAT KIND OF DETAIL?!
IT'S SUSPICIOUS! EVERYTHING ABOUT YOU IS SUSPICIOUS!!
HMPH.
IT IS **YOU** WHO ARE SUSPI-CIOUS...
AUGUST MORGAN.
AMADEUS HAD CLEARLY BEEN CAUGHT UP IN SOME KIND OF TROUBLE-- AND *DIED* FOR IT.
UNTIL NOW, I DID NOT KNOW WHAT THAT TROUBLE MIGHT HAVE BEEN.
HOWEVER, IF IT HAD SOMETHING TO DO WITH THE OFFICIAL LIST...
THEN IT WAS HIGHLY PROBABLE THAT THE **OTHER HALF** OF THE LIST WAS STILL IN THAT ROOM.

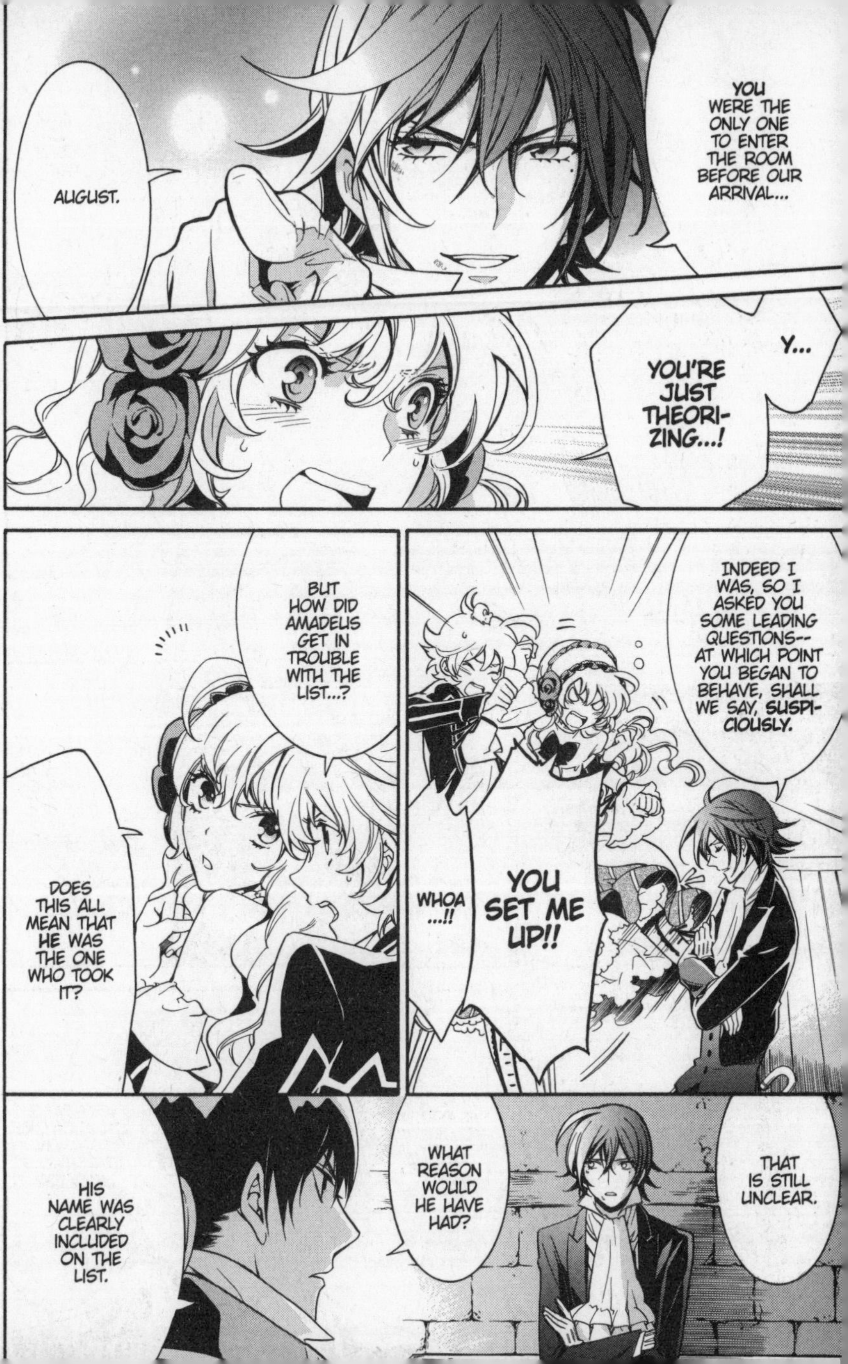
YOU WERE THE ONLY ONE TO ENTER THE ROOM BEFORE OUR ARRIVAL...
AUGUST.
Y...
YOU'RE JUST THEORI-ZING...!
INDEED I WAS, SO I ASKED YOU SOME LEADING QUESTIONS-- AT WHICH POINT YOU BEGAN TO BEHAVE, SHALL WE SAY, SUSPI-CIOUSLY.
YOU SET ME UP!!
WHOA ...!!
BUT HOW DID AMADEUS GET IN TROUBLE WITH THE LIST...?
DOES THIS ALL MEAN THAT HE WAS THE ONE WHO TOOK IT?
THAT IS STILL UNCLEAR.
WHAT REASON WOULD HE HAVE HAD?
HIS NAME WAS CLEARLY INCLUDED ON THE LIST.

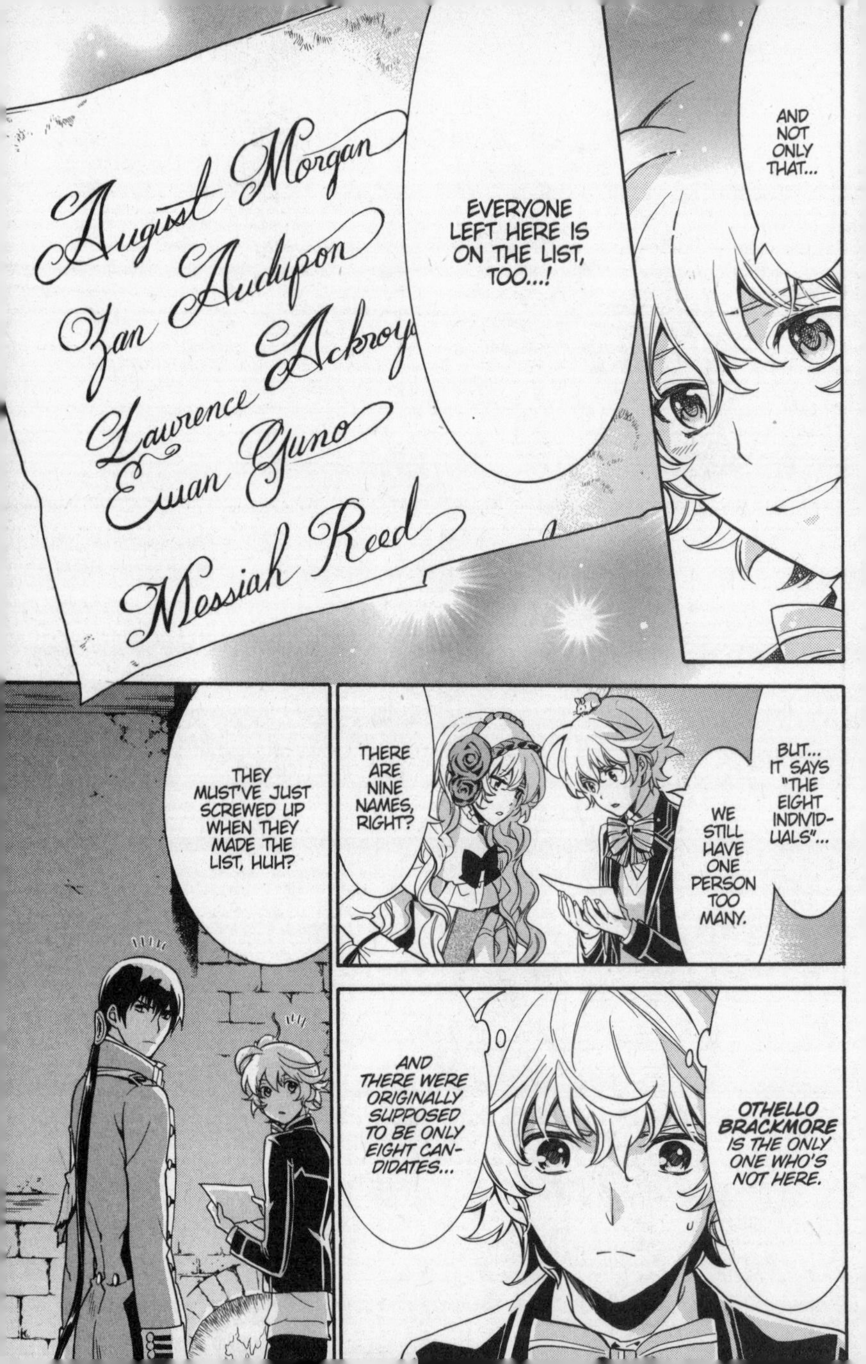
AND NOT ONLY THAT...
EVERYONE LEFT HERE IS ON THE LIST, TOO...!
August Morgan
Zan Audupon
Laurence Ackroy
Ewan Guno
Messiah Reed
BUT... IT SAYS "THE EIGHT INDIVID-UALS"...
WE STILL HAVE ONE PERSON TOO MANY.
THERE ARE NINE NAMES, RIGHT?
OTHELLO BRACKMORE IS THE ONLY ONE WHO'S NOT HERE.
AND THERE WERE ORIGINALLY SUPPOSED TO BE ONLY EIGHT CAN-DIDATES...
THEY MUST'VE JUST SCREWED UP WHEN THEY MADE THE LIST, HUH?

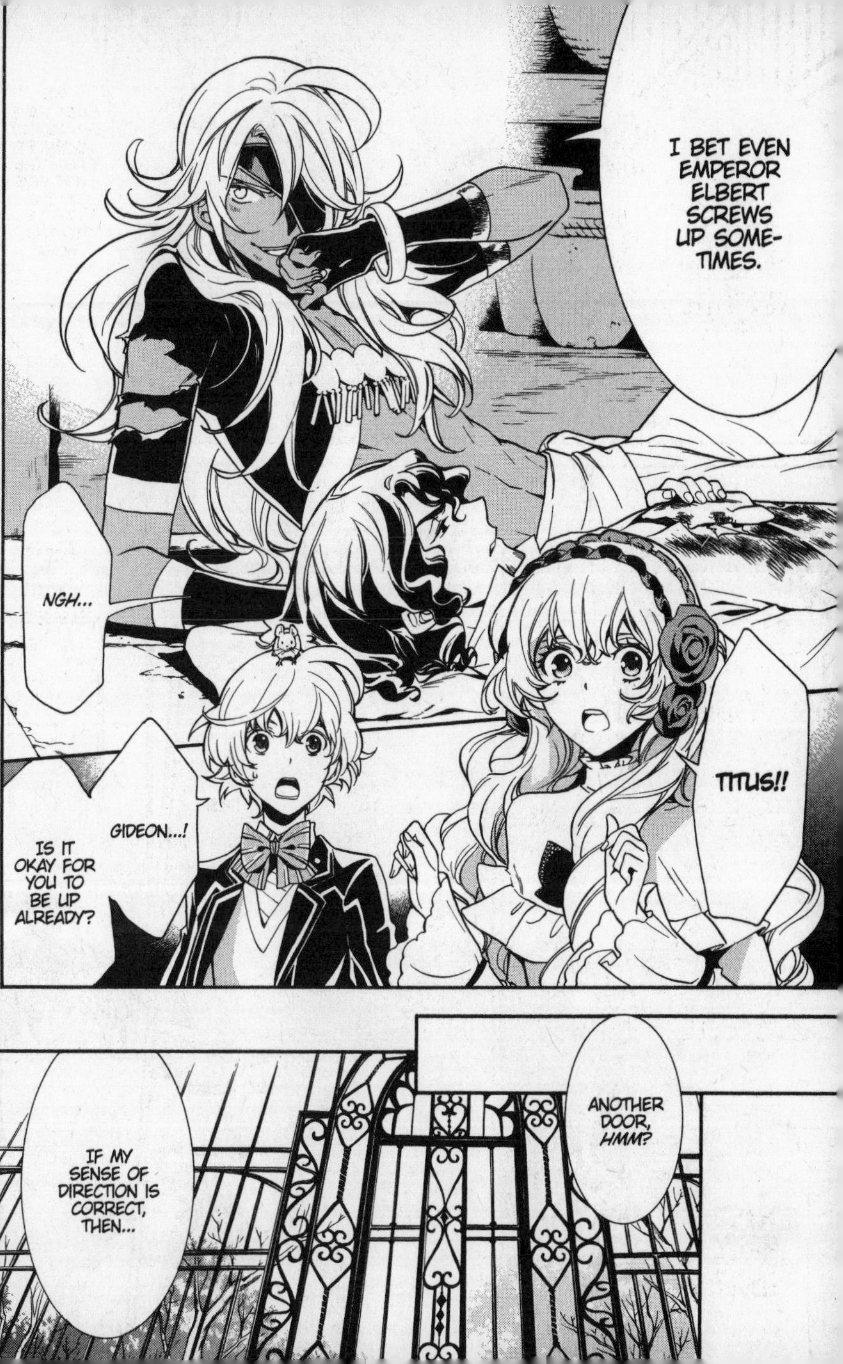
I BET EVEN EMPEROR ELBERT SCREWS UP SOME-TIMES.
NGH...
TITUS!!
GIDEON...!
IS IT OKAY FOR YOU TO BE UP ALREADY?
ANOTHER DOOR, HMM?
IF MY SENSE OF DIRECTION IS CORRECT, THEN...

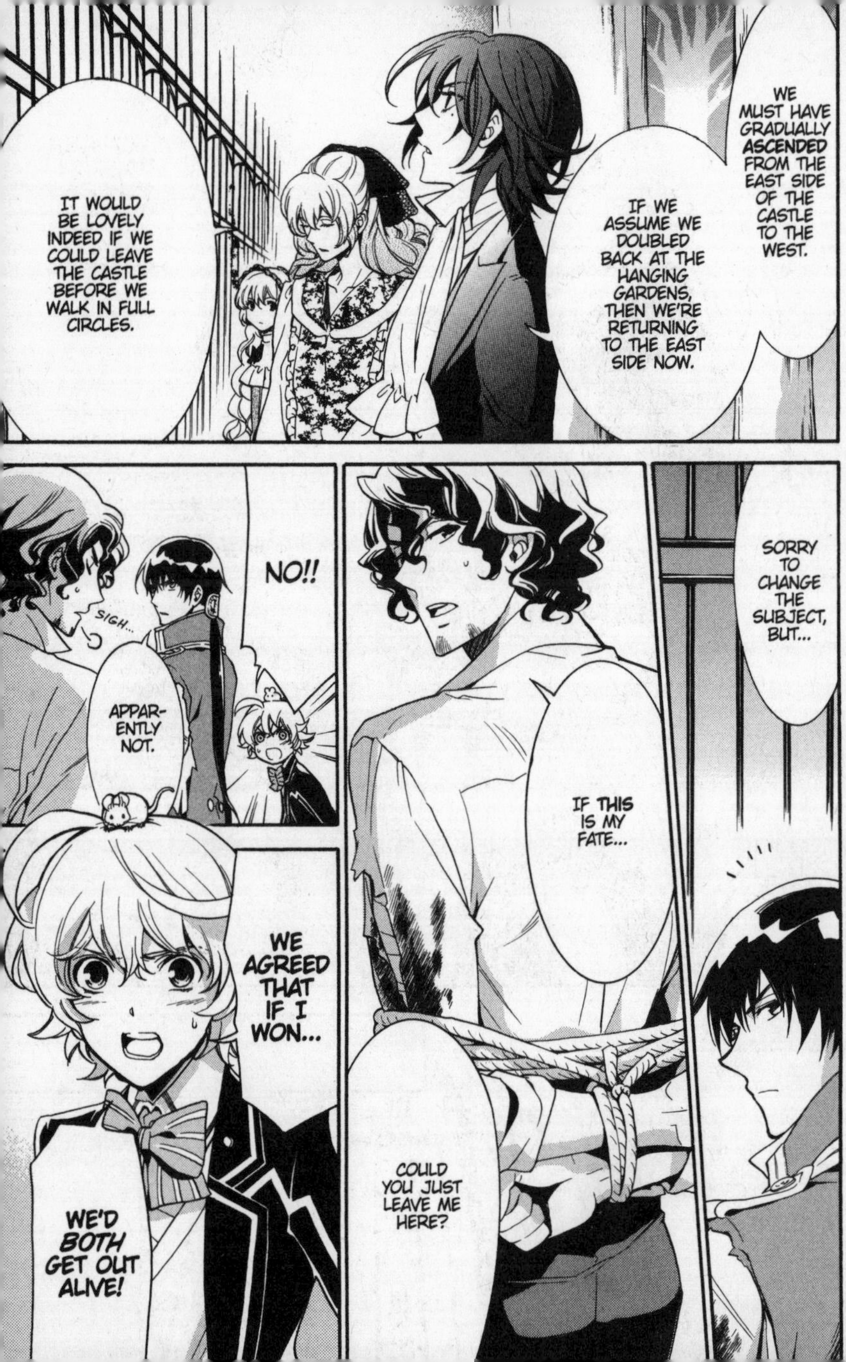
WE MUST HAVE GRADUALLY ASCENDED FROM THE EAST SIDE OF THE CASTLE TO THE WEST.
IF WE ASSUME WE DOUBLED BACK AT THE HANGING GARDENS, THEN WE'RE RETURNING TO THE EAST SIDE NOW.
IT WOULD BE LOVELY INDEED IF WE COULD LEAVE THE CASTLE BEFORE WE WALK IN FULL CIRCLES.
SORRY TO CHANGE THE SUBJECT, BUT...
IF THIS IS MY FATE...
COULD YOU JUST LEAVE ME HERE?
NO!!
SIGH...
APPARENTLY NOT.
WE AGREED THAT IF I WON...
WE'D BOTH GET OUT ALIVE!

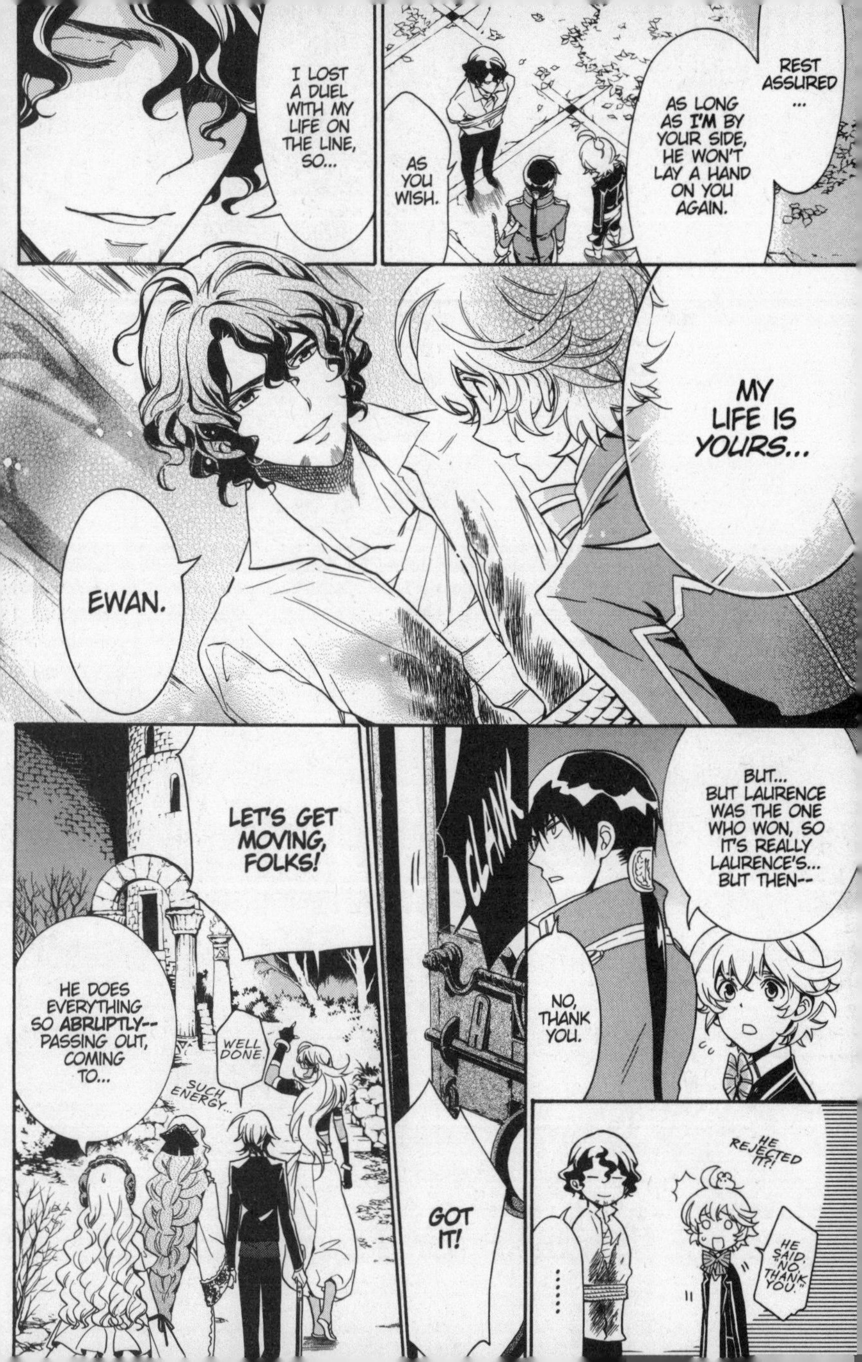
REST ASSURED...
AS LONG AS I'M BY YOUR SIDE, HE WON'T LAY A HAND ON YOU AGAIN.
AS YOU WISH.
I LOST A DUEL WITH MY LIFE ON THE LINE, SO...
MY LIFE IS YOURS...
EWAN.
BUT... BUT LAURENCE WAS THE ONE WHO WON, SO IT'S REALLY LAURENCE'S... BUT THEN--
NO, THANK YOU.
HE REJECTED IT?!
HE SAID, "NO THANK YOU."
......
CLANK
GOT IT!
LET'S GET MOVING, FOLKS!
WELL DONE.
HE DOES EVERYTHING SO ABRUPTLY-- PASSING OUT, COMING TO...
SUCH ENERGY...

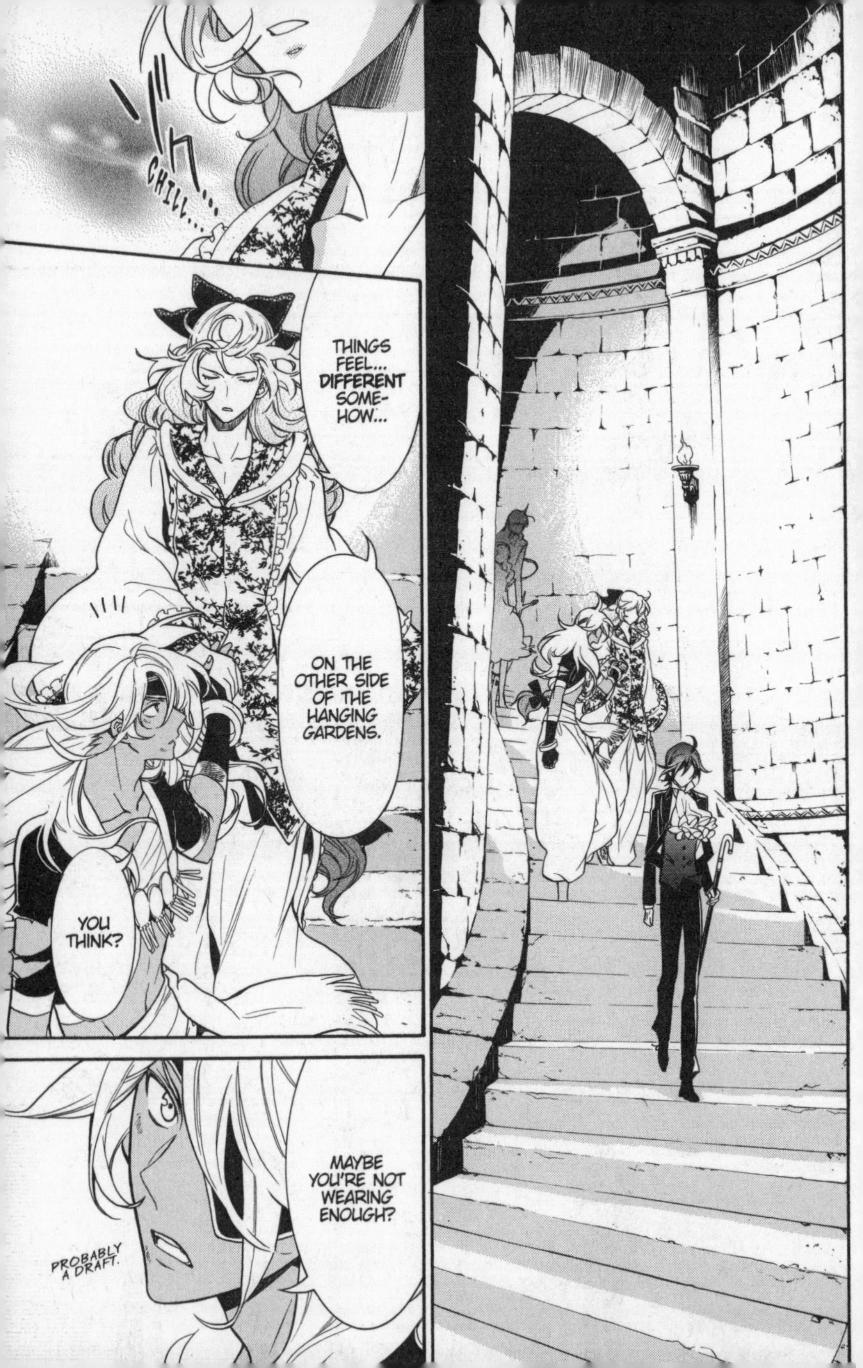
CHILL...
THINGS FEEL... DIFFERENT SOME-HOW...
ON THE OTHER SIDE OF THE HANGING GARDENS.
YOU THINK?
MAYBE YOU'RE NOT WEARING ENOUGH?
PROBABLY A DRAFT.

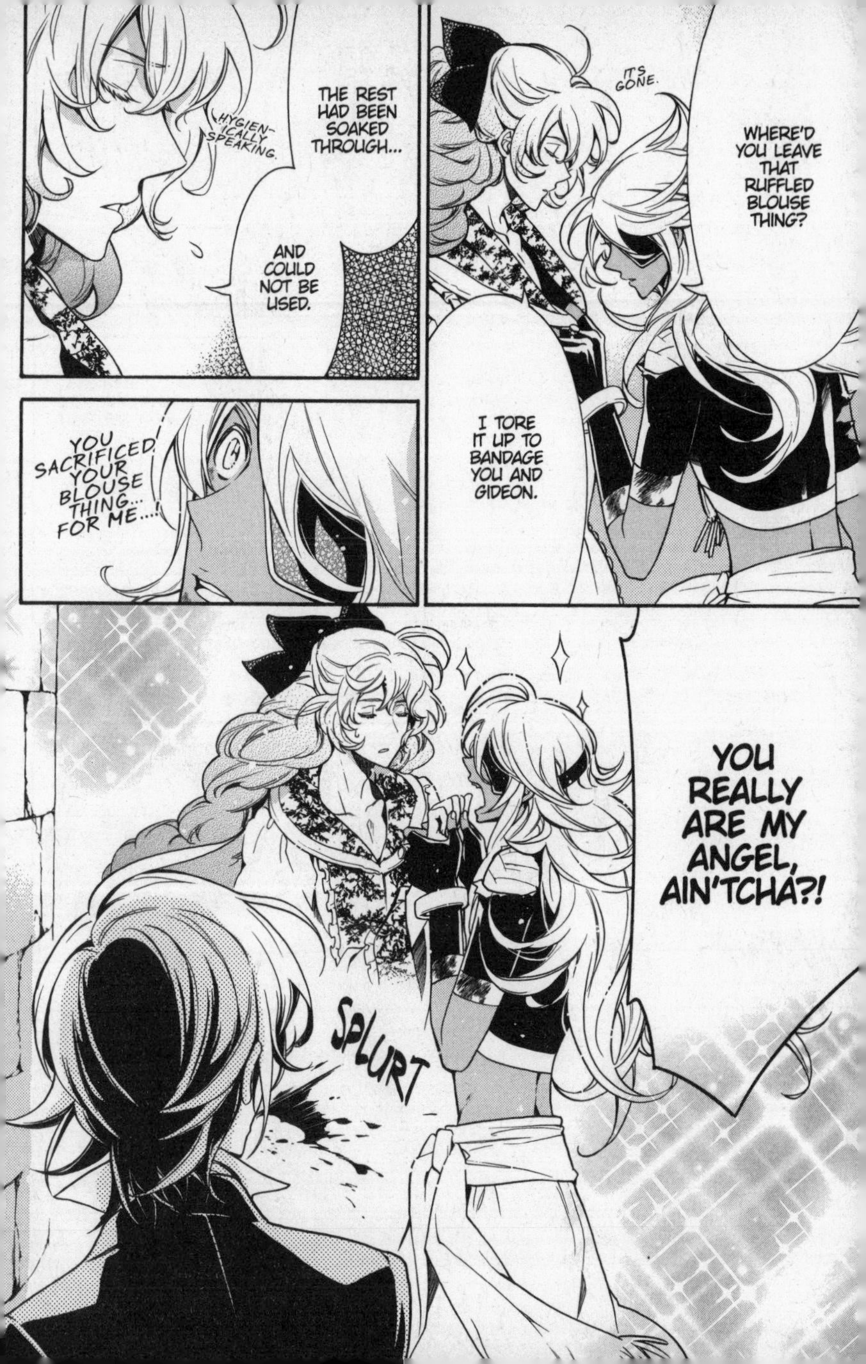
WHERE'D YOU LEAVE THAT RUFFLED BLOUSE THING?
IT'S GONE.
I TORE IT UP TO BANDAGE YOU AND GIDEON.
THE REST HAD BEEN SOAKED THROUGH...
HYGIEN-ICALLY SPEAKING.
AND COULD NOT BE USED.
YOU SACRIFICED YOUR BLOUSE THING... FOR ME...!
YOU REALLY ARE MY ANGEL, AIN'TCHA?!
SPLURT

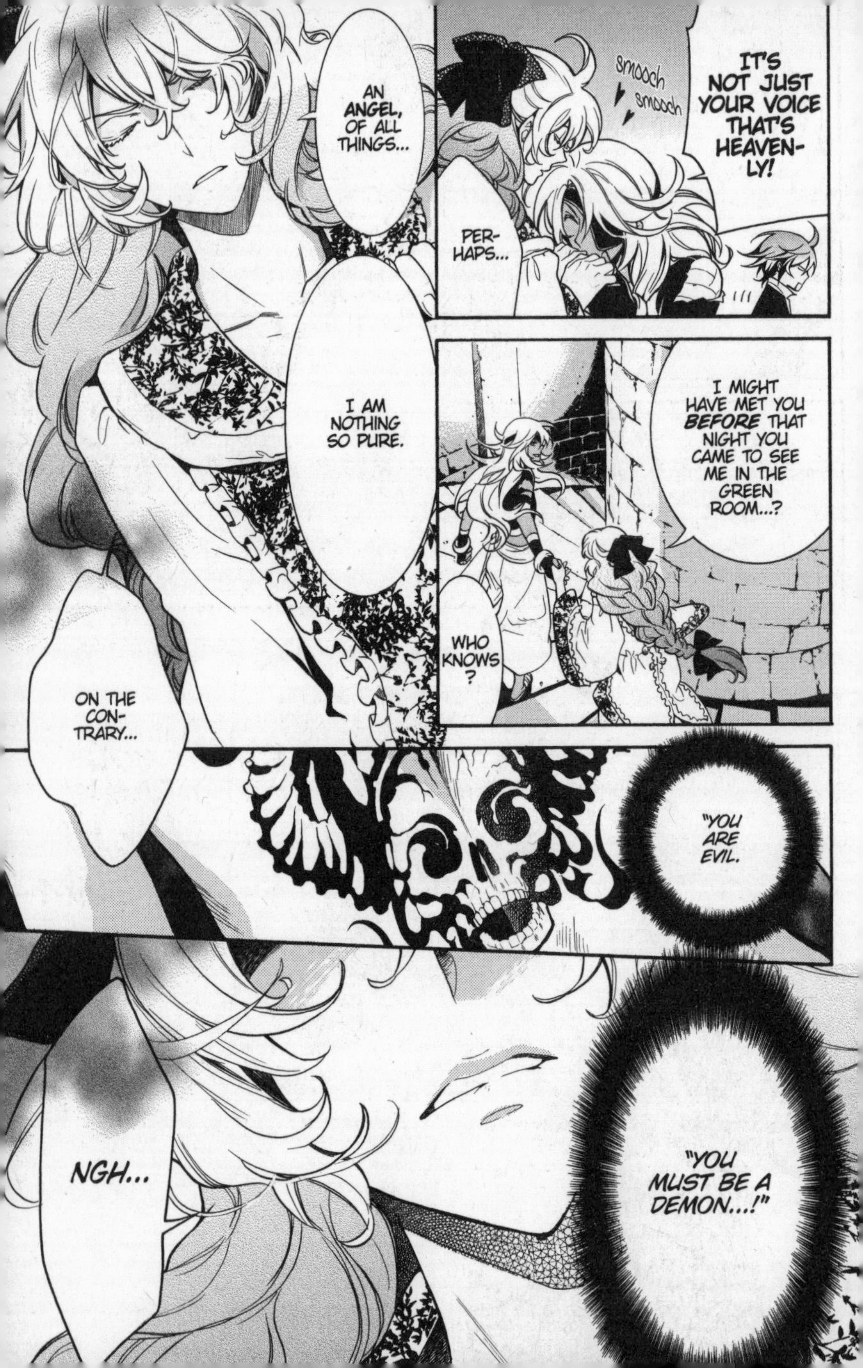
IT'S NOT JUST YOUR VOICE THAT'S HEAVEN-LY!
smooch smooch
PER-HAPS...
I MIGHT HAVE MET YOU BEFORE THAT NIGHT YOU CAME TO SEE ME IN THE GREEN ROOM...?
WHO KNOWS?
AN ANGEL, OF ALL THINGS...
I AM NOTHING SO PURE.
ON THE CON-TRARY...
"YOU ARE EVIL.
"YOU MUST BE A DEMON...!"
NGH...

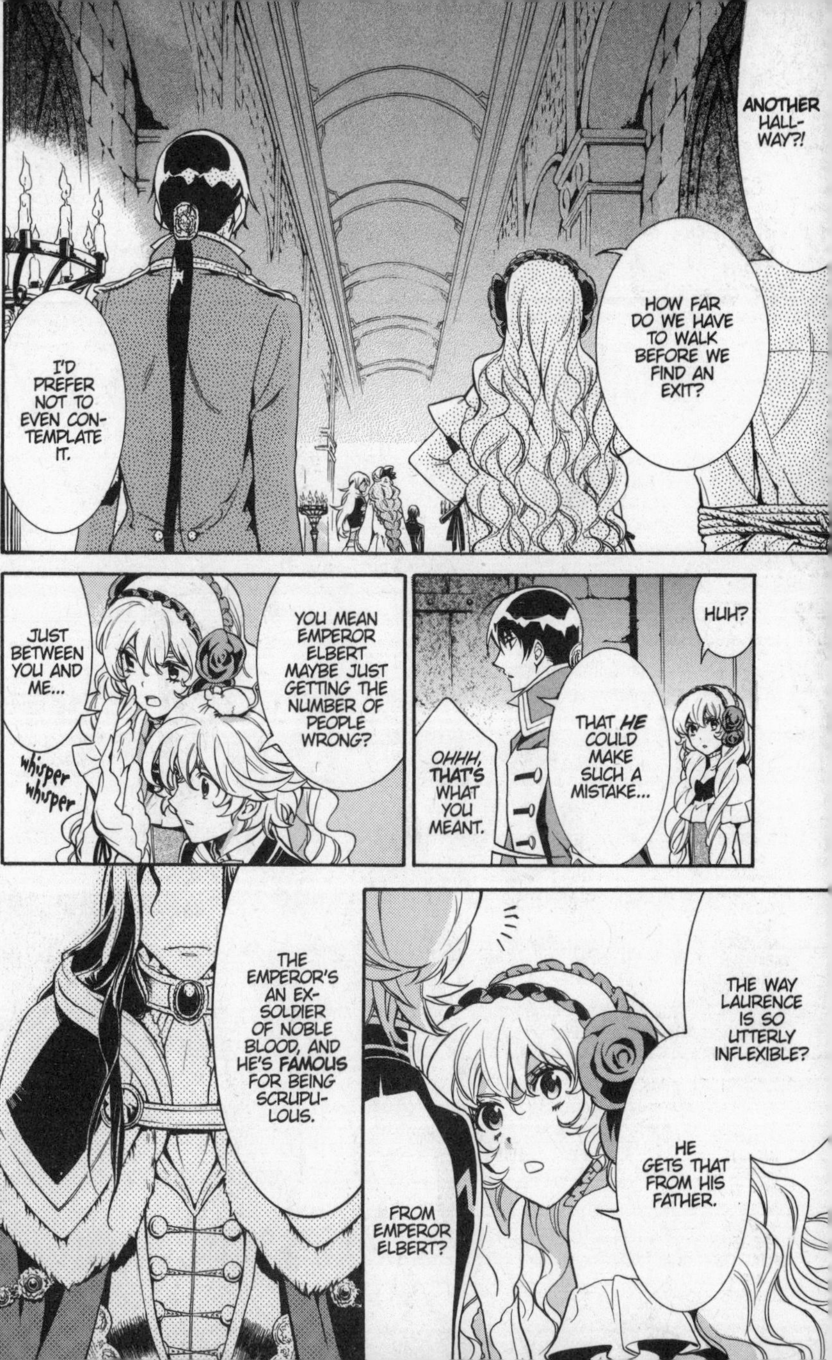
ANOTHER HALL-WAY?!
HOW FAR DO WE HAVE TO WALK BEFORE WE FIND AN EXIT?
I'D PREFER NOT TO EVEN CON-TEMPLATE IT.
HUH?
THAT *HE* COULD MAKE SUCH A MISTAKE...
OHHH, THAT'S WHAT YOU MEANT.
YOU MEAN EMPEROR ELBERT MAYBE JUST GETTING THE NUMBER OF PEOPLE WRONG?
JUST BETWEEN YOU AND ME...
whisper whisper
THE WAY LAURENCE IS SO UTTERLY INFLEXIBLE?
HE GETS THAT FROM HIS FATHER.
FROM EMPEROR ELBERT?
THE EMPEROR'S AN EX-SOLDIER OF NOBLE BLOOD, AND HE'S **FAMOUS** FOR BEING SCRUPULOUS.

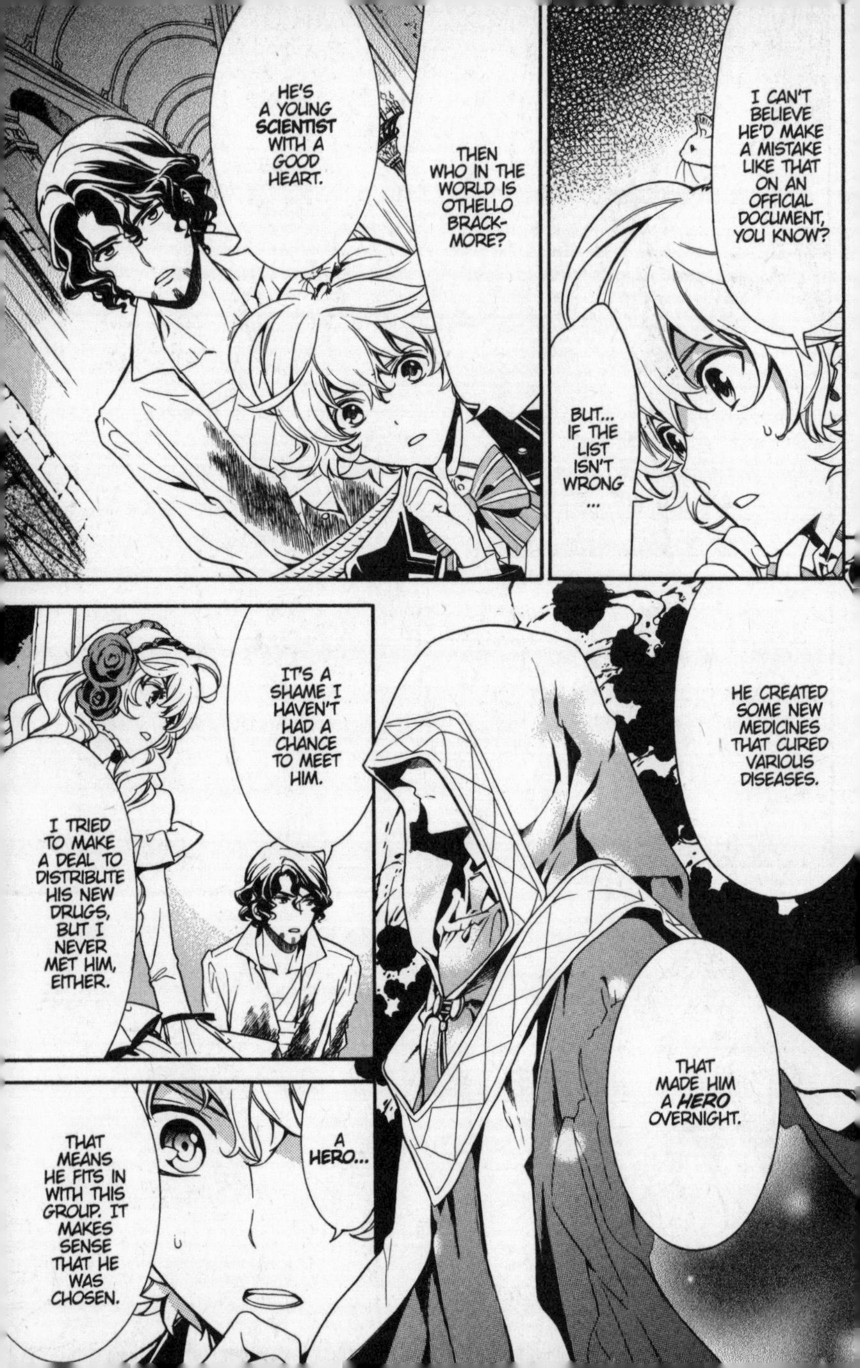
I CAN'T BELIEVE HE'D MAKE A MISTAKE LIKE THAT ON AN OFFICIAL DOCUMENT, YOU KNOW?
BUT... IF THE LIST ISN'T WRONG ...
THEN WHO IN THE WORLD IS OTHELLO BRACK-MORE?
HE'S A YOUNG SCIENTIST WITH A GOOD HEART.
HE CREATED SOME NEW MEDICINES THAT CURED VARIOUS DISEASES.
THAT MADE HIM A *HERO* OVERNIGHT.
IT'S A SHAME I HAVEN'T HAD A CHANCE TO MEET HIM.
I TRIED TO MAKE A DEAL TO DISTRIBUTE HIS NEW DRUGS, BUT I NEVER MET HIM, EITHER.
A HERO...
THAT MEANS HE FITS IN WITH THIS GROUP. IT MAKES SENSE THAT HE WAS CHOSEN.

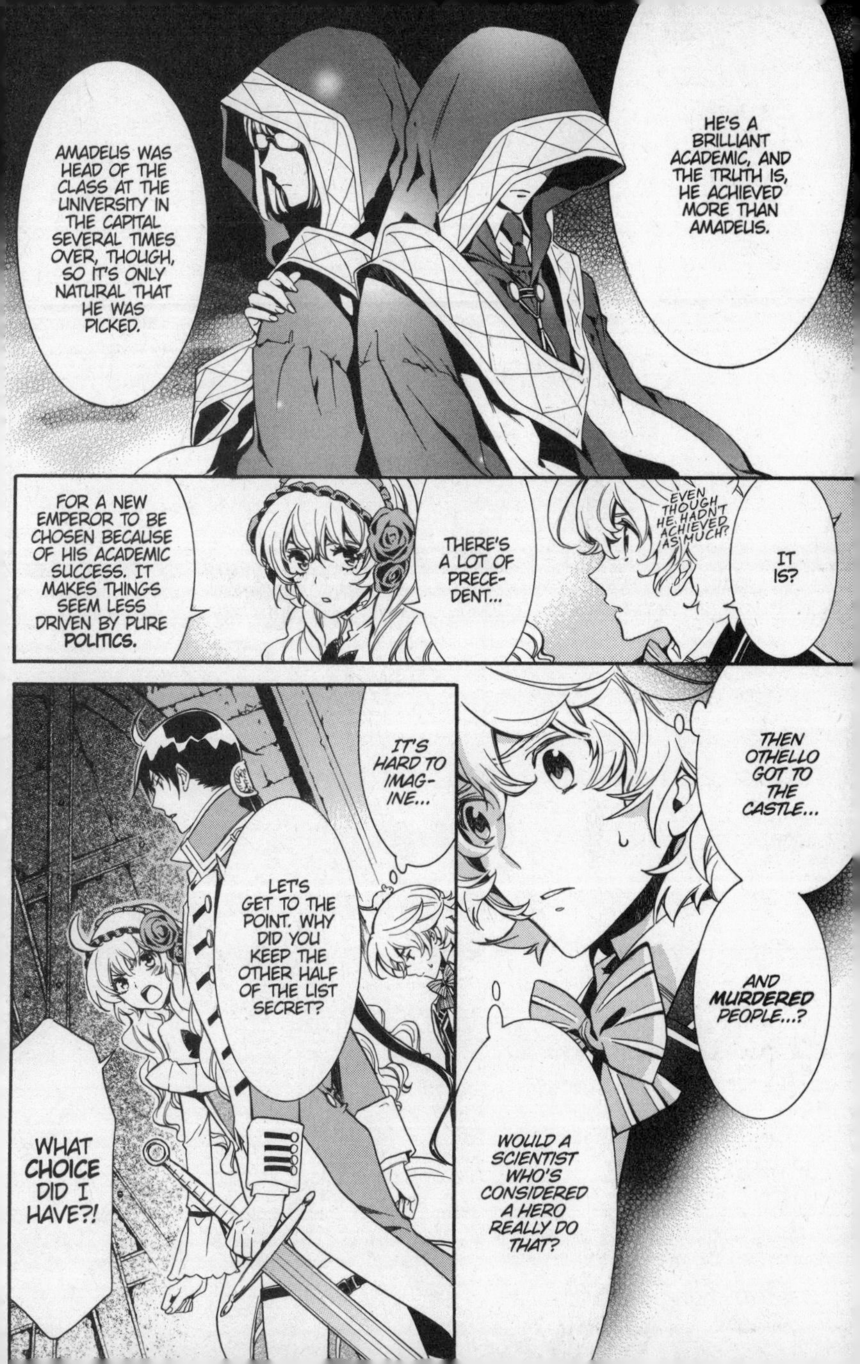
HE'S A BRILLIANT ACADEMIC, AND THE TRUTH IS, HE ACHIEVED MORE THAN AMADEUS.
AMADEUS WAS HEAD OF THE CLASS AT THE UNIVERSITY IN THE CAPITAL SEVERAL TIMES OVER, THOUGH, SO IT'S ONLY NATURAL THAT HE WAS PICKED.
IT IS?
EVEN THOUGH HE HADN'T ACHIEVED AS MUCH?
THERE'S A LOT OF PRECE-DENT...
FOR A NEW EMPEROR TO BE CHOSEN BECAUSE OF HIS ACADEMIC SUCCESS. IT MAKES THINGS SEEM LESS DRIVEN BY PURE POLITICS.
THEN OTHELLO GOT TO THE CASTLE...
AND MURDERED PEOPLE...?
WOULD A SCIENTIST WHO'S CONSIDERED A HERO REALLY DO THAT?
IT'S HARD TO IMAG-INE...
LET'S GET TO THE POINT. WHY DID YOU KEEP THE OTHER HALF OF THE LIST SECRET?
WHAT CHOICE DID I HAVE?!

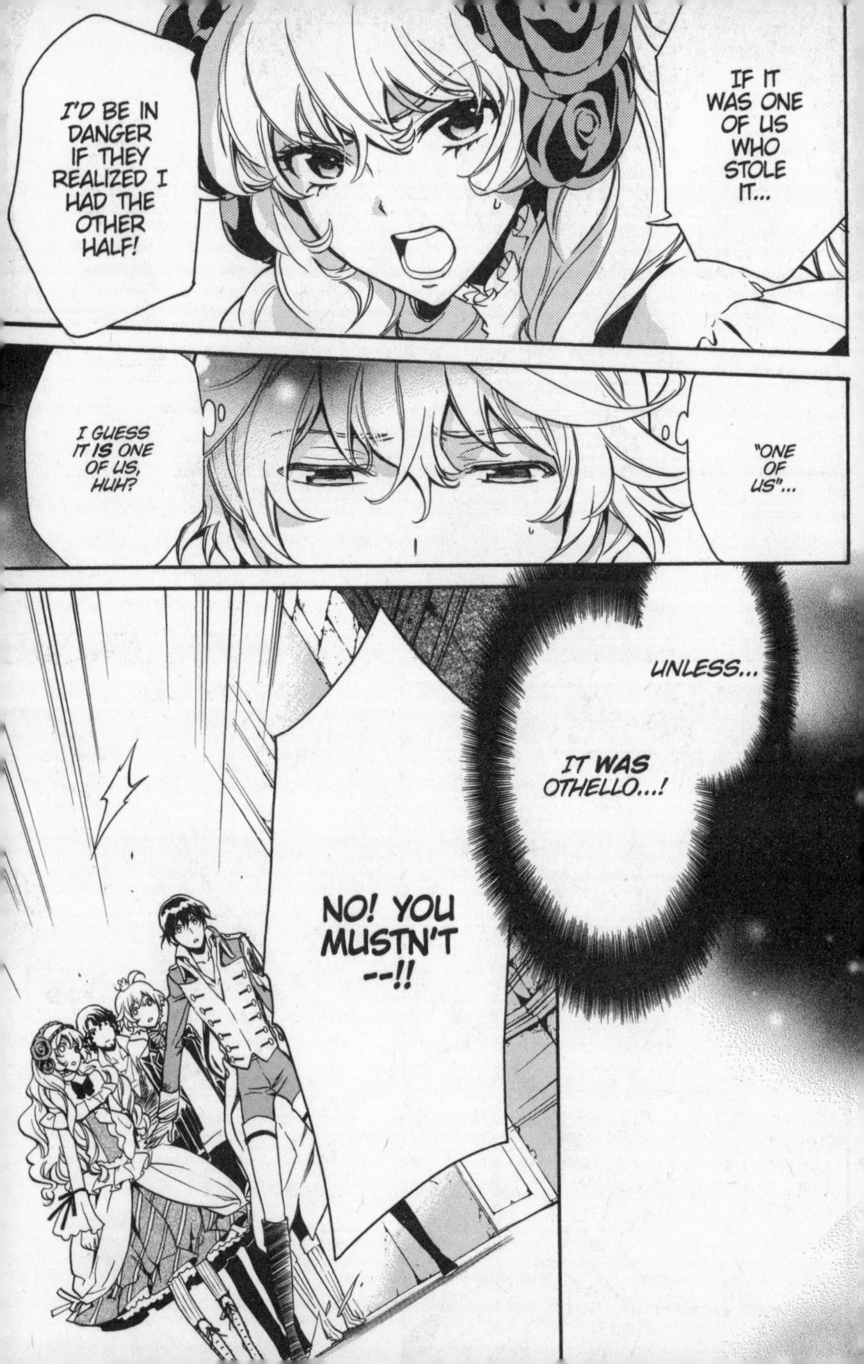
IF IT WAS ONE OF US WHO STOLE IT...
I'D BE IN DANGER IF THEY REALIZED I HAD THE OTHER HALF!
"ONE OF US"...
I GUESS IT IS ONE OF US, HUH?
UNLESS...
IT WAS OTHELLO...!
NO! YOU MUSTN'T --!!

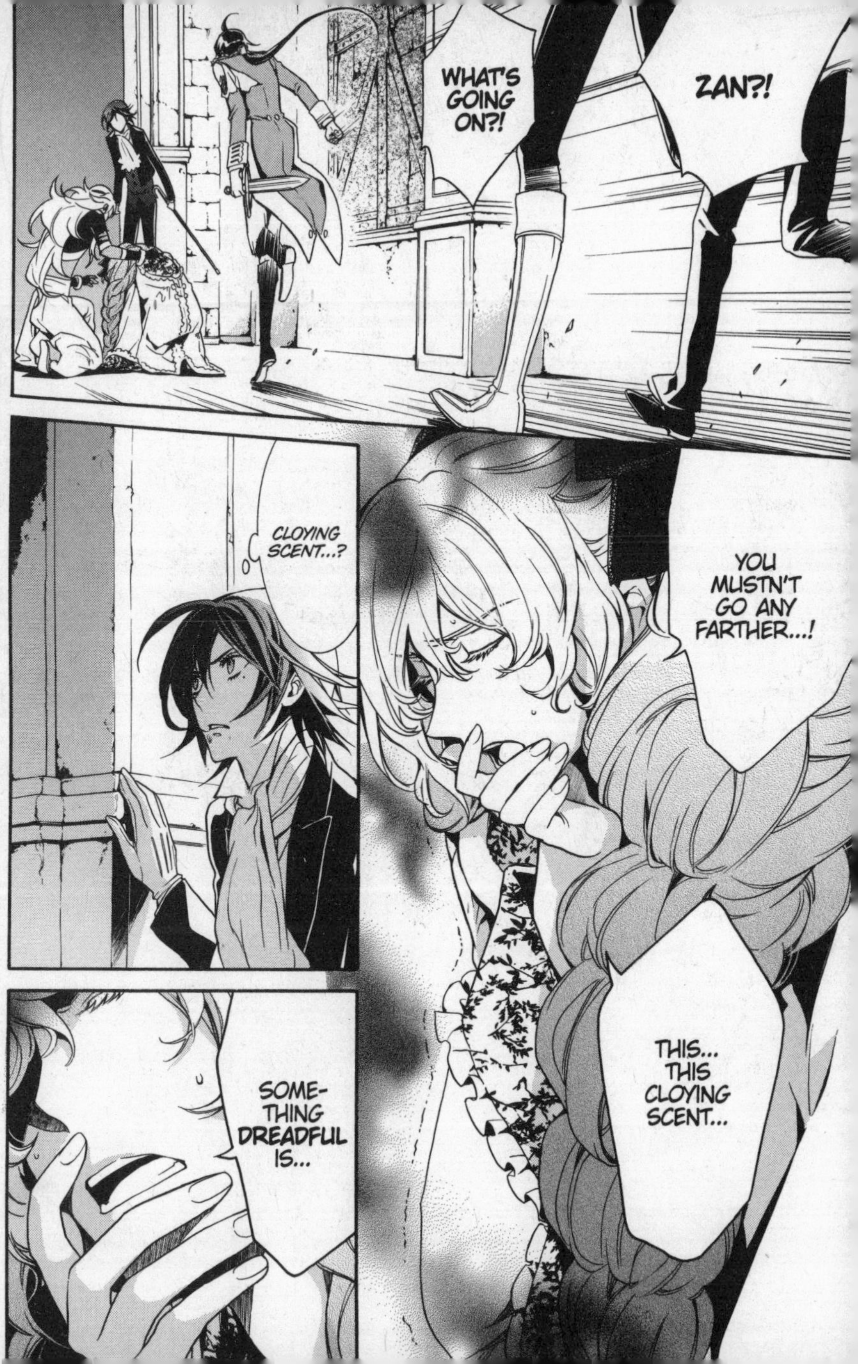
ZAN?!
WHAT'S GOING ON?!
YOU MUSTN'T GO ANY FARTHER...!
THIS... THIS CLOYING SCENT...
CLOYING SCENT...?
SOME-THING DREADFUL IS...

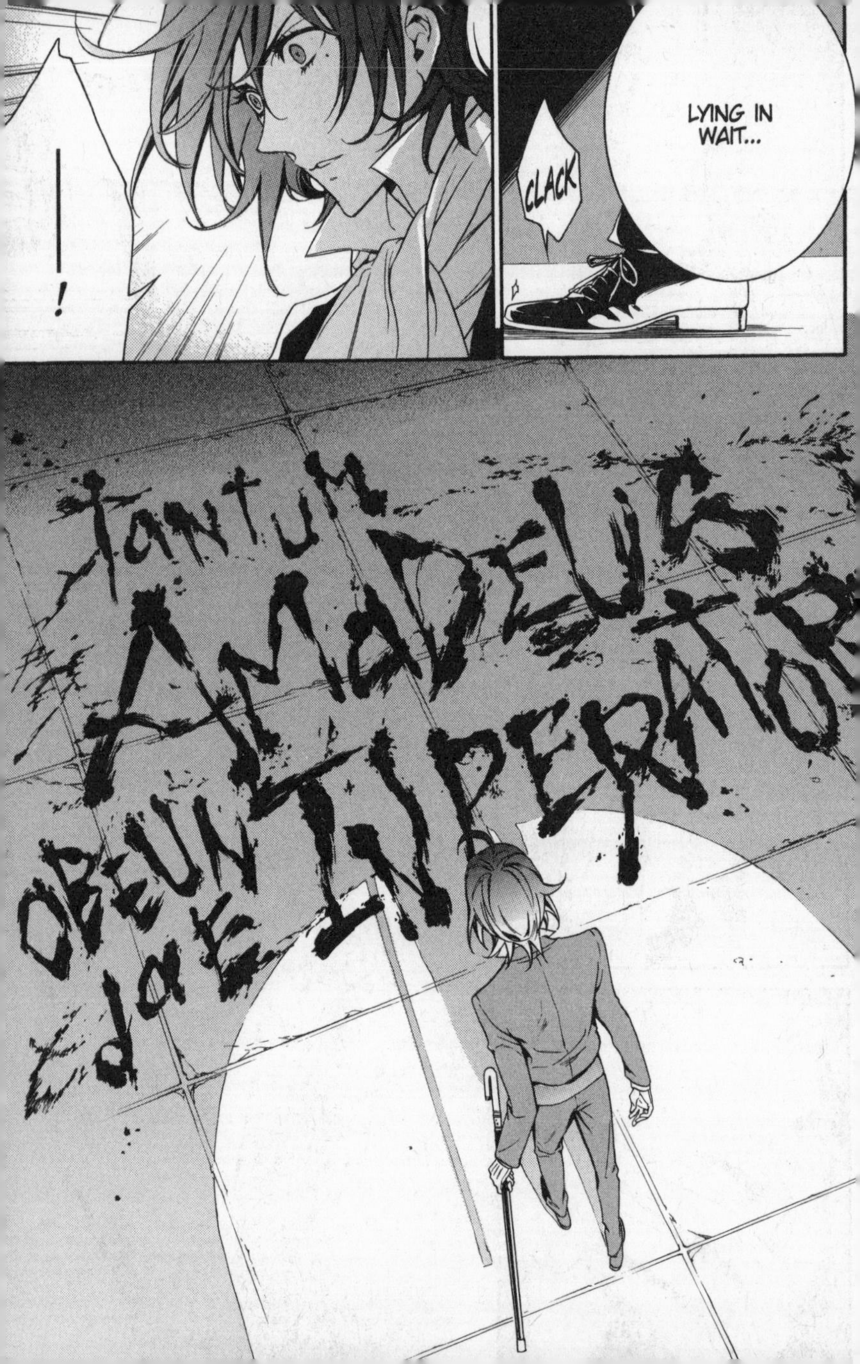
LYING IN WAIT...
CLACK
—!

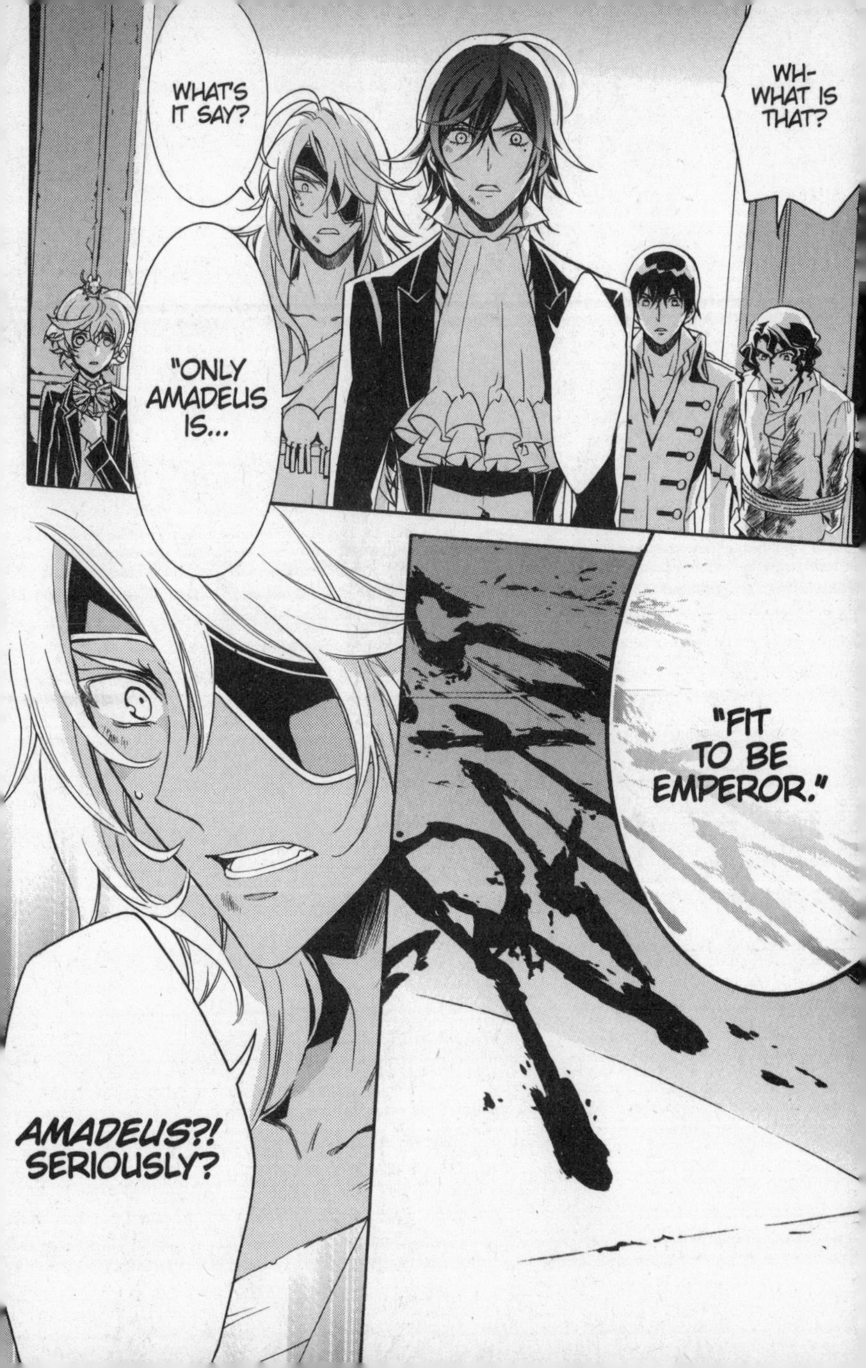
WH- WHAT IS THAT?
WHAT'S IT SAY?
"ONLY AMADEUS IS...
"FIT TO BE EMPEROR."
AMADEUS?! SERIOUSLY?

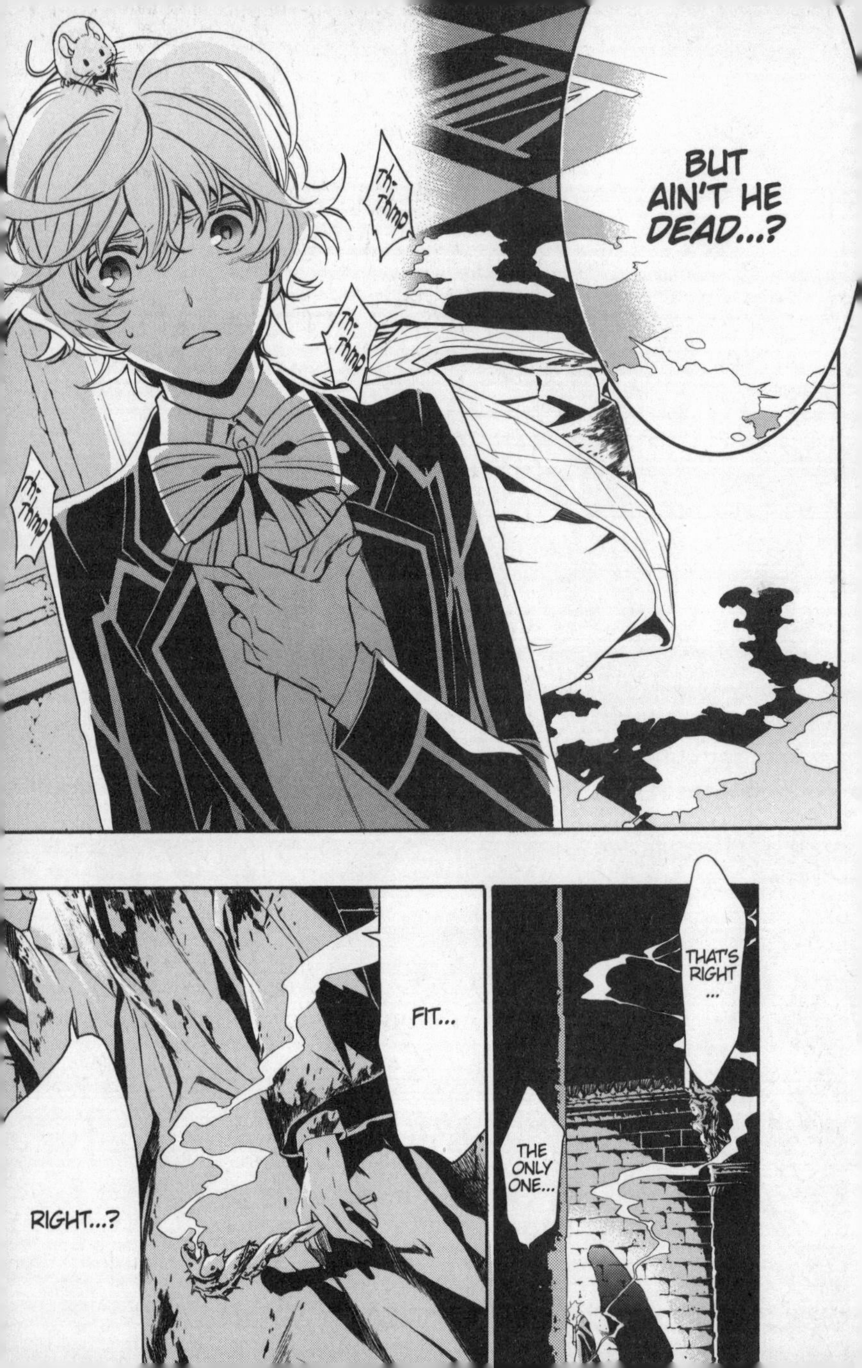
BUT AIN'T HE DEAD...?
thi-thmp
thi-thmp
thi-thmp
THAT'S RIGHT ...
THE ONLY ONE...
FIT...
RIGHT...?

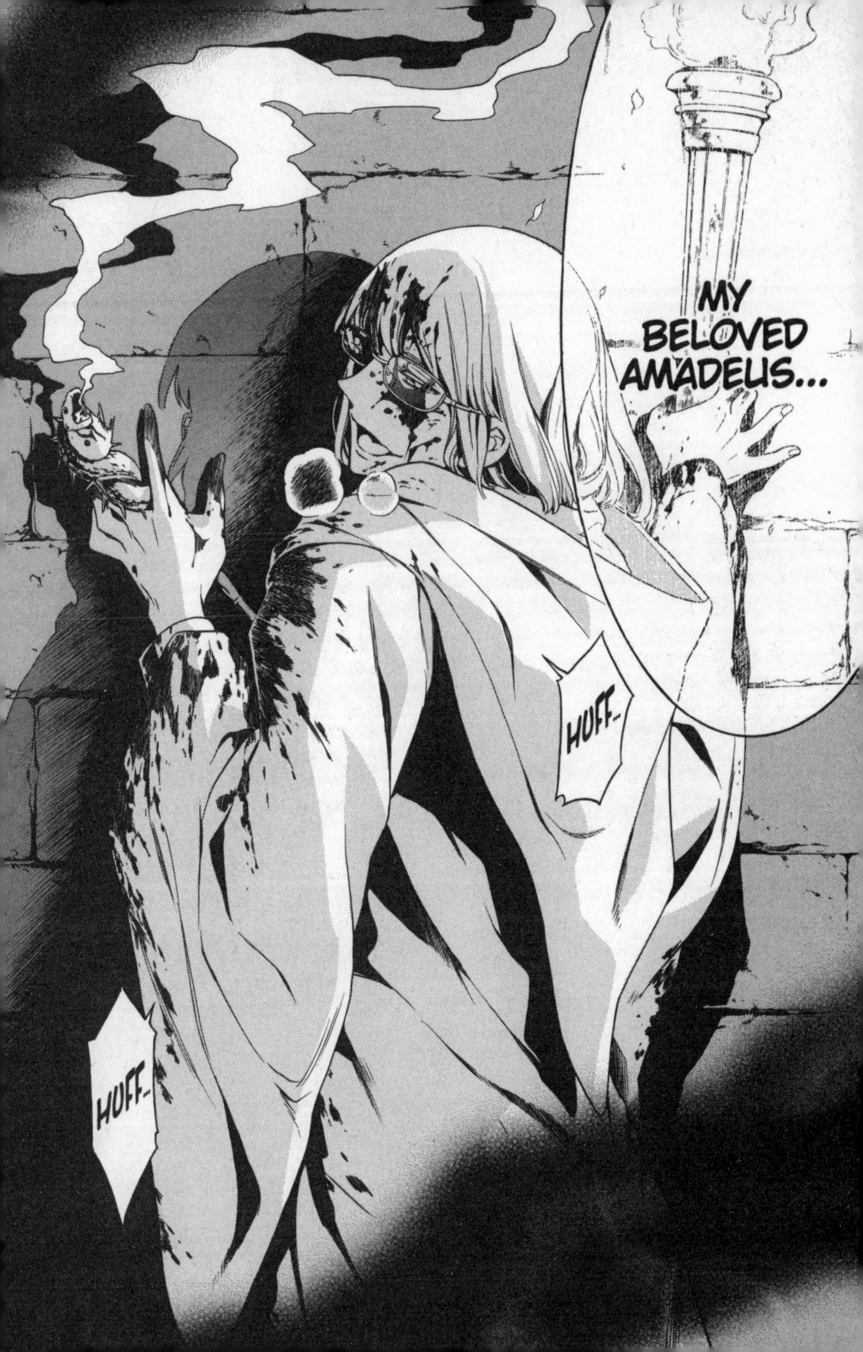
MY BELOVED AMADEUS...
HUFF...
HUFF...

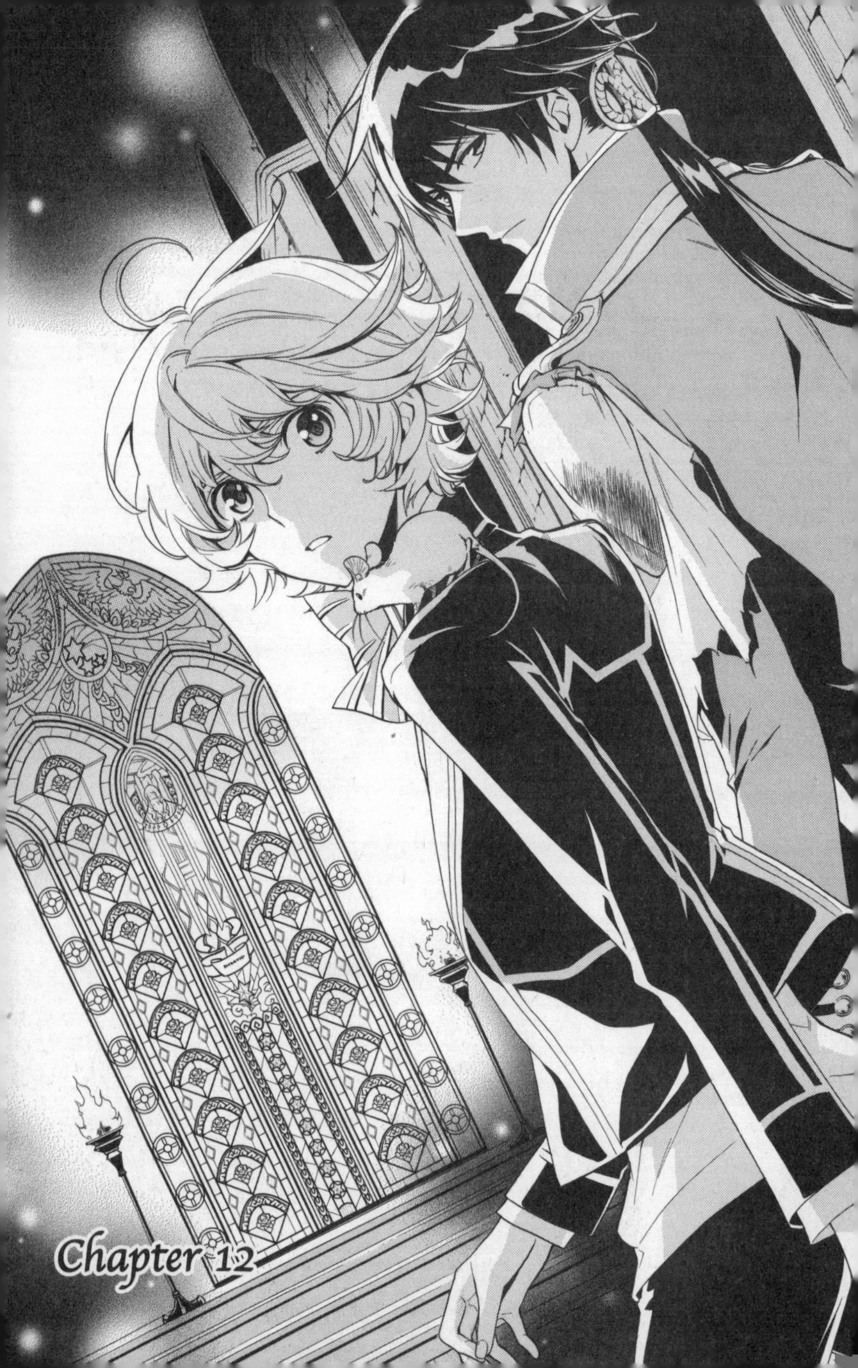
Chapter 12

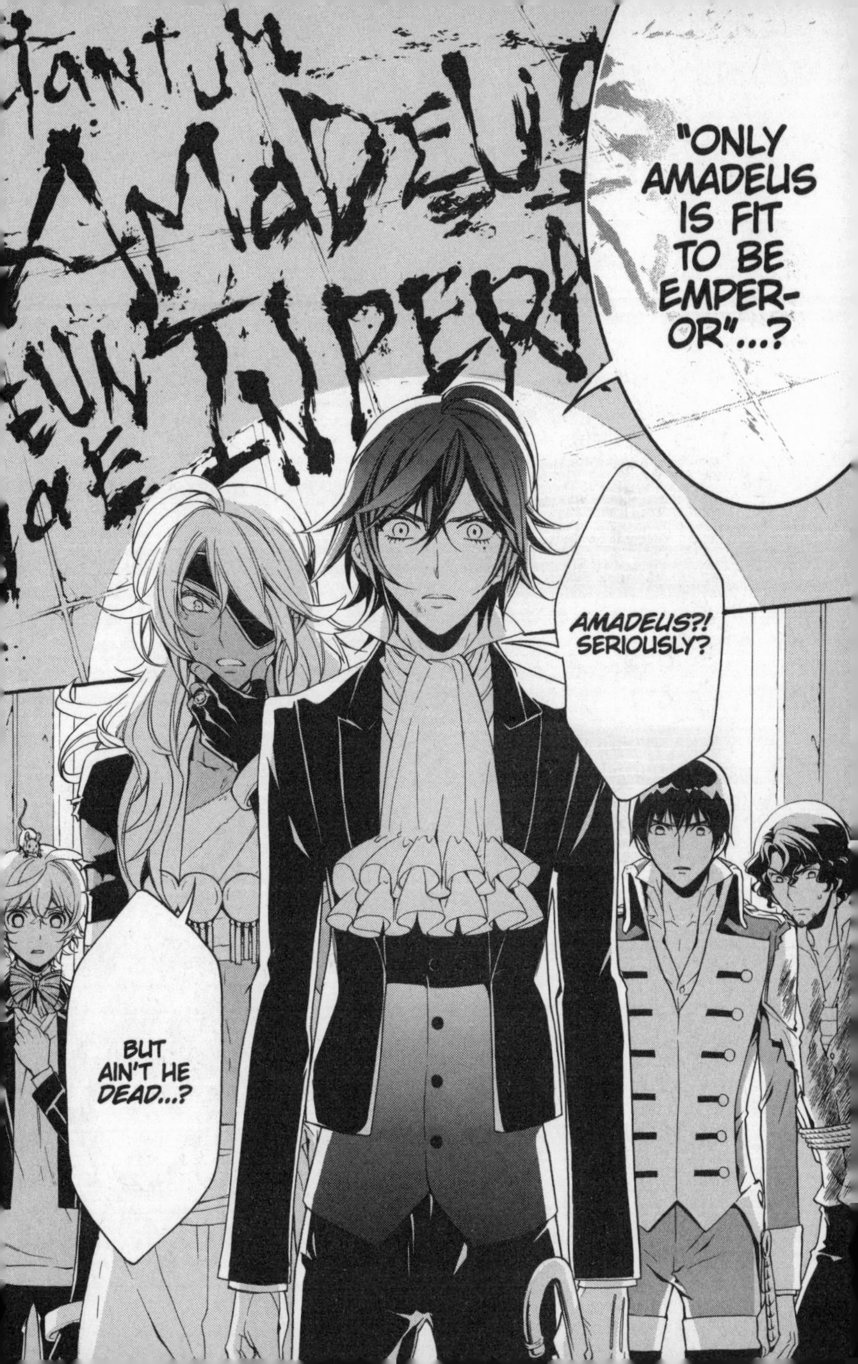
"ONLY AMADEUS IS FIT TO BE EMPER-OR"...?
AMADEUS?! SERIOUSLY?
BUT AIN'T HE DEAD...?

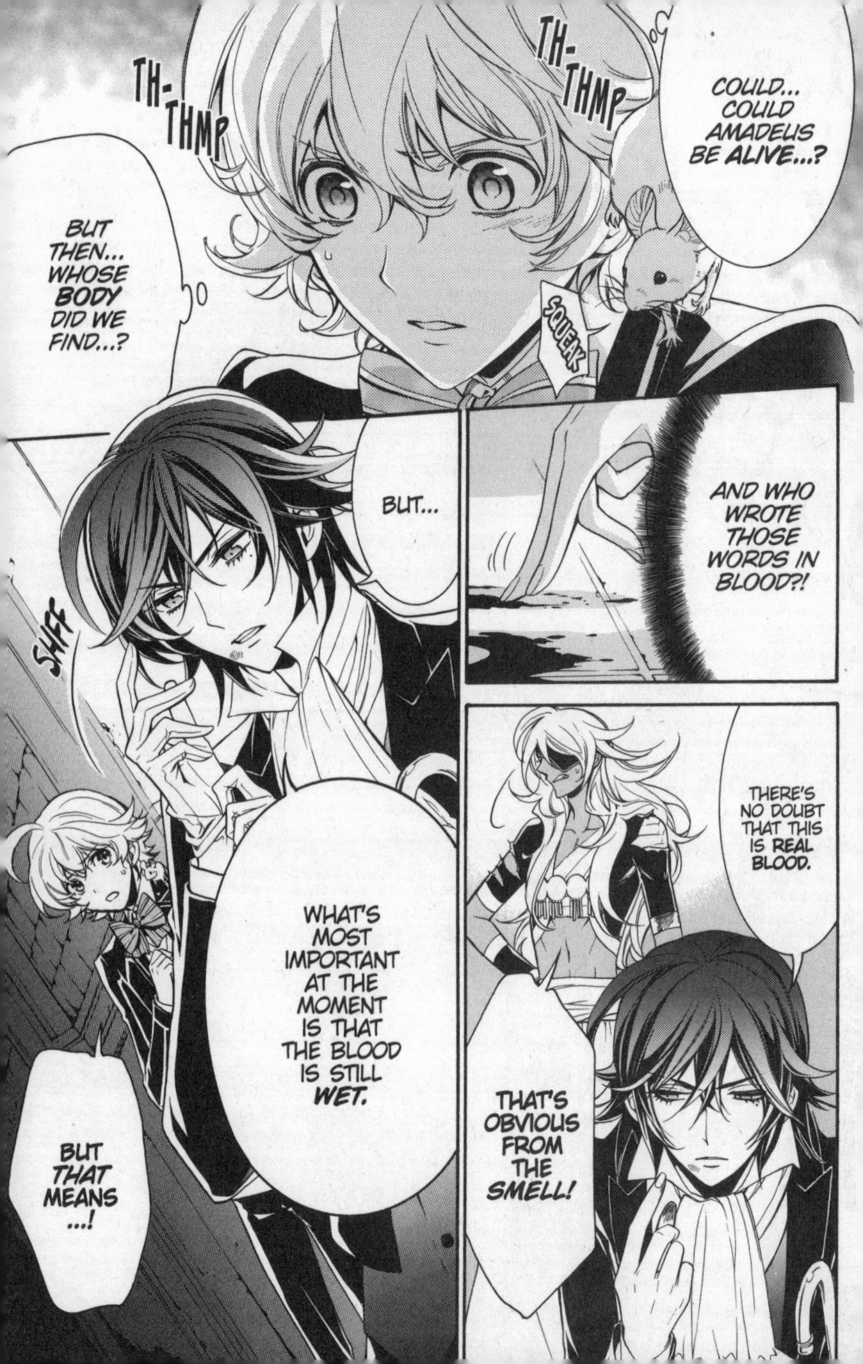

COULD... COULD AMADEUS BE ALIVE...?
TH-THMP
TH-THMP
SQUEAK
BUT THEN... WHOSE BODY DID WE FIND...?
AND WHO WROTE THOSE WORDS IN BLOOD?!
THERE'S NO DOUBT THAT THIS IS REAL BLOOD.
THAT'S OBVIOUS FROM THE SMELL!
BUT...
SHFF
WHAT'S MOST IMPORTANT AT THE MOMENT IS THAT THE BLOOD IS STILL WET.
BUT THAT MEANS ...!

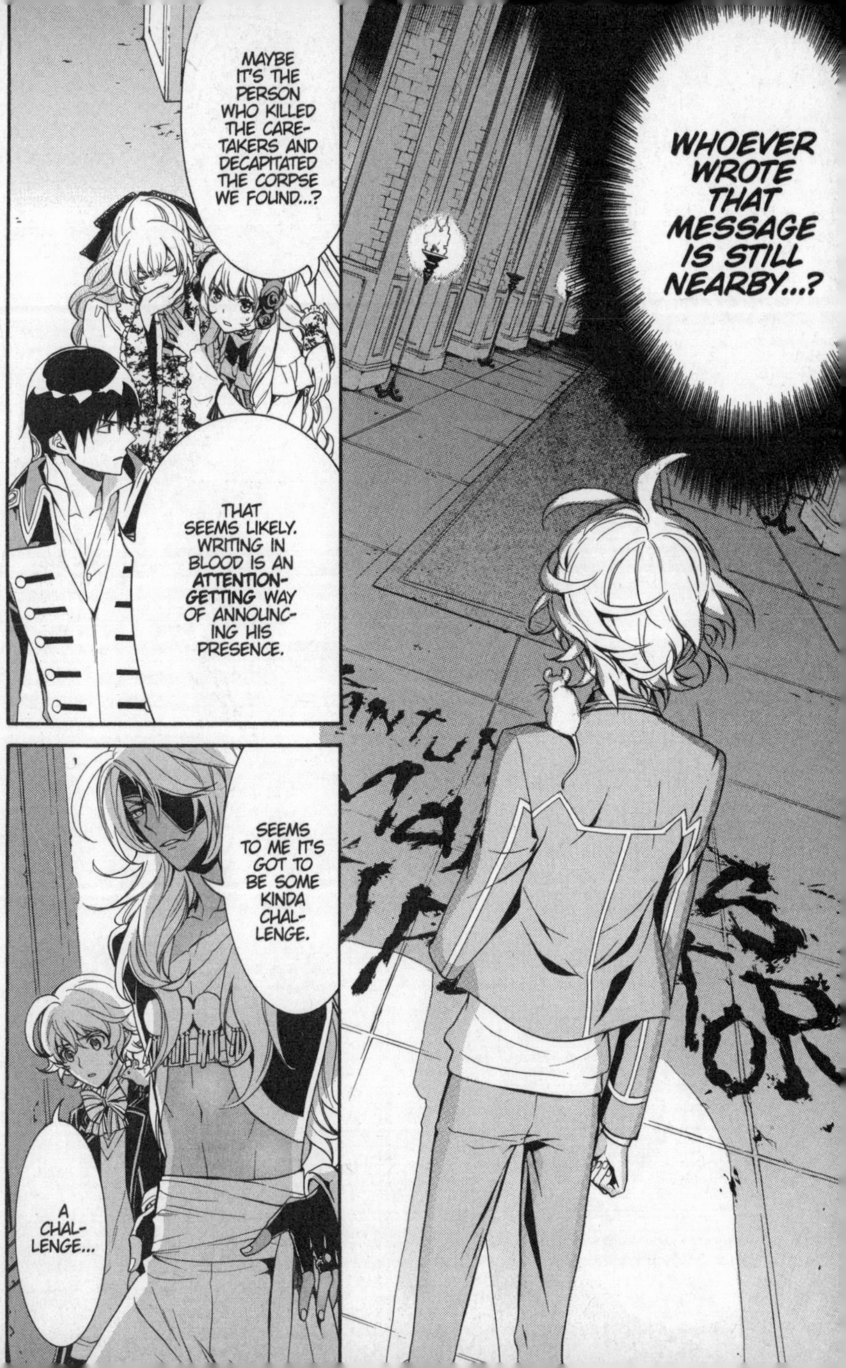
WHOEVER WROTE THAT MESSAGE IS STILL NEARBY...?
MAYBE IT'S THE PERSON WHO KILLED THE CARE-TAKERS AND DECAPITATED THE CORPSE WE FOUND...?
THAT SEEMS LIKELY. WRITING IN BLOOD IS AN ATTENTION-GETTING WAY OF ANNOUNC-ING HIS PRESENCE.
SEEMS TO ME IT'S GOT TO BE SOME KINDA CHAL-LENGE.
A CHAL-LENGE...

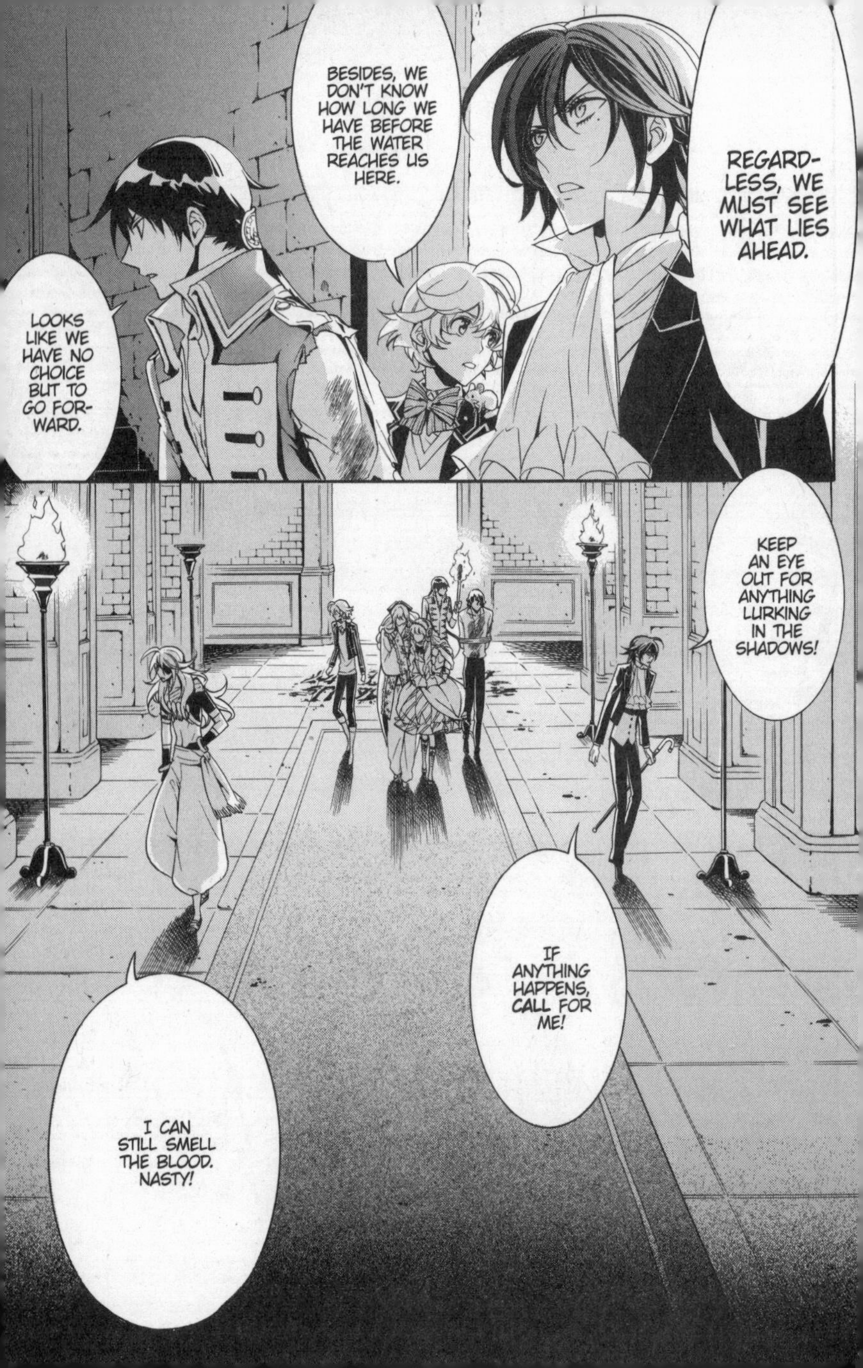
REGARDLESS, WE MUST SEE WHAT LIES AHEAD.
BESIDES, WE DON'T KNOW HOW LONG WE HAVE BEFORE THE WATER REACHES US HERE.
LOOKS LIKE WE HAVE NO CHOICE BUT TO GO FORWARD.
KEEP AN EYE OUT FOR ANYTHING LURKING IN THE SHADOWS!
IF ANYTHING HAPPENS, CALL FOR ME!
I CAN STILL SMELL THE BLOOD. NASTY!

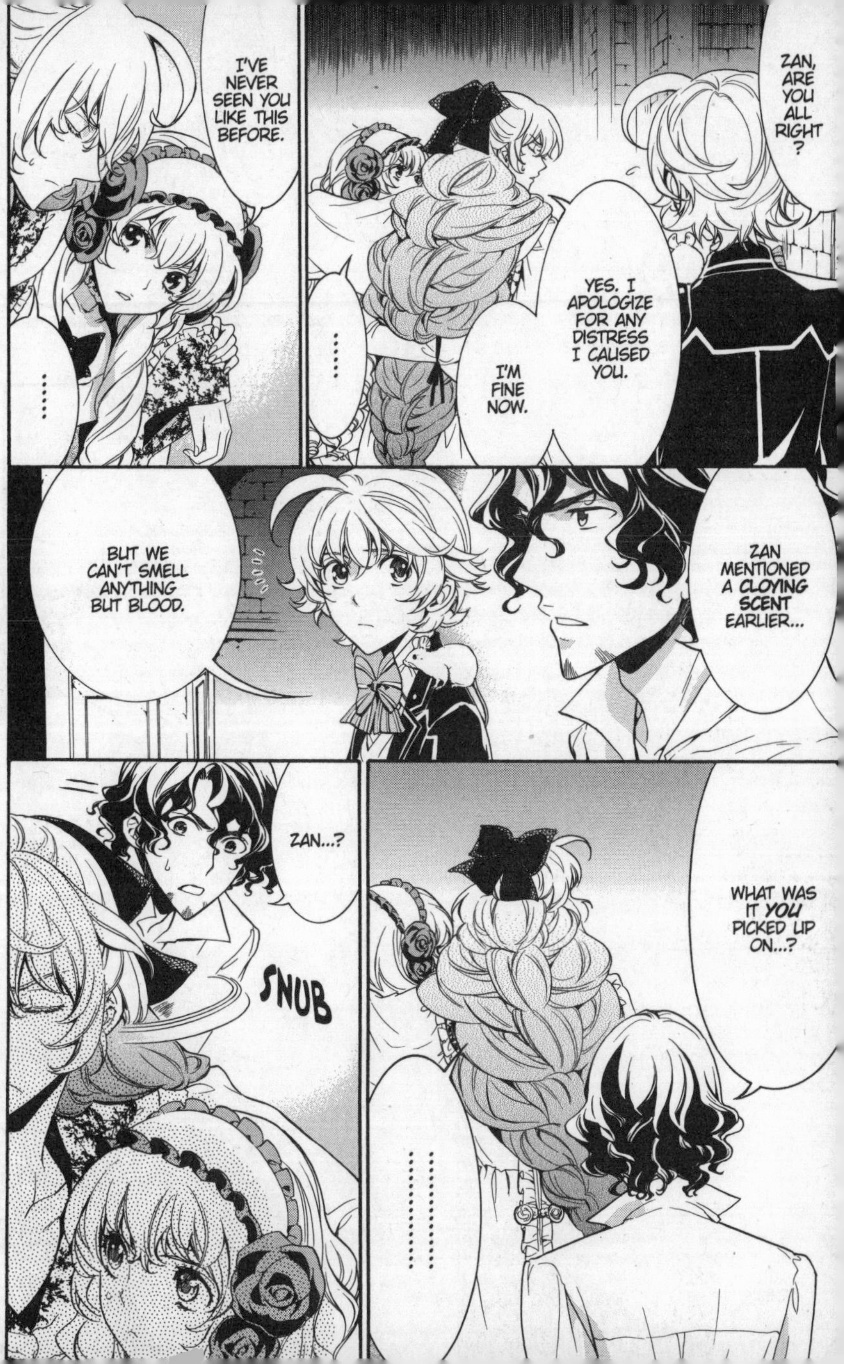
ZAN, ARE YOU ALL RIGHT?
YES. I APOLOGIZE FOR ANY DISTRESS I CAUSED YOU.
I'M FINE NOW.
......
I'VE NEVER SEEN YOU LIKE THIS BEFORE.
......
ZAN MENTIONED A CLOYING SCENT EARLIER...
BUT WE CAN'T SMELL ANYTHING BUT BLOOD.
WHAT WAS IT YOU PICKED UP ON...?
......
ZAN...?
SNUB

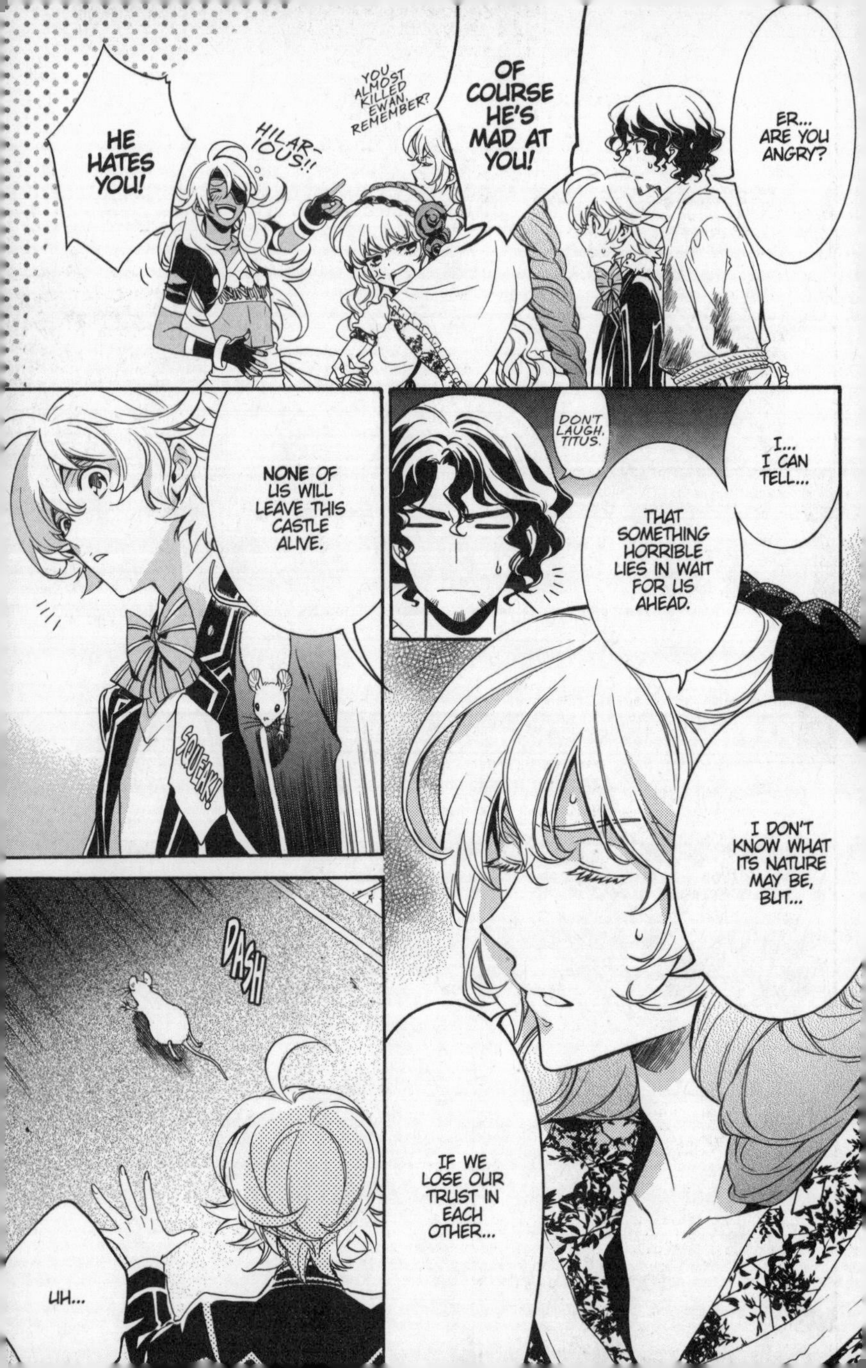
ER... ARE YOU ANGRY?
OF COURSE HE'S MAD AT YOU!
YOU ALMOST KILLED EWAN, REMEMBER?
HILAR-IOUS!!
HE HATES YOU!
I... I CAN TELL...
DON'T LAUGH, TITUS.
THAT SOMETHING HORRIBLE LIES IN WAIT FOR US AHEAD.
I DON'T KNOW WHAT ITS NATURE MAY BE, BUT...
IF WE LOSE OUR TRUST IN EACH OTHER...
NONE OF US WILL LEAVE THIS CASTLE ALIVE.
SQUEAK!
DASH
UH...

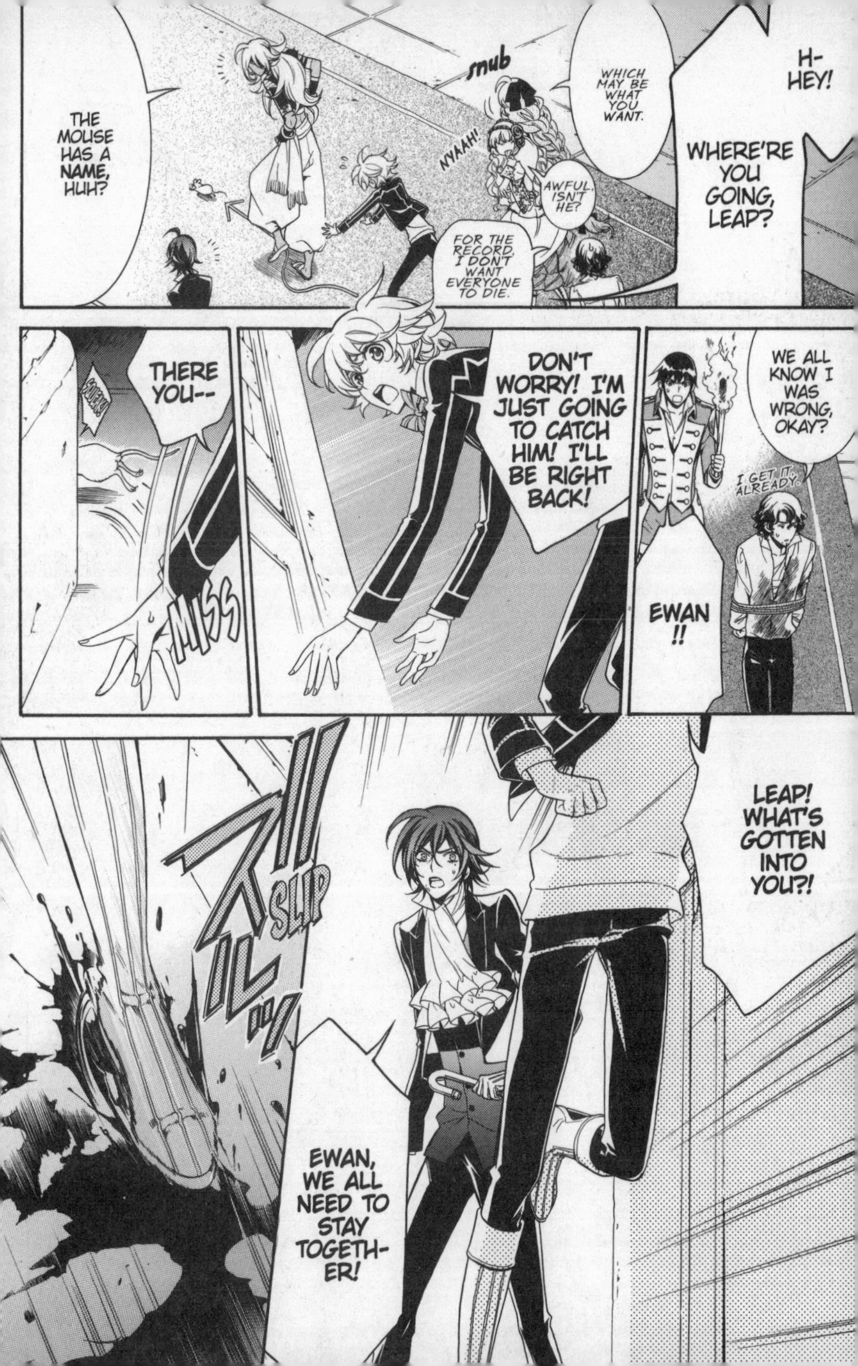
H-
HEY!
WHERE'RE YOU GOING, LEAP?
WHICH MAY BE WHAT YOU WANT.
snub
AWFUL, ISN'T HE?
NYAAH!
FOR THE RECORD, I DON'T WANT EVERYONE TO DIE.
THE MOUSE HAS A NAME, HUH?
WE ALL KNOW I WAS WRONG, OKAY?
I GET IT, ALREADY.
EWAN !!
DON'T WORRY! I'M JUST GOING TO CATCH HIM! I'LL BE RIGHT BACK!
THERE YOU--
SQUEAK!
MISS
LEAP! WHAT'S GOTTEN INTO YOU?!
SLIP
EWAN, WE ALL NEED TO STAY TOGETH-ER!

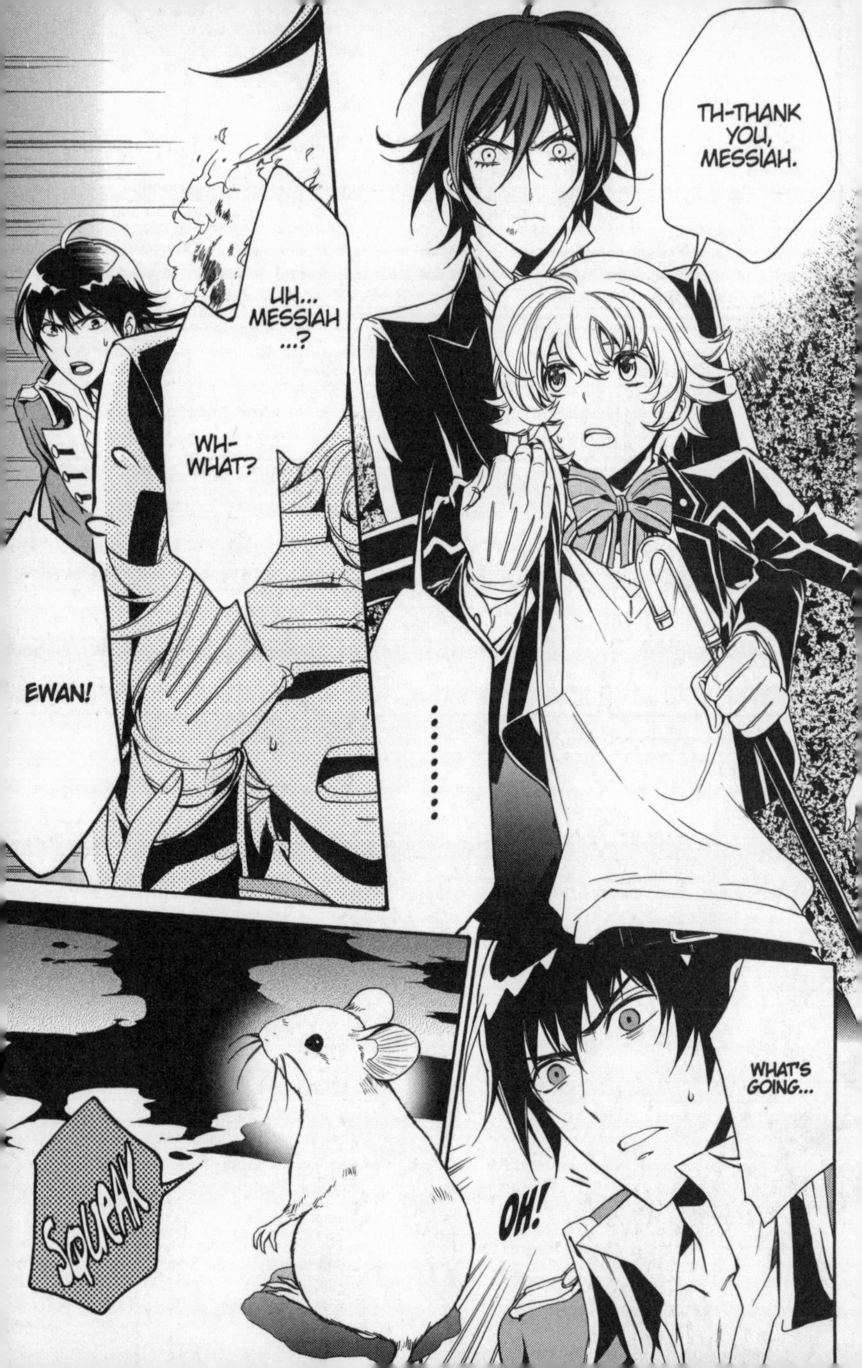
TH-THANK YOU, MESSIAH.
......
UH... MESSIAH ...?
WH-WHAT?
EWAN!
WHAT'S GOING...
OH!
SQUEAK

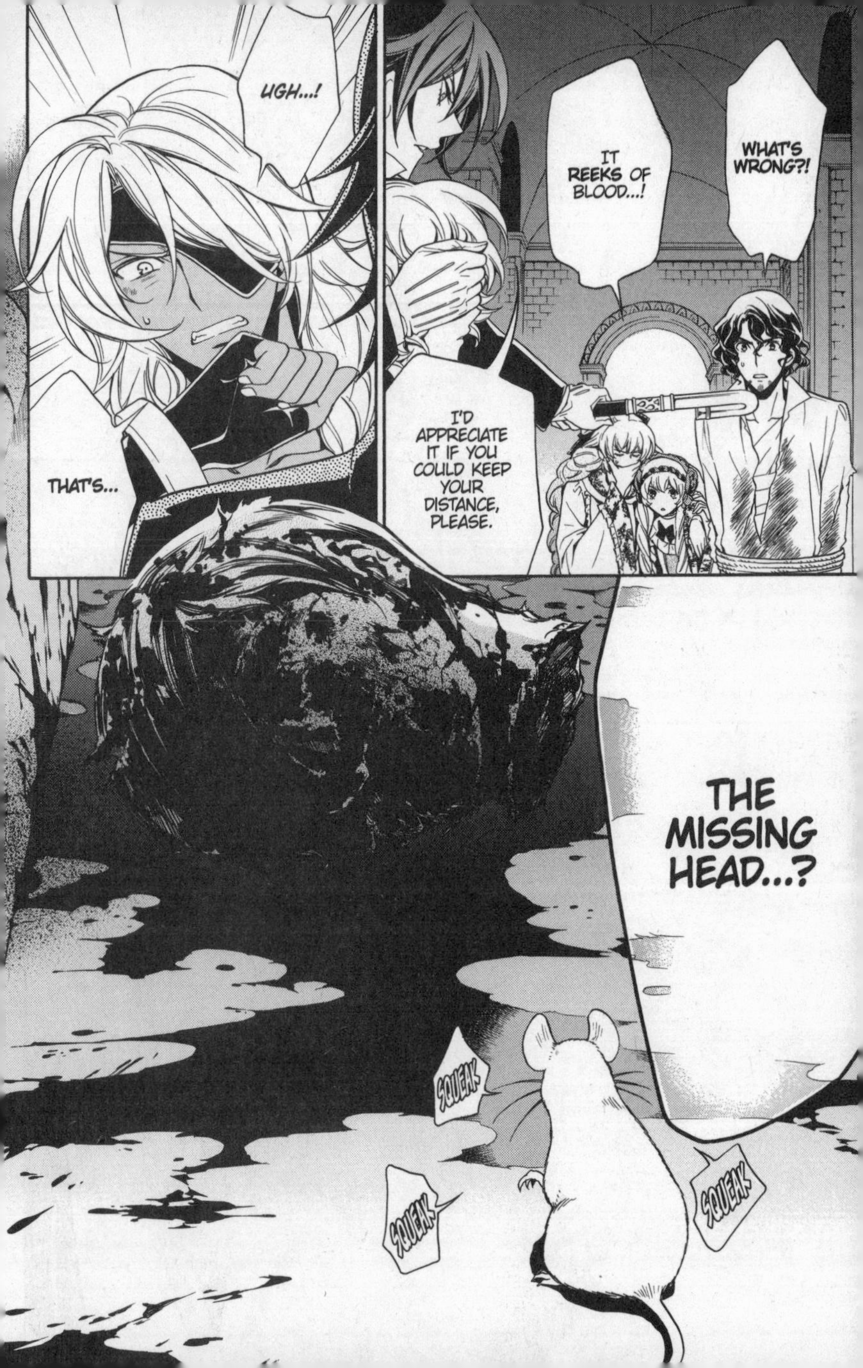
WHAT'S WRONG?!
IT REEKS OF BLOOD...!
I'D APPRECIATE IT IF YOU COULD KEEP YOUR DISTANCE, PLEASE.
UGH...!
THAT'S...
THE MISSING HEAD...?
SQUEAK
SQUEAK
SQUEAK

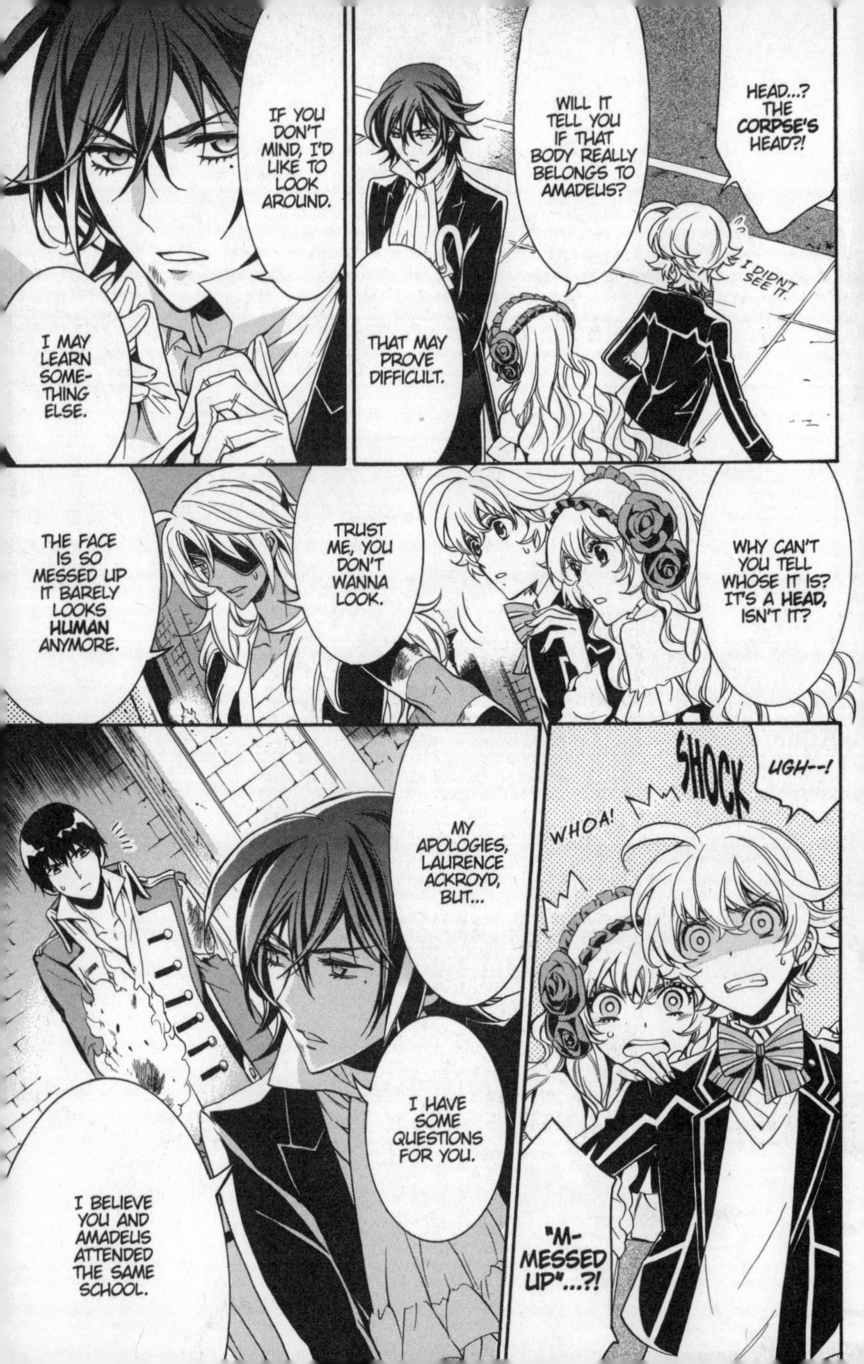
HEAD...? THE CORPSE'S HEAD?!
WILL IT TELL YOU IF THAT BODY REALLY BELONGS TO AMADEUS?
I DIDN'T SEE IT.
THAT MAY PROVE DIFFICULT.
IF YOU DON'T MIND, I'D LIKE TO LOOK AROUND.
I MAY LEARN SOME-THING ELSE.
WHY CAN'T YOU TELL WHOSE IT IS? IT'S A HEAD, ISN'T IT?
TRUST ME, YOU DON'T WANNA LOOK.
THE FACE IS SO MESSED UP IT BARELY LOOKS HUMAN ANYMORE.
UGH--!
SHOCK
WHOA!
"M-MESSED UP"...?!
MY APOLOGIES, LAURENCE ACKROYD, BUT...
I HAVE SOME QUESTIONS FOR YOU.
I BELIEVE YOU AND AMADEUS ATTENDED THE SAME SCHOOL.

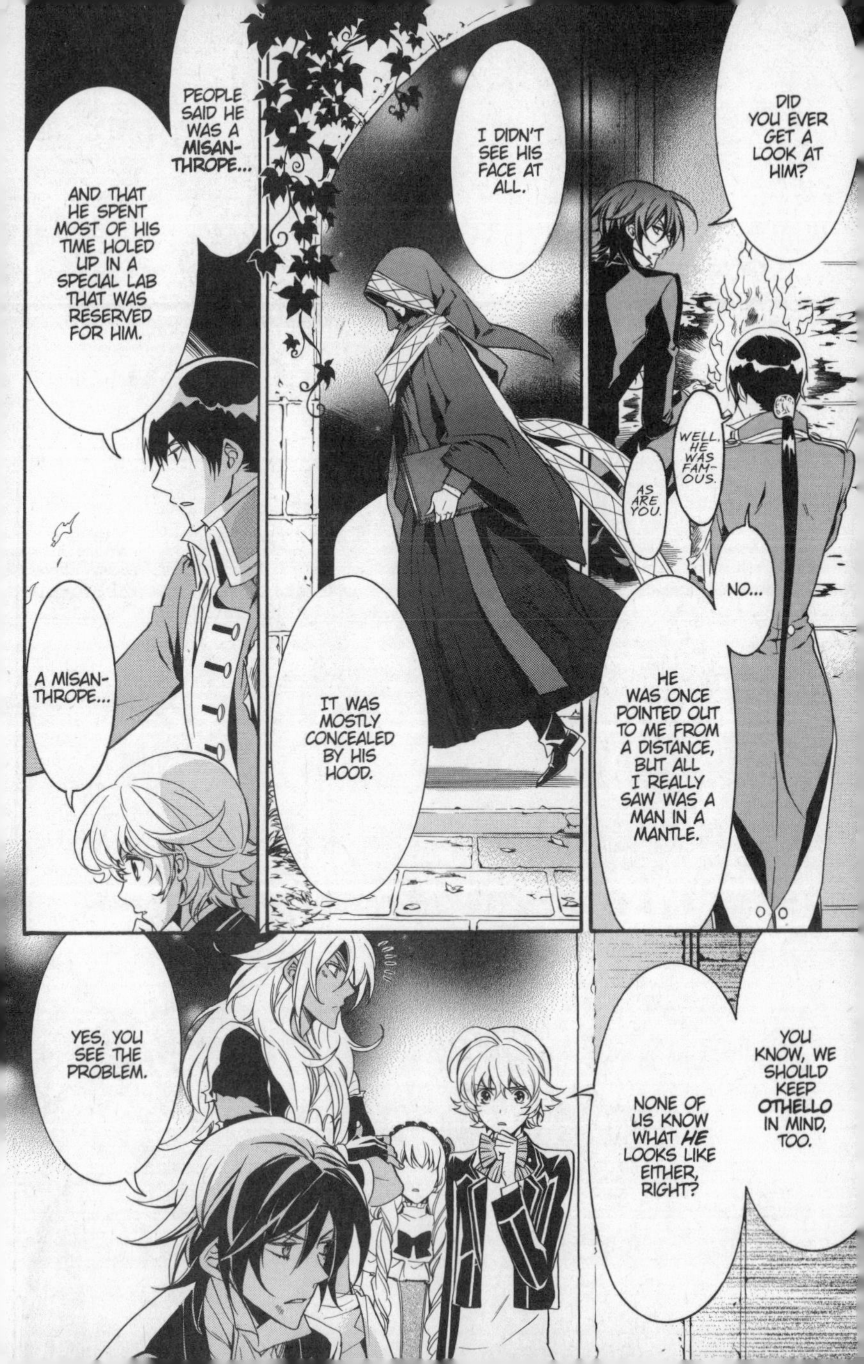
DID YOU EVER GET A LOOK AT HIM?
WELL, HE WAS FAMOUS.
AS ARE YOU.
NO...
HE WAS ONCE POINTED OUT TO ME FROM A DISTANCE, BUT ALL I REALLY SAW WAS A MAN IN A MANTLE.
I DIDN'T SEE HIS FACE AT ALL.
IT WAS MOSTLY CONCEALED BY HIS HOOD.
PEOPLE SAID HE WAS A MISANTHROPE...
AND THAT HE SPENT MOST OF HIS TIME HOLED UP IN A SPECIAL LAB THAT WAS RESERVED FOR HIM.
A MISANTHROPE...
YOU KNOW, WE SHOULD KEEP **OTHELLO** IN MIND, TOO.
NONE OF US KNOW WHAT ***HE*** LOOKS LIKE EITHER, RIGHT?
YES, YOU SEE THE PROBLEM.

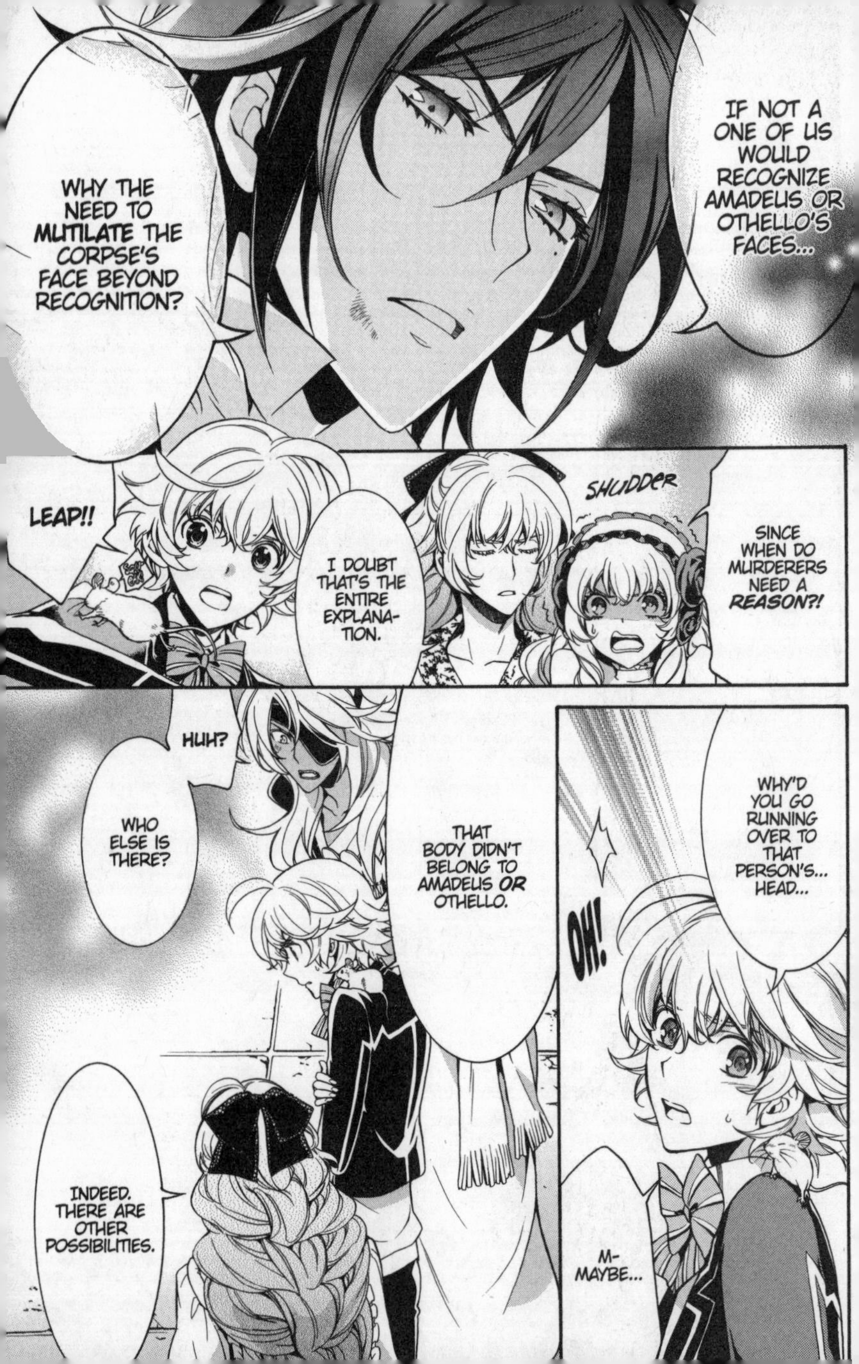
IF NOT A ONE OF US WOULD RECOGNIZE AMADEUS OR OTHELLO'S FACES...
WHY THE NEED TO MUTILATE THE CORPSE'S FACE BEYOND RECOGNITION?
SINCE WHEN DO MURDERERS NEED A REASON?!
SHUDDER
I DOUBT THAT'S THE ENTIRE EXPLANATION.
LEAP!!
WHY'D YOU GO RUNNING OVER TO THAT PERSON'S... HEAD...
OH!
M-MAYBE...
THAT BODY DIDN'T BELONG TO AMADEUS OR OTHELLO.
HUH?
WHO ELSE IS THERE?
INDEED. THERE ARE OTHER POSSIBILITIES.

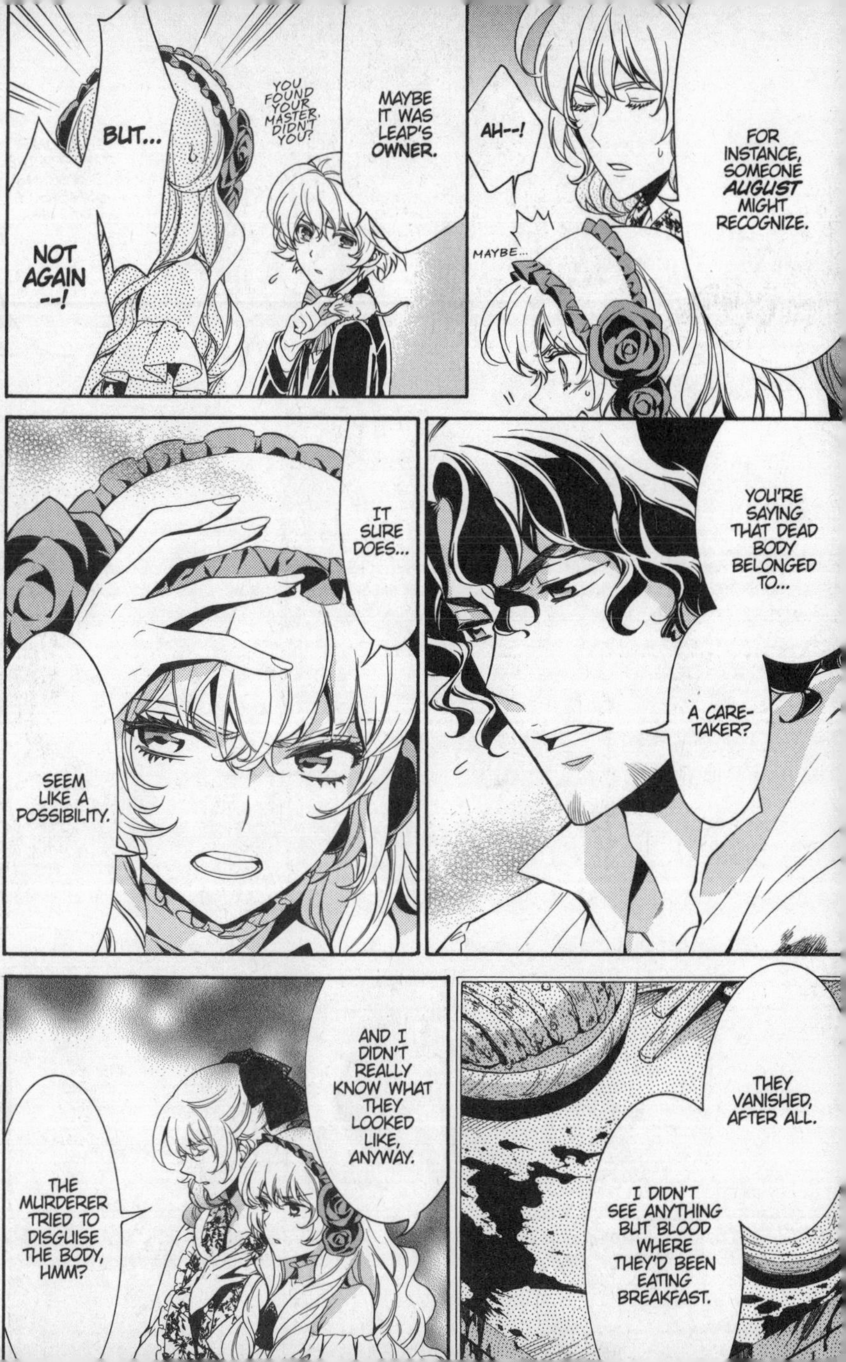
FOR INSTANCE, SOMEONE AUGUST MIGHT RECOGNIZE.
AH--!
MAYBE...
MAYBE IT WAS LEAP'S OWNER.
YOU FOUND YOUR MASTER, DIDN'T YOU?
BUT...
NOT AGAIN--!
YOU'RE SAYING THAT DEAD BODY BELONGED TO...
A CARE-TAKER?
IT SURE DOES...
SEEM LIKE A POSSIBILITY.
THEY VANISHED, AFTER ALL.
I DIDN'T SEE ANYTHING BUT BLOOD WHERE THEY'D BEEN EATING BREAKFAST.
AND I DIDN'T REALLY KNOW WHAT THEY LOOKED LIKE, ANYWAY.
THE MURDERER TRIED TO DISGUISE THE BODY, HMM?

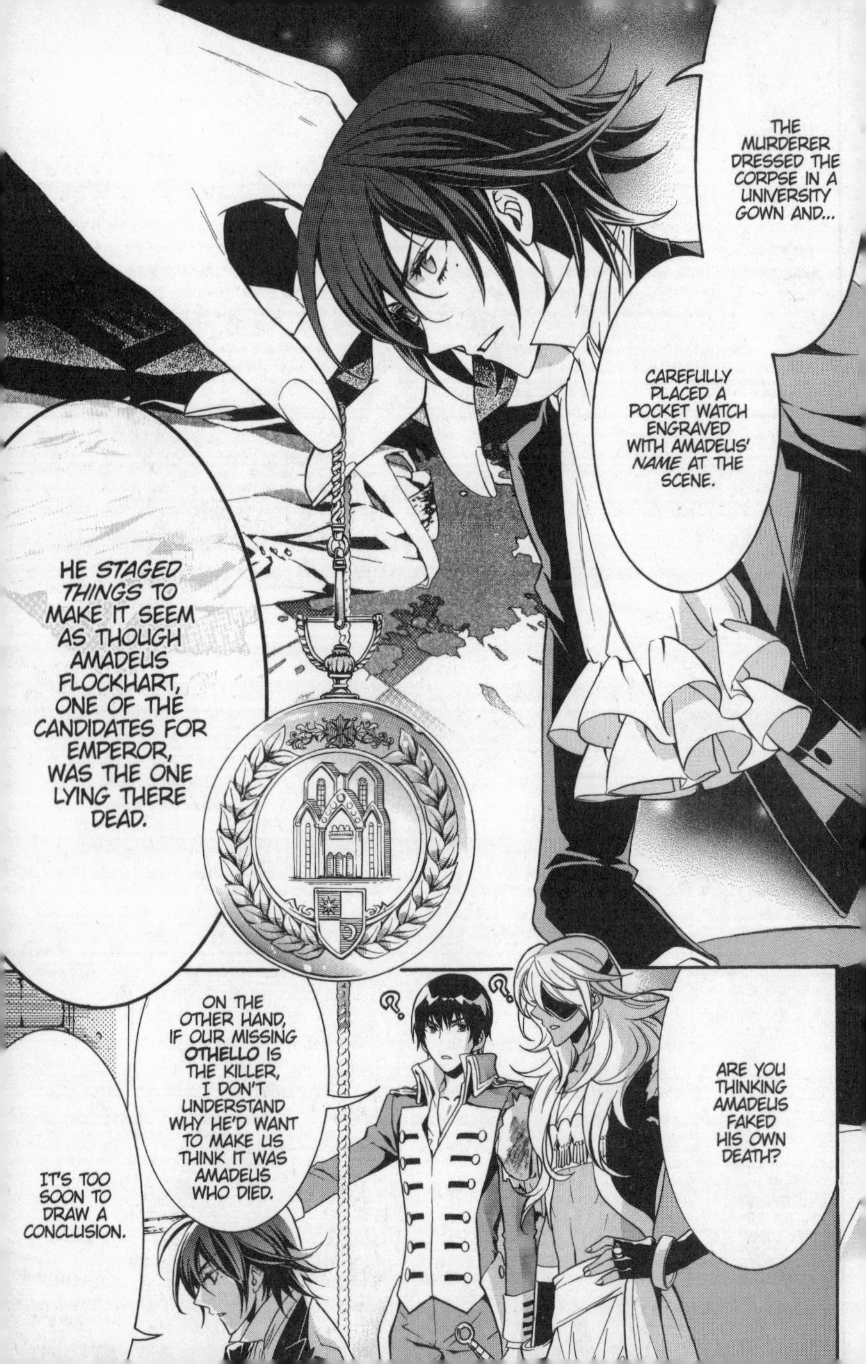
THE MURDERER DRESSED THE CORPSE IN A UNIVERSITY GOWN AND...
CAREFULLY PLACED A POCKET WATCH ENGRAVED WITH AMADEUS' *NAME* AT THE SCENE.
HE *STAGED THINGS* TO MAKE IT SEEM AS THOUGH AMADEUS FLOCKHART, ONE OF THE CANDIDATES FOR EMPEROR, WAS THE ONE LYING THERE DEAD.
ARE YOU THINKING AMADEUS FAKED HIS OWN DEATH?
ON THE OTHER HAND, IF OUR MISSING OTHELLO IS THE KILLER, I DON'T UNDERSTAND WHY HE'D WANT TO MAKE US THINK IT WAS AMADEUS WHO DIED.
IT'S TOO SOON TO DRAW A CONCLUSION.

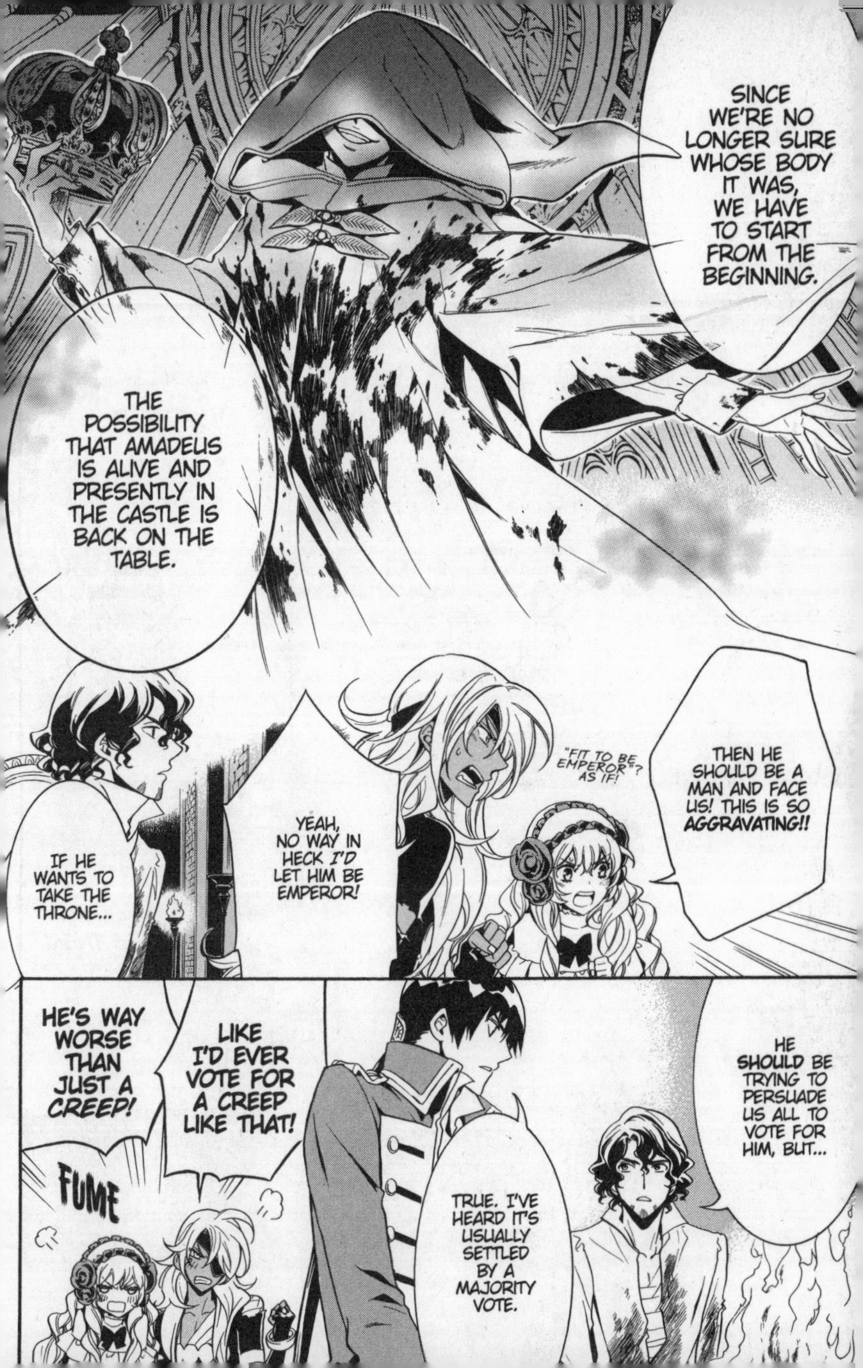
SINCE WE'RE NO LONGER SURE WHOSE BODY IT WAS, WE HAVE TO START FROM THE BEGINNING.
THE POSSIBILITY THAT AMADEUS IS ALIVE AND PRESENTLY IN THE CASTLE IS BACK ON THE TABLE.
THEN HE SHOULD BE A MAN AND FACE US! THIS IS SO AGGRAVATING!!
"FIT TO BE EMPEROR"? AS IF!
YEAH, NO WAY IN HECK I'D LET HIM BE EMPEROR!
IF HE WANTS TO TAKE THE THRONE...
HE SHOULD BE TRYING TO PERSUADE US ALL TO VOTE FOR HIM, BUT...
TRUE. I'VE HEARD IT'S USUALLY SETTLED BY A MAJORITY VOTE.
LIKE I'D EVER VOTE FOR A CREEP LIKE THAT!
HE'S WAY WORSE THAN JUST A CREEP!
FUME

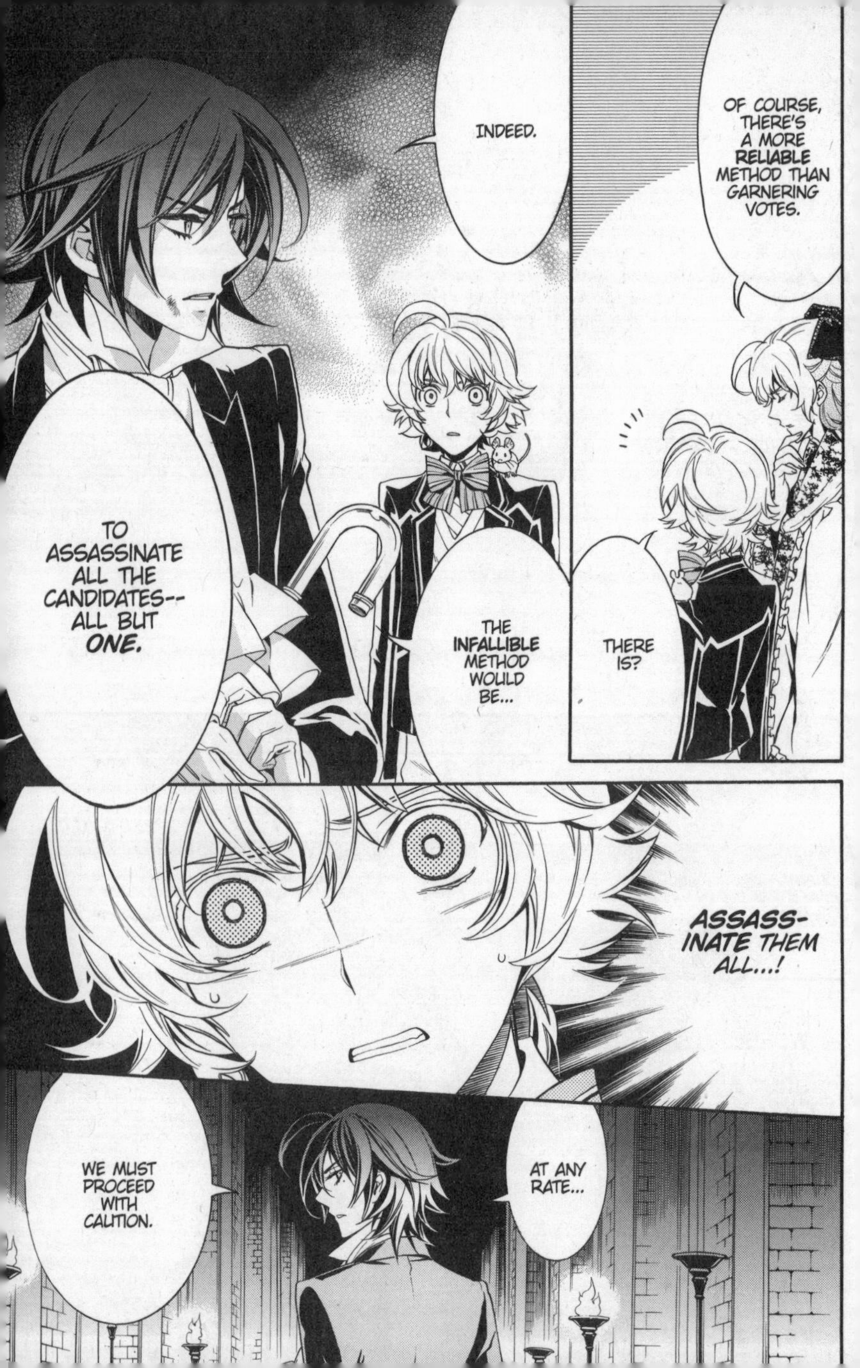
OF COURSE, THERE'S A MORE RELIABLE METHOD THAN GARNERING VOTES.
THERE IS?
INDEED.
THE INFALLIBLE METHOD WOULD BE...
TO ASSASSINATE ALL THE CANDIDATES--ALL BUT ONE.
ASSASS-INATE THEM ALL...!
AT ANY RATE...
WE MUST PROCEED WITH CAUTION.

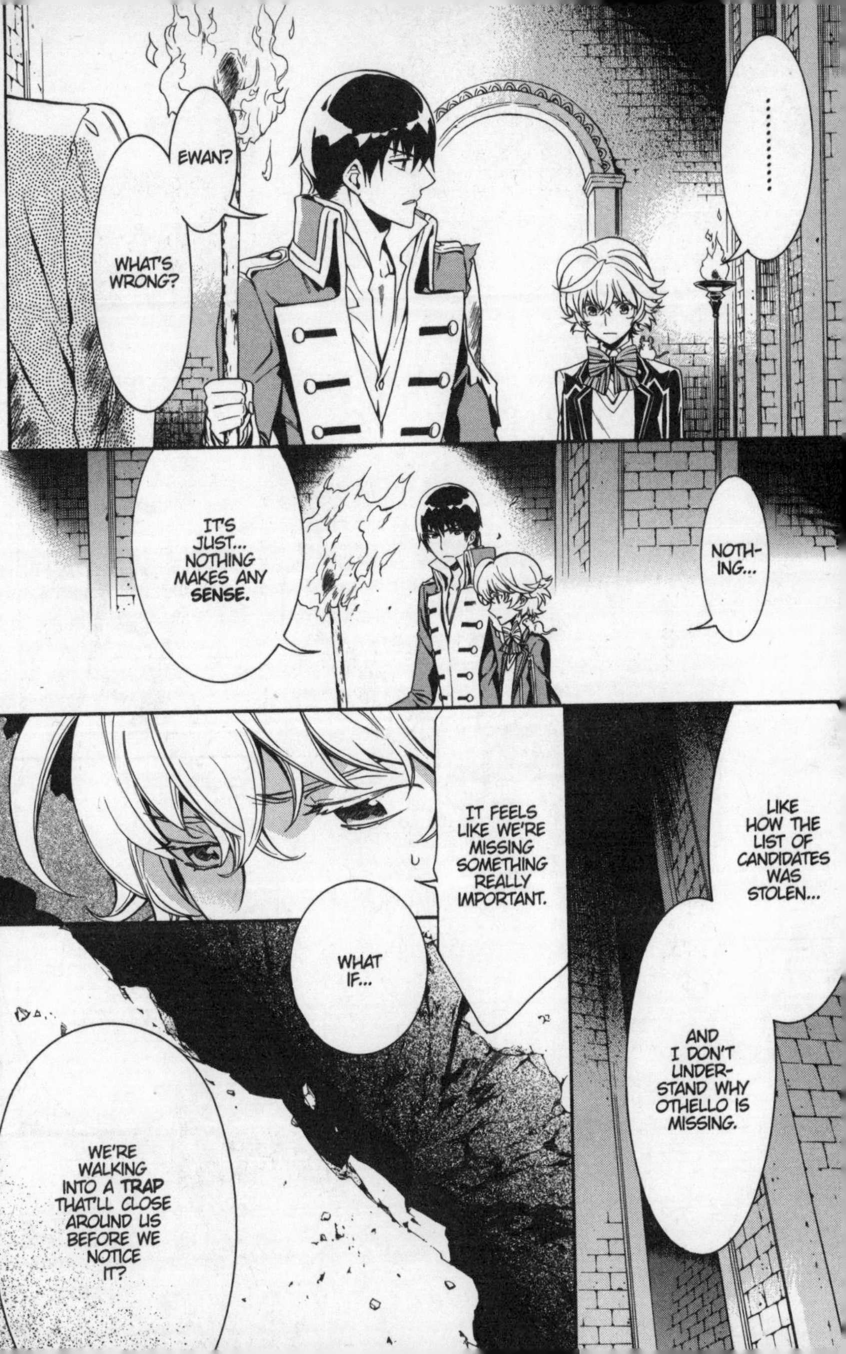
......
EWAN?
WHAT'S WRONG?
NOTH-ING...
IT'S JUST... NOTHING MAKES ANY SENSE.
LIKE HOW THE LIST OF CANDIDATES WAS STOLEN...
AND I DON'T UNDER-STAND WHY OTHELLO IS MISSING.
IT FEELS LIKE WE'RE MISSING SOMETHING REALLY IMPORTANT.
WHAT IF...
WE'RE WALKING INTO A TRAP THAT'LL CLOSE AROUND US BEFORE WE NOTICE IT?

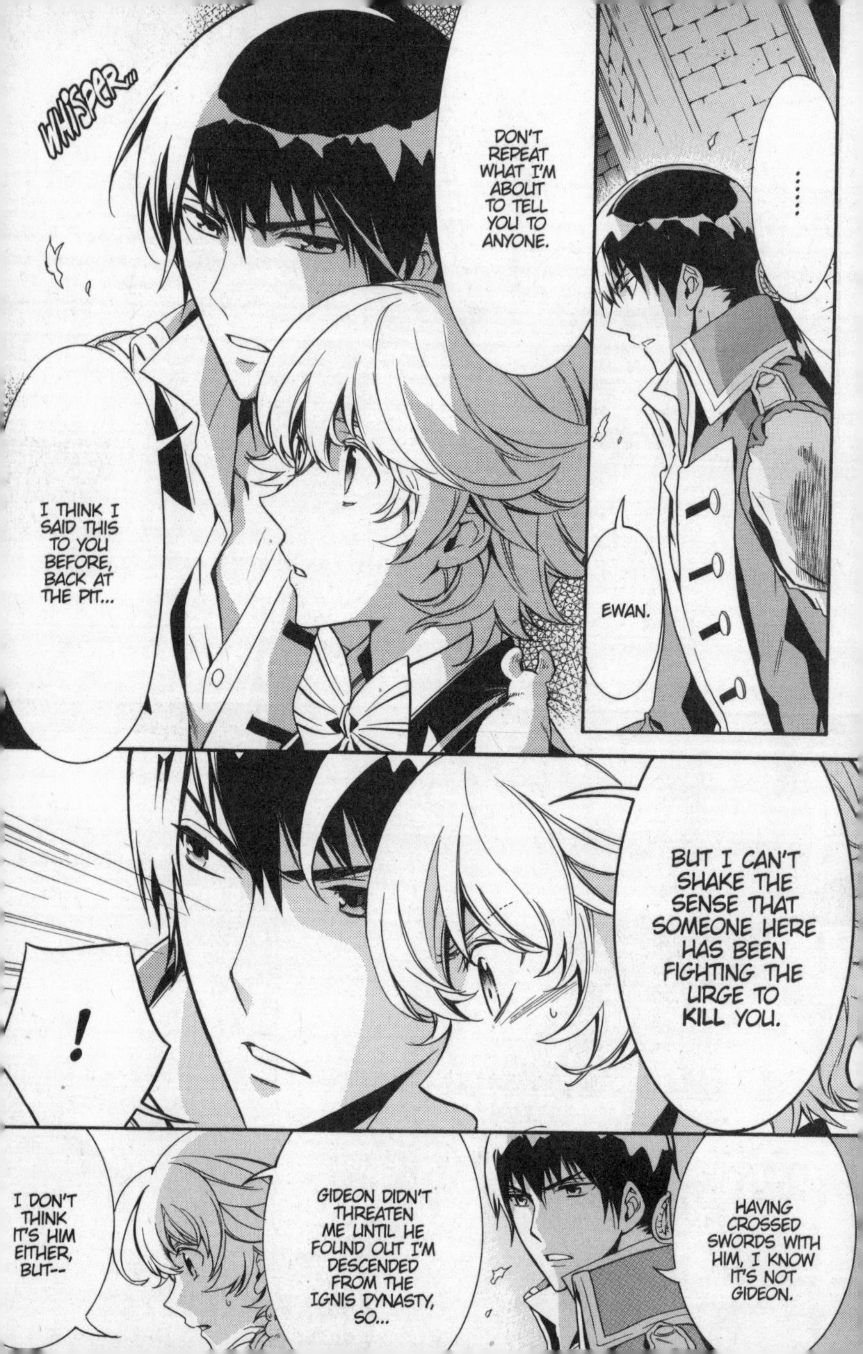
......
EWAN.
DON'T REPEAT WHAT I'M ABOUT TO TELL YOU TO ANYONE.
WHISPER...
I THINK I SAID THIS TO YOU BEFORE, BACK AT THE PIT...
BUT I CAN'T SHAKE THE SENSE THAT SOMEONE HERE HAS BEEN FIGHTING THE URGE TO KILL YOU.
!
HAVING CROSSED SWORDS WITH HIM, I KNOW IT'S NOT GIDEON.
GIDEON DIDN'T THREATEN ME UNTIL HE FOUND OUT I'M DESCENDED FROM THE IGNIS DYNASTY, SO...
I DON'T THINK IT'S HIM EITHER, BUT--

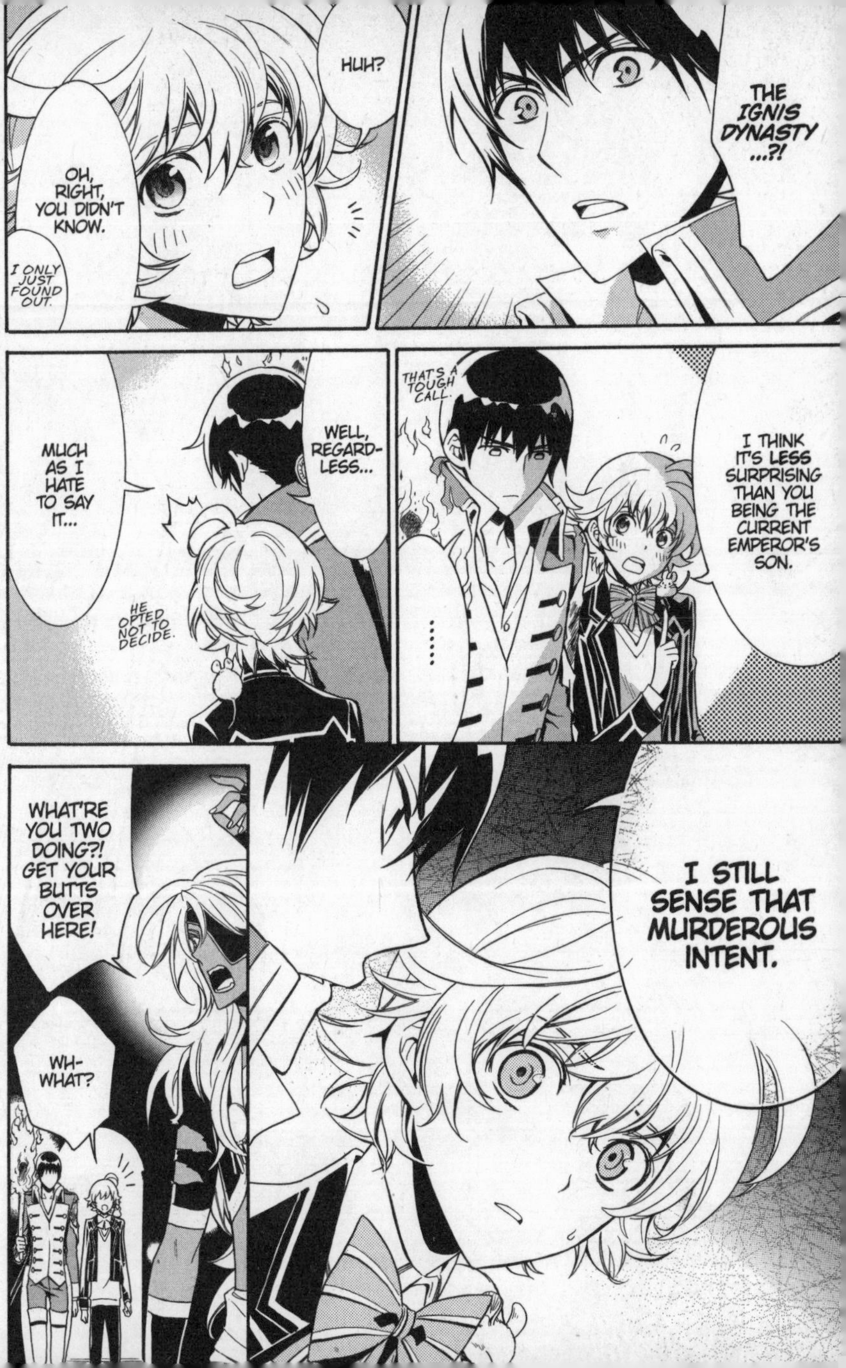
THE IGNIS DYNASTY ...?!
HUH?
OH, RIGHT, YOU DIDN'T KNOW.
I ONLY JUST FOUND OUT.
I THINK IT'S LESS SURPRISING THAN YOU BEING THE CURRENT EMPEROR'S SON.
THAT'S A TOUGH CALL.
......
WELL, REGARDLESS...
MUCH AS I HATE TO SAY IT...
HE OPTED NOT TO DECIDE.
I STILL SENSE THAT MURDEROUS INTENT.
WHAT'RE YOU TWO DOING?! GET YOUR BUTTS OVER HERE!
WH-WHAT?

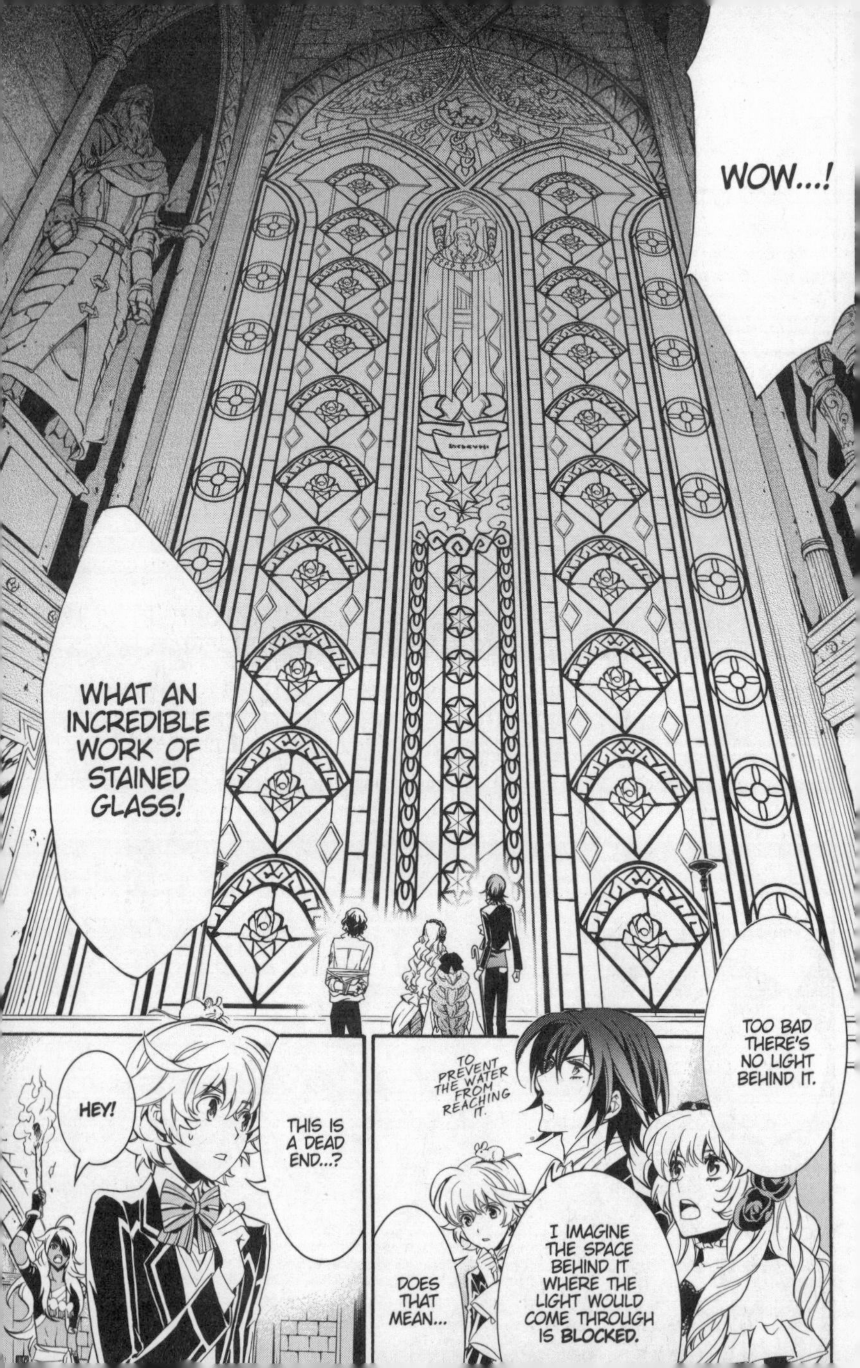
WOW...!
WHAT AN INCREDIBLE WORK OF STAINED GLASS!
TOO BAD THERE'S NO LIGHT BEHIND IT.
I IMAGINE THE SPACE BEHIND IT WHERE THE LIGHT WOULD COME THROUGH IS BLOCKED.
TO PREVENT THE WATER FROM REACHING IT.
DOES THAT MEAN...
THIS IS A DEAD END...?
HEY!

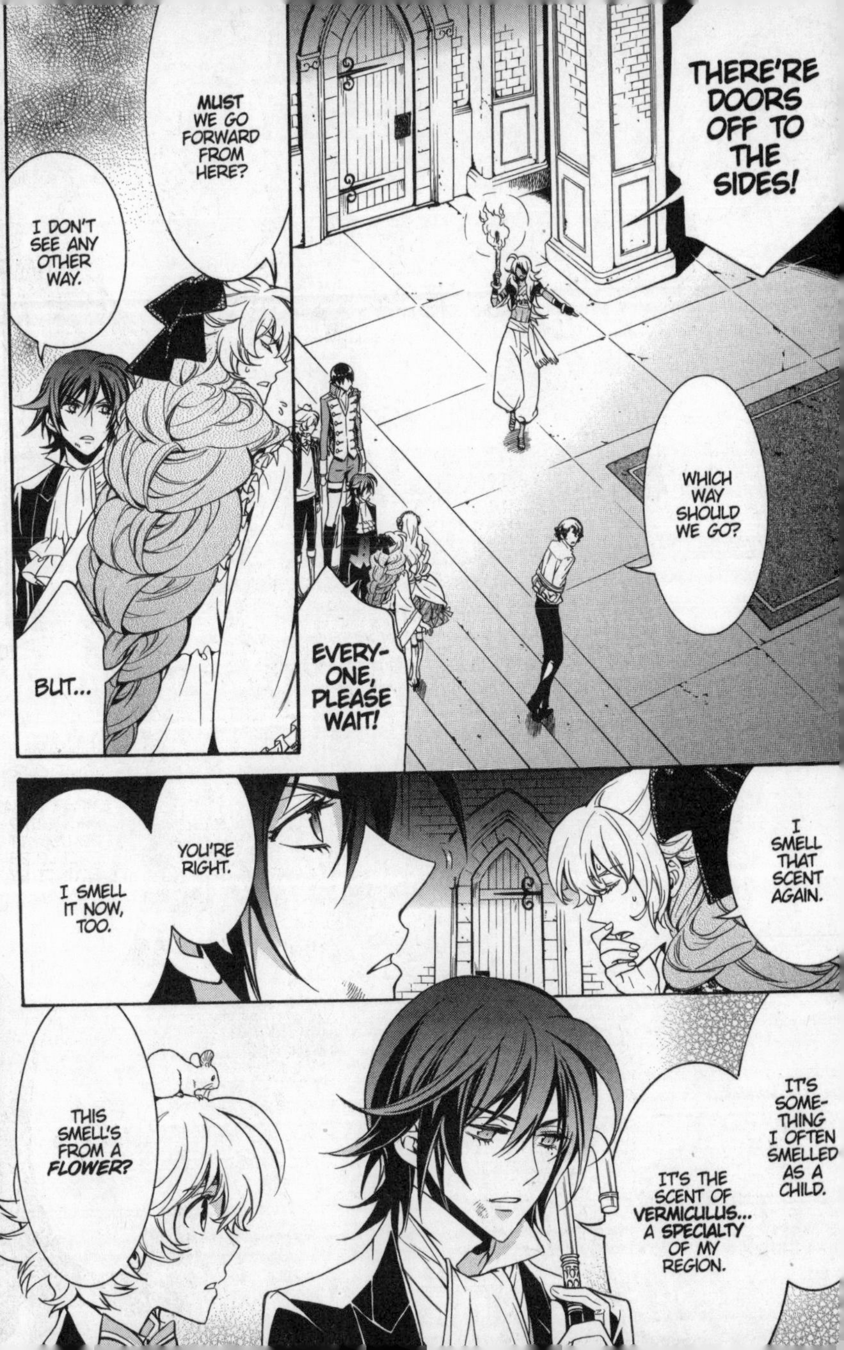
THERE'RE DOORS OFF TO THE SIDES!
WHICH WAY SHOULD WE GO?
EVERY-ONE, PLEASE WAIT!
MUST WE GO FORWARD FROM HERE?
I DON'T SEE ANY OTHER WAY.
BUT...
I SMELL THAT SCENT AGAIN.
YOU'RE RIGHT.
I SMELL IT NOW, TOO.
IT'S SOME-THING I OFTEN SMELLED AS A CHILD.
IT'S THE SCENT OF VERMICULUS... A SPECIALTY OF MY REGION.
THIS SMELL'S FROM A *FLOWER?*

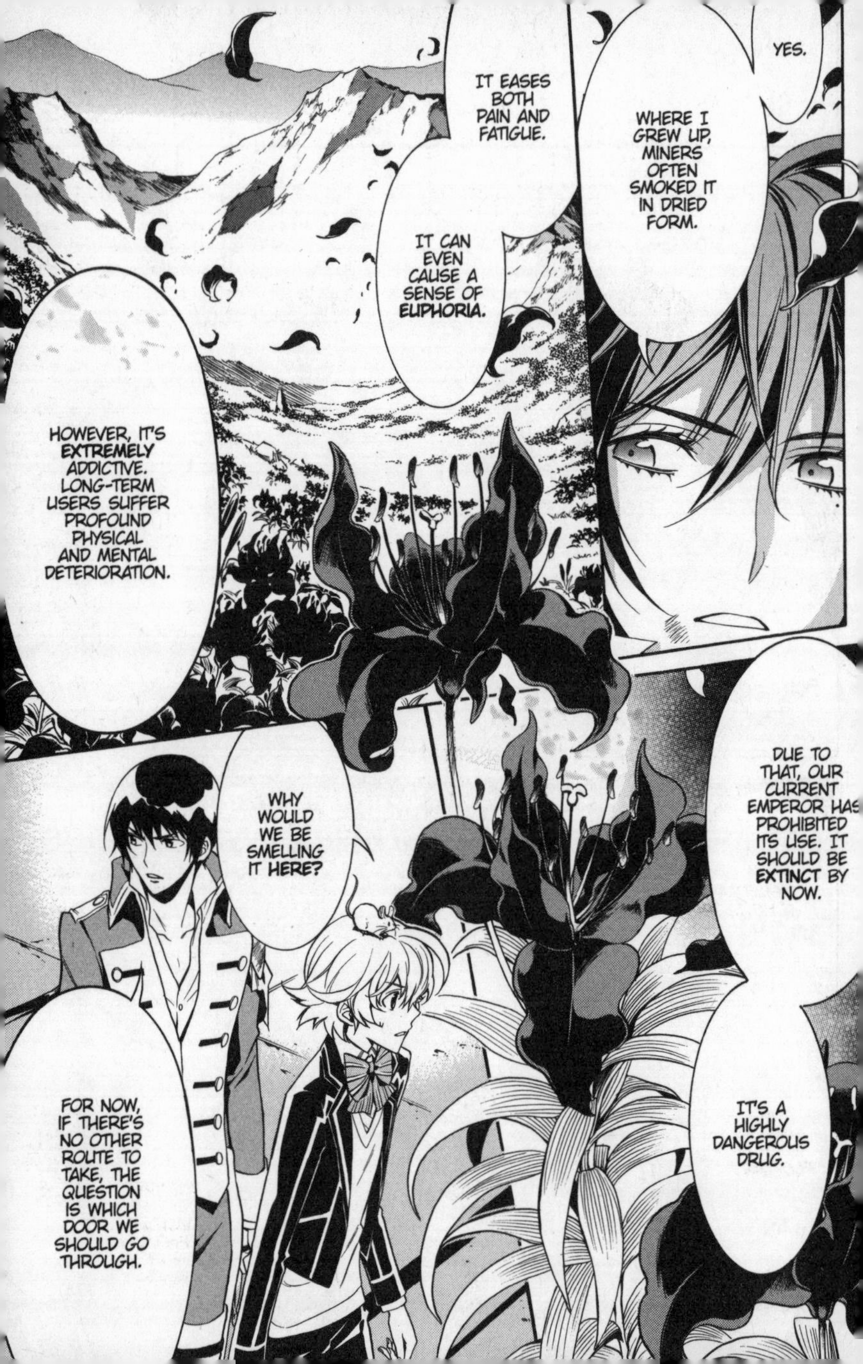
YES.
WHERE I GREW UP, MINERS OFTEN SMOKED IT IN DRIED FORM.
IT EASES BOTH PAIN AND FATIGUE.
IT CAN EVEN CAUSE A SENSE OF **EUPHORIA.**
HOWEVER, IT'S **EXTREMELY** ADDICTIVE. LONG-TERM USERS SUFFER PROFOUND PHYSICAL AND MENTAL DETERIORATION.
DUE TO THAT, OUR CURRENT EMPEROR HAS PROHIBITED ITS USE. IT SHOULD BE **EXTINCT** BY NOW.
IT'S A HIGHLY DANGEROUS DRUG.
WHY WOULD WE BE SMELLING IT **HERE?**
FOR NOW, IF THERE'S NO OTHER ROUTE TO TAKE, THE QUESTION IS WHICH DOOR WE SHOULD GO THROUGH.

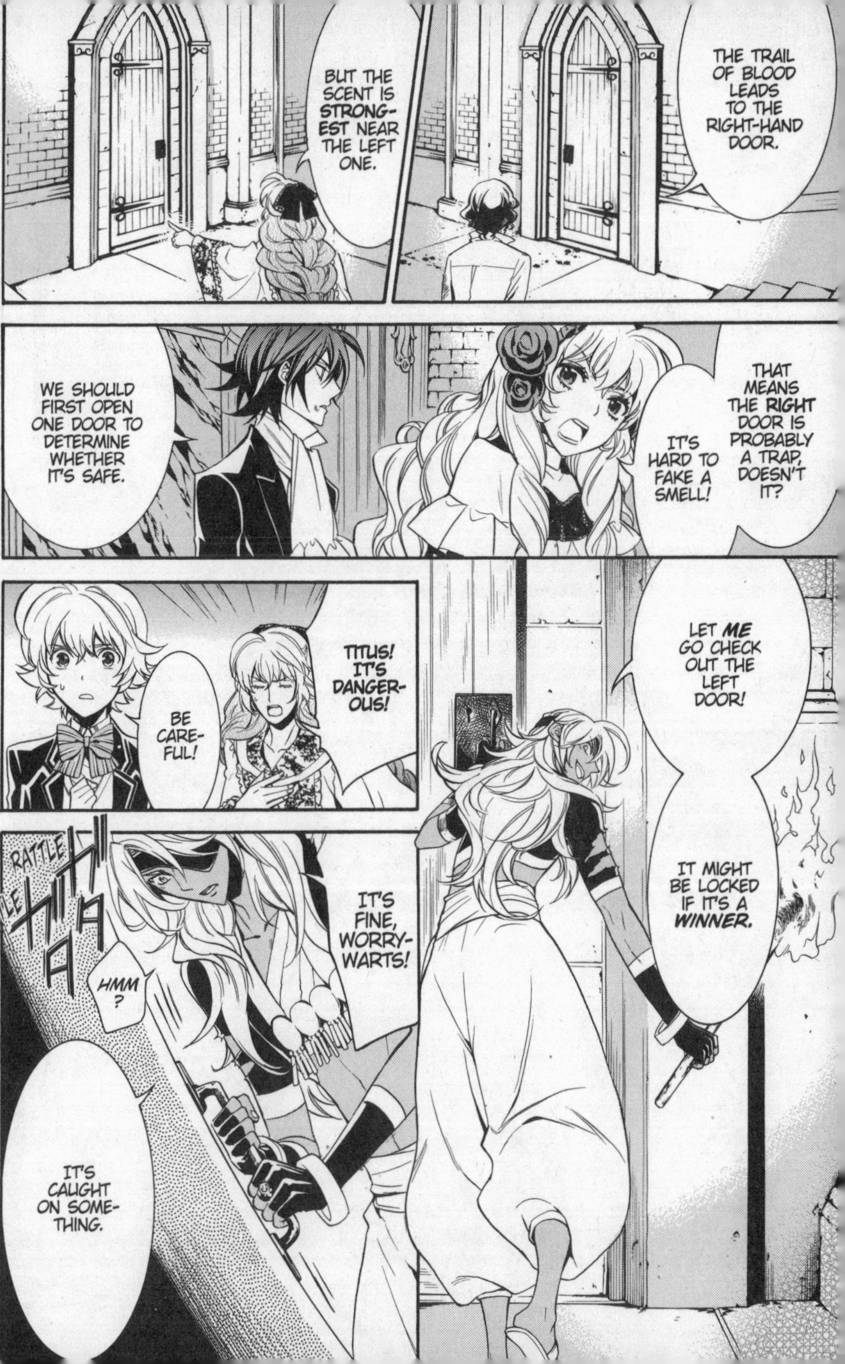
THE TRAIL OF BLOOD LEADS TO THE RIGHT-HAND DOOR.
BUT THE SCENT IS STRONGEST NEAR THE LEFT ONE.
THAT MEANS THE RIGHT DOOR IS PROBABLY A TRAP, DOESN'T IT?
IT'S HARD TO FAKE A SMELL!
WE SHOULD FIRST OPEN ONE DOOR TO DETERMINE WHETHER IT'S SAFE.
LET ME GO CHECK OUT THE LEFT DOOR!
IT MIGHT BE LOCKED IF IT'S A WINNER.
TITUS! IT'S DANGEROUS!
BE CAREFUL!
IT'S FINE, WORRY-WARTS!
RATTLE
TTLE
HMM?
IT'S CAUGHT ON SOMETHING.

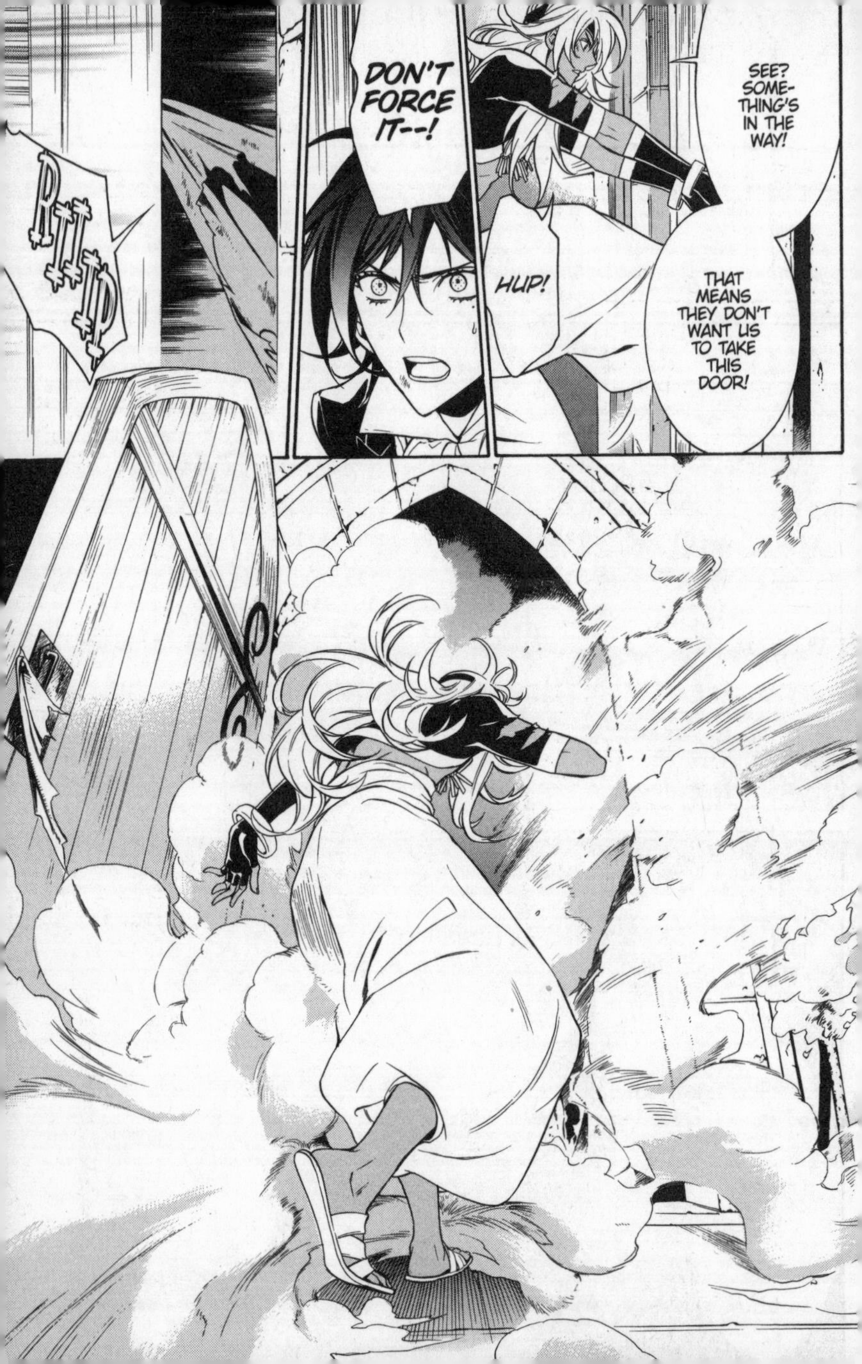
SEE? SOME-THING'S IN THE WAY!
THAT MEANS THEY DON'T WANT US TO TAKE THIS DOOR!
HUP!
DON'T FORCE IT--!
RIIIP

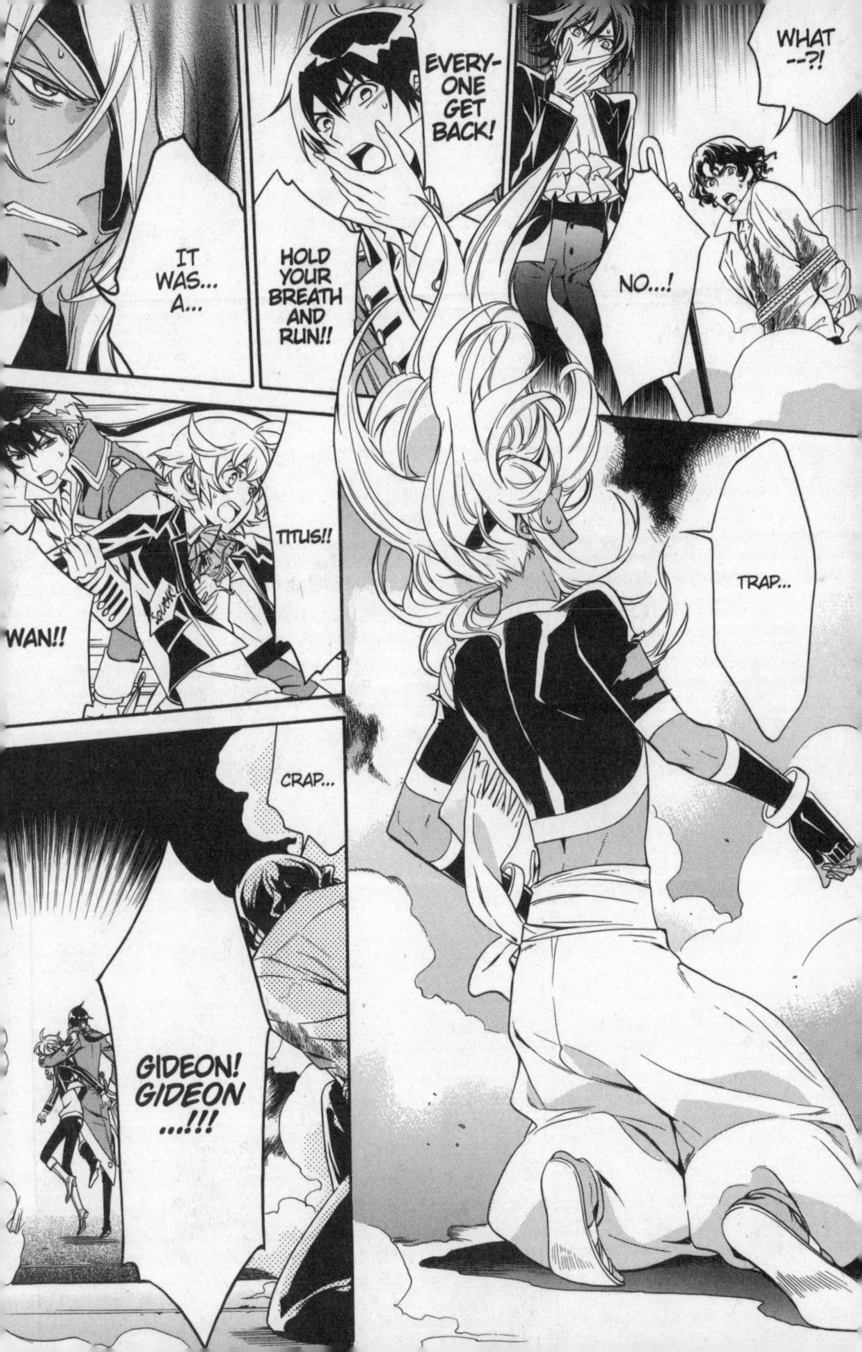
WHAT --?!
NO...!
EVERY-ONE GET BACK!
HOLD YOUR BREATH AND RUN!!
IT WAS... A...
TRAP...
TITUS!!
SQUAAK!
WAN!!
CRAP...
GIDEON! GIDEON ...!!!

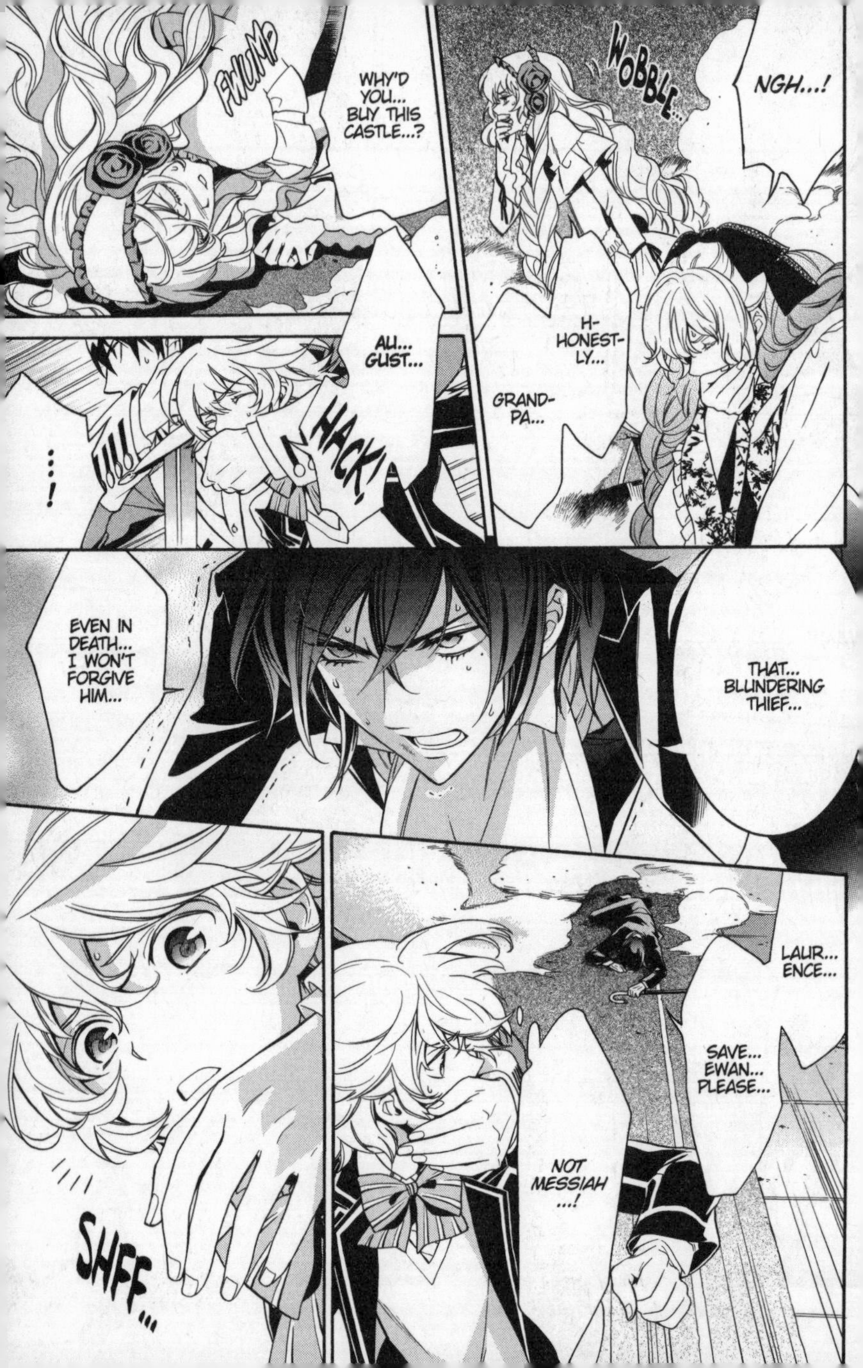

NGH...!
WOBBLE...
H-HONEST-LY...
GRAND-PA...
WHY'D YOU... BUY THIS CASTLE...?
FWUMP
AU... GUST...
HACK!
!!!
...!
THAT... BLUNDERING THIEF...
EVEN IN DEATH... I WON'T FORGIVE HIM...
LAUR... ENCE...
SAVE... EWAN... PLEASE...
NOT MESSIAH ...!
SHFF...

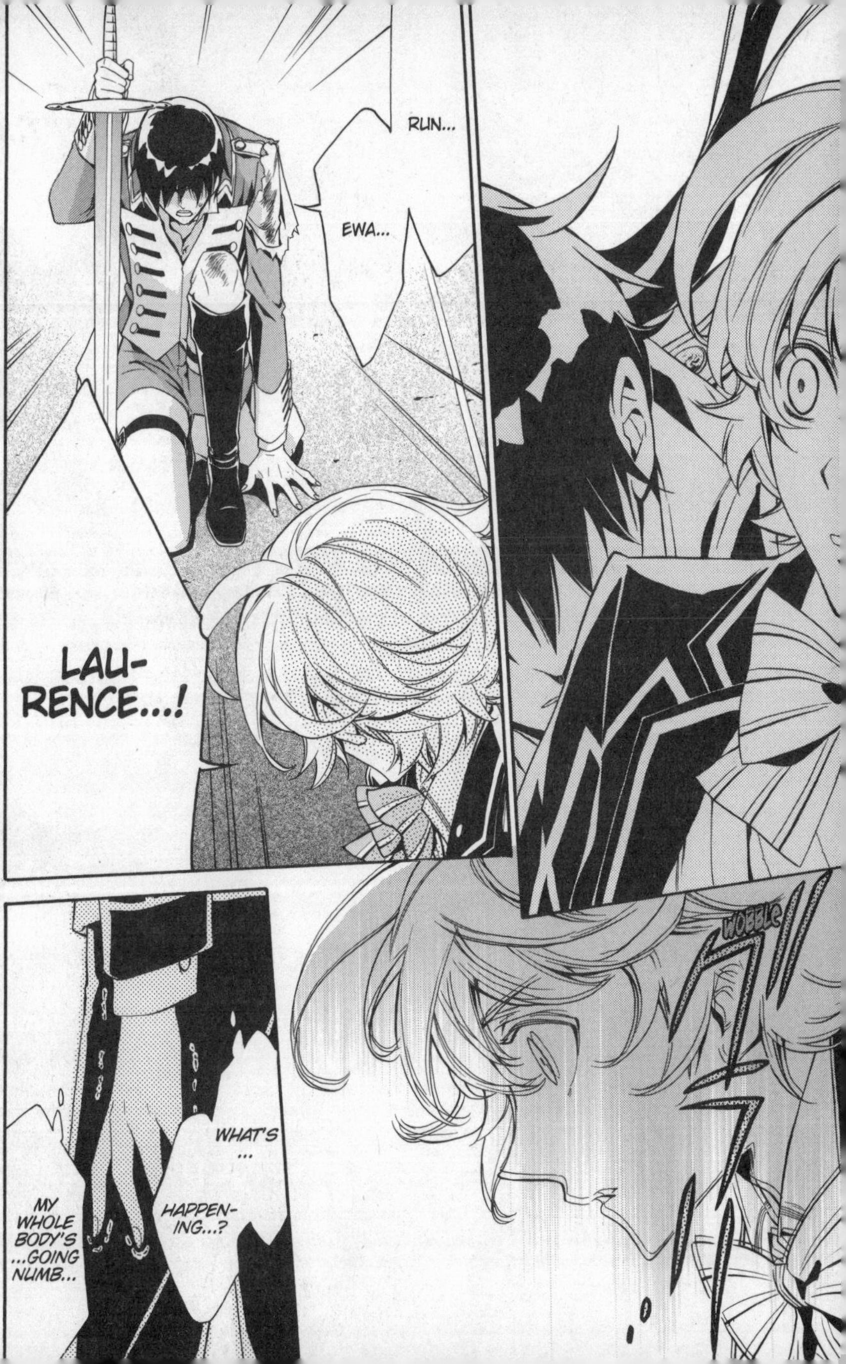
WOBBLE
RUN...
EWA...
LAU-RENCE...!
WHAT'S... HAPPEN-ING...?
MY WHOLE BODY'S ...GOING NUMB...

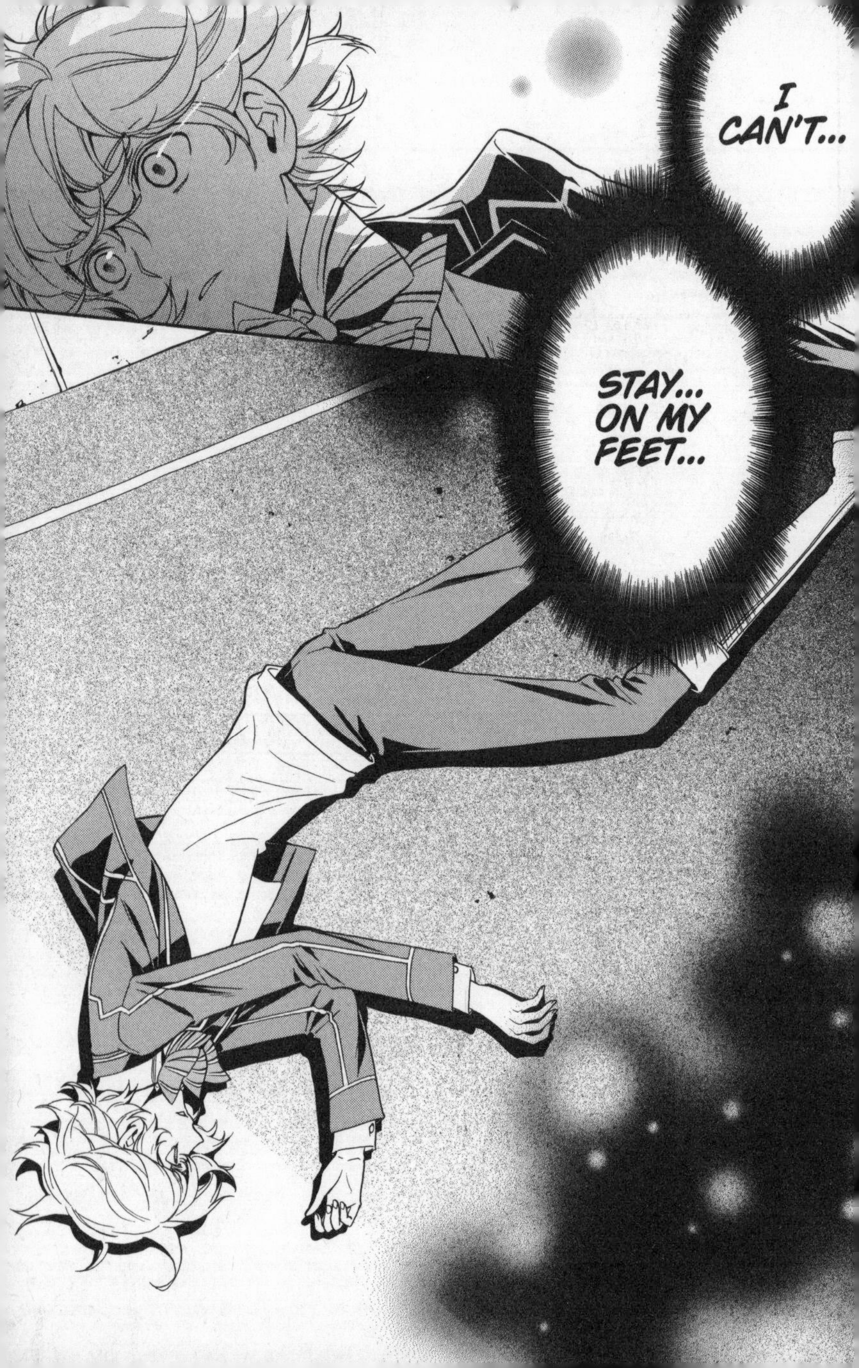
I CAN'T...
STAY... ON MY FEET...

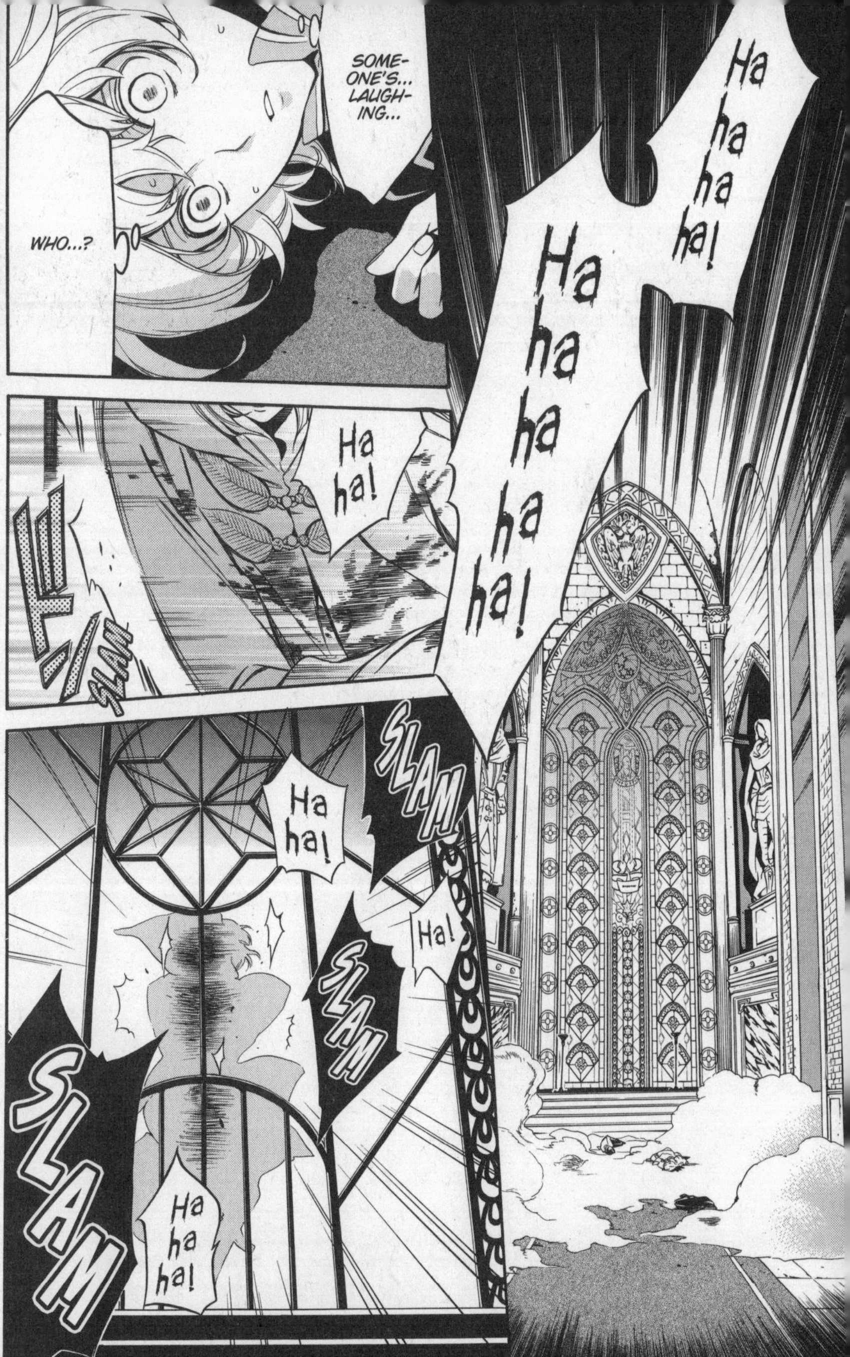

Ha ha ha ha!
Ha ha ha ha ha ha ha!
SOME-ONE'S... LAUGH-ING...
WHO...?
Ha ha!
SLAM
SLAM
Ha ha!
Ha!
SLAM
SLAM
Ha ha ha!

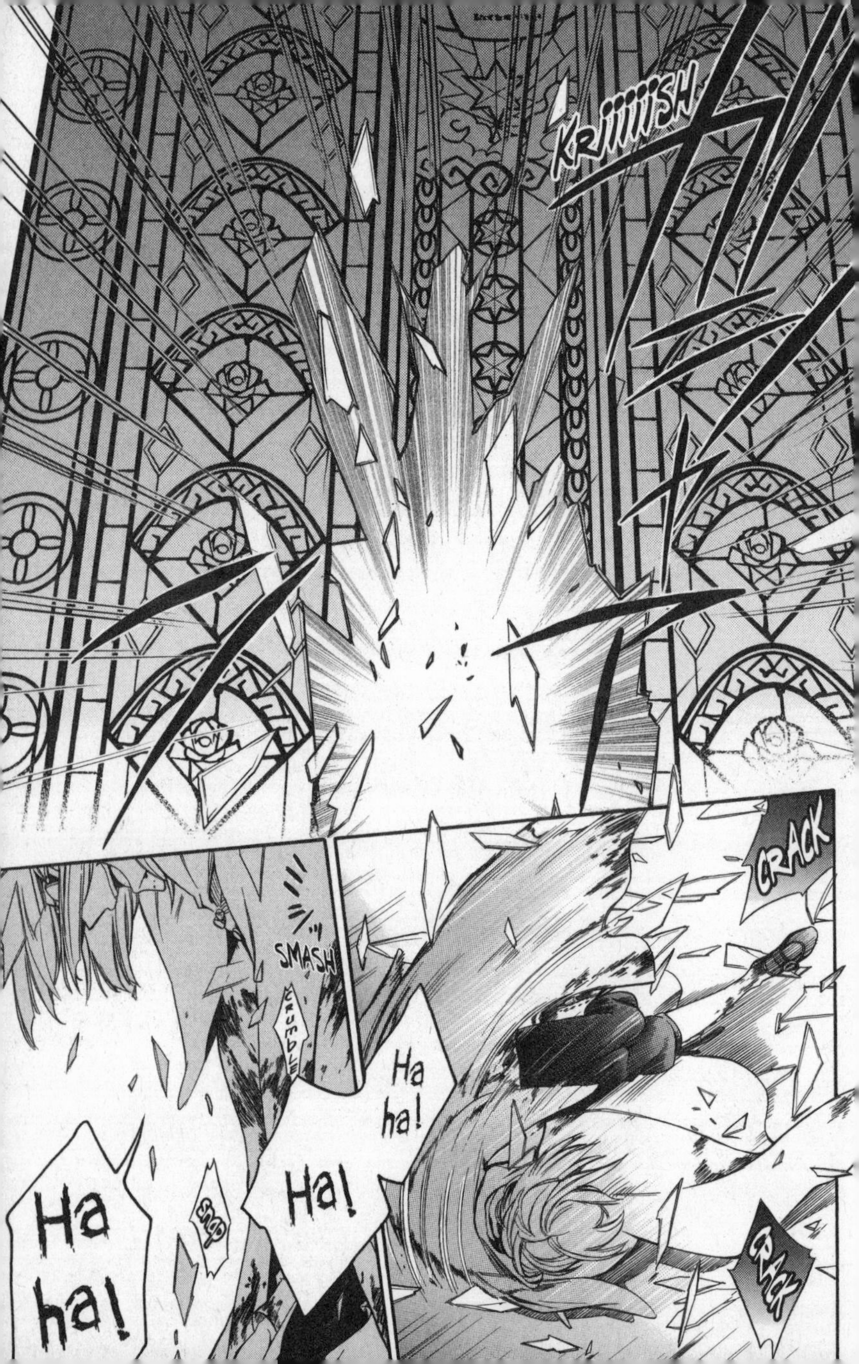
KRIIIIIISH
CRACK
Ha ha!
Ha!
CRACK
SMASH
CRUMBLE
snap
Ha ha!

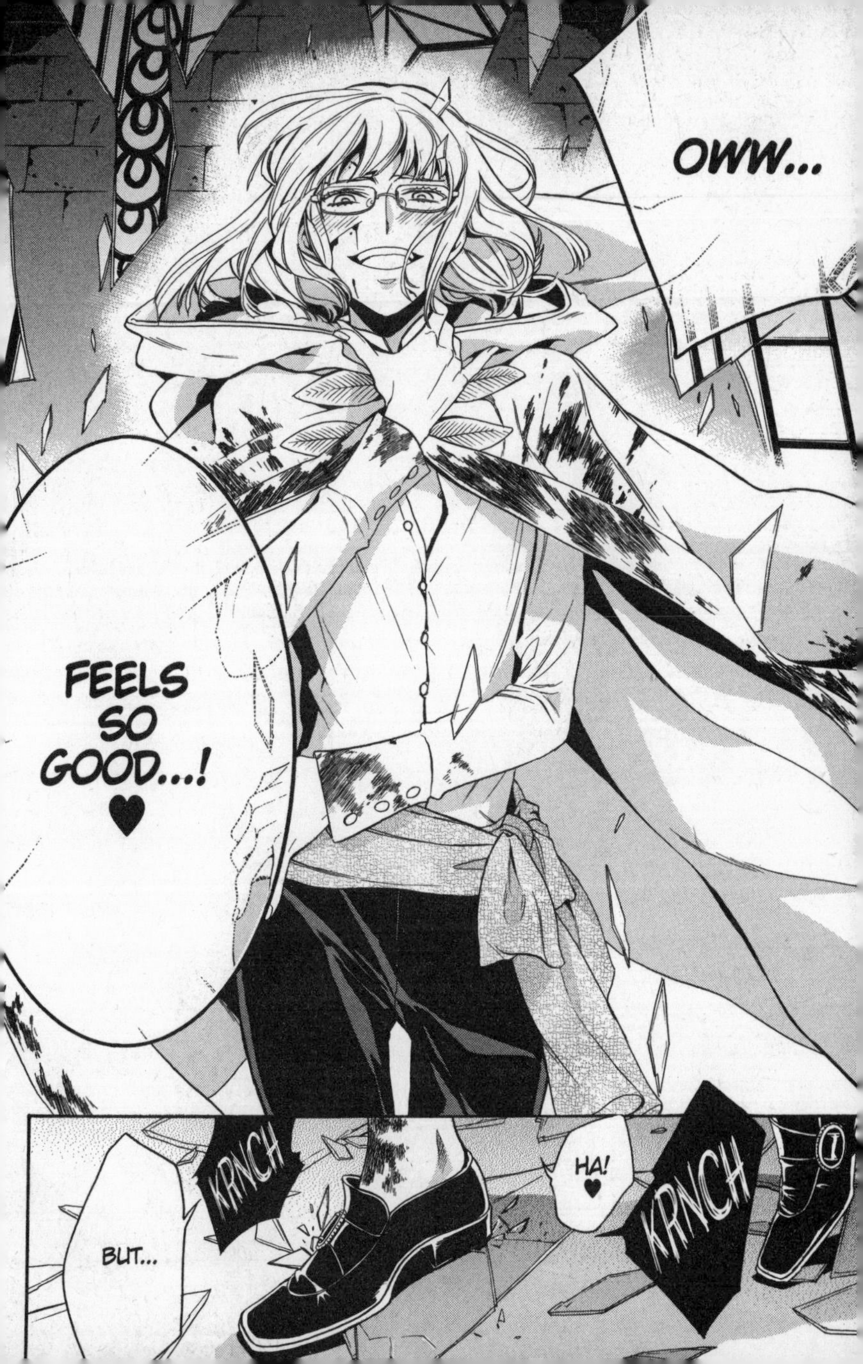
OWW...
FEELS SO GOOD...! ♥
KRNCH
HA! ♥
KRNCH
BUT...

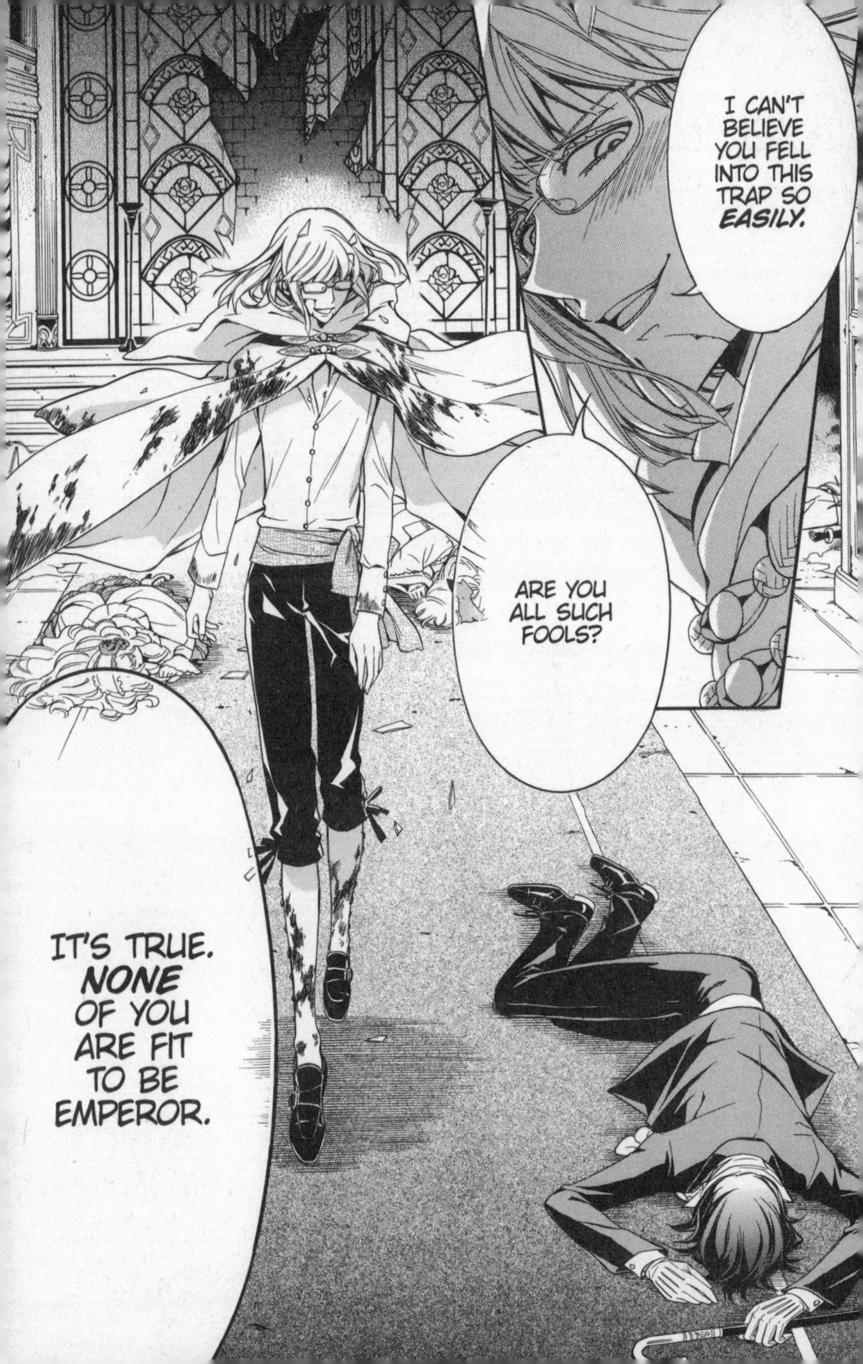
I CAN'T BELIEVE YOU FELL INTO THIS TRAP SO *EASILY.*
ARE YOU ALL SUCH FOOLS?
IT'S TRUE. *NONE* OF YOU ARE FIT TO BE EMPEROR.

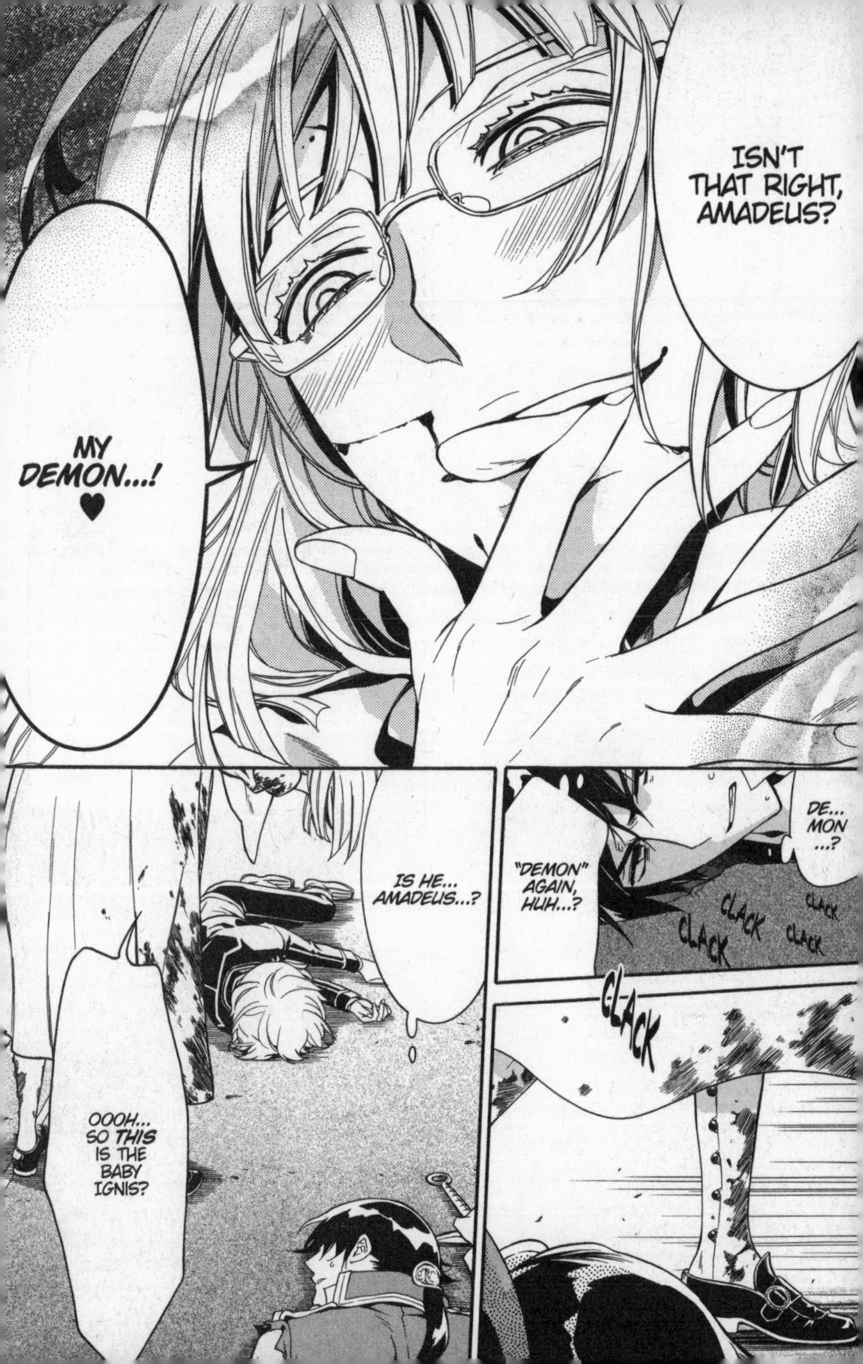
ISN'T THAT RIGHT, AMADEUS?
MY DEMON...! ♥
DE... MON ...?
CLACK CLACK CLACK CLACK
"DEMON" AGAIN, HUH...?
CLACK
IS HE... AMADEUS...?
OOOH... SO THIS IS THE BABY IGNIS?

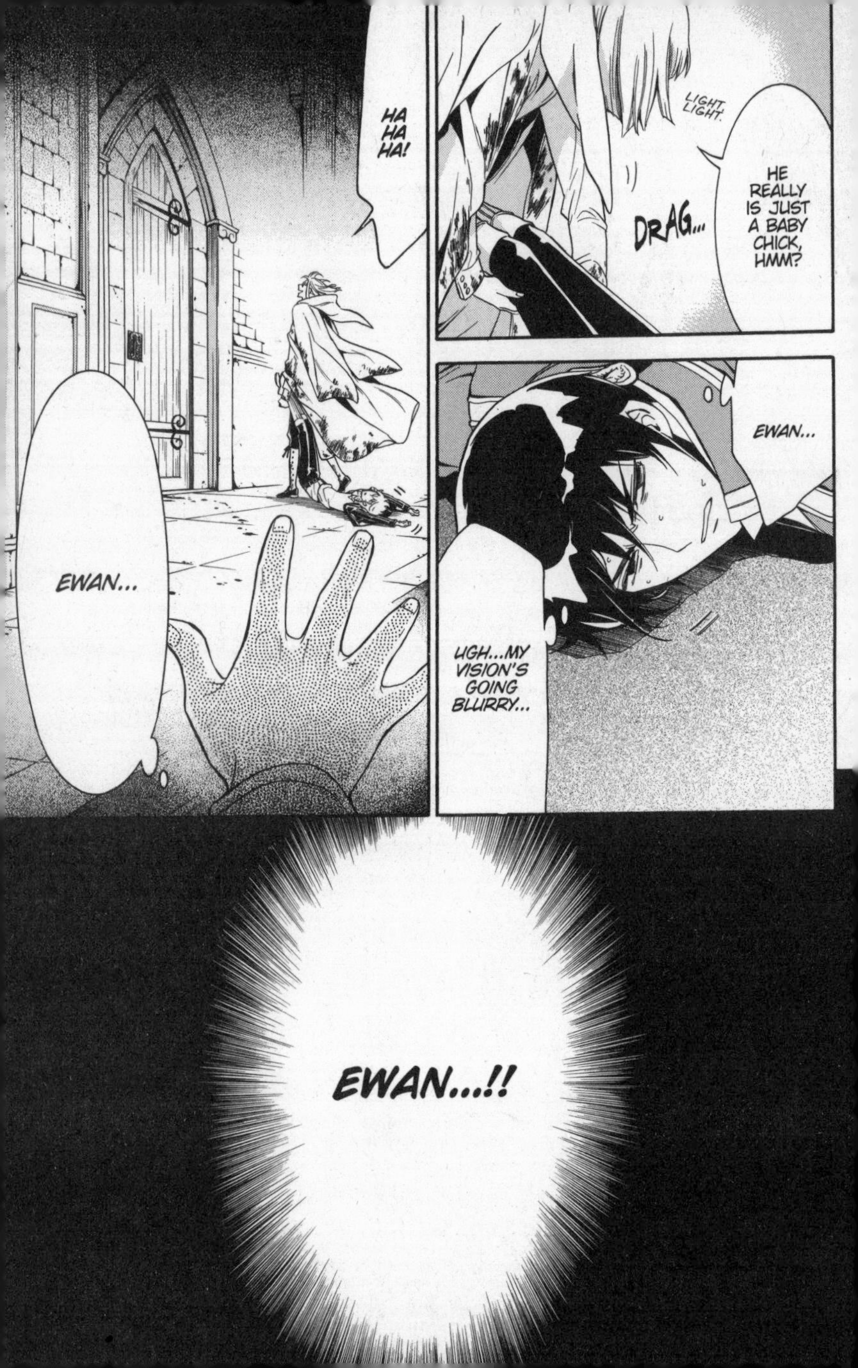
LIGHT, LIGHT.
HE REALLY IS JUST A BABY CHICK, HMM?
DRAG...
EWAN...
UGH...MY VISION'S GOING BLURRY...
HA HA HA!
EWAN...
EWAN...!!

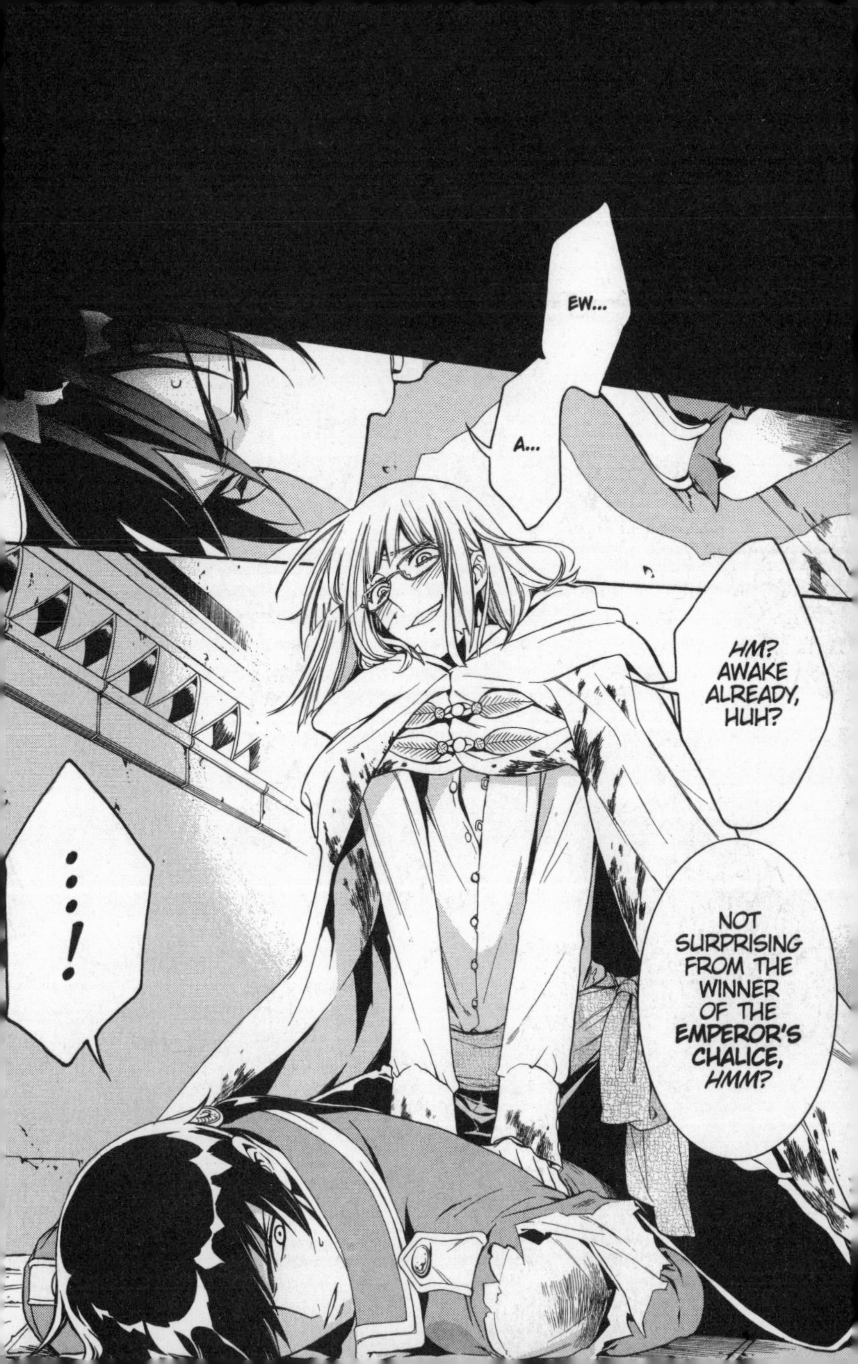
EW...
A...
HM? AWAKE ALREADY, HUH?
NOT SURPRISING FROM THE WINNER OF THE EMPEROR'S CHALICE, HMM?
...!

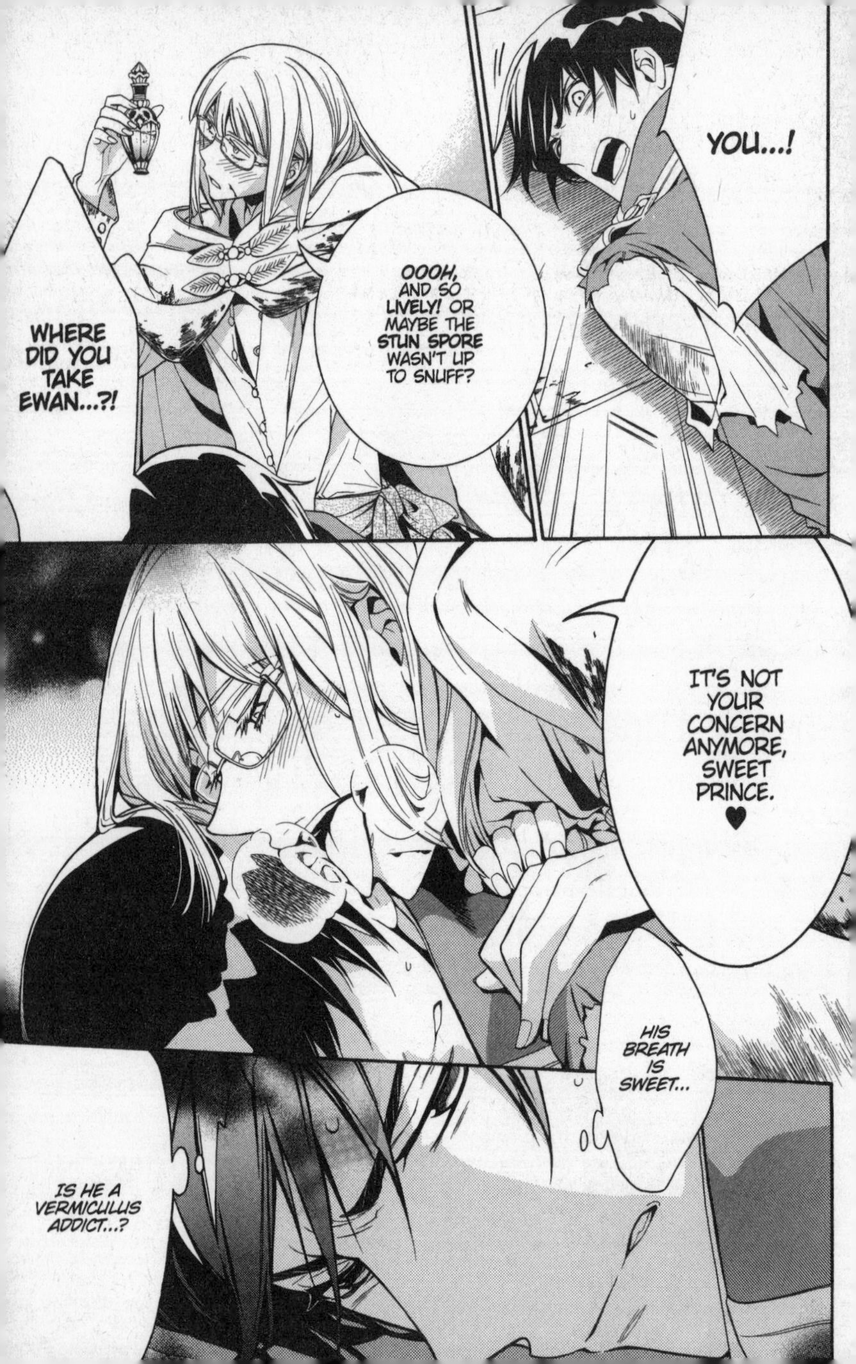
YOU...!
OOOH, AND SO LIVELY! OR MAYBE THE STUN SPORE WASN'T UP TO SNUFF?
WHERE DID YOU TAKE EWAN...?!
IT'S NOT YOUR CONCERN ANYMORE, SWEET PRINCE. ♥
HIS BREATH IS SWEET...
IS HE A VERMICULUS ADDICT...?

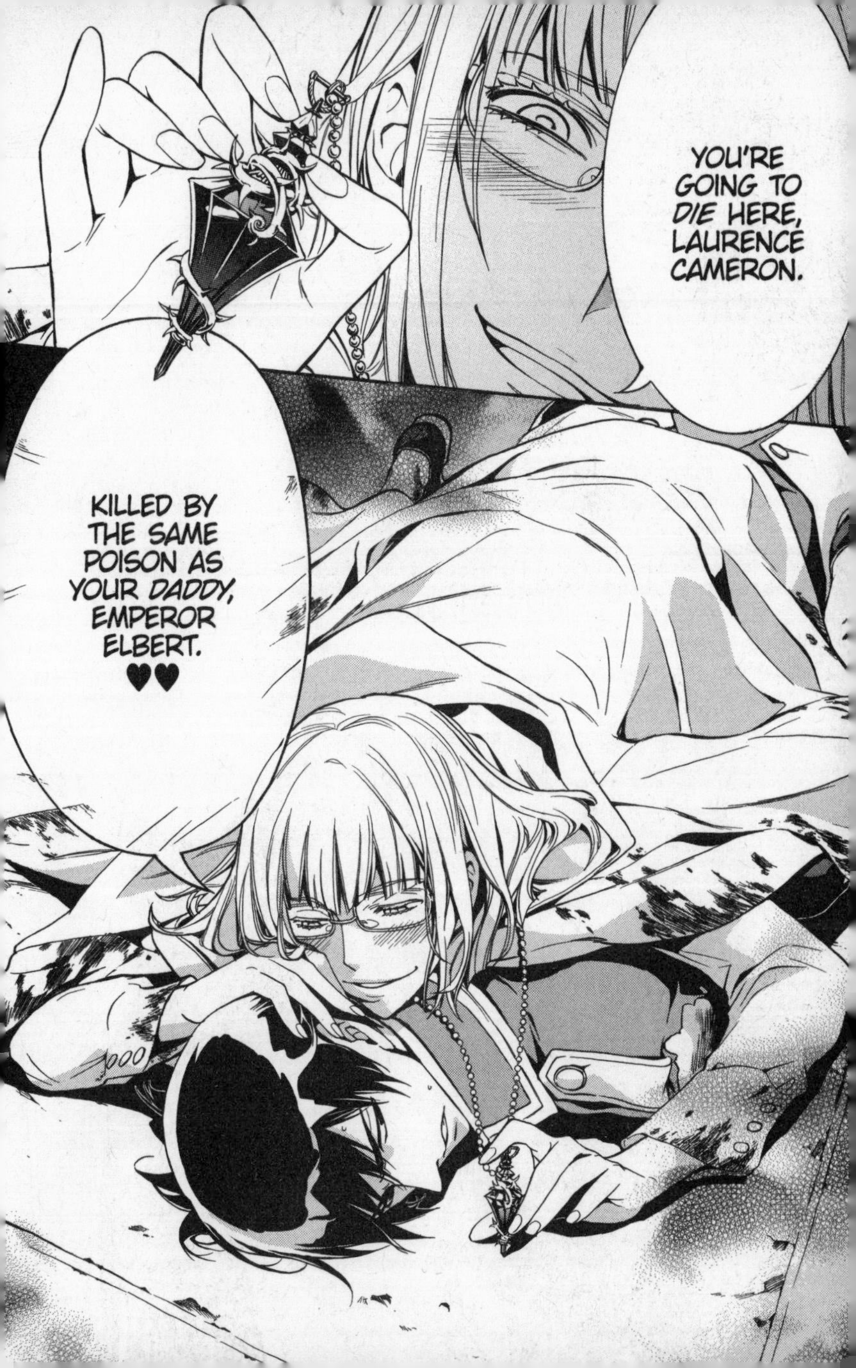
YOU'RE GOING TO *DIE* HERE, LAURENCE CAMERON.
KILLED BY THE SAME POISON AS YOUR *DADDY*, EMPEROR ELBERT. ♥♥

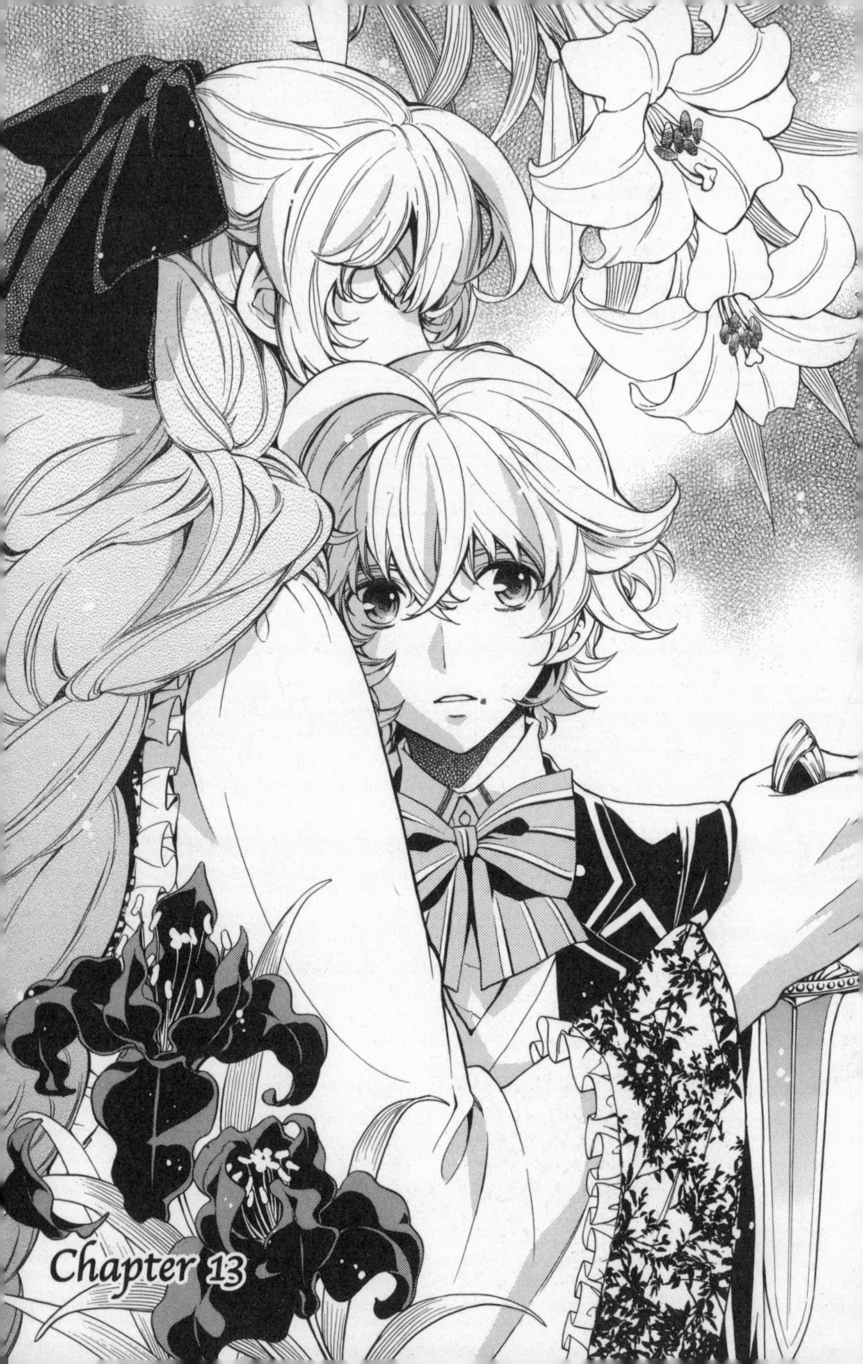
Chapter 13

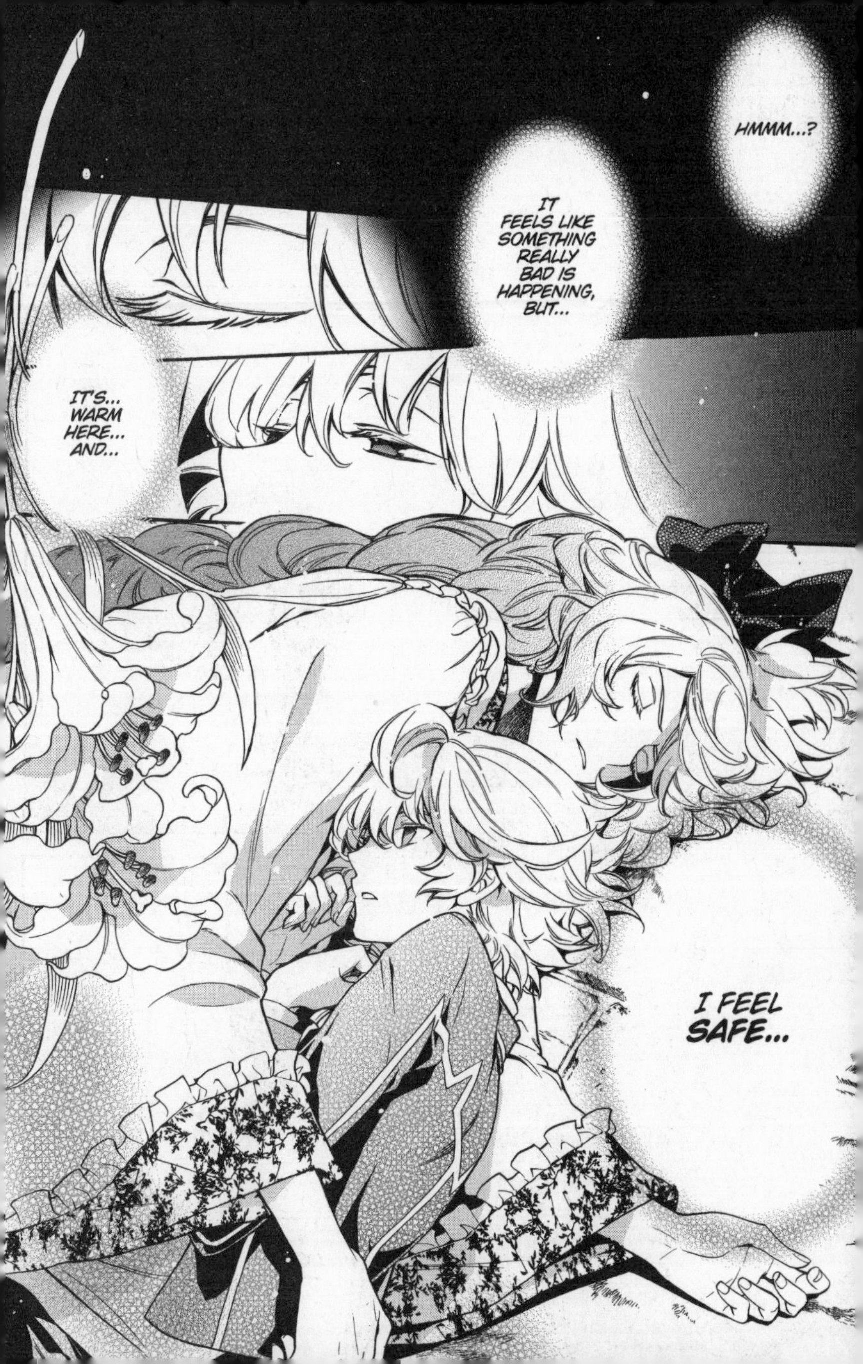
HMMM...?
IT FEELS LIKE SOMETHING REALLY BAD IS HAPPENING, BUT...
IT'S... WARM HERE... AND...
I FEEL SAFE...

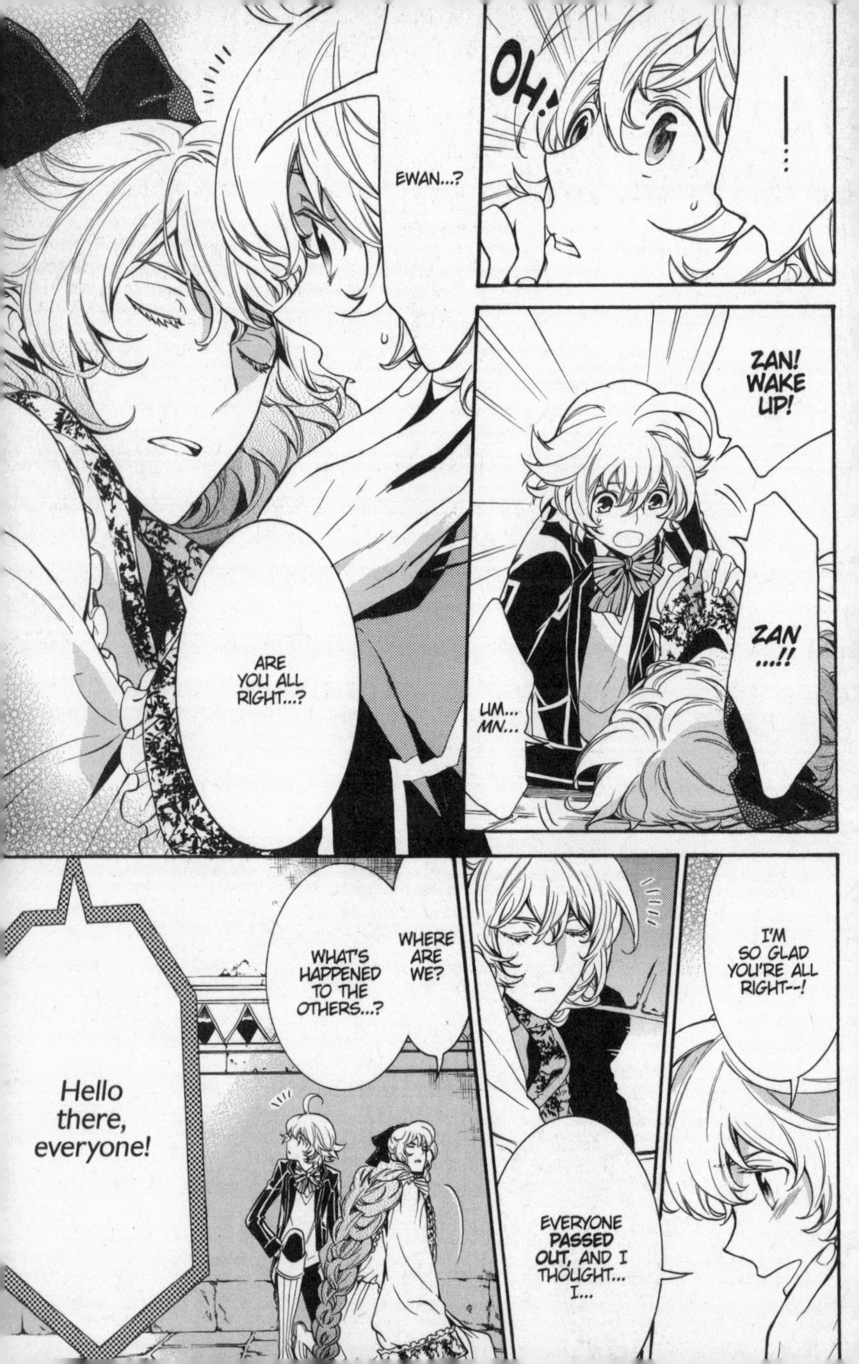
OH!
......
ZAN! WAKE UP!
ZAN ...!!
UM... MN...
EWAN...?
ARE YOU ALL RIGHT...?
I'M SO GLAD YOU'RE ALL RIGHT--!
EVERYONE PASSED OUT, AND I THOUGHT... I...
WHERE ARE WE?
WHAT'S HAPPENED TO THE OTHERS...?
Hello there, everyone!

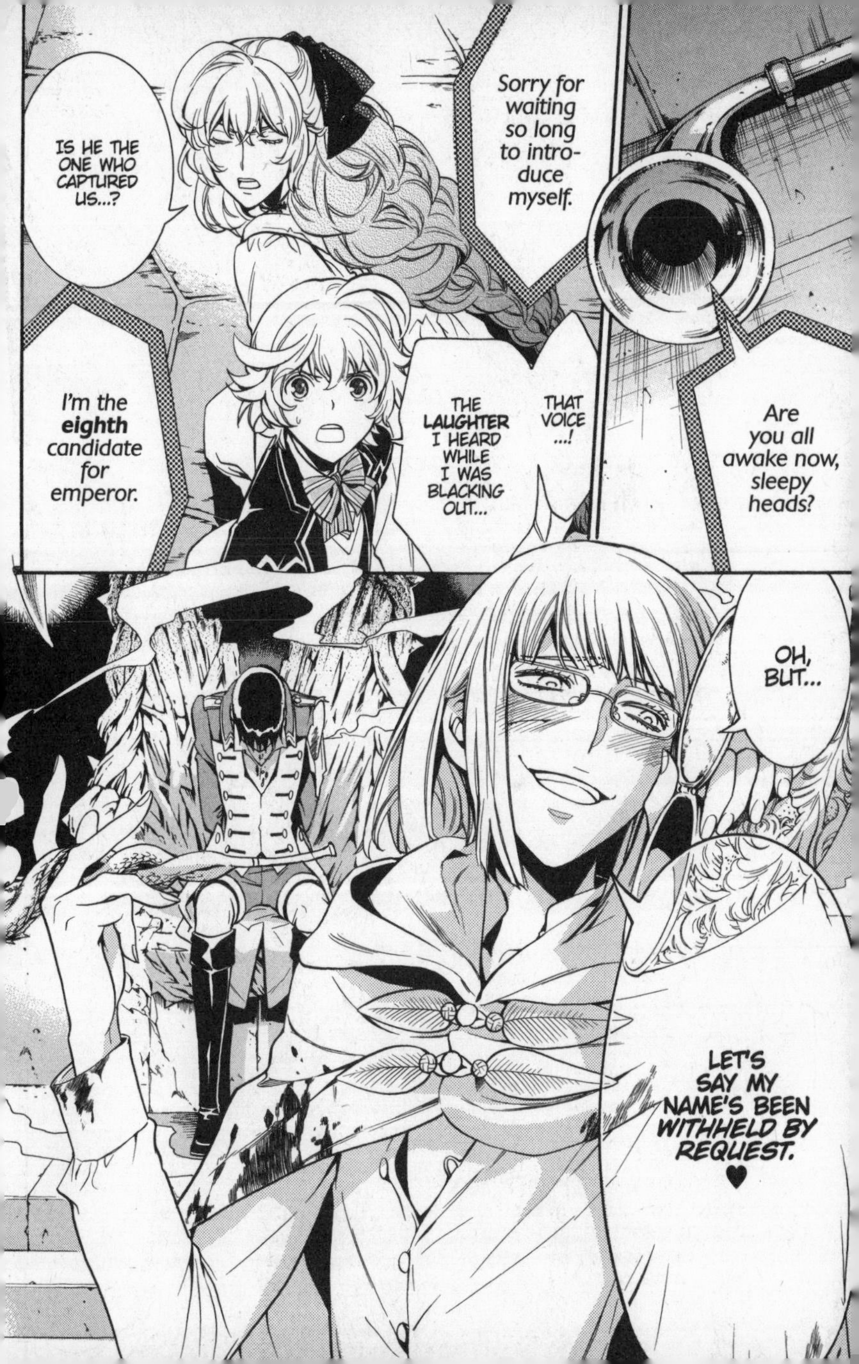
Are you all awake now, sleepy heads?
THAT VOICE ...!
THE LAUGHTER I HEARD WHILE I WAS BLACKING OUT...
Sorry for waiting so long to intro-duce myself.
IS HE THE ONE WHO CAPTURED US...?
I'm the **eighth** candidate for emperor.
OH, BUT...
LET'S SAY MY NAME'S BEEN WITHHELD BY REQUEST. ♥

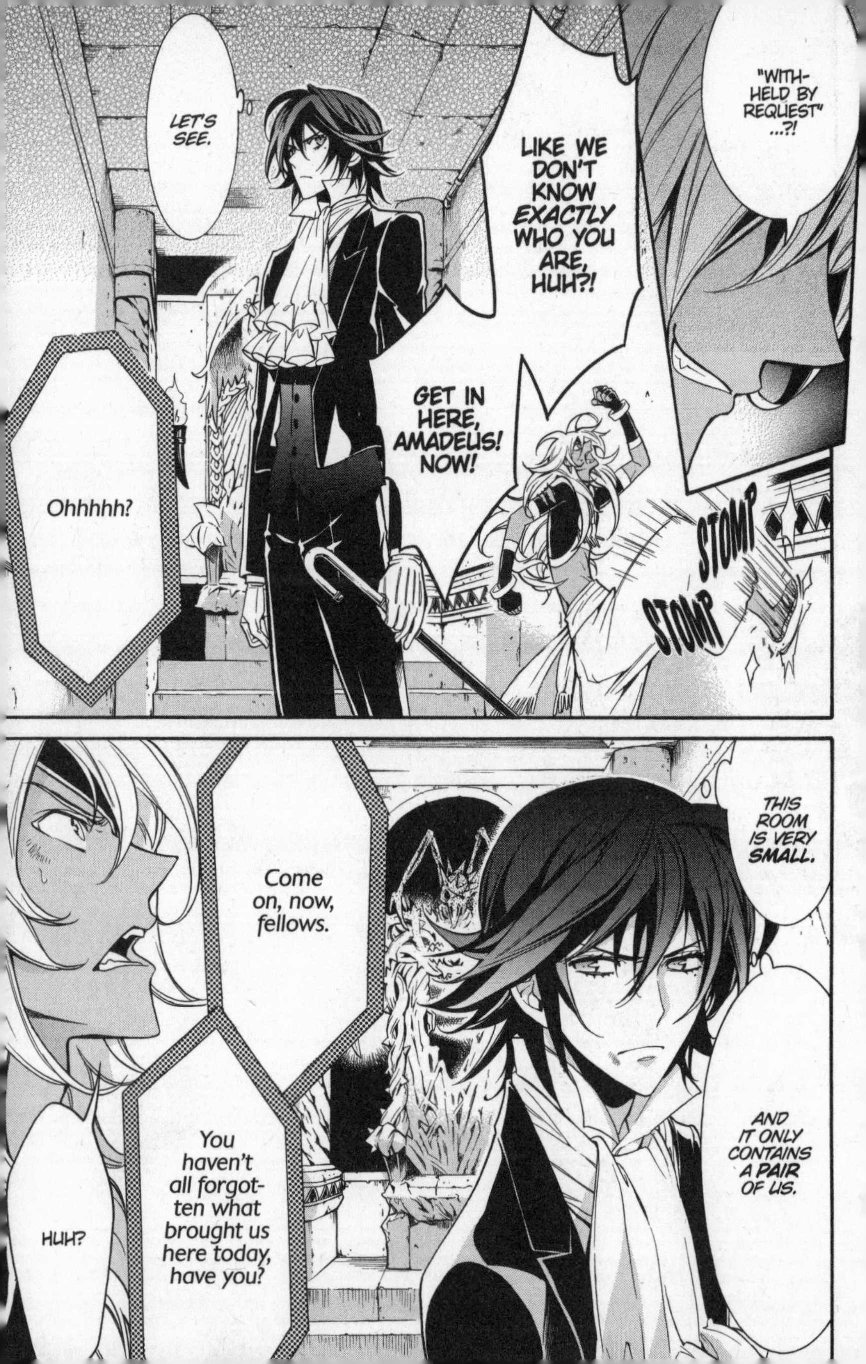
"WITH-HELD BY REQUEST" ...?!
LIKE WE DON'T KNOW EXACTLY WHO YOU ARE, HUH?!
GET IN HERE, AMADEUS! NOW!
STOMP
STOMP
LET'S SEE.
Ohhhhh?
THIS ROOM IS VERY SMALL.
AND IT ONLY CONTAINS A PAIR OF US.
Come on, now, fellows.
You haven't all forgot-ten what brought us here today, have you?
HUH?

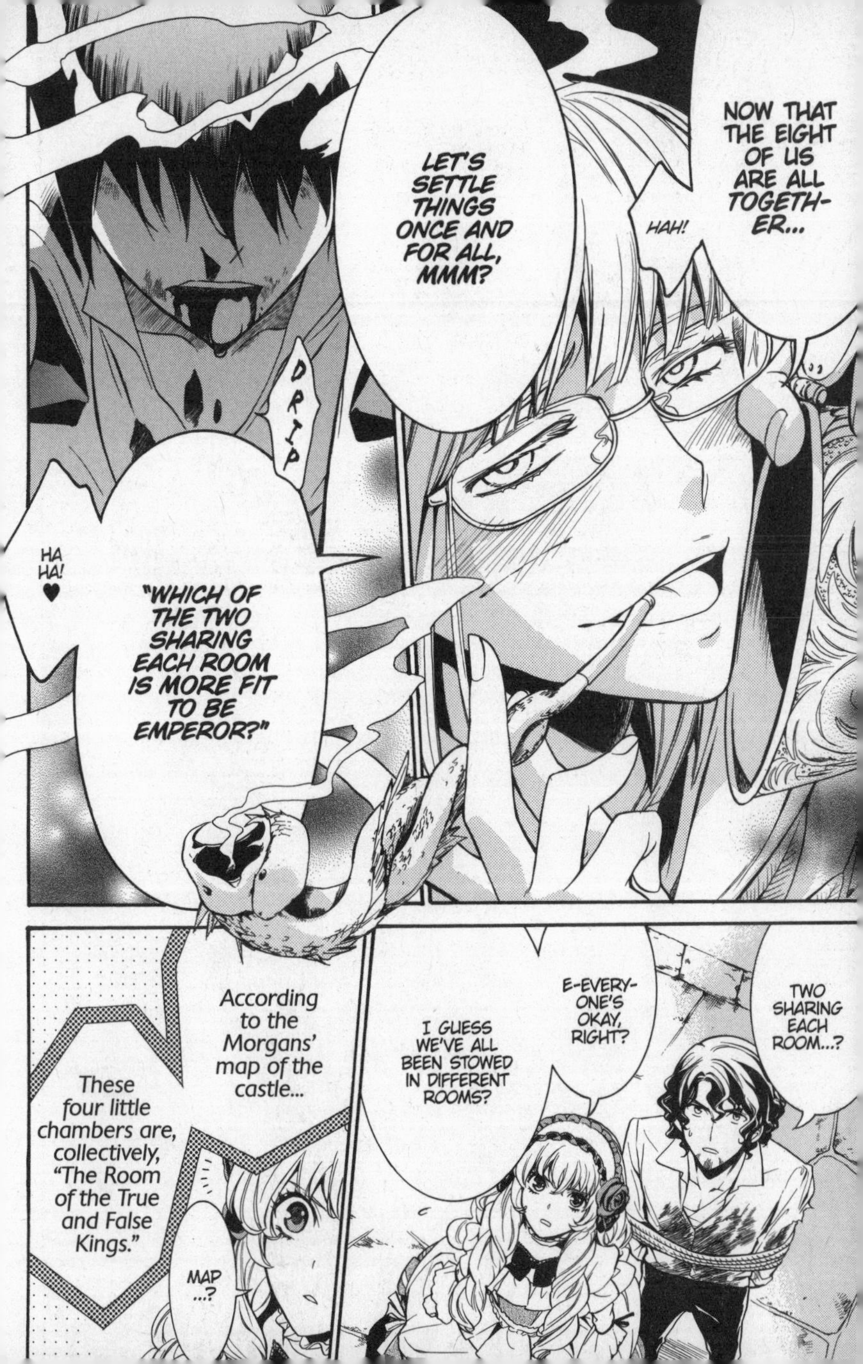
NOW THAT THE EIGHT OF US ARE ALL TOGETH-ER...
HAH!
LET'S SETTLE THINGS ONCE AND FOR ALL, MMM?
DRIP
HA HA! ♥
"WHICH OF THE TWO SHARING EACH ROOM IS MORE FIT TO BE EMPEROR?"
TWO SHARING EACH ROOM...?
E-EVERY-ONE'S OKAY, RIGHT?
I GUESS WE'VE ALL BEEN STOWED IN DIFFERENT ROOMS?
According to the Morgans' map of the castle...
These four little chambers are, collectively, "The Room of the True and False Kings."
MAP ...?

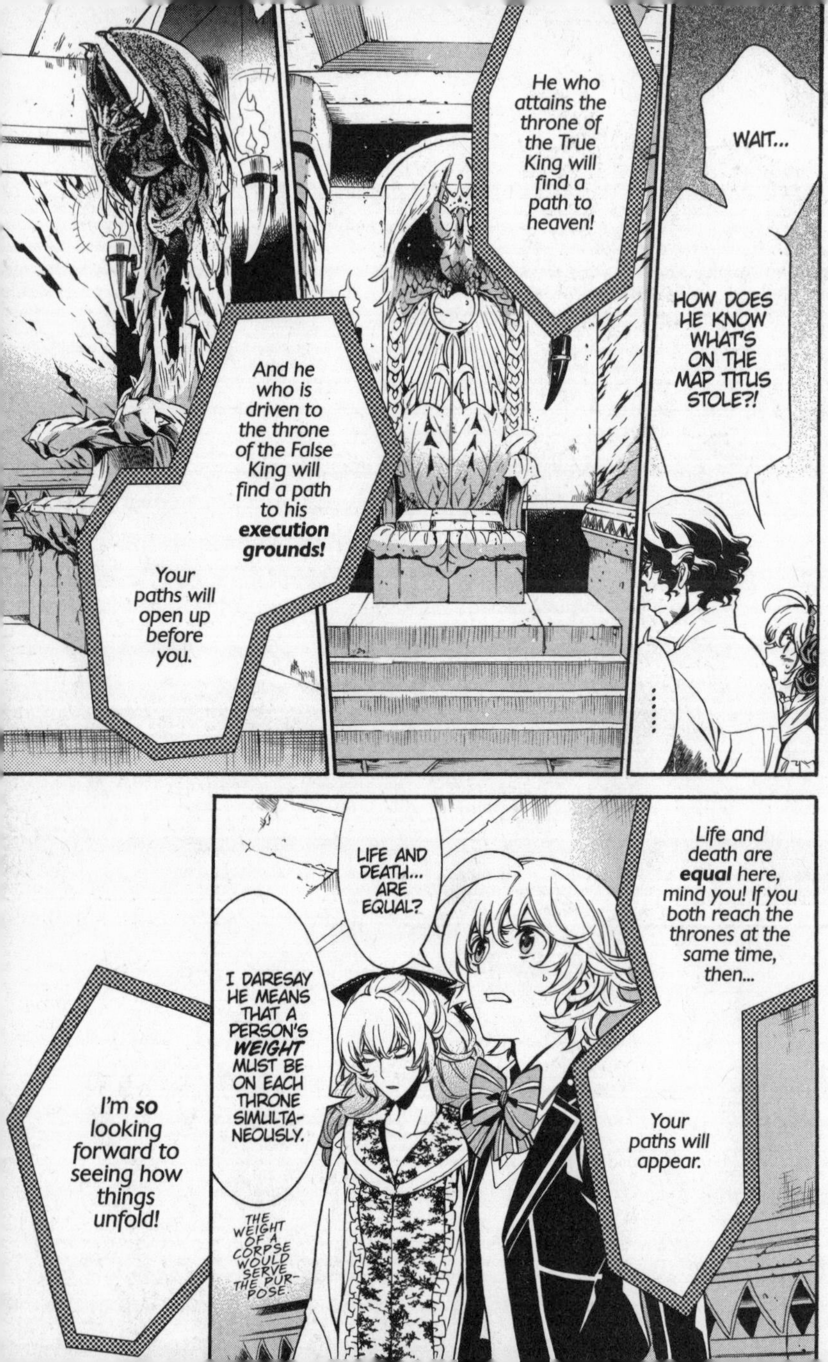

WAIT...
HOW DOES HE KNOW WHAT'S ON THE MAP TITUS STOLE?!
......
He who attains the throne of the True King will find a path to heaven!
And he who is driven to the throne of the False King will find a path to his **execution grounds!**
Your paths will open up before you.
Life and death are **equal** here, mind you! If you both reach the thrones at the same time, then...
Your paths will appear.
LIFE AND DEATH... ARE EQUAL?
I DARESAY HE MEANS THAT A PERSON'S *WEIGHT* MUST BE ON EACH THRONE SIMULTANEOUSLY.
THE WEIGHT OF A CORPSE WOULD SERVE THE PURPOSE.
I'm **so** looking forward to seeing how things unfold!

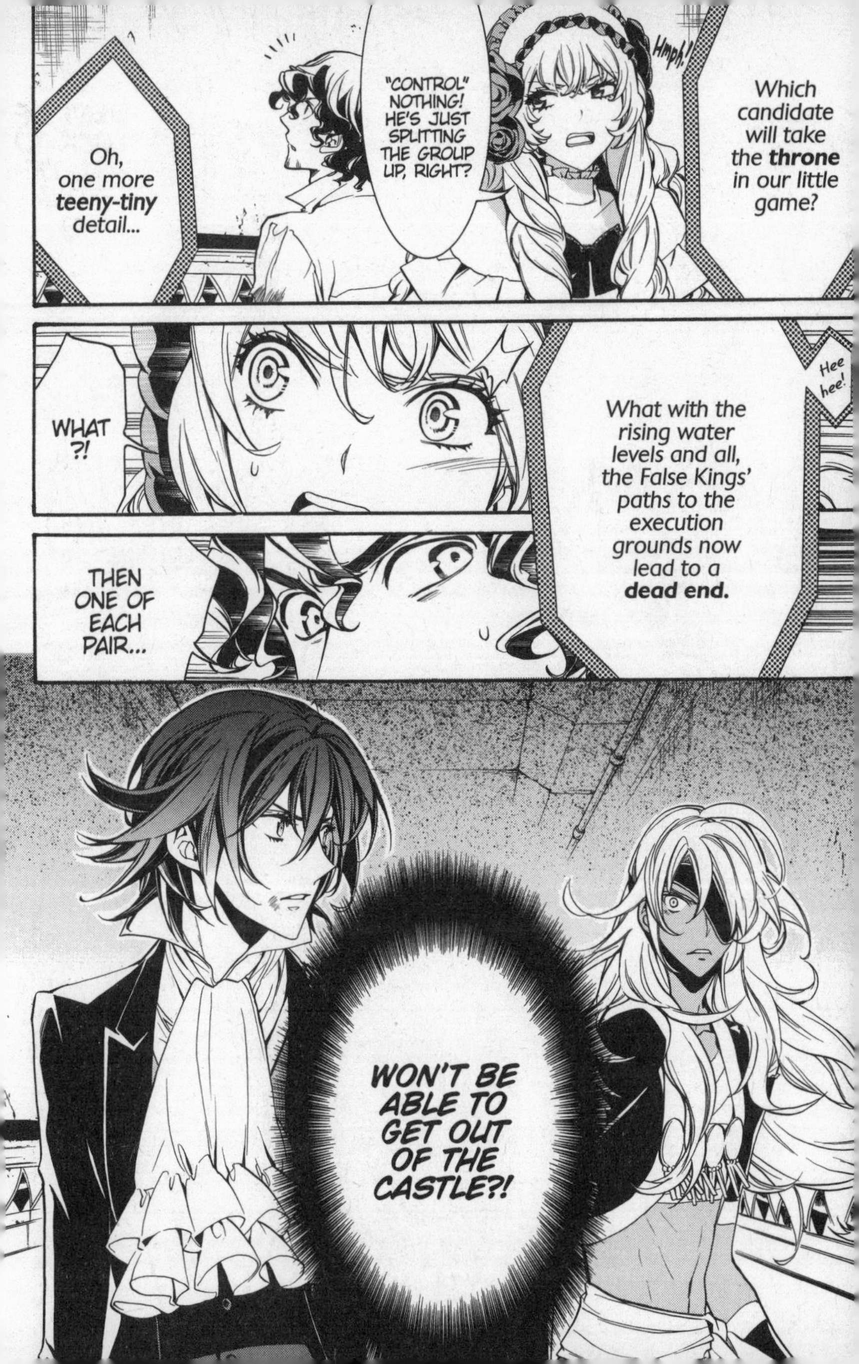
Which candidate will take the **throne** in our little game?
Hmph!
"CONTROL" NOTHING! HE'S JUST SPLITTING THE GROUP UP, RIGHT?
Oh, one more **teeny-tiny** detail...
Hee hee!
What with the rising water levels and all, the False Kings' paths to the execution grounds now lead to a **dead end.**
WHAT ?!
THEN ONE OF EACH PAIR...
WON'T BE ABLE TO GET OUT OF THE CASTLE?!

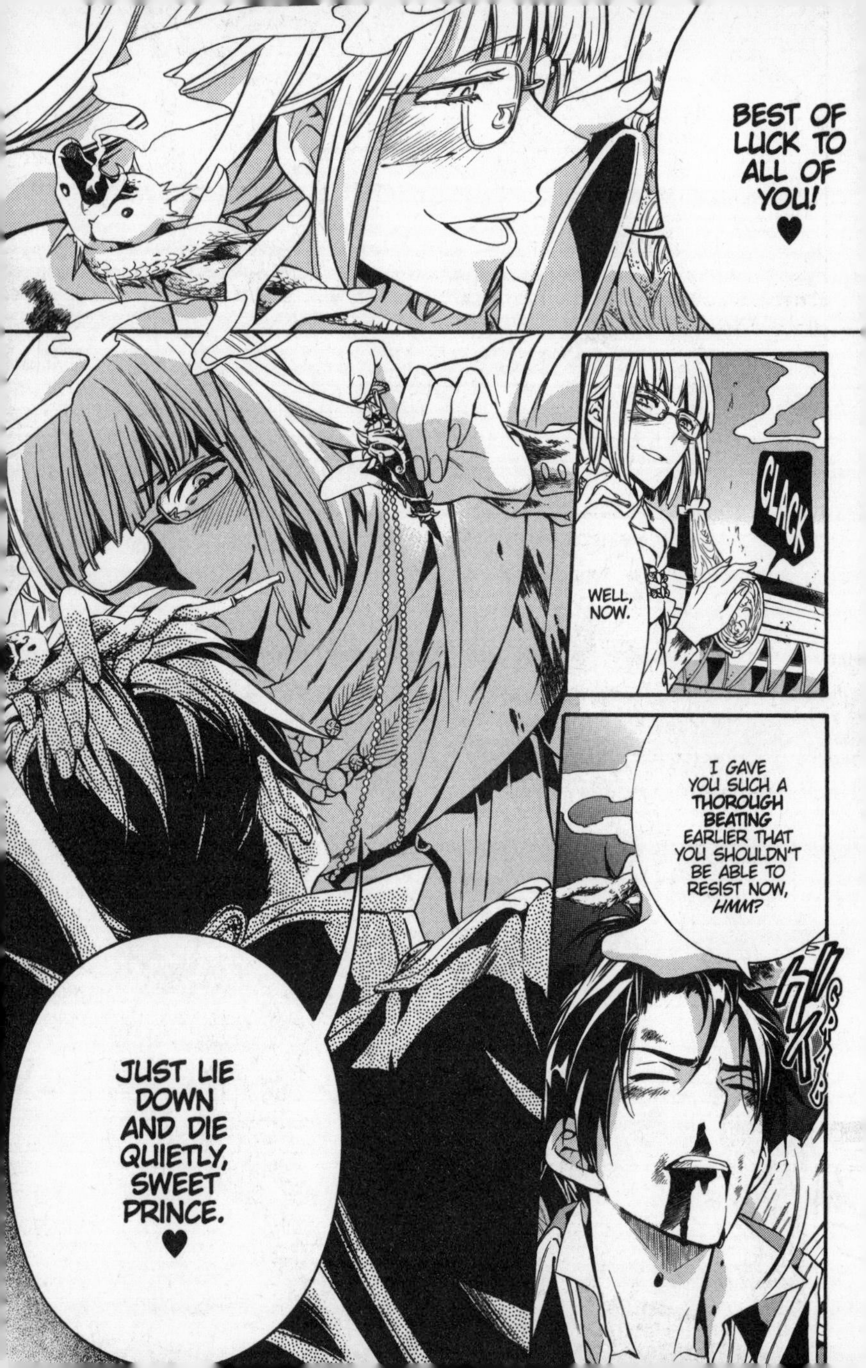
BEST OF LUCK TO ALL OF YOU! ♥
CLACK
WELL, NOW.
I GAVE YOU SUCH A THOROUGH BEATING EARLIER THAT YOU SHOULDN'T BE ABLE TO RESIST NOW, *HMM?*
GRAB
JUST LIE DOWN AND DIE QUIETLY, SWEET PRINCE. ♥

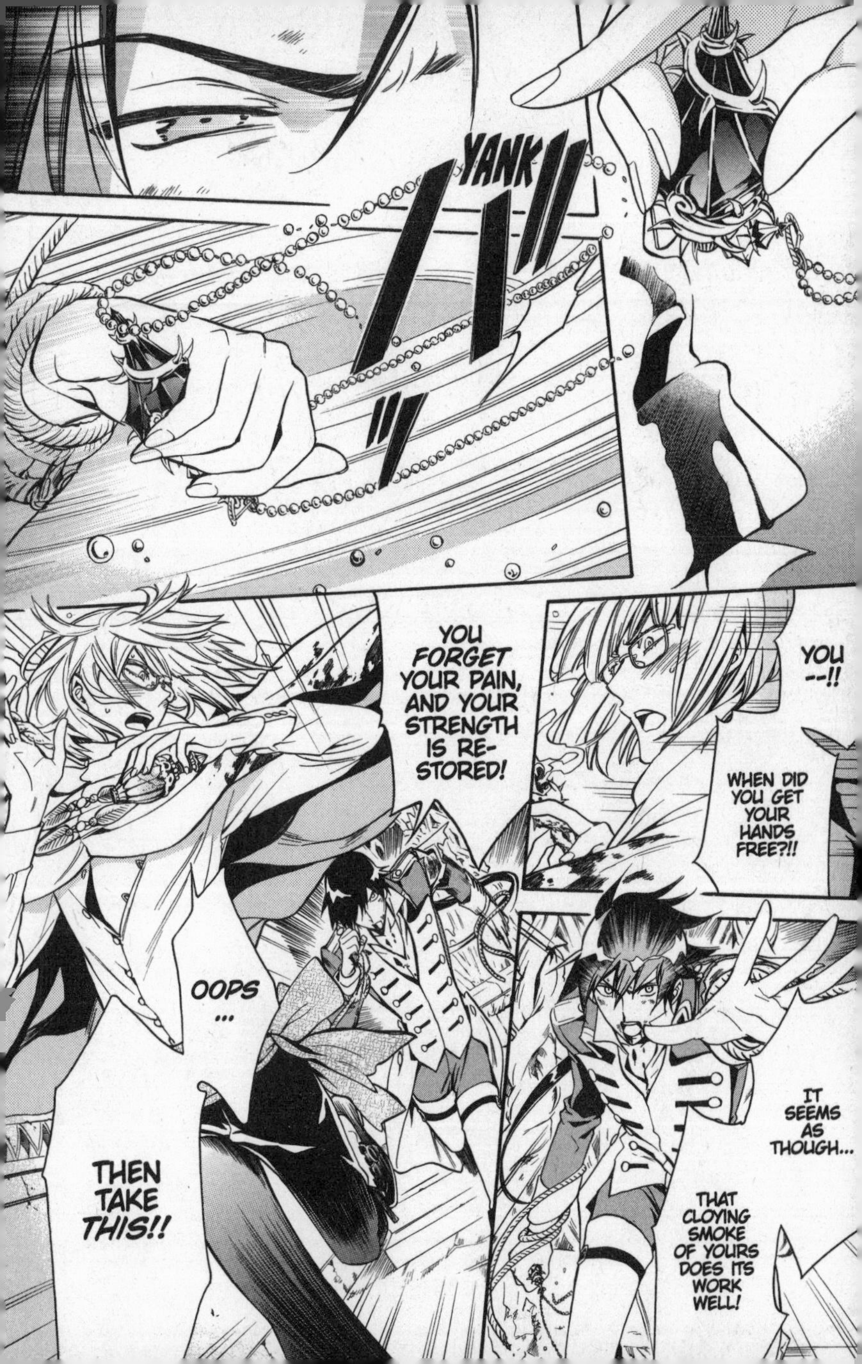
YANK!!
YOU--!!
WHEN DID YOU GET YOUR HANDS FREE?!!
IT SEEMS AS THOUGH...
THAT CLOYING SMOKE OF YOURS DOES ITS WORK WELL!
YOU FORGET YOUR PAIN, AND YOUR STRENGTH IS RE-STORED!
OOPS...
THEN TAKE THIS!!

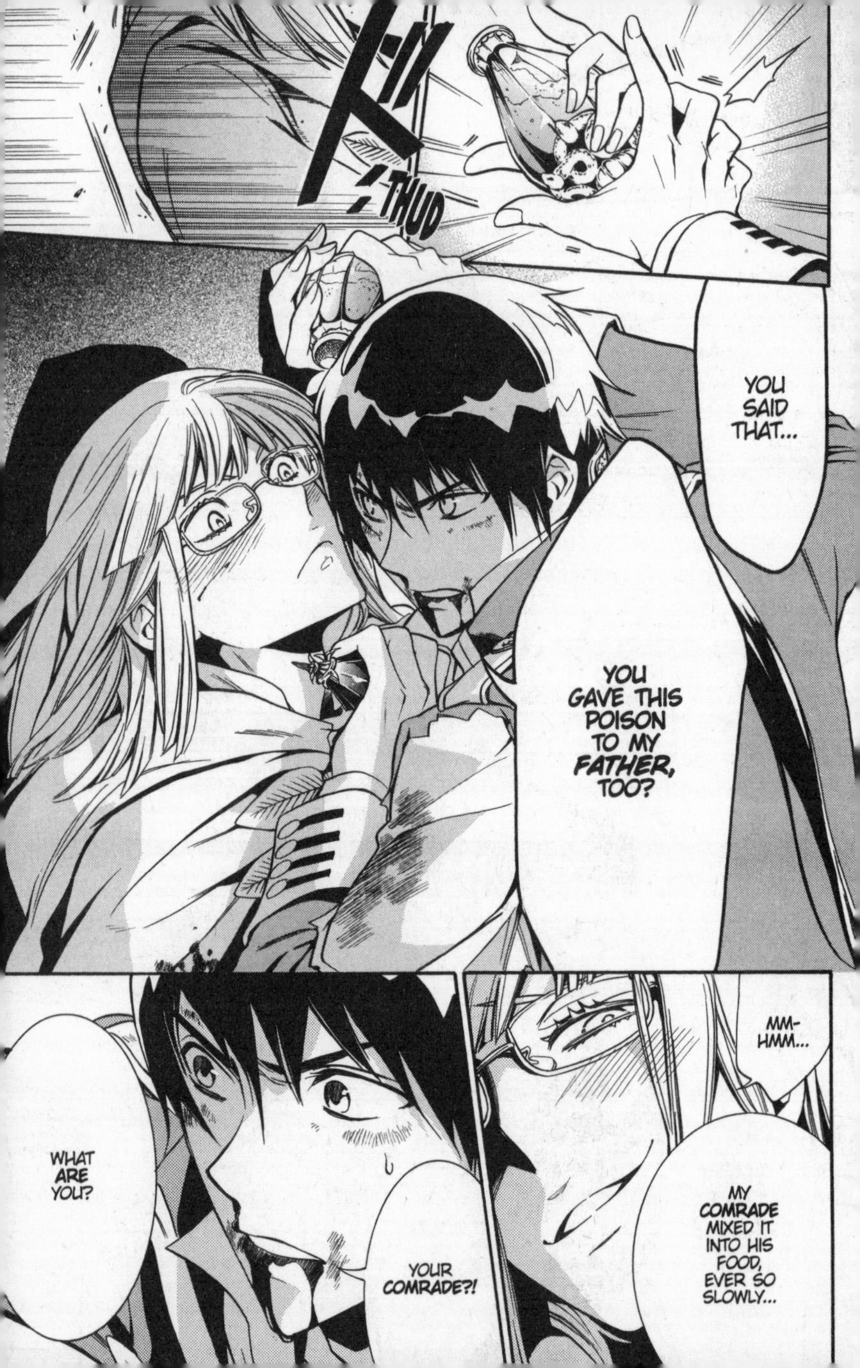
THUD
YOU SAID THAT...
YOU GAVE THIS POISON TO MY *FATHER*, TOO?
MM-HMM...
MY COMRADE MIXED IT INTO HIS FOOD, EVER SO SLOWLY...
YOUR COMRADE?!
WHAT ARE YOU?

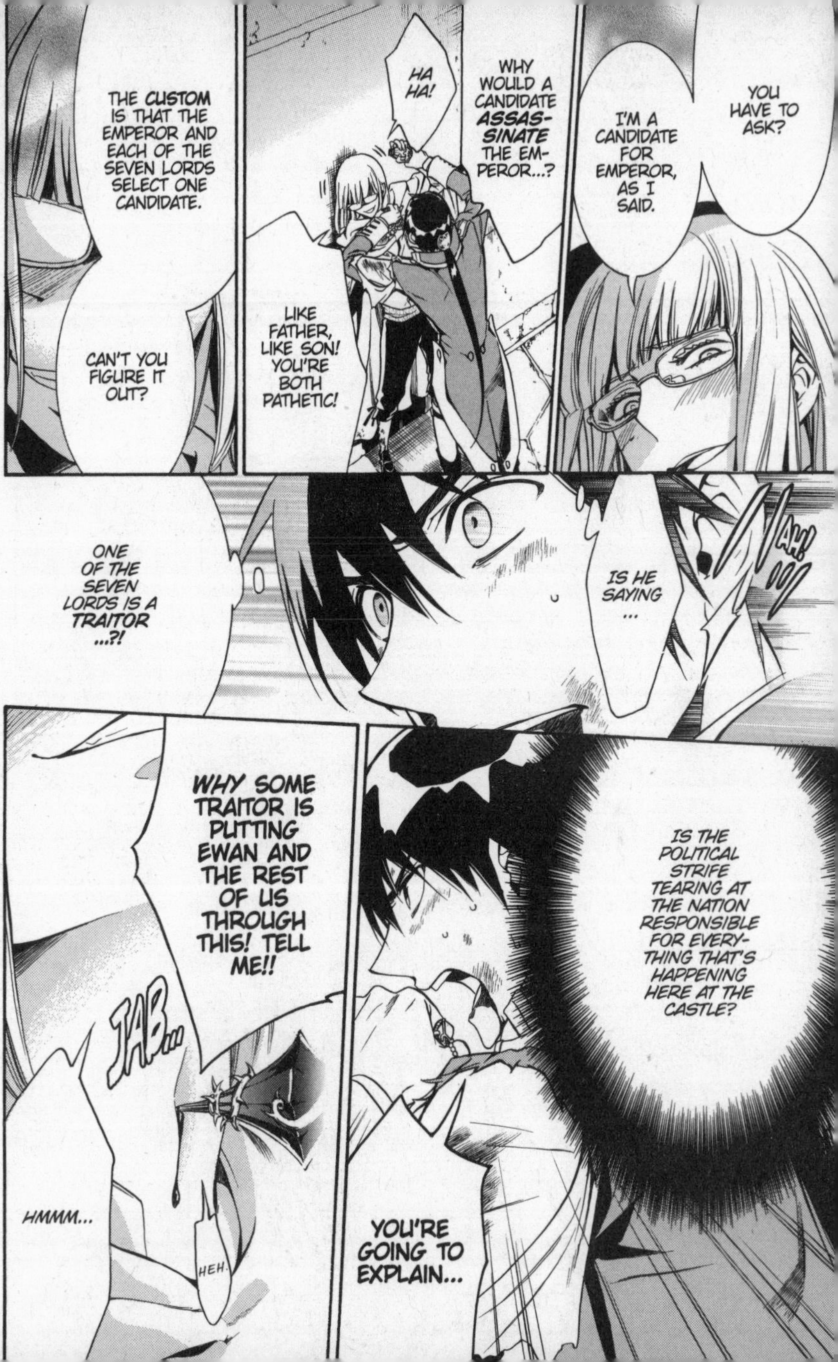
YOU HAVE TO ASK?
I'M A CANDIDATE FOR EMPEROR, AS I SAID.
WHY WOULD A CANDIDATE ASSAS-SINATE THE EM-PEROR...?
HA HA!
LIKE FATHER, LIKE SON! YOU'RE BOTH PATHETIC!
THE CUSTOM IS THAT THE EMPEROR AND EACH OF THE SEVEN LORDS SELECT ONE CANDIDATE.
CAN'T YOU FIGURE IT OUT?
AH!!
IS HE SAYING ...
ONE OF THE SEVEN LORDS IS A TRAITOR ...?!
IS THE POLITICAL STRIFE TEARING AT THE NATION RESPONSIBLE FOR EVERY-THING THAT'S HAPPENING HERE AT THE CASTLE?
YOU'RE GOING TO EXPLAIN...
WHY SOME TRAITOR IS PUTTING EWAN AND THE REST OF US THROUGH THIS! TELL ME!!
JAB...
HMMM...
HEH.

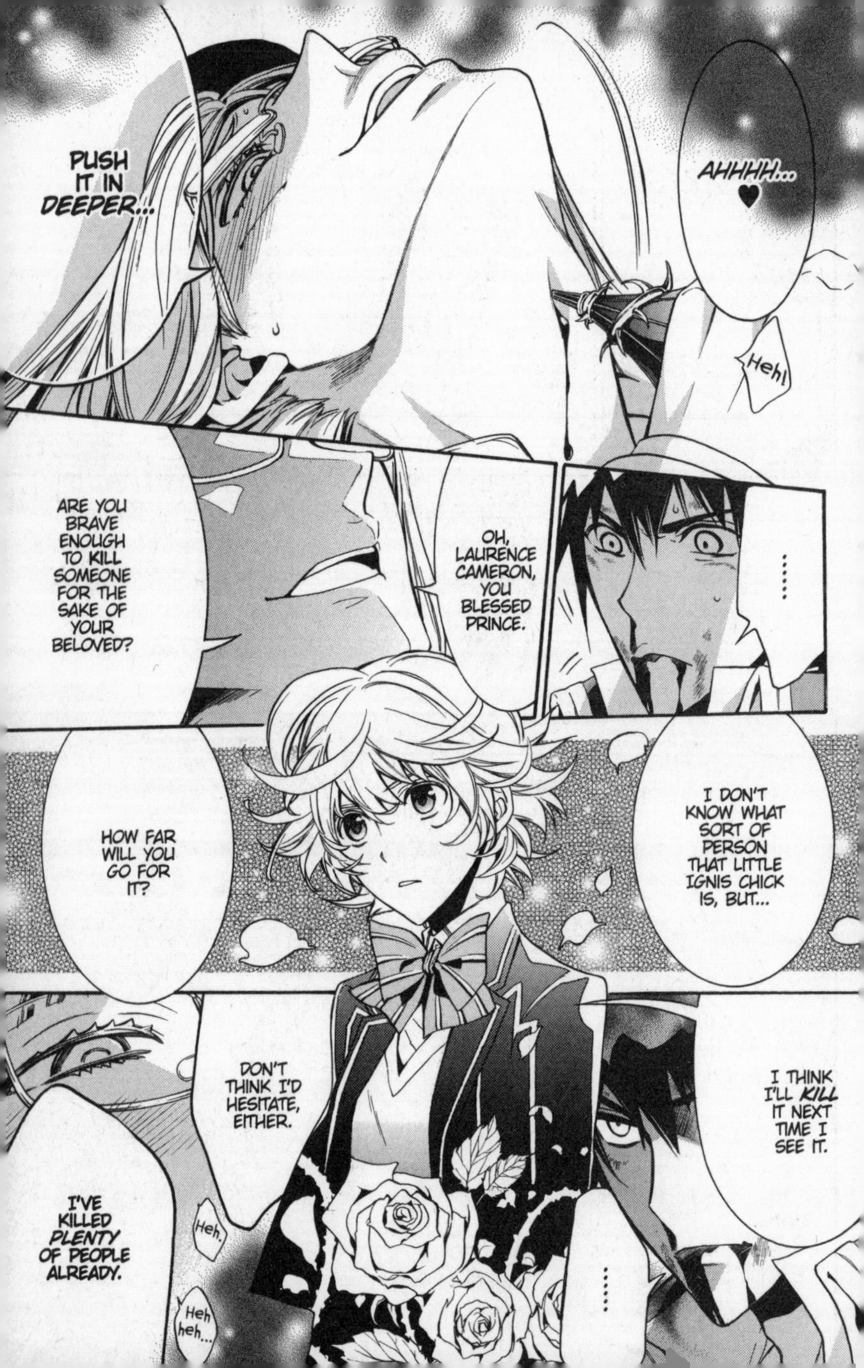
AHHHH... ♥
Heh!
PUSH IT IN DEEPER...
......
OH, LAURENCE CAMERON, YOU BLESSED PRINCE.
ARE YOU BRAVE ENOUGH TO KILL SOMEONE FOR THE SAKE OF YOUR BELOVED?
I DON'T KNOW WHAT SORT OF PERSON THAT LITTLE IGNIS CHICK IS, BUT...
HOW FAR WILL YOU GO FOR IT?
I THINK I'LL *KILL* IT NEXT TIME I SEE IT.
......
DON'T THINK I'D HESITATE, EITHER.
Heh.
I'VE KILLED *PLENTY* OF PEOPLE ALREADY.
Heh heh...

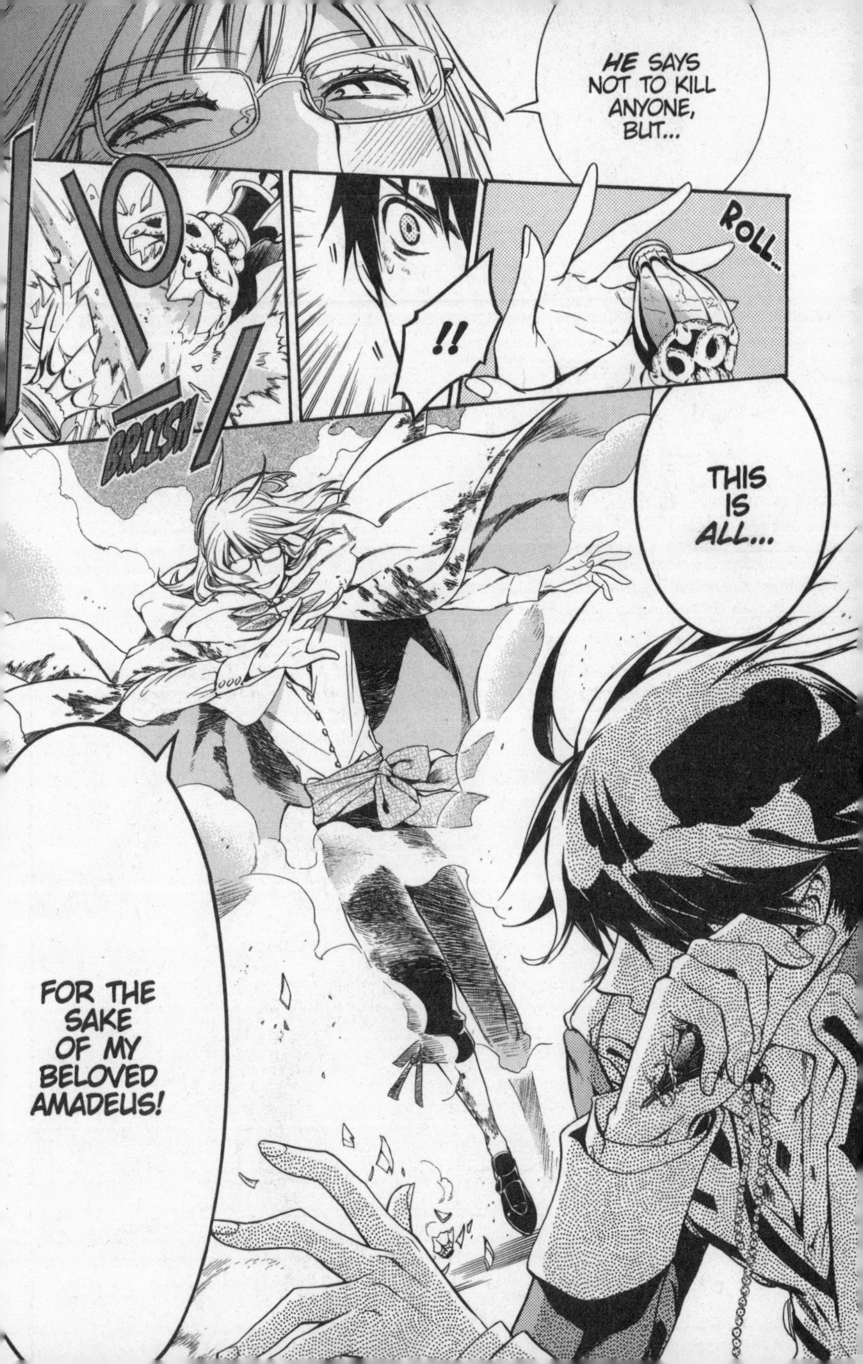
HE SAYS NOT TO KILL ANYONE, BUT...
ROLL...
!!
BRIISH
THIS IS ALL...
FOR THE SAKE OF MY BELOVED AMADEUS!

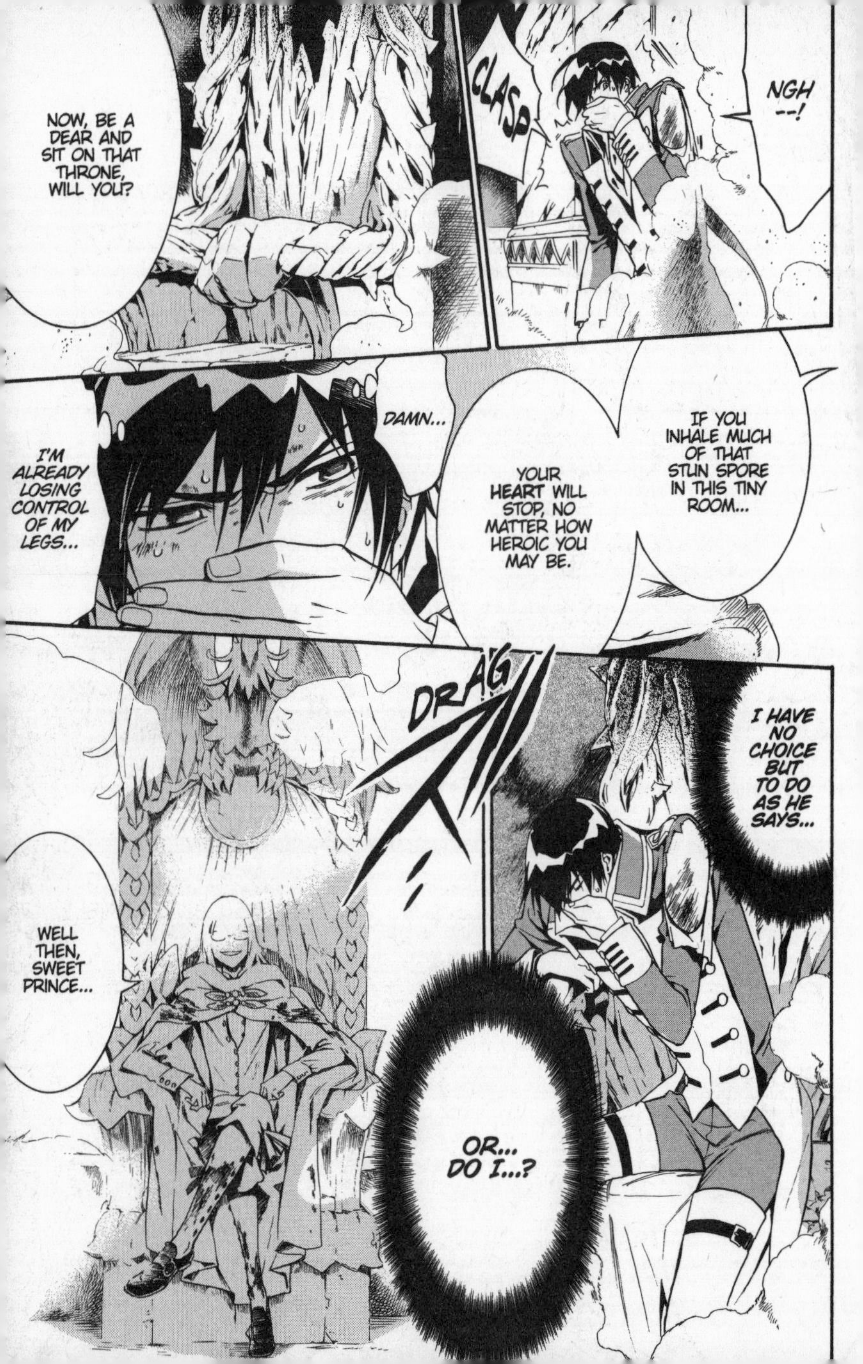
CLASP
NGH--!
NOW, BE A DEAR AND SIT ON THAT THRONE, WILL YOU?
IF YOU INHALE MUCH OF THAT STUN SPORE IN THIS TINY ROOM...
YOUR HEART WILL STOP, NO MATTER HOW HEROIC YOU MAY BE.
DAMN...
I'M ALREADY LOSING CONTROL OF MY LEGS...
I HAVE NO CHOICE BUT TO DO AS HE SAYS...
OR... DO I...?
DRAG
WELL THEN, SWEET PRINCE...

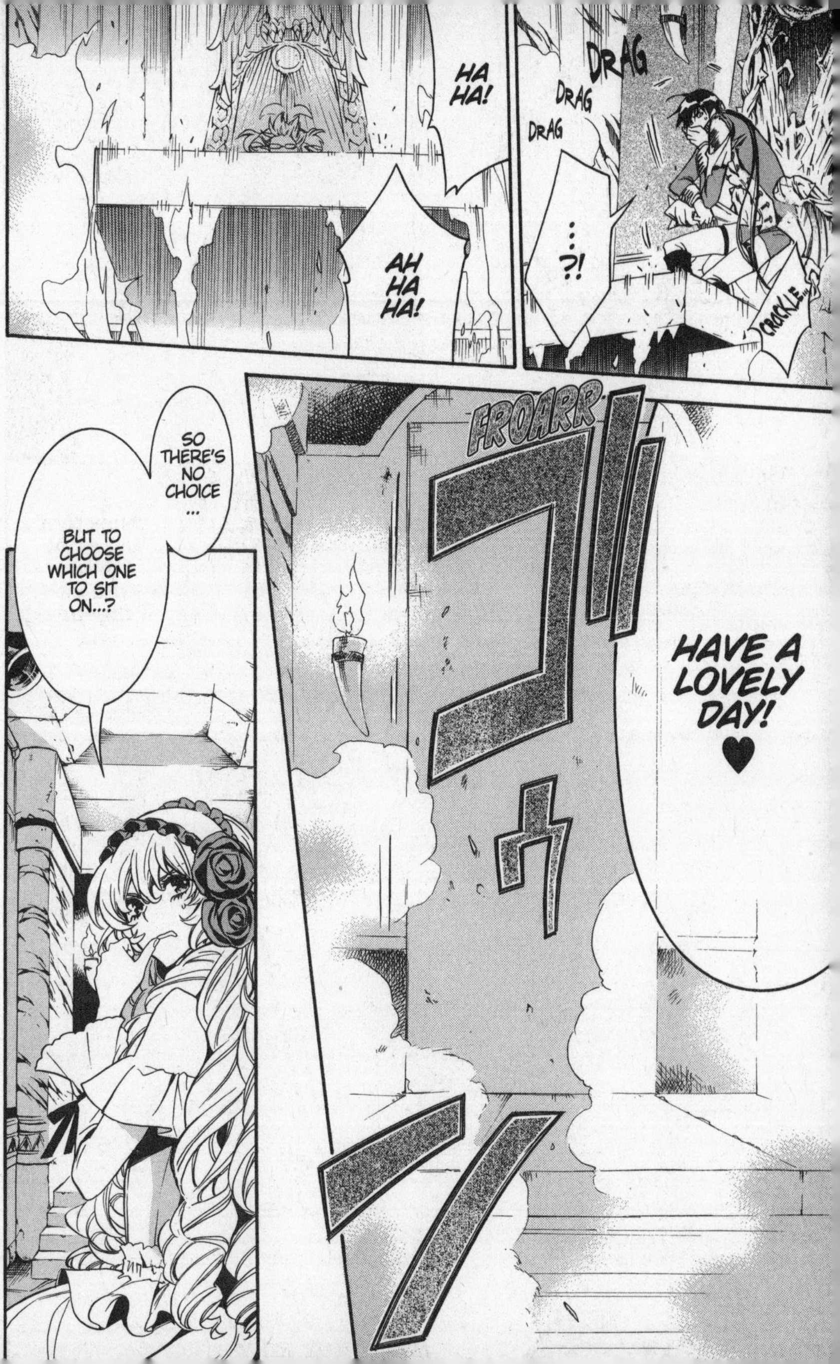
DRAG
DRAG
DRAG
...?!
CRACKLE...
HA HA!
AH HA HA!
HAVE A LOVELY DAY! ♥
FROARR
SO THERE'S NO CHOICE...
BUT TO CHOOSE WHICH ONE TO SIT ON...?

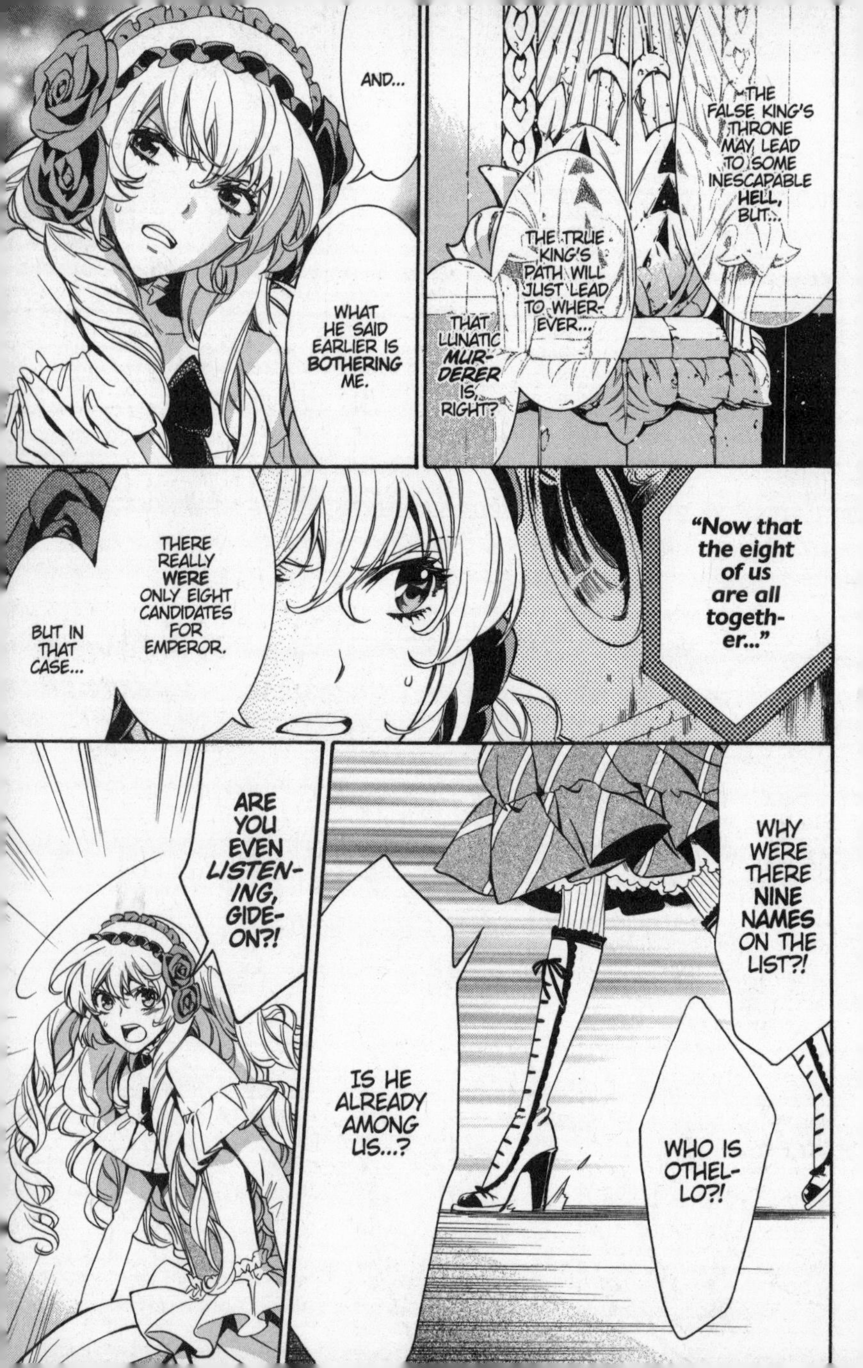
THE FALSE KING'S THRONE MAY LEAD TO SOME INESCAPABLE HELL, BUT...
THE TRUE KING'S PATH WILL JUST LEAD TO WHER-EVER...
THAT LUNATIC *MUR-DERER* IS RIGHT?
AND...
WHAT HE SAID EARLIER IS BOTHERING ME.
"Now that the eight of us are all togeth-er..."
THERE REALLY WERE ONLY EIGHT CANDIDATES FOR EMPEROR.
BUT IN THAT CASE...
WHY WERE THERE NINE NAMES ON THE LIST?!
WHO IS OTHEL-LO?!
IS HE ALREADY AMONG US...?
ARE YOU EVEN *LISTEN-ING,* GIDE-ON?!

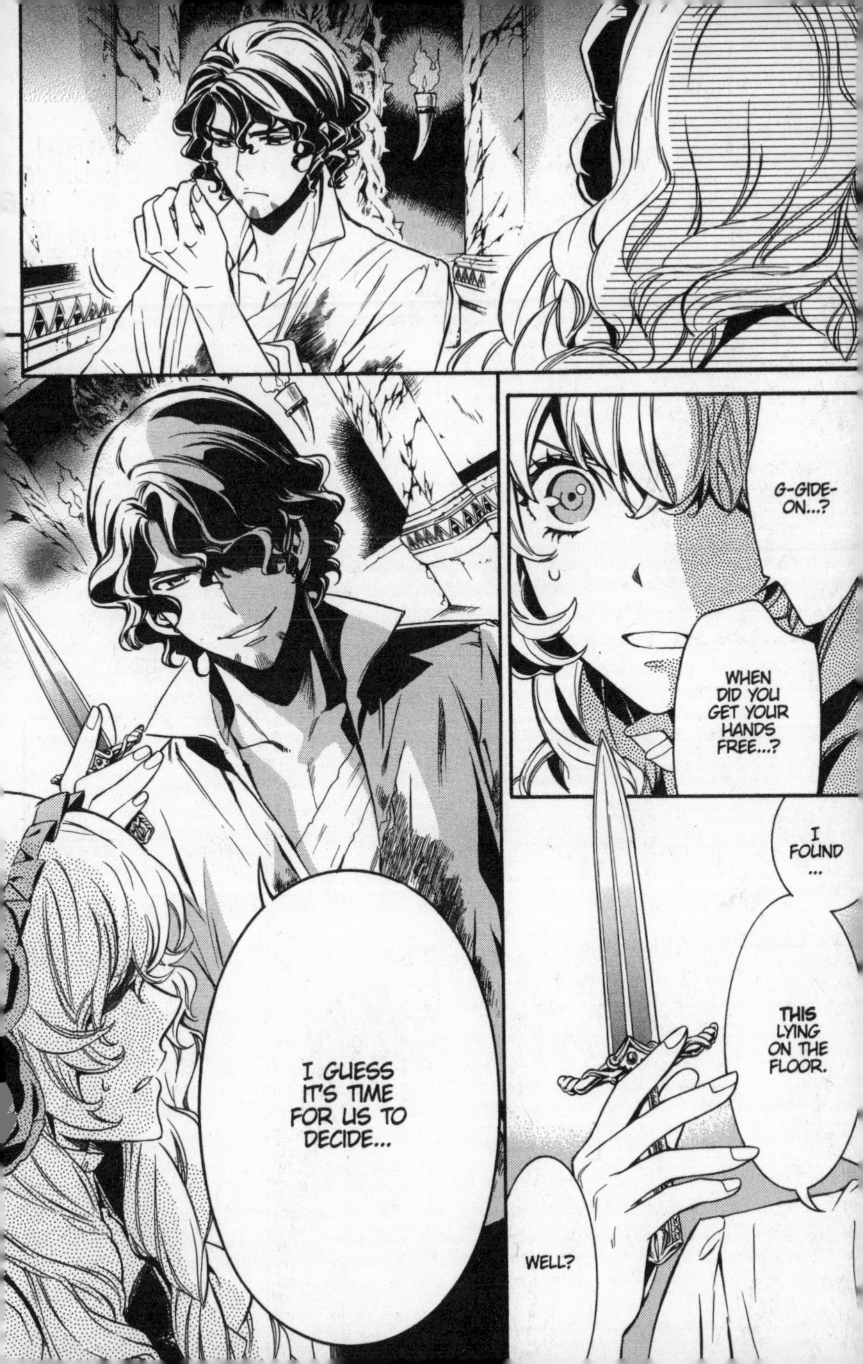
G-GIDE-ON...?
WHEN DID YOU GET YOUR HANDS FREE...?
I FOUND ...
THIS LYING ON THE FLOOR.
WELL?
I GUESS IT'S TIME FOR US TO DECIDE...

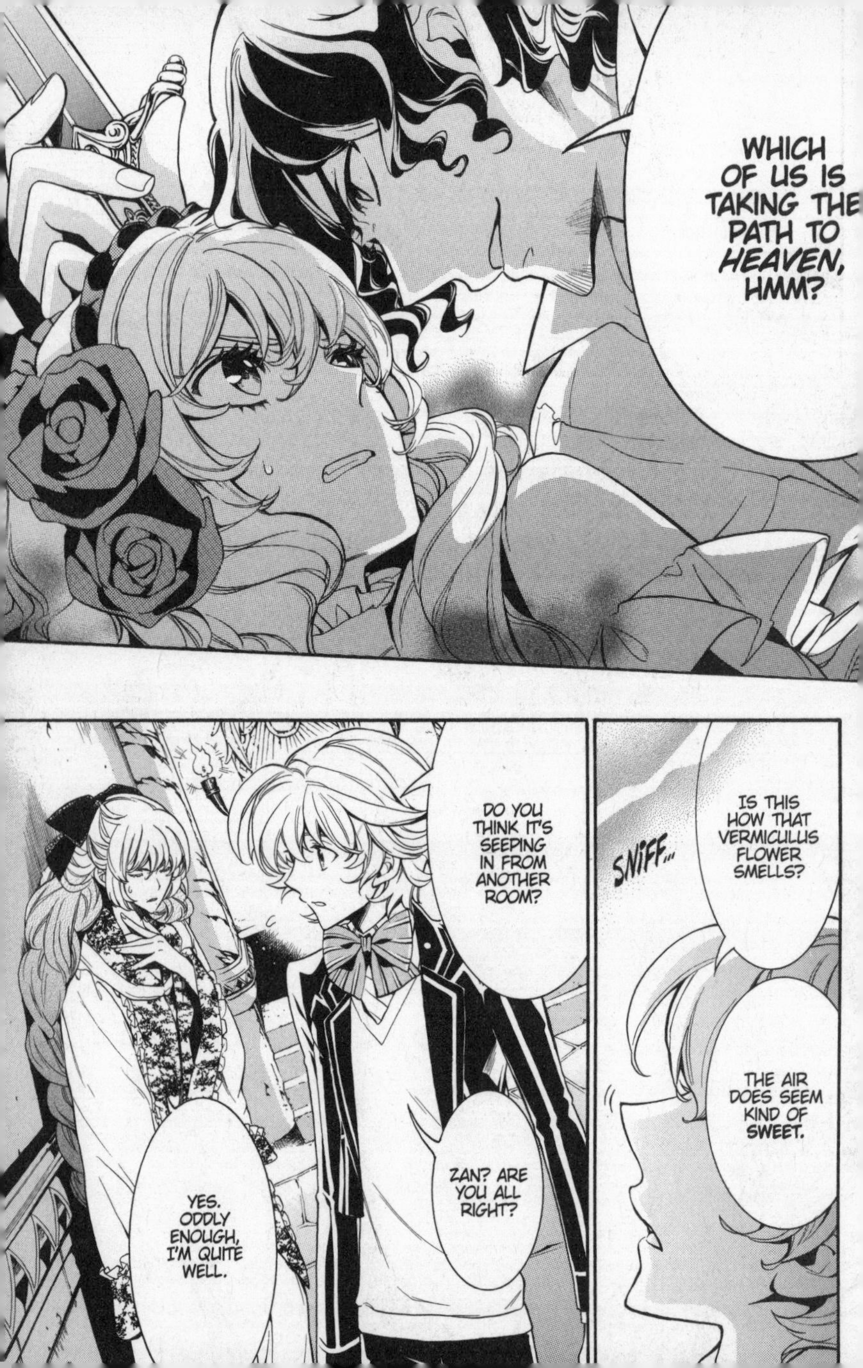
WHICH OF US IS TAKING THE PATH TO *HEAVEN*, HMM?
IS THIS HOW THAT VERMICULUS FLOWER SMELLS?
SNIFF...
THE AIR DOES SEEM KIND OF SWEET.
DO YOU THINK IT'S SEEPING IN FROM ANOTHER ROOM?
ZAN? ARE YOU ALL RIGHT?
YES. ODDLY ENOUGH, I'M QUITE WELL.

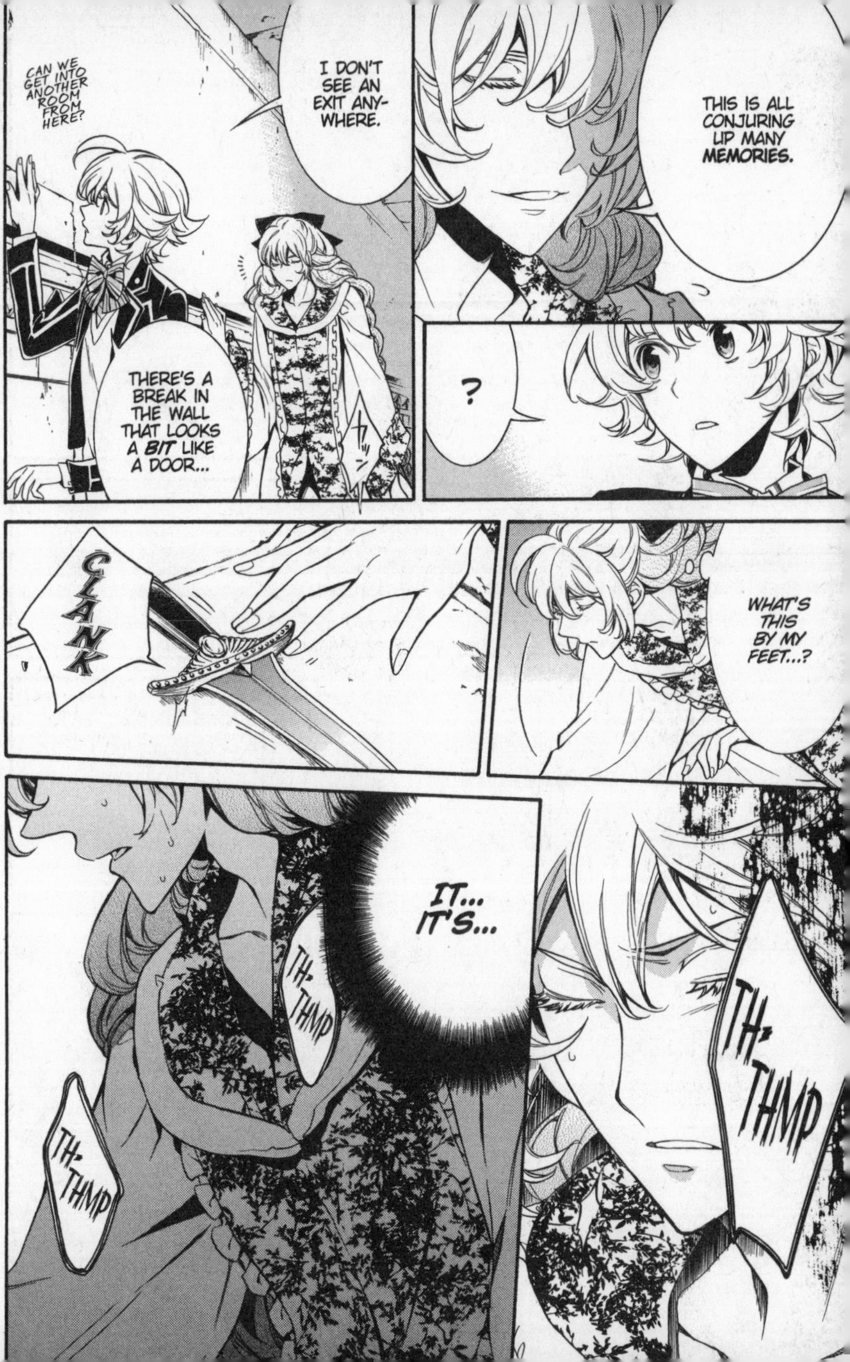
THIS IS ALL CONJURING UP MANY MEMORIES.
?
I DON'T SEE AN EXIT ANY-WHERE.
CAN WE GET INTO ANOTHER ROOM FROM HERE?
THERE'S A BREAK IN THE WALL THAT LOOKS A *BIT* LIKE A DOOR...
WHAT'S THIS BY MY FEET...?
CLANK
TH-THMP
IT... IT'S...
TH-THMP
TH-THMP

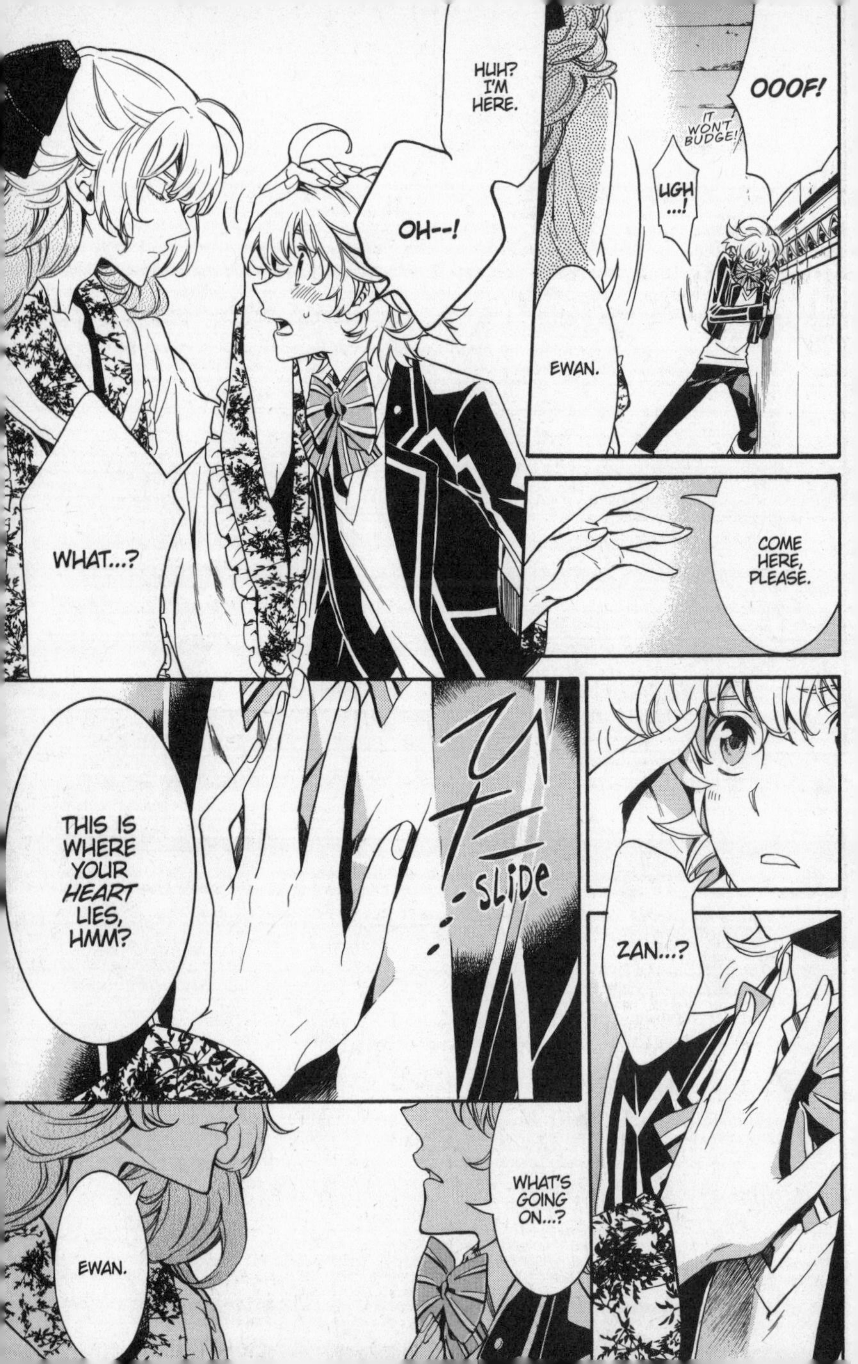
OOOF!
IT WON'T BUDGE!
UGH...!
EWAN.
COME HERE, PLEASE.
HUH? I'M HERE.
OH--!
WHAT...?
ZAN...?
SLIDE
THIS IS WHERE YOUR *HEART* LIES, HMM?
WHAT'S GOING ON...?
EWAN.

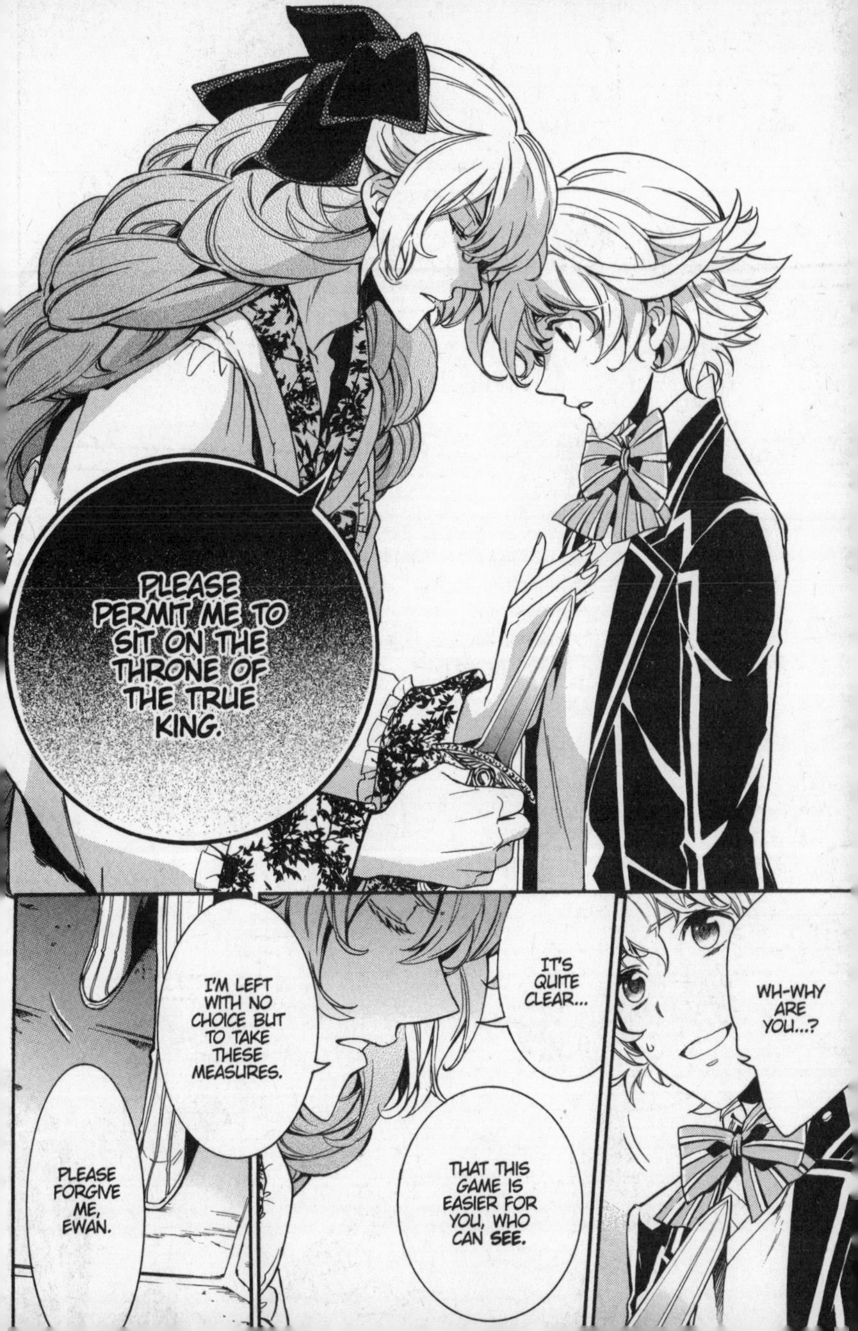
PLEASE PERMIT ME TO SIT ON THE THRONE OF THE TRUE KING.
WH-WHY ARE YOU...?
IT'S QUITE CLEAR...
THAT THIS GAME IS EASIER FOR YOU, WHO CAN SEE.
I'M LEFT WITH NO CHOICE BUT TO TAKE THESE MEASURES.
PLEASE FORGIVE ME, EWAN.

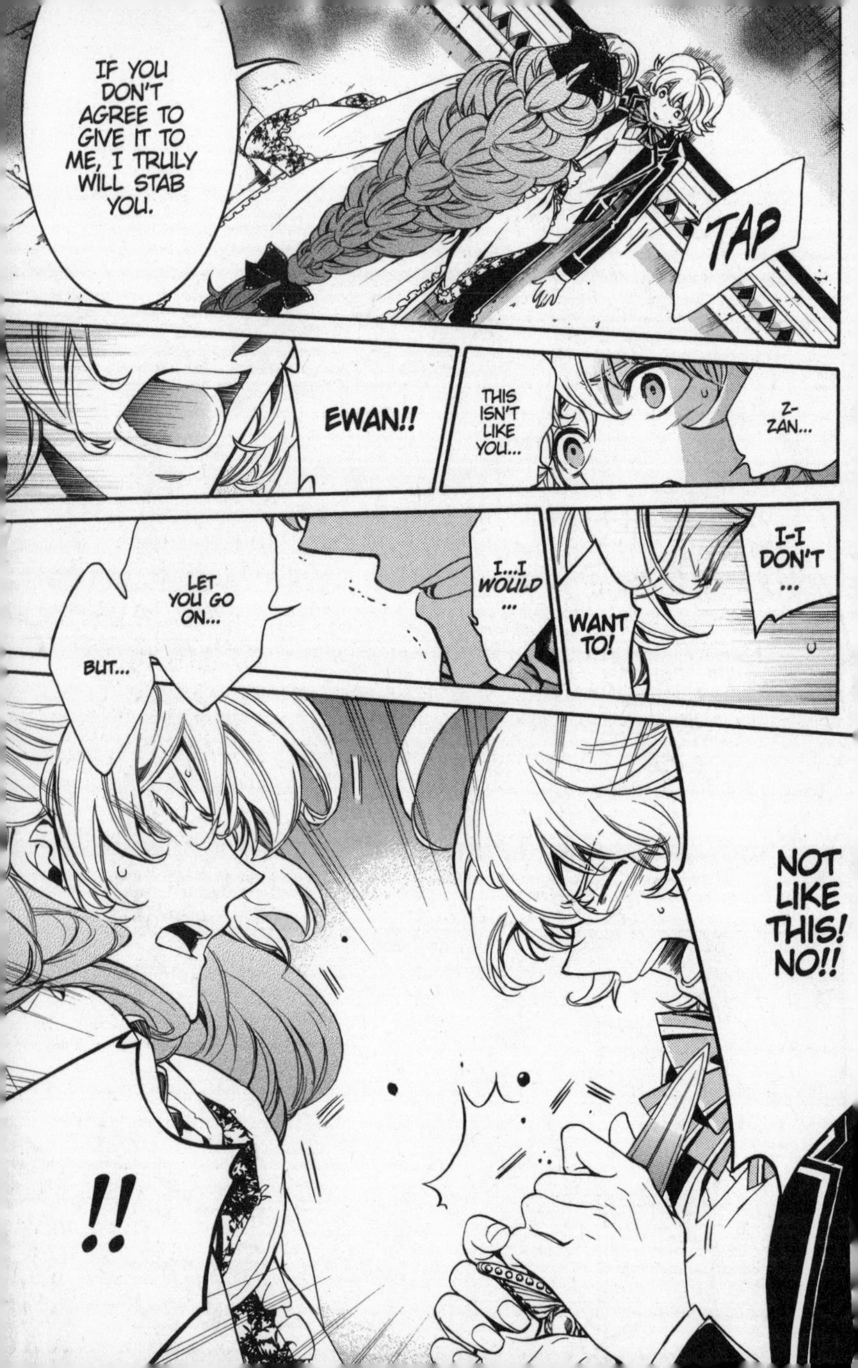
IF YOU DON'T AGREE TO GIVE IT TO ME, I TRULY WILL STAB YOU.
TAP
Z-ZAN...
THIS ISN'T LIKE YOU...
EWAN!!
I-I DON'T ...
WANT TO!
I...I WOULD ...
LET YOU GO ON...
BUT...
NOT LIKE THIS! NO!!
!!

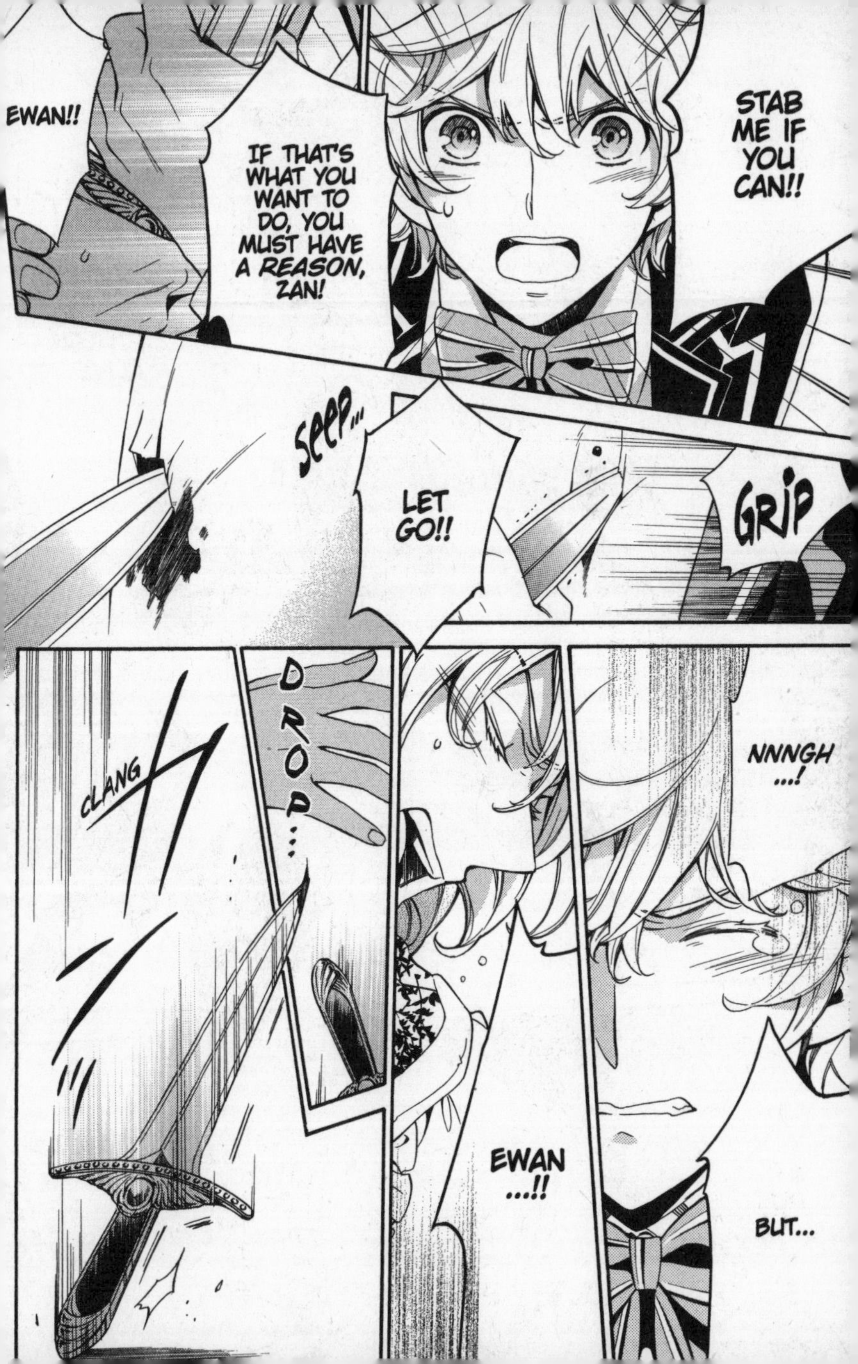
STAB ME IF YOU CAN!!
IF THAT'S WHAT YOU WANT TO DO, YOU MUST HAVE A *REASON,* ZAN!
EWAN!!
GRIP
LET GO!!
SEEP...
NNNGH ...!
BUT...
EWAN ...!!
DROP...
CLANG

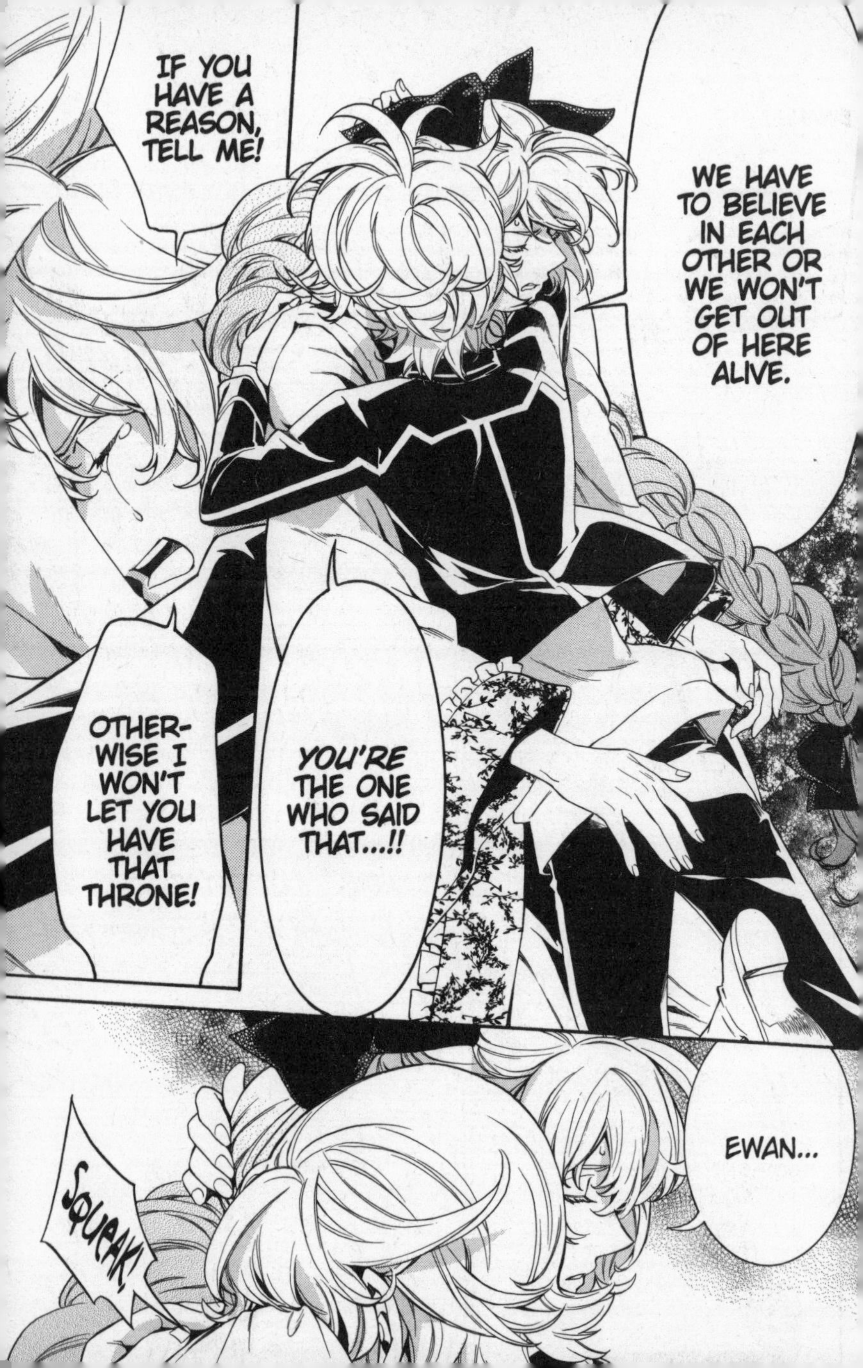
WE HAVE TO BELIEVE IN EACH OTHER OR WE WON'T GET OUT OF HERE ALIVE.
IF YOU HAVE A REASON, TELL ME!
YOU'RE THE ONE WHO SAID THAT...!!
OTHER-WISE I WON'T LET YOU HAVE THAT THRONE!
EWAN...
SQUEAK!

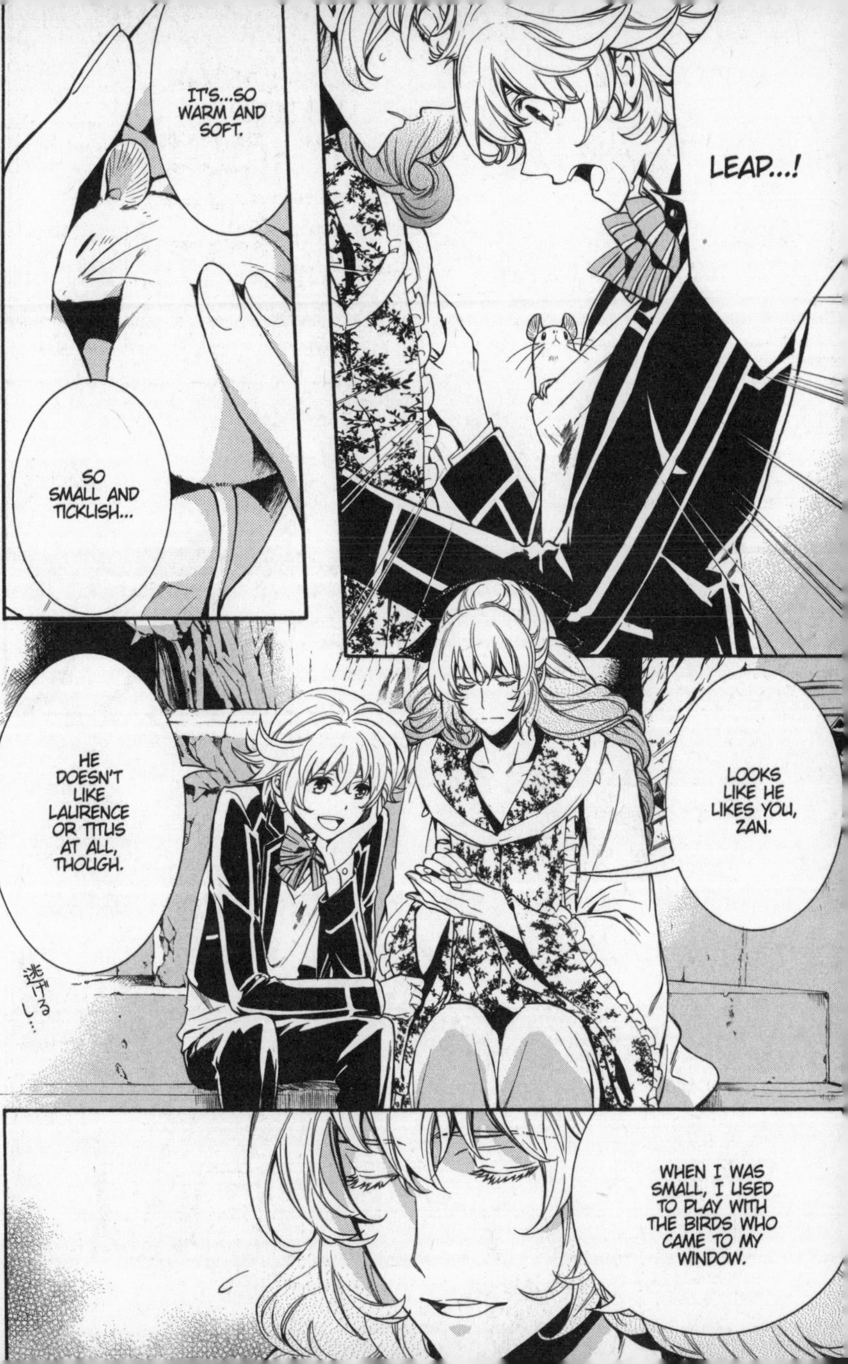
LEAP...!
IT'S...SO WARM AND SOFT.
SO SMALL AND TICKLISH...
LOOKS LIKE HE LIKES YOU, ZAN.
HE DOESN'T LIKE LAURENCE OR TITUS AT ALL, THOUGH.
逃げるし…
WHEN I WAS SMALL, I USED TO PLAY WITH THE BIRDS WHO CAME TO MY WINDOW.

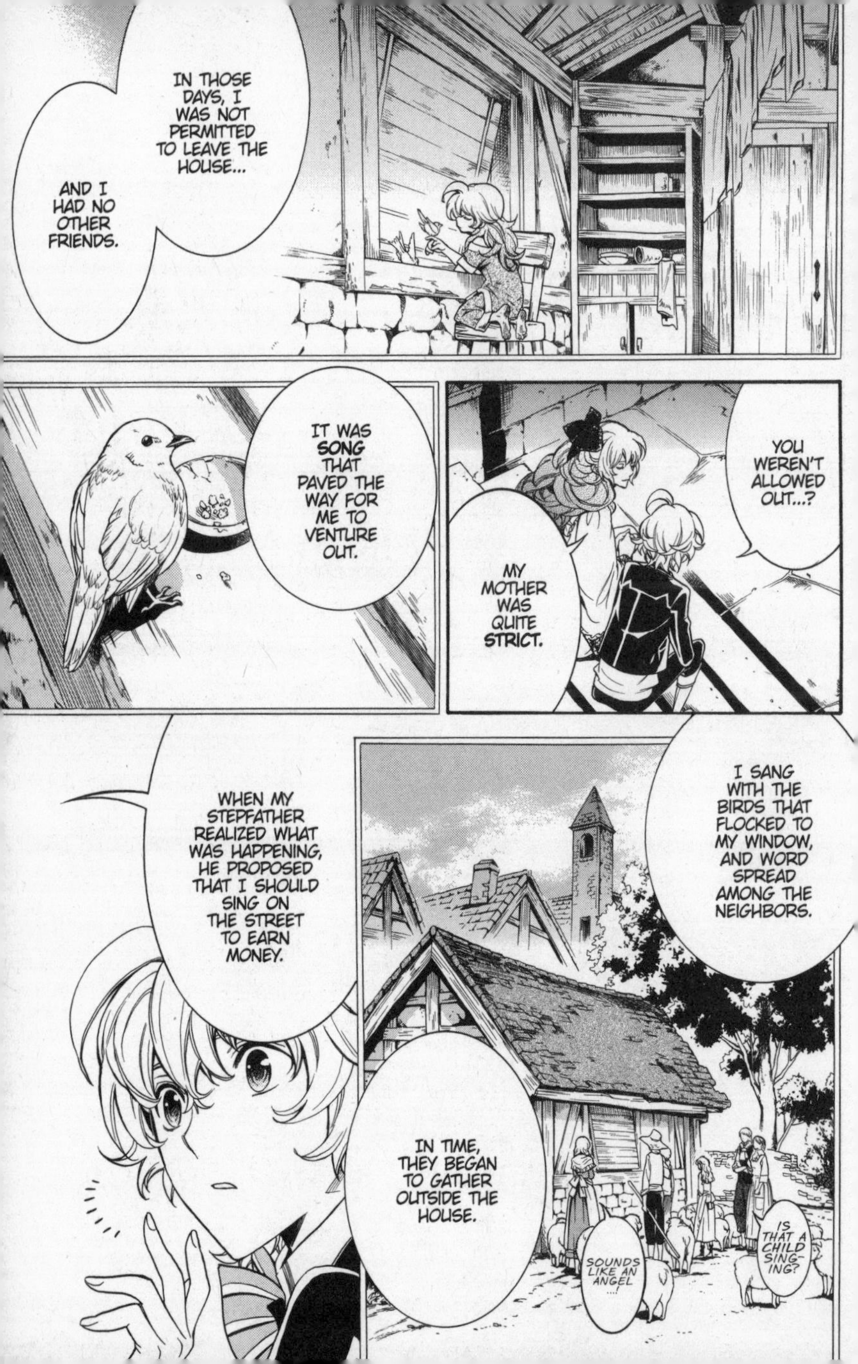
IN THOSE DAYS, I WAS NOT PERMITTED TO LEAVE THE HOUSE...
AND I HAD NO OTHER FRIENDS.
YOU WEREN'T ALLOWED OUT...?
MY MOTHER WAS QUITE STRICT.
IT WAS SONG THAT PAVED THE WAY FOR ME TO VENTURE OUT.
I SANG WITH THE BIRDS THAT FLOCKED TO MY WINDOW, AND WORD SPREAD AMONG THE NEIGHBORS.
IS THAT A CHILD SING-ING?
SOUNDS LIKE AN ANGEL...!
IN TIME, THEY BEGAN TO GATHER OUTSIDE THE HOUSE.
WHEN MY STEPFATHER REALIZED WHAT WAS HAPPENING, HE PROPOSED THAT I SHOULD SING ON THE STREET TO EARN MONEY.

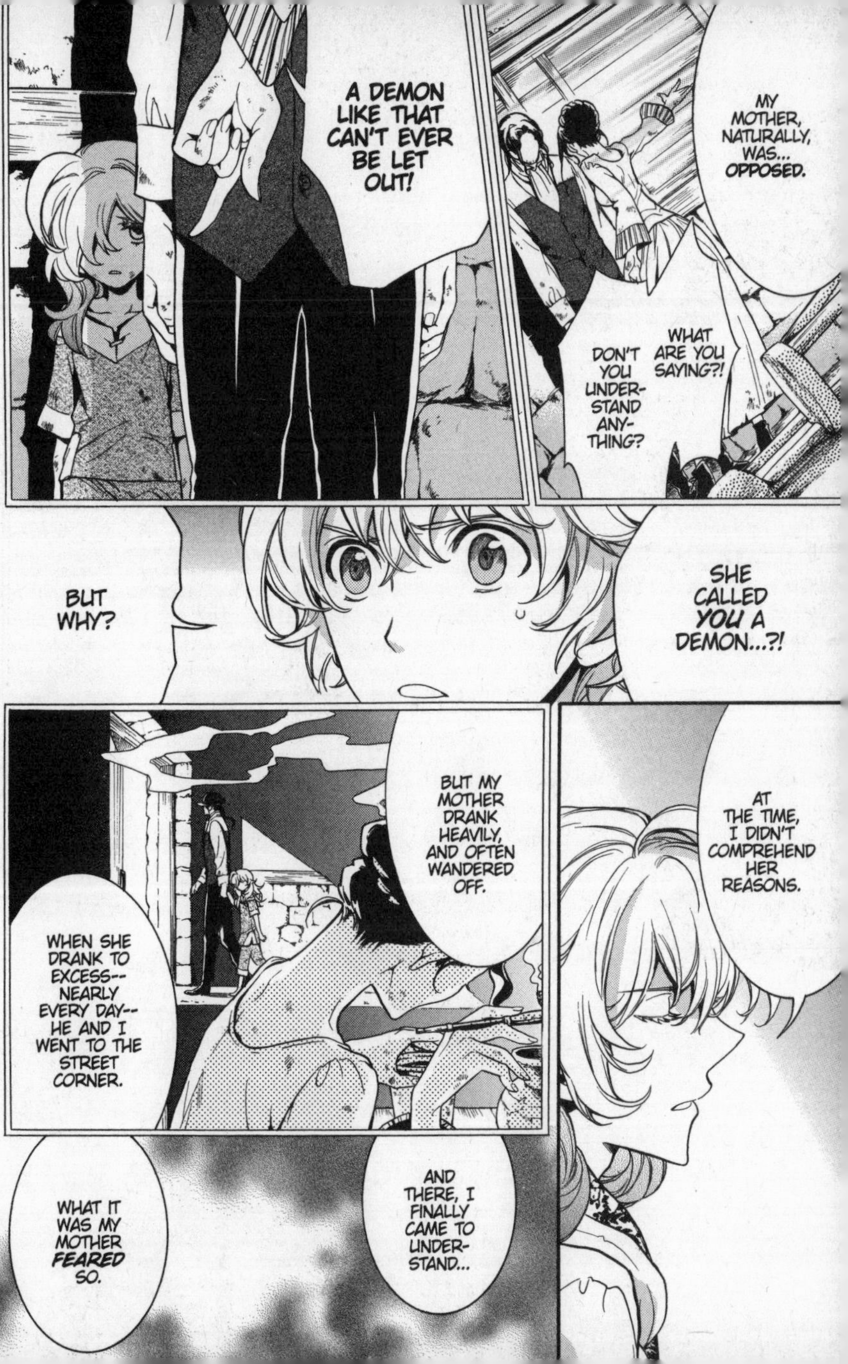
MY MOTHER, NATURALLY, WAS... OPPOSED.
WHAT ARE YOU SAYING?!
DON'T YOU UNDER-STAND ANY-THING?
A DEMON LIKE THAT CAN'T EVER BE LET OUT!
SHE CALLED *YOU* A DEMON...?!
BUT WHY?
AT THE TIME, I DIDN'T COMPREHEND HER REASONS.
BUT MY MOTHER DRANK HEAVILY, AND OFTEN WANDERED OFF.
WHEN SHE DRANK TO EXCESS-- NEARLY EVERY DAY-- HE AND I WENT TO THE STREET CORNER.
AND THERE, I FINALLY CAME TO UNDER-STAND...
WHAT IT WAS MY MOTHER *FEARED* SO.

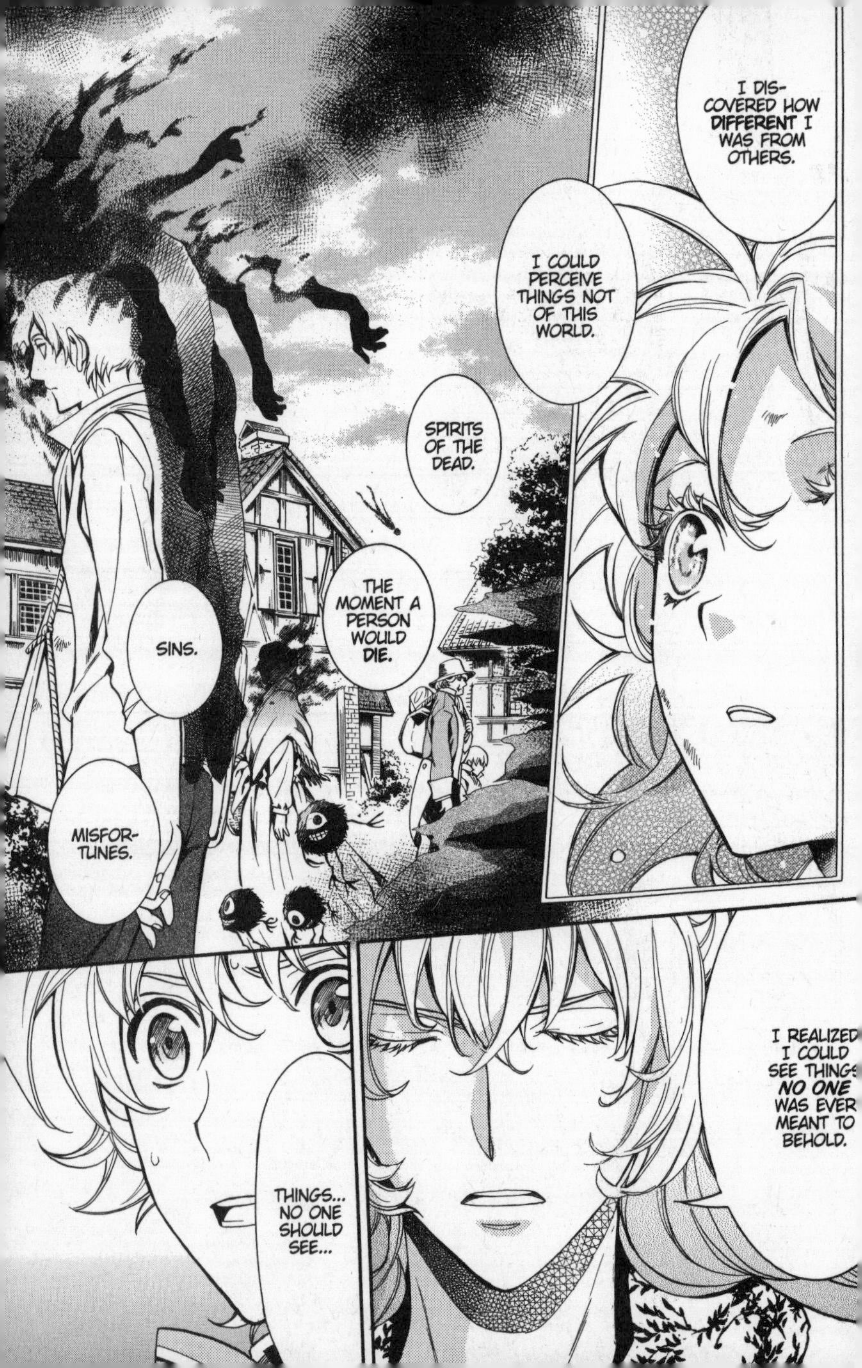
I DIS-COVERED HOW DIFFERENT I WAS FROM OTHERS.
I COULD PERCEIVE THINGS NOT OF THIS WORLD.
SPIRITS OF THE DEAD.
THE MOMENT A PERSON WOULD DIE.
SINS.
MISFOR-TUNES.
I REALIZED I COULD SEE THINGS ***NO ONE*** WAS EVER MEANT TO BEHOLD.
THINGS... NO ONE SHOULD SEE...

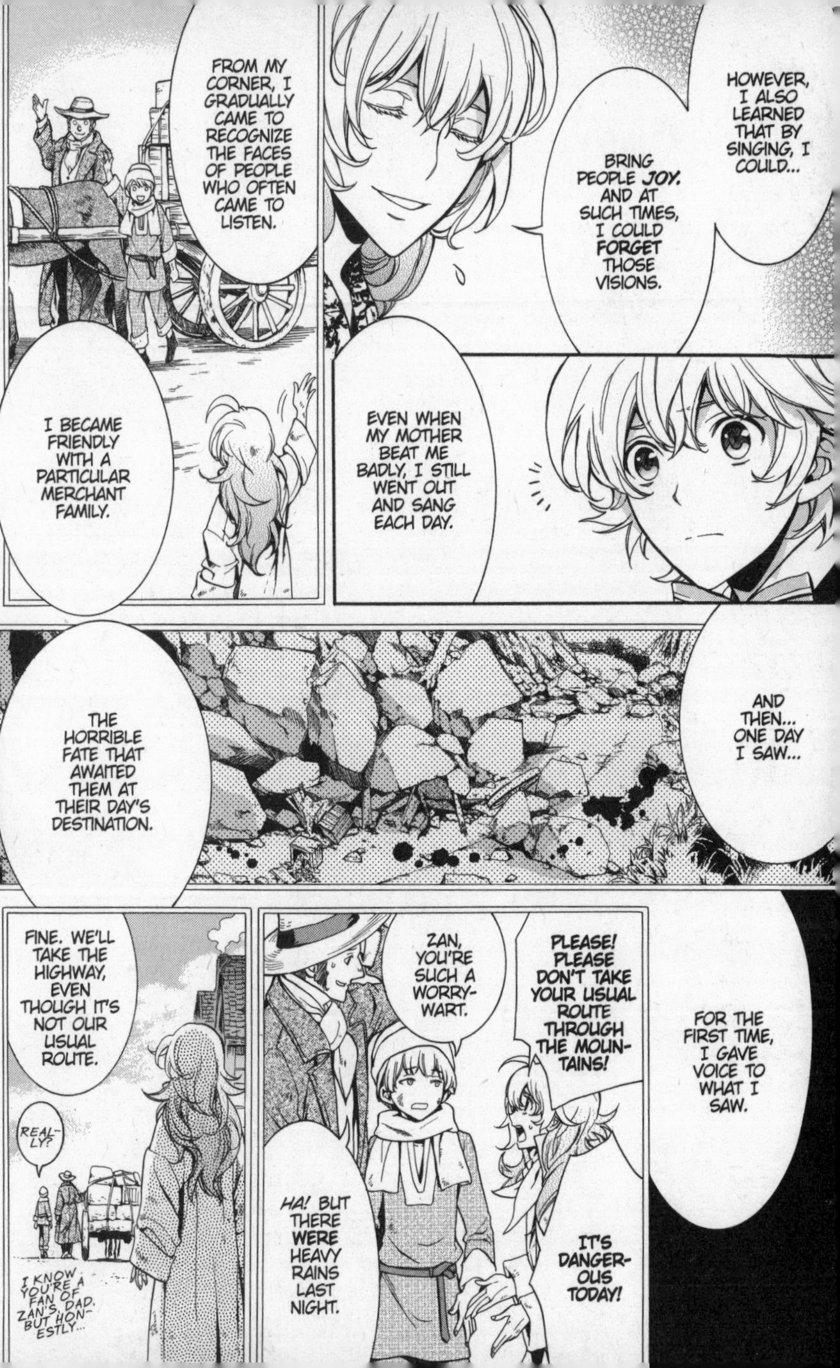
HOWEVER, I ALSO LEARNED THAT BY SINGING, I COULD...
BRING PEOPLE JOY. AND AT SUCH TIMES, I COULD FORGET THOSE VISIONS.
EVEN WHEN MY MOTHER BEAT ME BADLY, I STILL WENT OUT AND SANG EACH DAY.
FROM MY CORNER, I GRADUALLY CAME TO RECOGNIZE THE FACES OF PEOPLE WHO OFTEN CAME TO LISTEN.
I BECAME FRIENDLY WITH A PARTICULAR MERCHANT FAMILY.
AND THEN... ONE DAY I SAW...
THE HORRIBLE FATE THAT AWAITED THEM AT THEIR DAY'S DESTINATION.
FOR THE FIRST TIME, I GAVE VOICE TO WHAT I SAW.
PLEASE! PLEASE DON'T TAKE YOUR USUAL ROUTE THROUGH THE MOUN-TAINS!
IT'S DANGER-OUS TODAY!
ZAN, YOU'RE SUCH A WORRY-WART.
HA! BUT THERE WERE HEAVY RAINS LAST NIGHT.
FINE. WE'LL TAKE THE HIGHWAY, EVEN THOUGH IT'S NOT OUR USUAL ROUTE.
REAL-LY?
I KNOW YOU'RE A FAN OF ZAN'S, DAD. BUT HON-ESTLY...

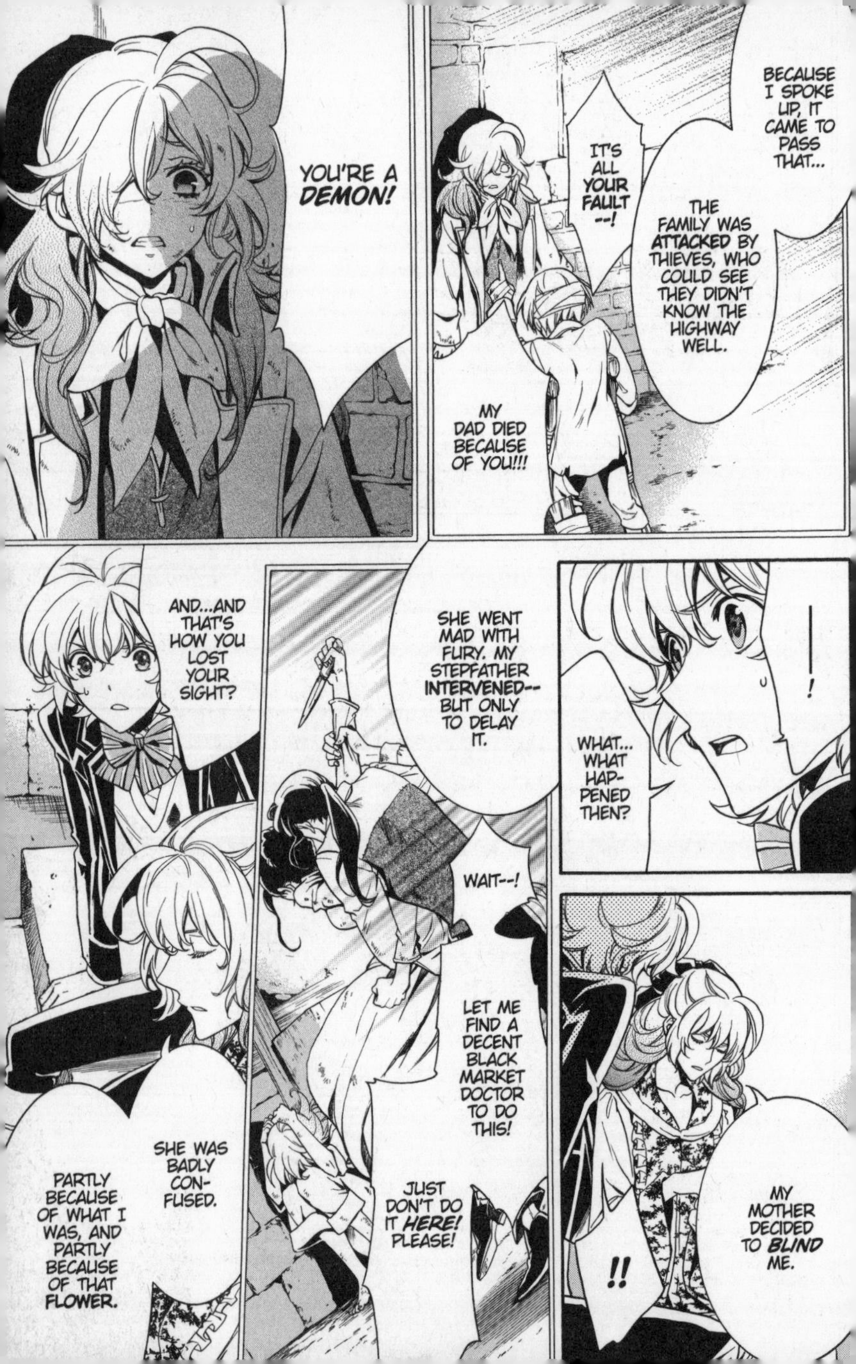
BECAUSE I SPOKE UP, IT CAME TO PASS THAT...
THE FAMILY WAS ATTACKED BY THIEVES, WHO COULD SEE THEY DIDN'T KNOW THE HIGHWAY WELL.
IT'S ALL YOUR FAULT--!
MY DAD DIED BECAUSE OF YOU!!!
YOU'RE A DEMON!
—!
WHAT... WHAT HAP-PENED THEN?
MY MOTHER DECIDED TO BLIND ME.
!!
SHE WENT MAD WITH FURY. MY STEPFATHER INTERVENED--BUT ONLY TO DELAY IT.
WAIT--!
LET ME FIND A DECENT BLACK MARKET DOCTOR TO DO THIS!
JUST DON'T DO IT HERE! PLEASE!
AND...AND THAT'S HOW YOU LOST YOUR SIGHT?
SHE WAS BADLY CON-FUSED.
PARTLY BECAUSE OF WHAT I WAS, AND PARTLY BECAUSE OF THAT FLOWER.

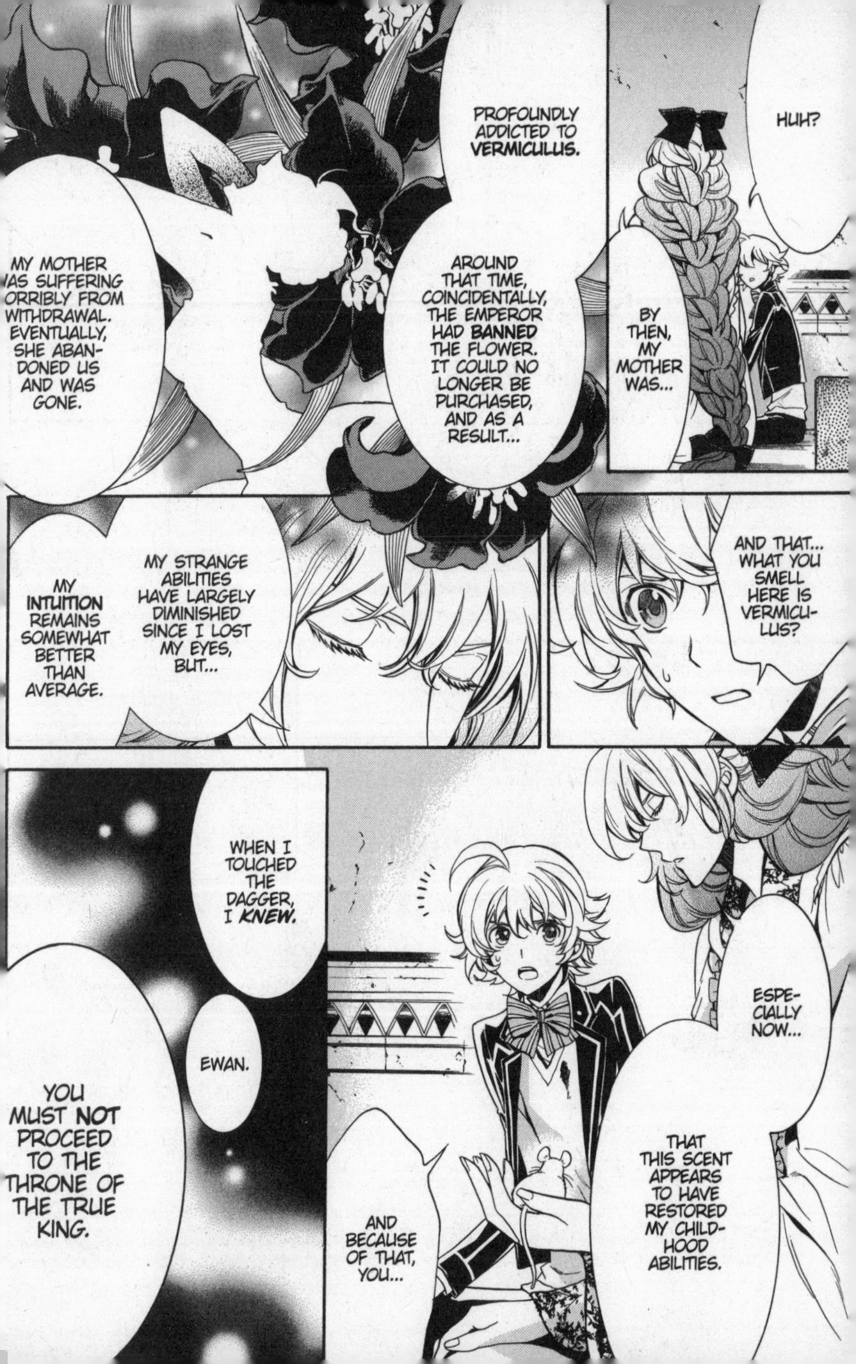
HUH?
BY THEN, MY MOTHER WAS...
PROFOUNDLY ADDICTED TO VERMICULUS.
AROUND THAT TIME, COINCIDENTALLY, THE EMPEROR HAD BANNED THE FLOWER. IT COULD NO LONGER BE PURCHASED, AND AS A RESULT...
MY MOTHER WAS SUFFERING ORRIBLY FROM WITHDRAWAL. EVENTUALLY, SHE ABANDONED US AND WAS GONE.
AND THAT... WHAT YOU SMELL HERE IS VERMICULUS?
MY STRANGE ABILITIES HAVE LARGELY DIMINISHED SINCE I LOST MY EYES, BUT...
MY INTUITION REMAINS SOMEWHAT BETTER THAN AVERAGE.
ESPECIALLY NOW...
THAT THIS SCENT APPEARS TO HAVE RESTORED MY CHILDHOOD ABILITIES.
AND BECAUSE OF THAT, YOU...
WHEN I TOUCHED THE DAGGER, I KNEW.
EWAN.
YOU MUST NOT PROCEED TO THE THRONE OF THE TRUE KING.

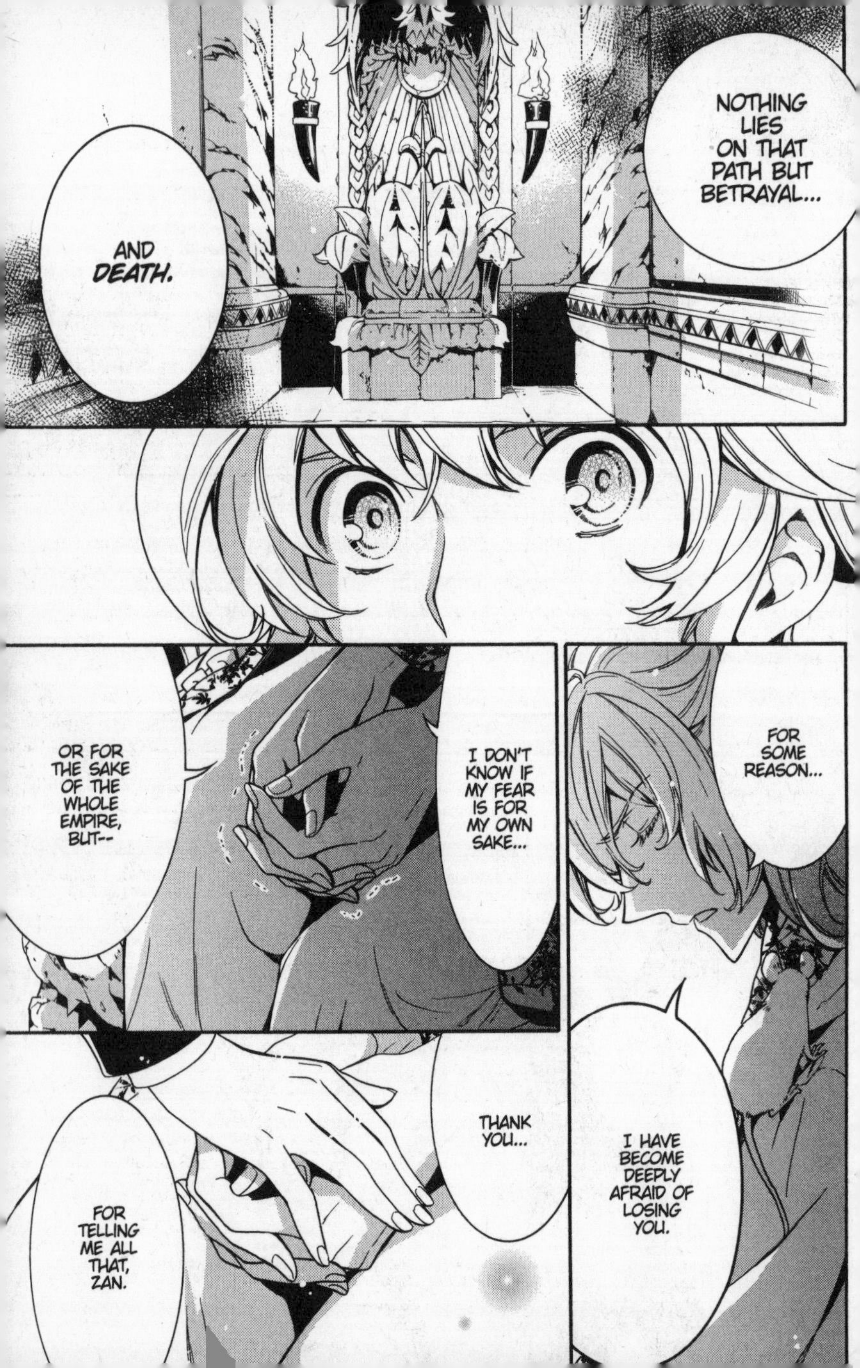
NOTHING LIES ON THAT PATH BUT BETRAYAL...
AND DEATH.
FOR SOME REASON...
I HAVE BECOME DEEPLY AFRAID OF LOSING YOU.
I DON'T KNOW IF MY FEAR IS FOR MY OWN SAKE...
OR FOR THE SAKE OF THE WHOLE EMPIRE, BUT--
THANK YOU...
FOR TELLING ME ALL THAT, ZAN.

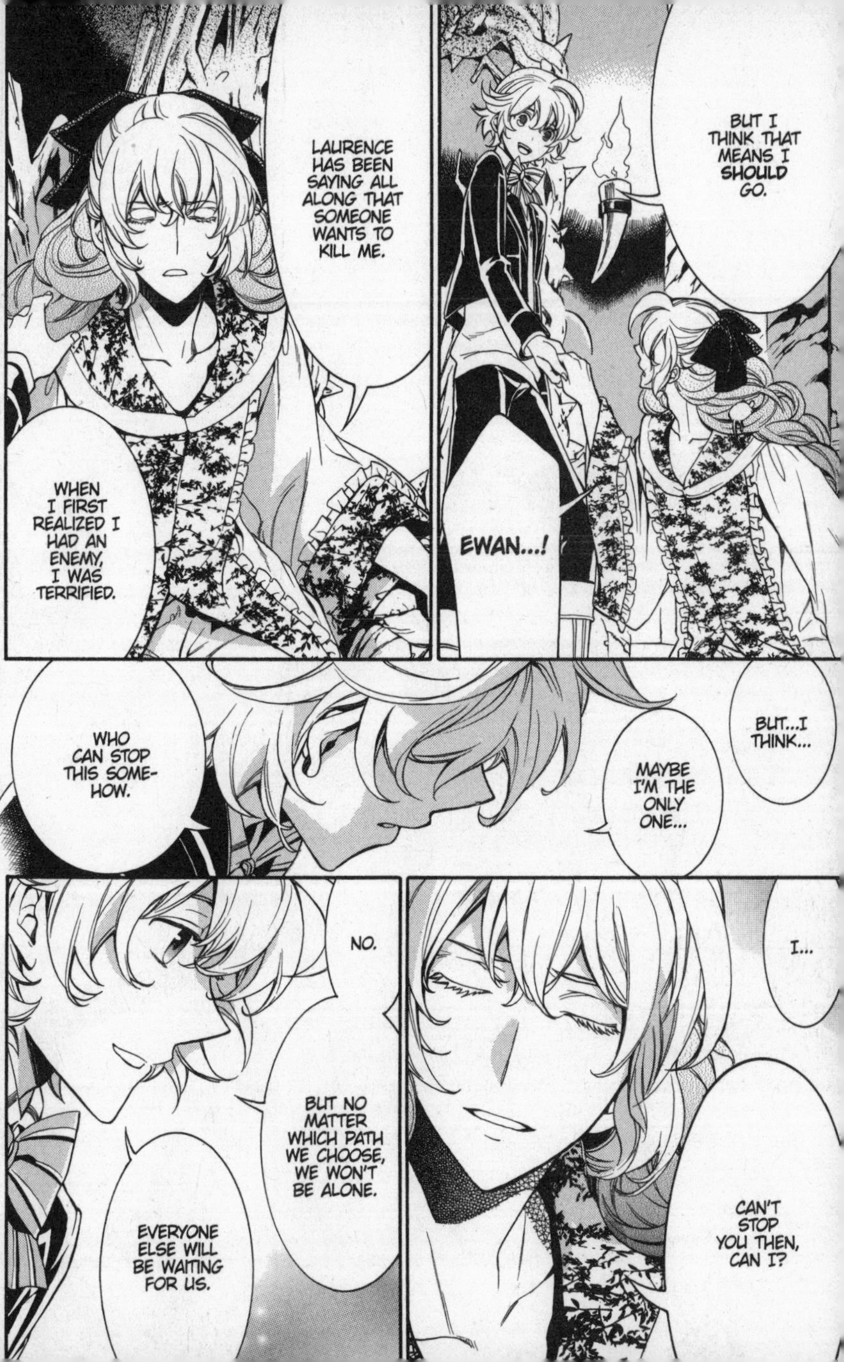
BUT I THINK THAT MEANS I SHOULD GO.
EWAN...!
LAURENCE HAS BEEN SAYING ALL ALONG THAT SOMEONE WANTS TO KILL ME.
WHEN I FIRST REALIZED I HAD AN ENEMY, I WAS TERRIFIED.
BUT...I THINK...
MAYBE I'M THE ONLY ONE...
WHO CAN STOP THIS SOME-HOW.
I...
CAN'T STOP YOU THEN, CAN I?
NO.
BUT NO MATTER WHICH PATH WE CHOOSE, WE WON'T BE ALONE.
EVERYONE ELSE WILL BE WAITING FOR US.

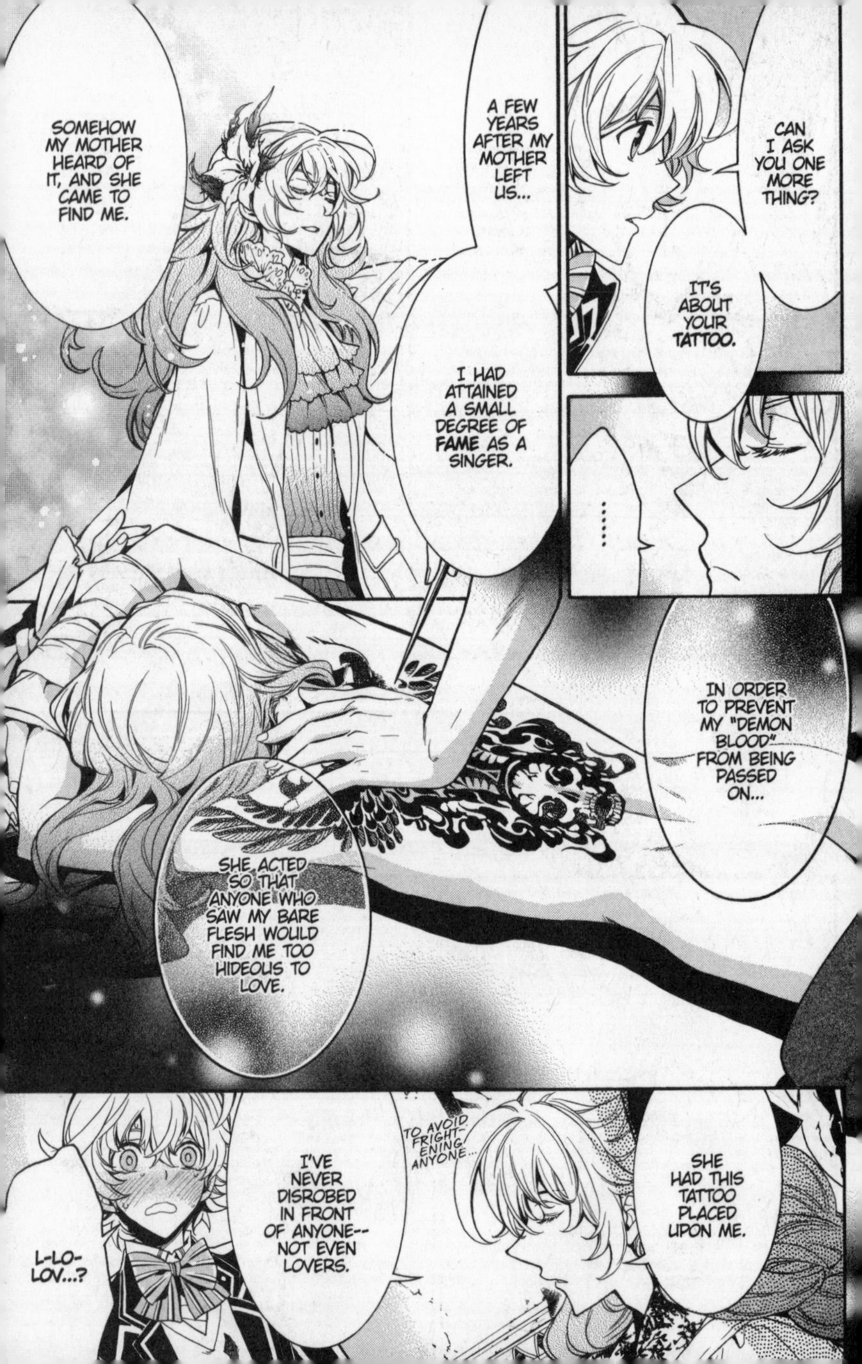
CAN I ASK YOU ONE MORE THING?
IT'S ABOUT YOUR TATTOO.
......
A FEW YEARS AFTER MY MOTHER LEFT US...
I HAD ATTAINED A SMALL DEGREE OF FAME AS A SINGER.
SOMEHOW MY MOTHER HEARD OF IT, AND SHE CAME TO FIND ME.
IN ORDER TO PREVENT MY "DEMON BLOOD" FROM BEING PASSED ON...
SHE ACTED SO THAT ANYONE WHO SAW MY BARE FLESH WOULD FIND ME TOO HIDEOUS TO LOVE.
SHE HAD THIS TATTOO PLACED UPON ME.
TO AVOID FRIGHTENING ANYONE...
I'VE NEVER DISROBED IN FRONT OF ANYONE-- NOT EVEN LOVERS.
L-LO-LOV...?

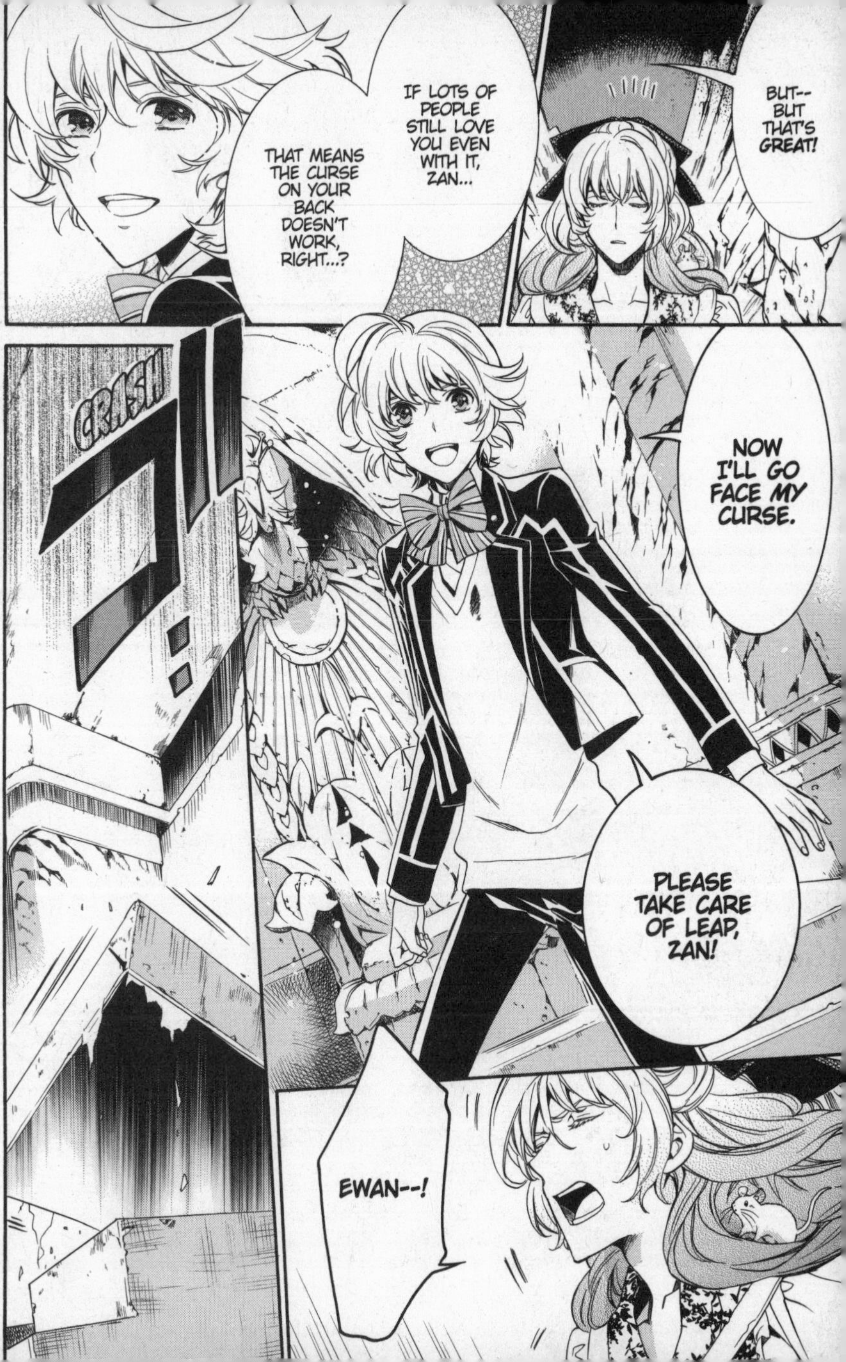
BUT-- BUT THAT'S GREAT!
IF LOTS OF PEOPLE STILL LOVE YOU EVEN WITH IT, ZAN...
THAT MEANS THE CURSE ON YOUR BACK DOESN'T WORK, RIGHT...?
NOW I'LL GO FACE MY CURSE.
PLEASE TAKE CARE OF LEAP, ZAN!
EWAN--!
CRASH

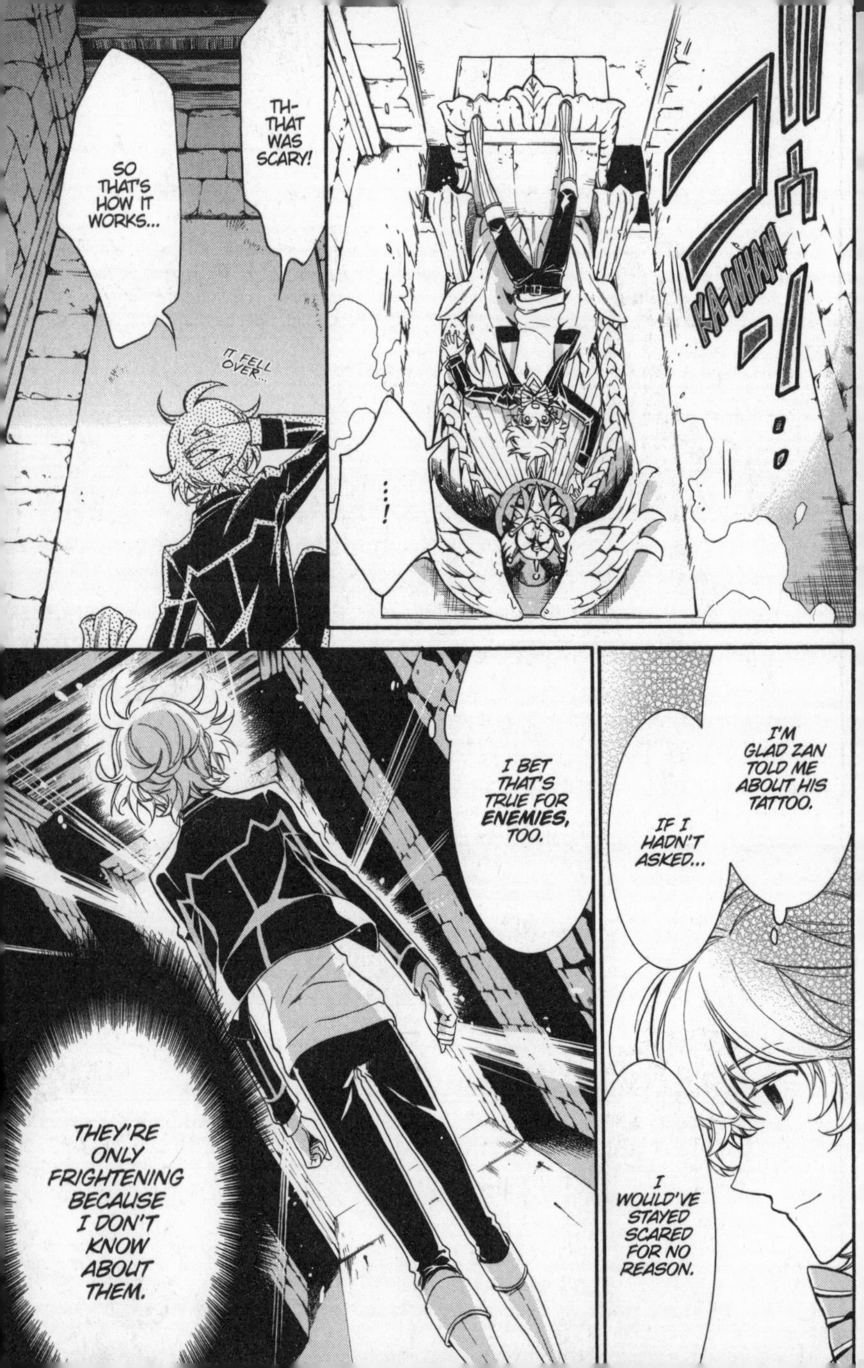
KA-WHAM
...!
TH-THAT WAS SCARY!
SO THAT'S HOW IT WORKS...
IT FELL OVER...
I'M GLAD ZAN TOLD ME ABOUT HIS TATTOO.
IF I HADN'T ASKED...
I WOULD'VE STAYED SCARED FOR NO REASON.
I BET THAT'S TRUE FOR ENEMIES, TOO.
THEY'RE ONLY FRIGHTENING BECAUSE I DON'T KNOW ABOUT THEM.

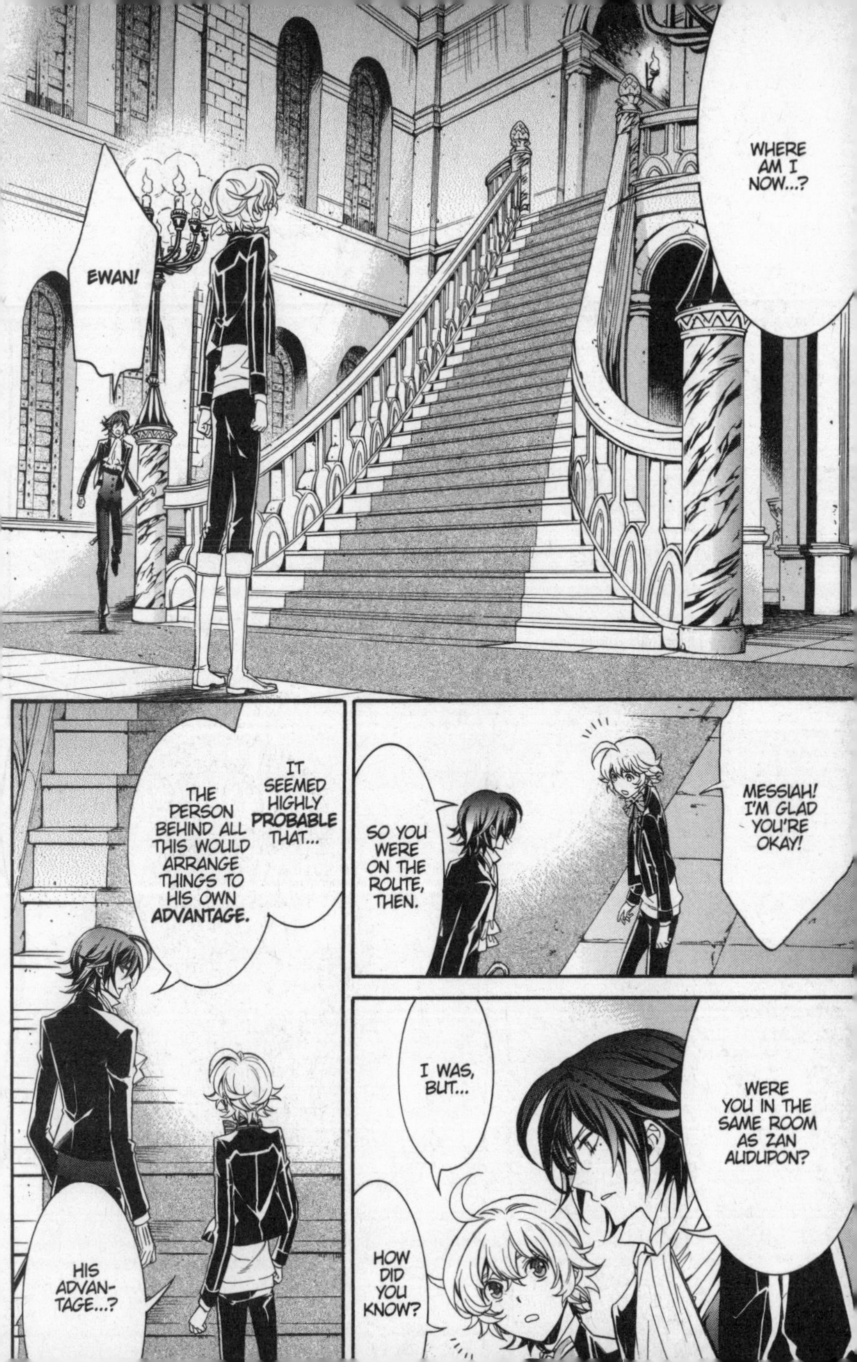
WHERE AM I NOW...?
EWAN!
MESSIAH! I'M GLAD YOU'RE OKAY!
SO YOU WERE ON THE ROUTE, THEN.
WERE YOU IN THE SAME ROOM AS ZAN AUDUPON?
I WAS, BUT...
HOW DID YOU KNOW?
IT SEEMED HIGHLY PROBABLE THAT...
THE PERSON BEHIND ALL THIS WOULD ARRANGE THINGS TO HIS OWN ADVANTAGE.
HIS ADVAN-TAGE...?

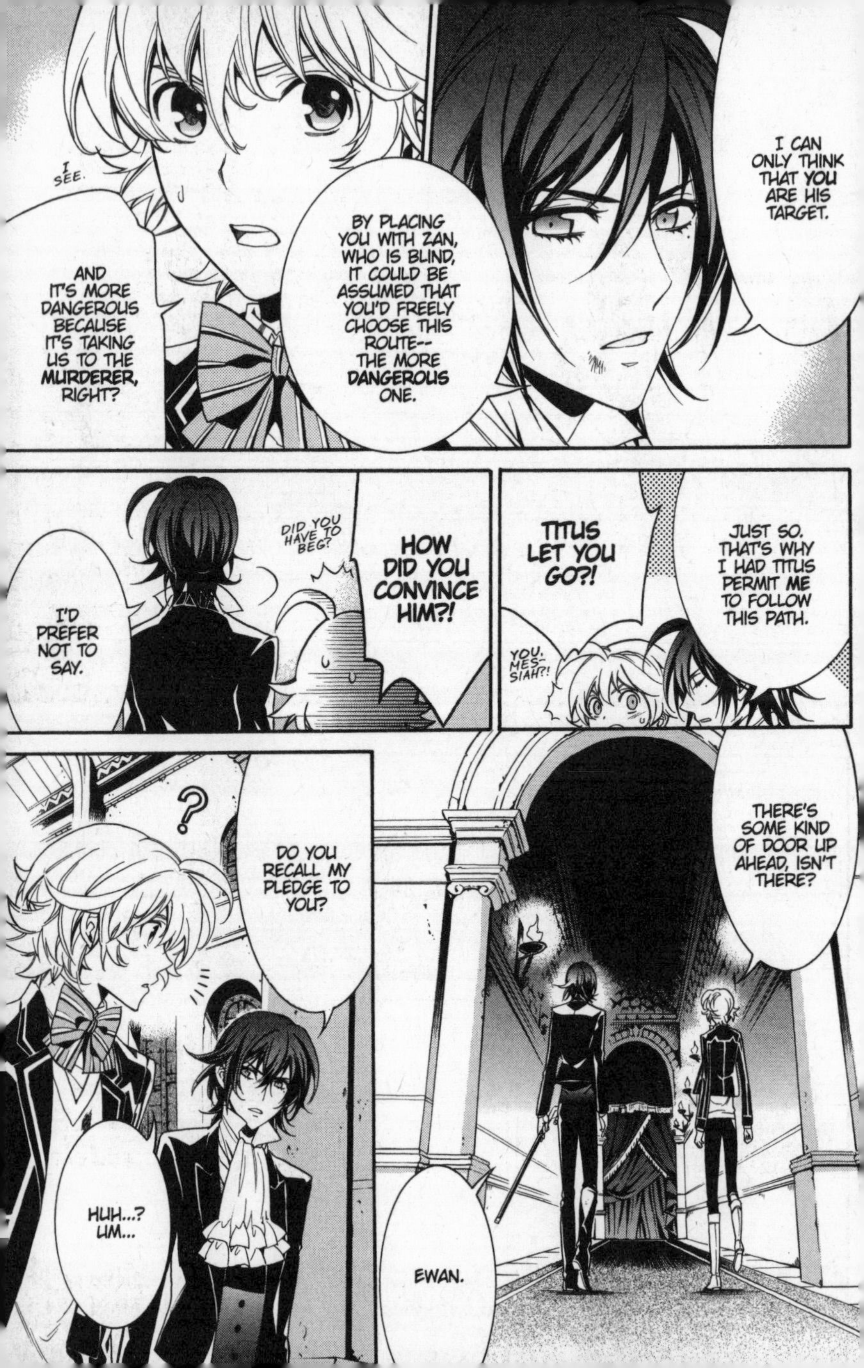
I CAN ONLY THINK THAT YOU ARE HIS TARGET.
BY PLACING YOU WITH ZAN, WHO IS BLIND, IT COULD BE ASSUMED THAT YOU'D FREELY CHOOSE THIS ROUTE-- THE MORE DANGEROUS ONE.
I SEE.
AND IT'S MORE DANGEROUS BECAUSE IT'S TAKING US TO THE MURDERER, RIGHT?
JUST SO. THAT'S WHY I HAD TITUS PERMIT ME TO FOLLOW THIS PATH.
TITUS LET YOU GO?!
YOU. MES-SIAH?!
HOW DID YOU CONVINCE HIM?!
DID YOU HAVE TO BEG?
I'D PREFER NOT TO SAY.
THERE'S SOME KIND OF DOOR UP AHEAD, ISN'T THERE?
EWAN.
DO YOU RECALL MY PLEDGE TO YOU?
?
HUH...? UM...

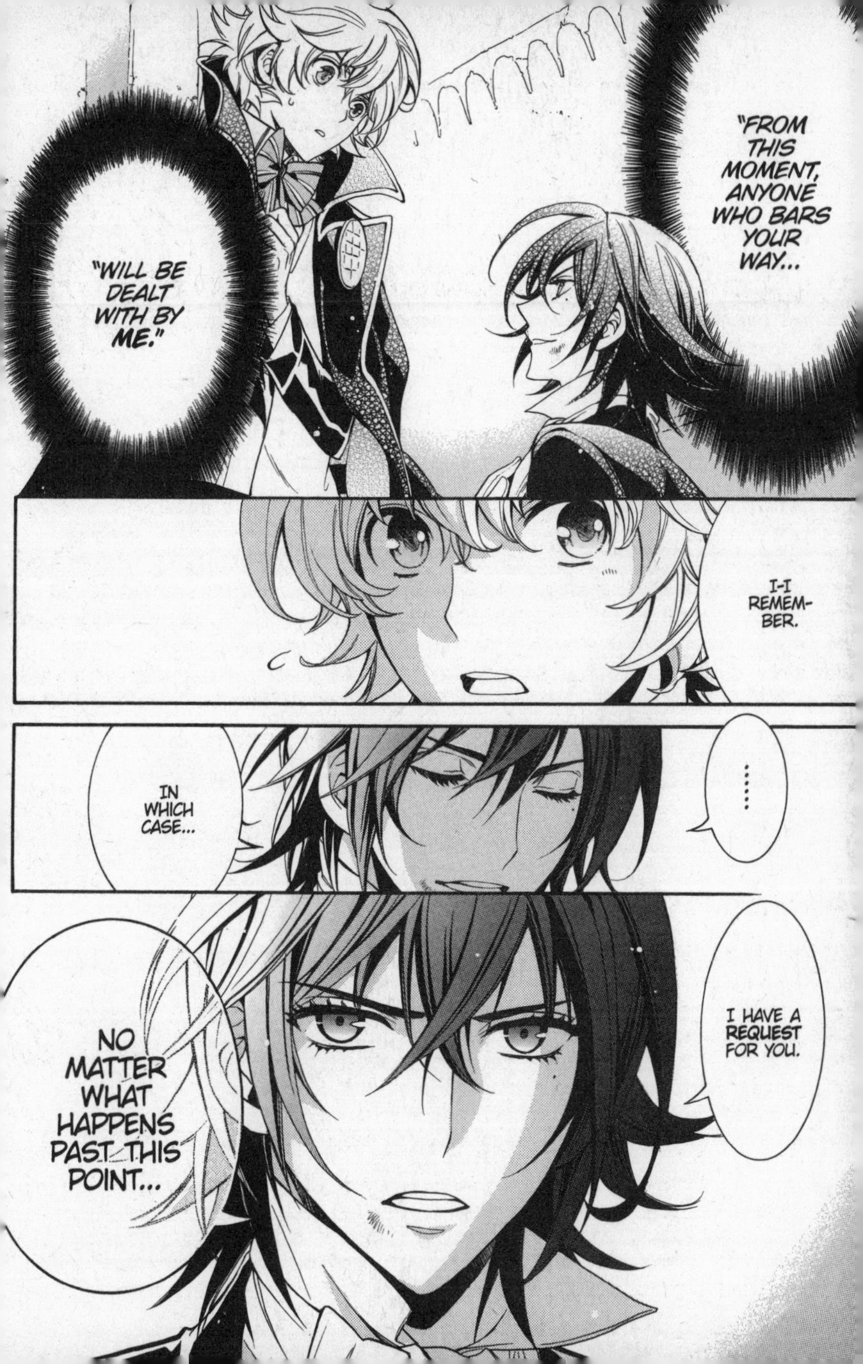
"FROM THIS MOMENT, ANYONE WHO BARS YOUR WAY...
"WILL BE DEALT WITH BY ME."
I-I REMEMBER.
......
IN WHICH CASE...
I HAVE A REQUEST FOR YOU.
NO MATTER WHAT HAPPENS PAST THIS POINT...

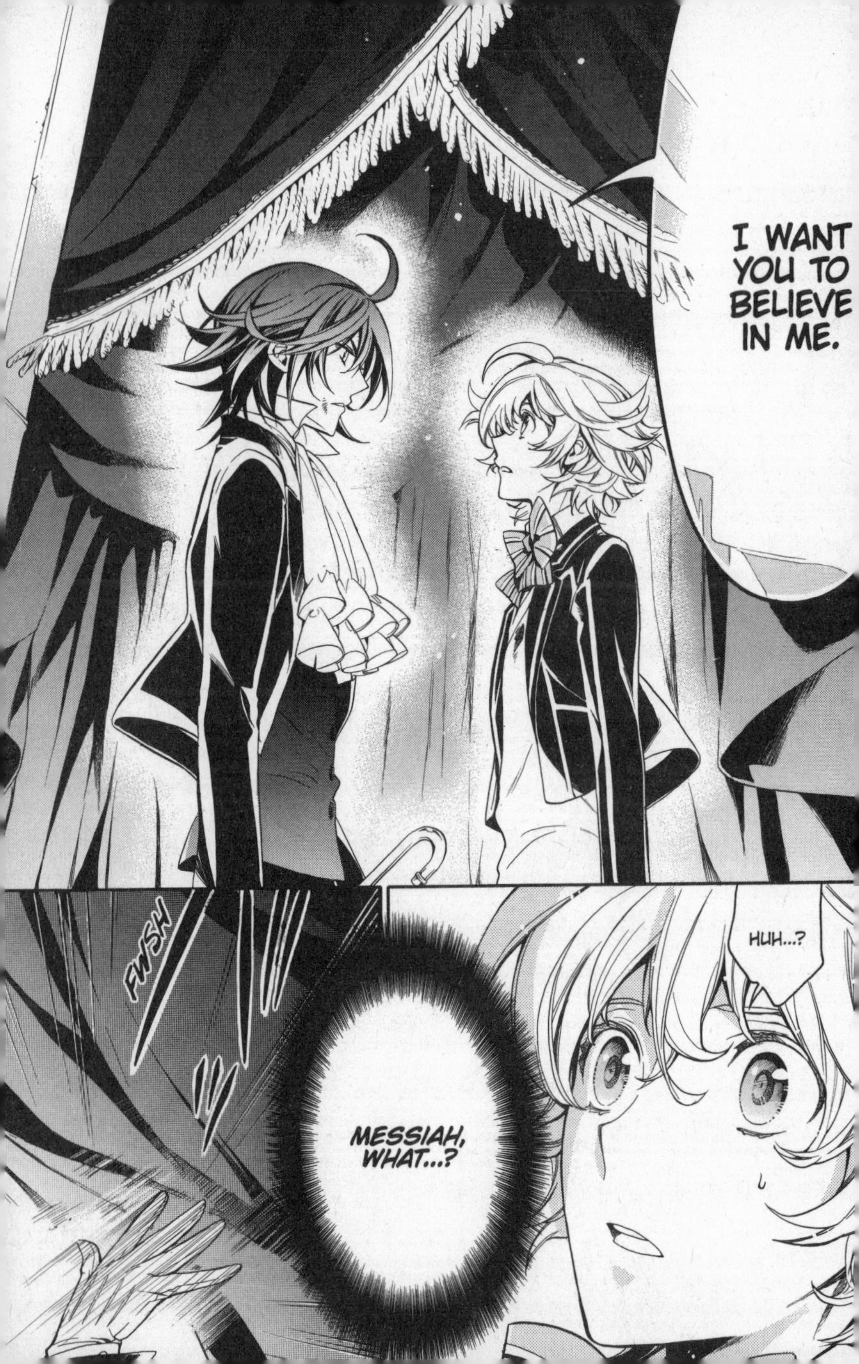
I WANT YOU TO BELIEVE IN ME.
HUH...?
MESSIAH, WHAT...?
FWSH

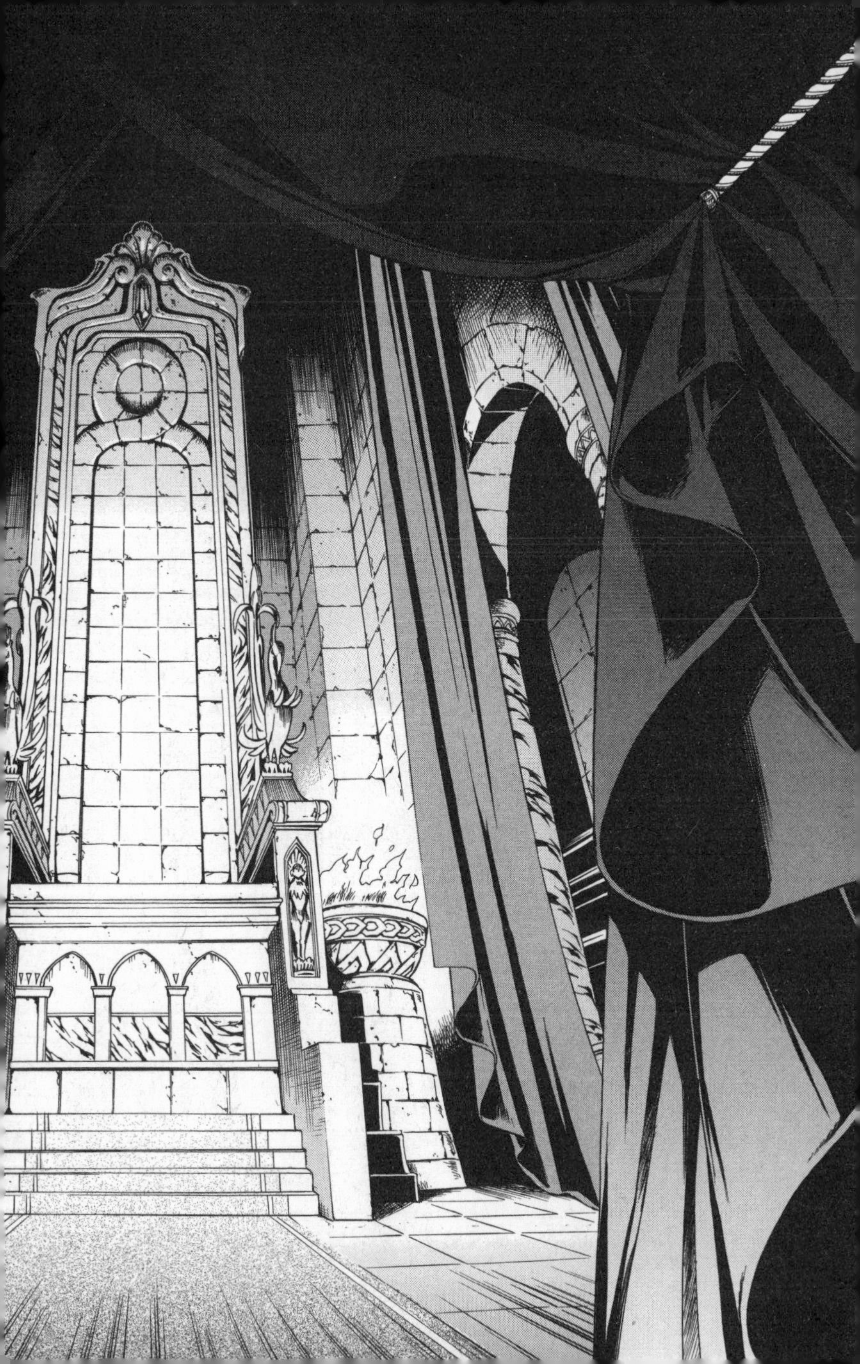

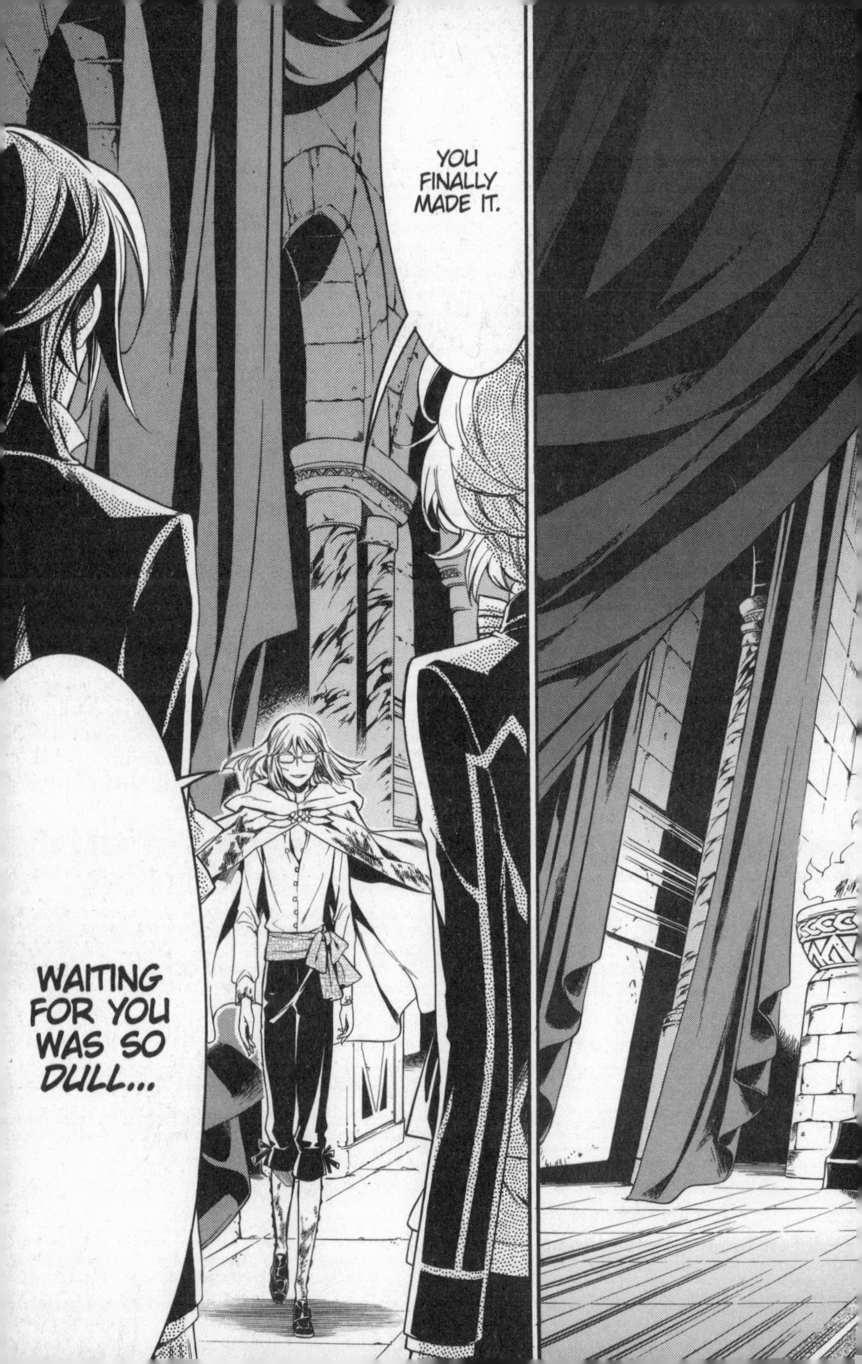
YOU FINALLY MADE IT.
WAITING FOR YOU WAS SO DULL...

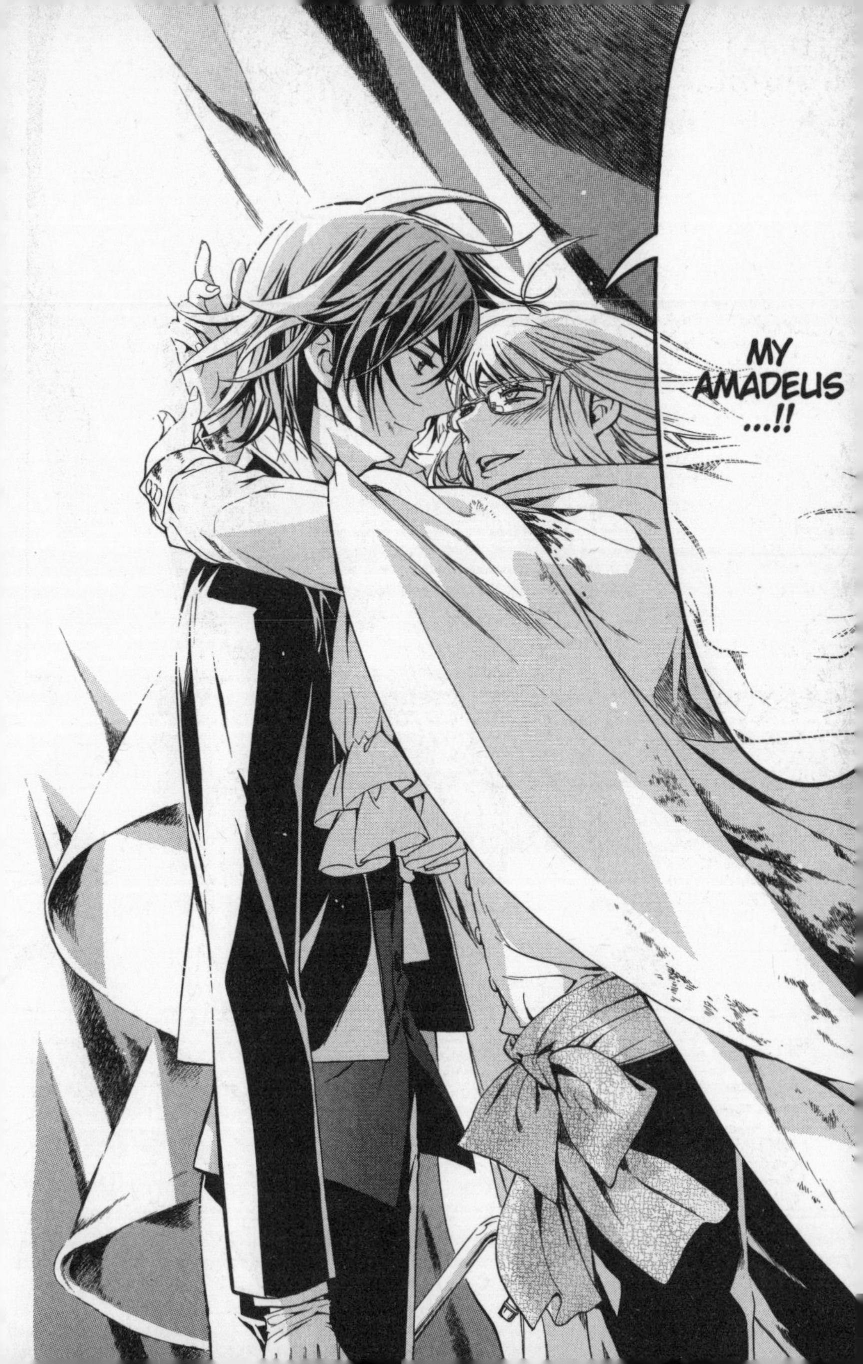
MY AMADEUS ...!!

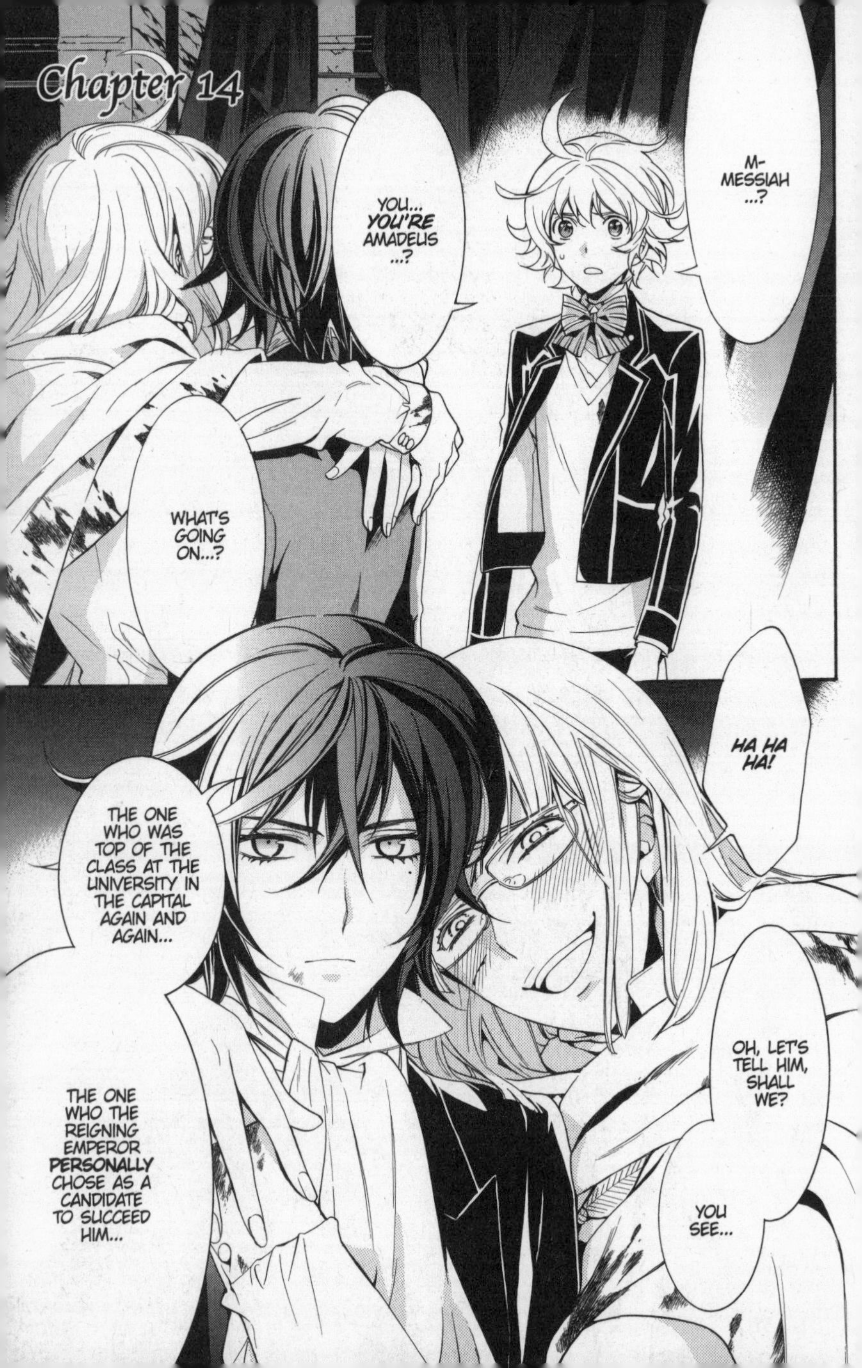
Chapter 14
M-MESSIAH ...?
YOU... *YOU'RE* AMADEUS ...?
WHAT'S GOING ON...?
HA HA HA!
THE ONE WHO WAS TOP OF THE CLASS AT THE UNIVERSITY IN THE CAPITAL AGAIN AND AGAIN...
OH, LET'S TELL HIM, SHALL WE?
THE ONE WHO THE REIGNING EMPEROR **PERSONALLY** CHOSE AS A CANDIDATE TO SUCCEED HIM...
YOU SEE...

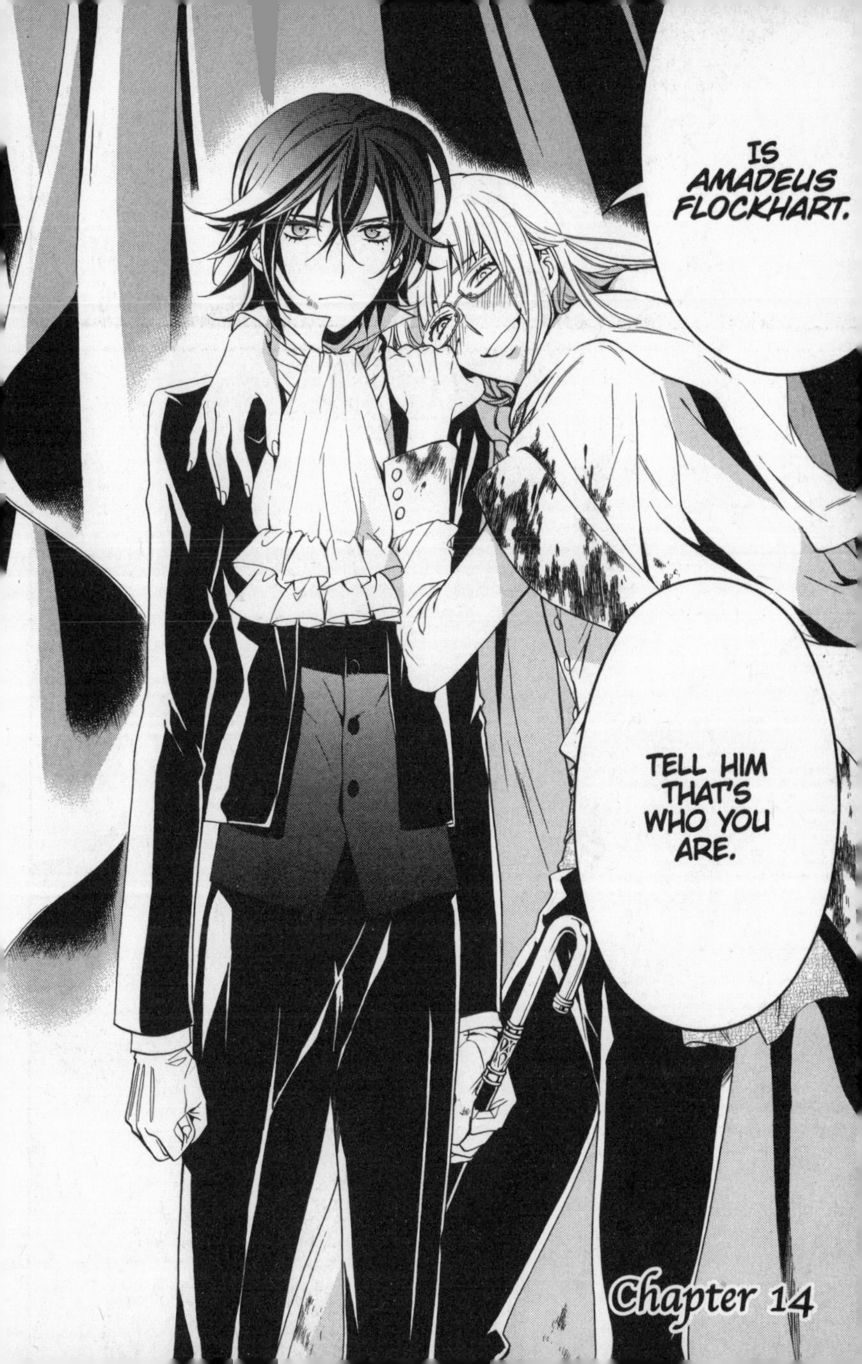
IS AMADEUS FLOCKHART.
TELL HIM THAT'S WHO YOU ARE.
Chapter 14

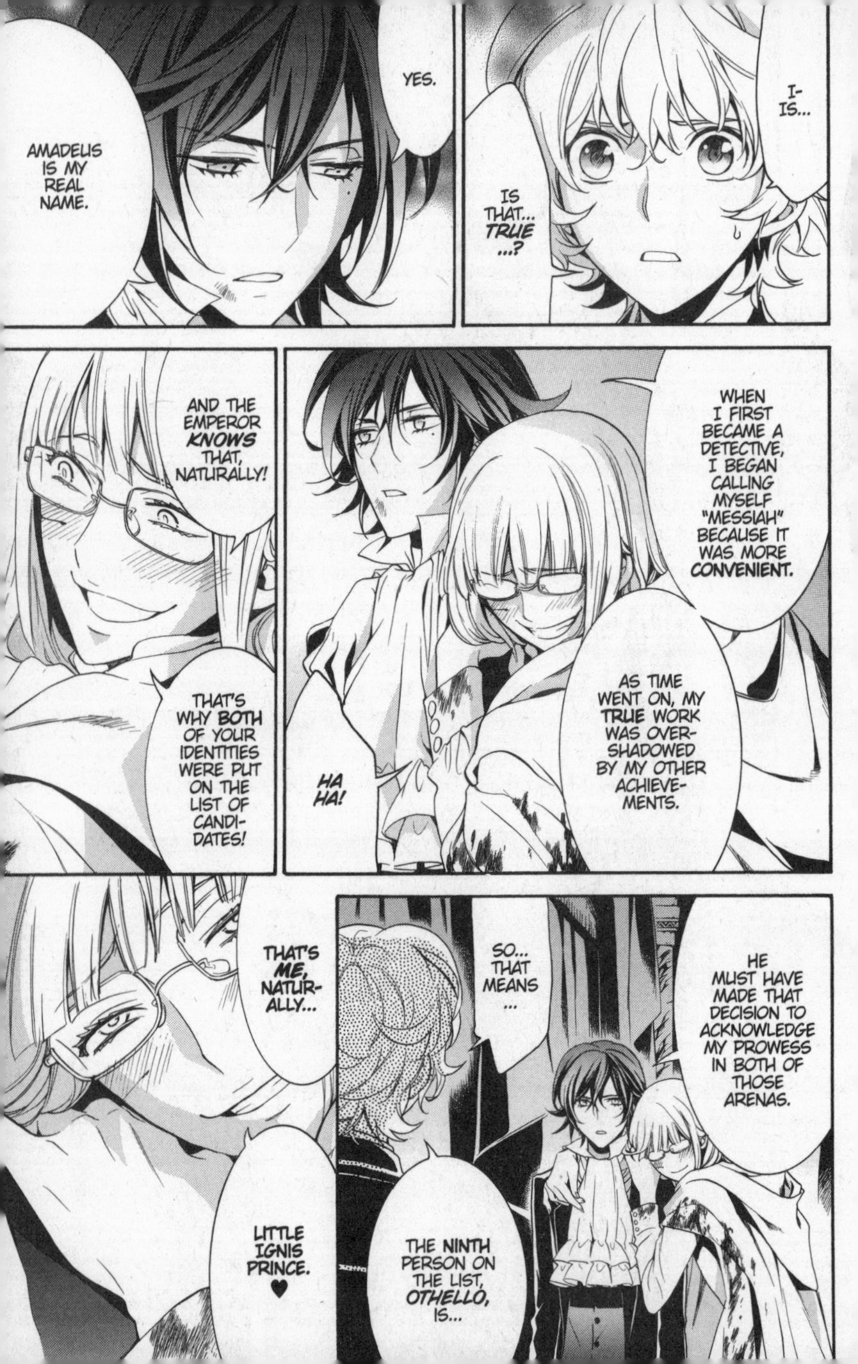
I- IS...
IS THAT... TRUE ...?
YES.
AMADEUS IS MY REAL NAME.
WHEN I FIRST BECAME A DETECTIVE, I BEGAN CALLING MYSELF "MESSIAH" BECAUSE IT WAS MORE CONVENIENT.
AS TIME WENT ON, MY TRUE WORK WAS OVER-SHADOWED BY MY OTHER ACHIEVE-MENTS.
HA HA!
AND THE EMPEROR KNOWS THAT, NATURALLY!
THAT'S WHY BOTH OF YOUR IDENTITIES WERE PUT ON THE LIST OF CANDI-DATES!
HE MUST HAVE MADE THAT DECISION TO ACKNOWLEDGE MY PROWESS IN BOTH OF THOSE ARENAS.
SO... THAT MEANS ...
THE NINTH PERSON ON THE LIST, OTHELLO, IS...
THAT'S ME, NATUR-ALLY...
LITTLE IGNIS PRINCE. ♥

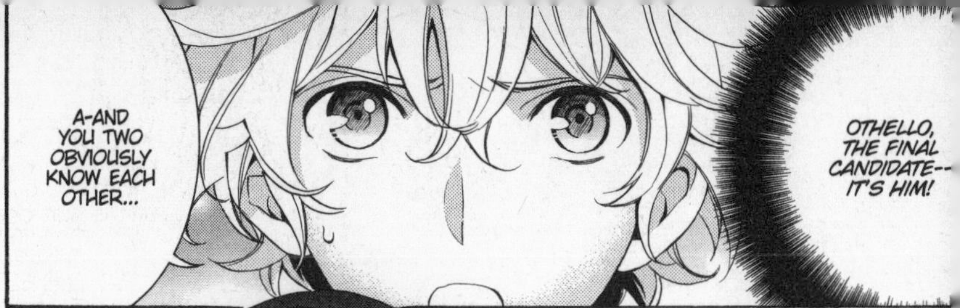
OTHELLO, THE FINAL CANDIDATE--IT'S HIM!
A-AND YOU TWO OBVIOUSLY KNOW EACH OTHER...
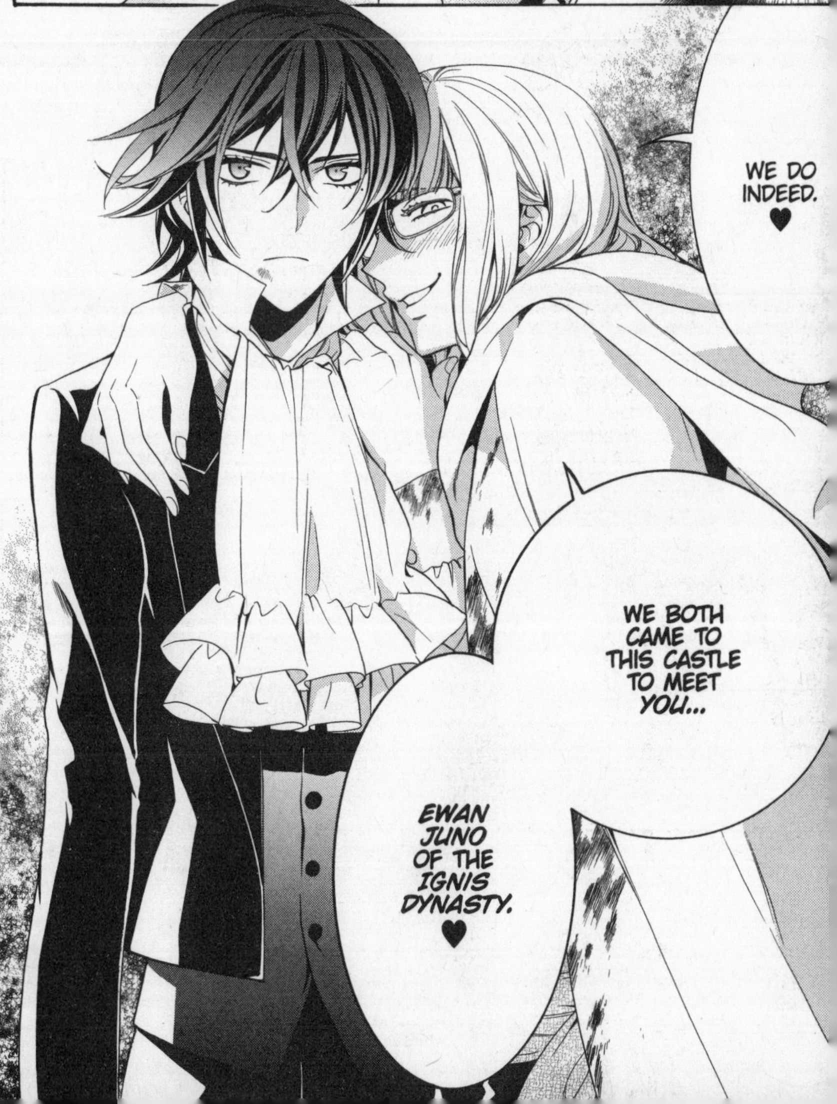
WE DO INDEED. ♥
WE BOTH CAME TO THIS CASTLE TO MEET YOU...
EWAN JUNO OF THE IGNIS DYNASTY. ♥

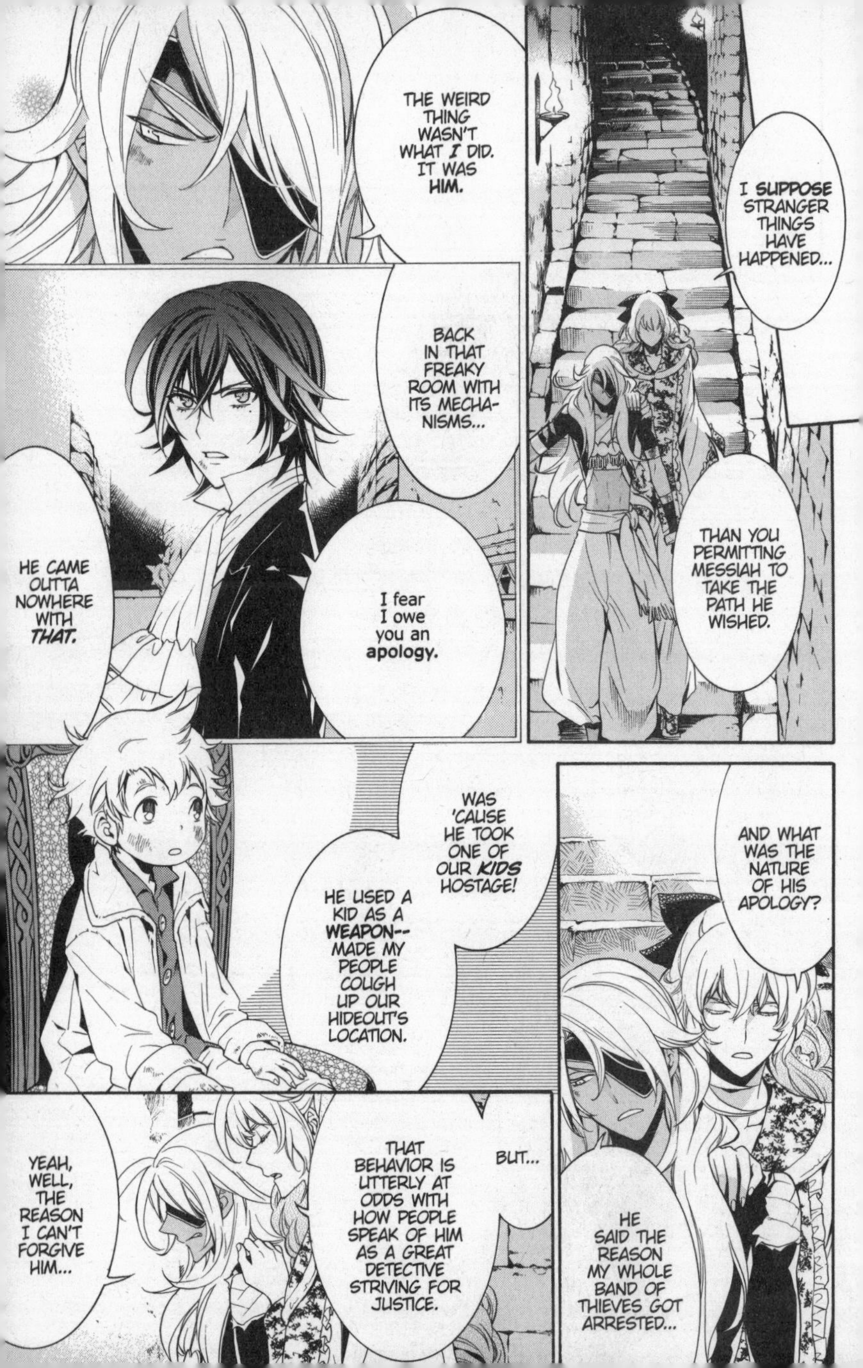
I SUPPOSE STRANGER THINGS HAVE HAPPENED...
THAN YOU PERMITTING MESSIAH TO TAKE THE PATH HE WISHED.
THE WEIRD THING WASN'T WHAT *I* DID. IT WAS **HIM.**
BACK IN THAT FREAKY ROOM WITH ITS MECHANISMS...
I fear I owe you an **apology.**
HE CAME OUTTA NOWHERE WITH ***THAT.***
AND WHAT WAS THE NATURE OF HIS APOLOGY?
HE SAID THE REASON MY WHOLE BAND OF THIEVES GOT ARRESTED...
WAS 'CAUSE HE TOOK ONE OF OUR ***KIDS*** HOSTAGE!
HE USED A KID AS A **WEAPON**--MADE MY PEOPLE COUGH UP OUR HIDEOUT'S LOCATION.
BUT...
THAT BEHAVIOR IS UTTERLY AT ODDS WITH HOW PEOPLE SPEAK OF HIM AS A GREAT DETECTIVE STRIVING FOR JUSTICE.
YEAH, WELL, THE REASON I CAN'T FORGIVE HIM...

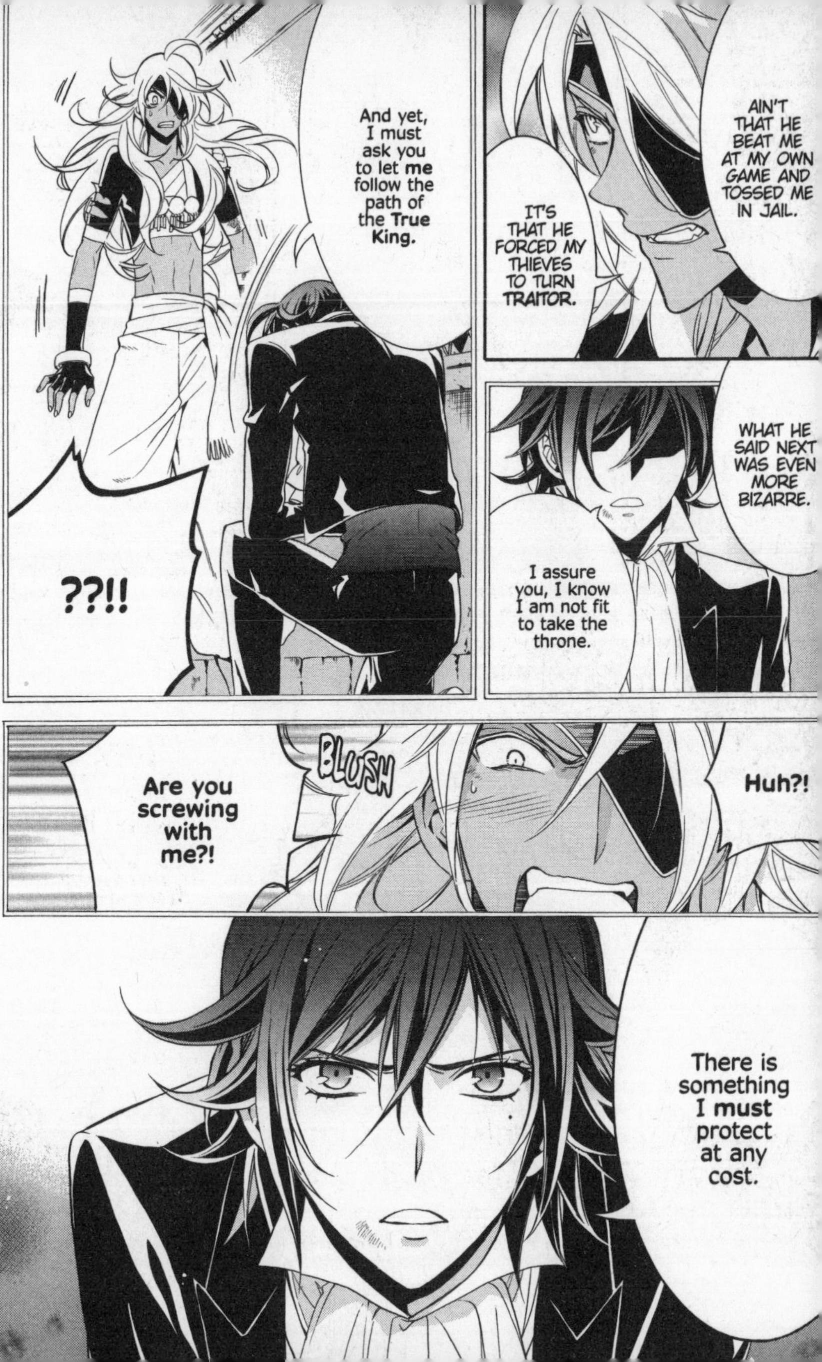
AIN'T THAT HE BEAT ME AT MY OWN GAME AND TOSSED ME IN JAIL.
IT'S THAT HE FORCED MY THIEVES TO TURN TRAITOR.
WHAT HE SAID NEXT WAS EVEN MORE BIZARRE.
I assure you, I know I am not fit to take the throne.
And yet, I must ask you to let me follow the path of the True King.
??!!
Huh?!
BLUSH
Are you screwing with me?!
There is something I must protect at any cost.

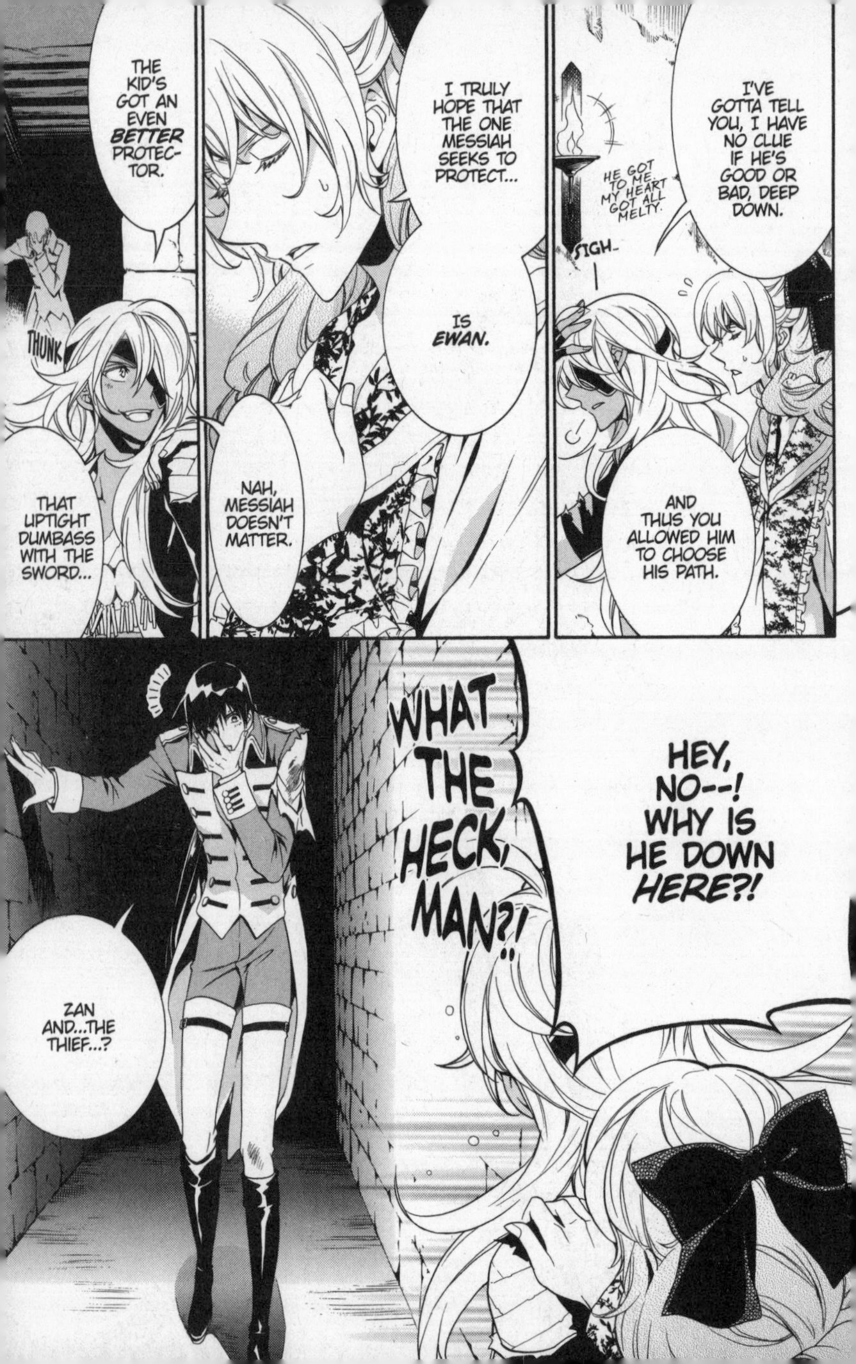
I'VE GOTTA TELL YOU, I HAVE NO CLUE IF HE'S GOOD OR BAD, DEEP DOWN.
HE GOT TO ME. MY HEART GOT ALL MELTY.
SIGH
AND THUS YOU ALLOWED HIM TO CHOOSE HIS PATH.
I TRULY HOPE THAT THE ONE MESSIAH SEEKS TO PROTECT...
IS *EWAN.*
NAH, MESSIAH DOESN'T MATTER.
THE KID'S GOT AN EVEN ***BETTER*** PROTECTOR.
THUNK
THAT UPTIGHT DUMBASS WITH THE SWORD...
WHAT THE HECK, MAN?!
HEY, NO--! WHY IS HE DOWN *HERE?!*
ZAN AND...THE THIEF...?

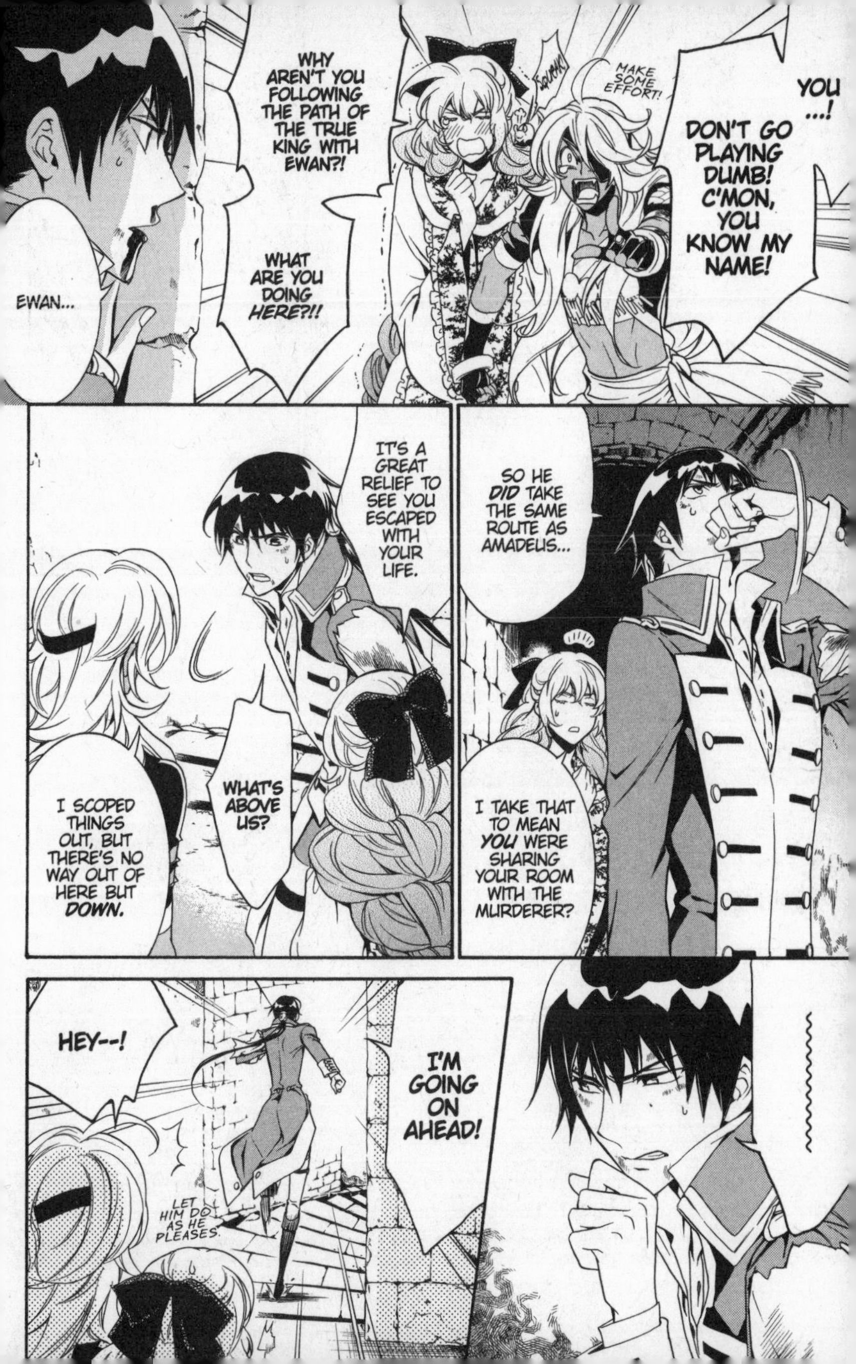
YOU ...!
DON'T GO PLAYING DUMB! C'MON, YOU KNOW MY NAME!
MAKE SOME EFFORT!
SQUAWK!
WHY AREN'T YOU FOLLOWING THE PATH OF THE TRUE KING WITH EWAN?!
WHAT ARE YOU DOING *HERE?!!*
EWAN...
SO HE *DID* TAKE THE SAME ROUTE AS AMADEUS...
I TAKE THAT TO MEAN *YOU* WERE SHARING YOUR ROOM WITH THE MURDERER?
IT'S A GREAT RELIEF TO SEE YOU ESCAPED WITH YOUR LIFE.
WHAT'S ABOVE US?
I SCOPED THINGS OUT, BUT THERE'S NO WAY OUT OF HERE BUT *DOWN.*
I'M GOING ON AHEAD!
HEY--!
LET HIM DO AS HE PLEASES.

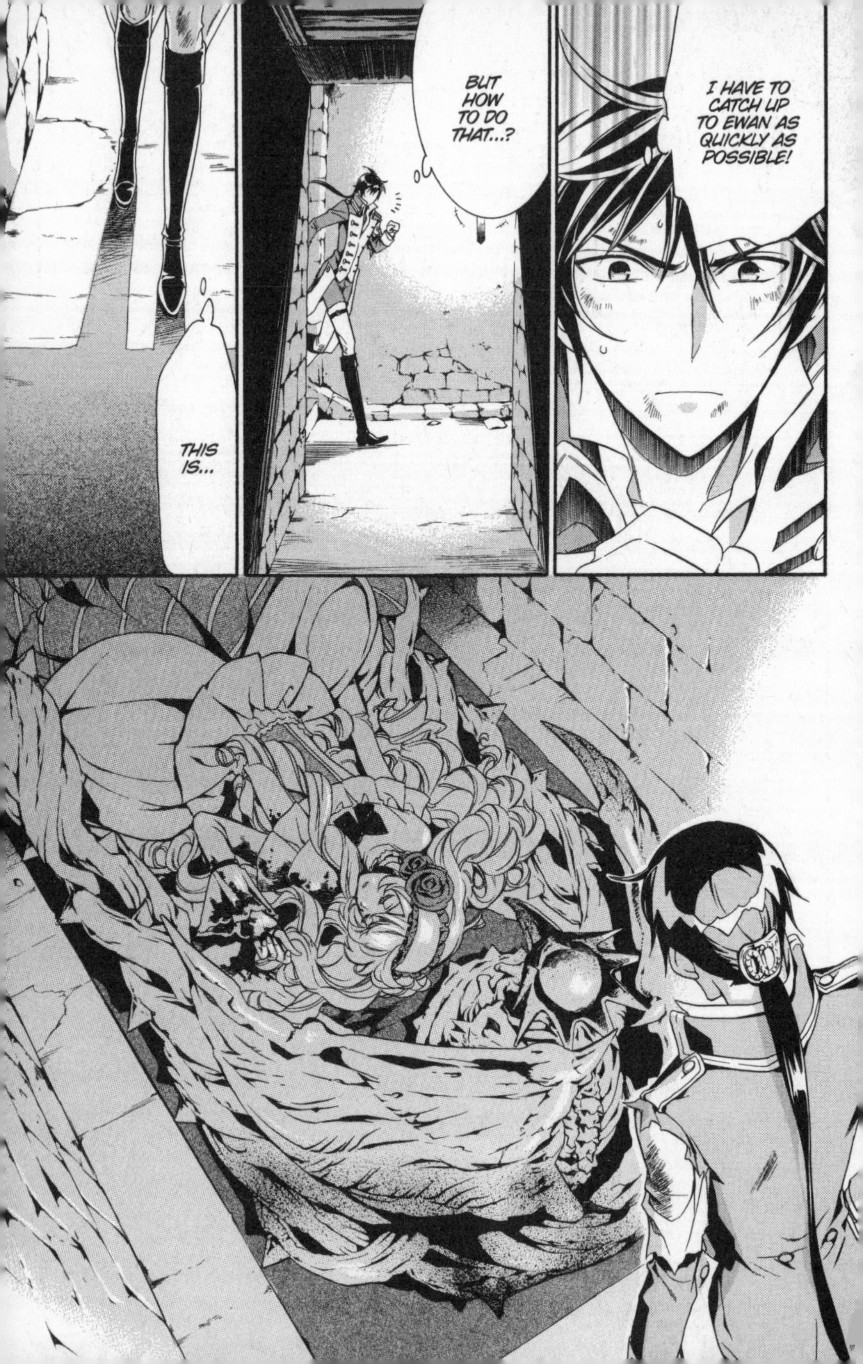
I HAVE TO CATCH UP TO EWAN AS QUICKLY AS POSSIBLE!
BUT HOW TO DO THAT...?
THIS IS...

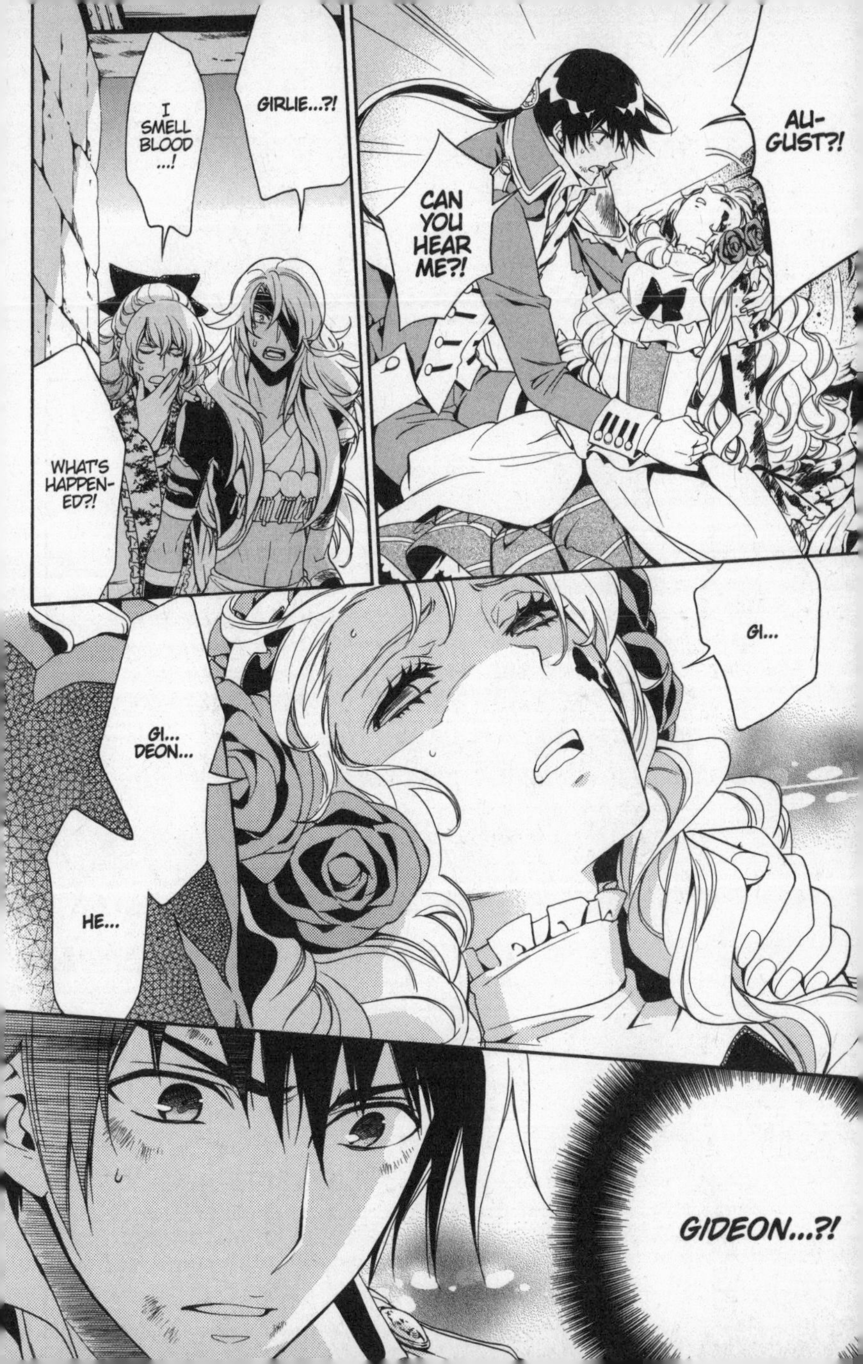

AU-GUST?!
CAN YOU HEAR ME?!
GIRLIE...?!
I SMELL BLOOD...!
WHAT'S HAPPEN-ED?!
GI...
GI... DEON...
HE...
GIDEON...?!

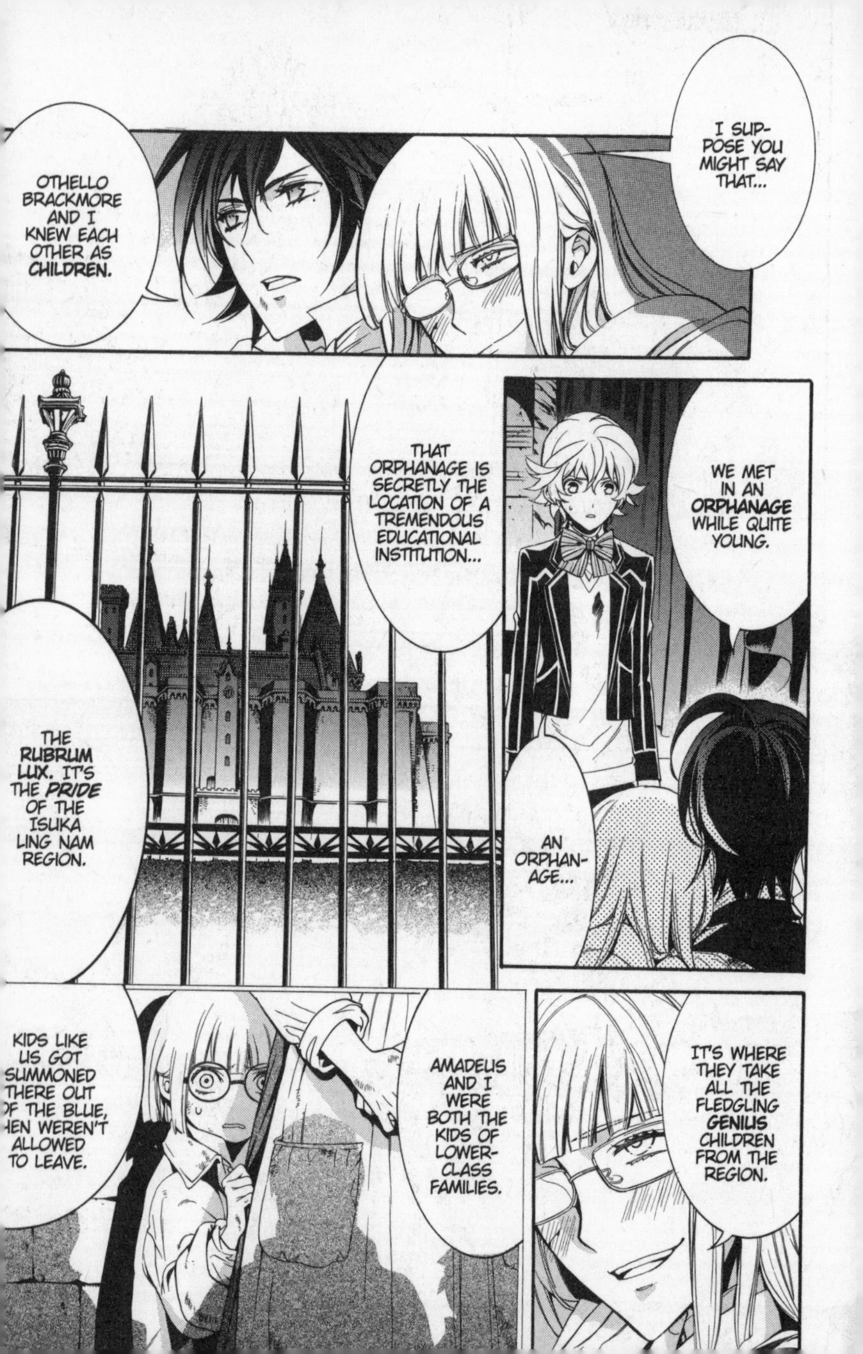
I SUP-POSE YOU MIGHT SAY THAT...
OTHELLO BRACKMORE AND I KNEW EACH OTHER AS CHILDREN.
WE MET IN AN ORPHANAGE WHILE QUITE YOUNG.
AN ORPHAN-AGE...
THAT ORPHANAGE IS SECRETLY THE LOCATION OF A TREMENDOUS EDUCATIONAL INSTITUTION...
THE RUBRUM LUX. IT'S THE PRIDE OF THE ISUKA LING NAM REGION.
IT'S WHERE THEY TAKE ALL THE FLEDGLING GENIUS CHILDREN FROM THE REGION.
AMADEUS AND I WERE BOTH THE KIDS OF LOWER-CLASS FAMILIES.
KIDS LIKE US GOT SUMMONED THERE OUT OF THE BLUE, HEN WEREN'T ALLOWED TO LEAVE.

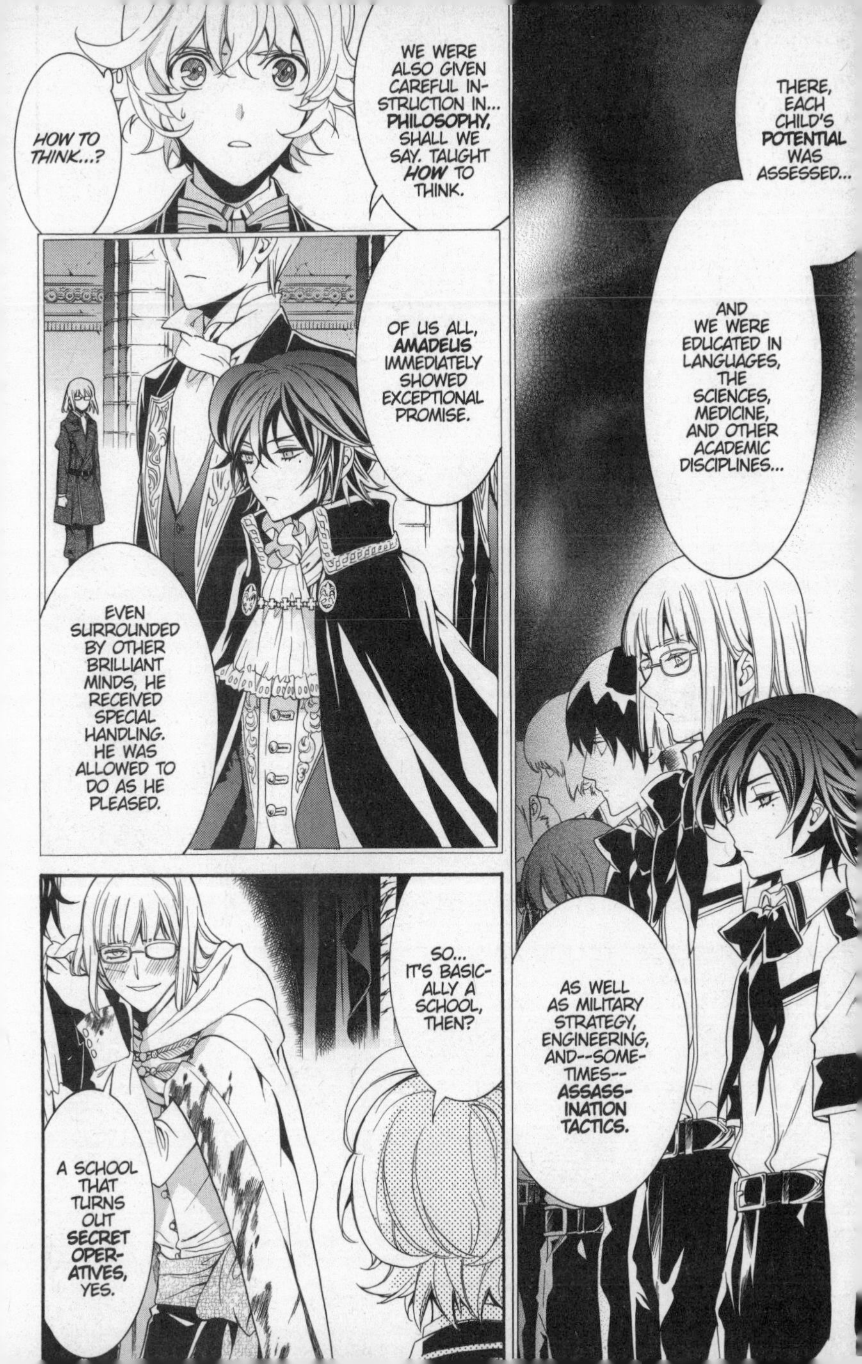
THERE, EACH CHILD'S POTENTIAL WAS ASSESSED...
AND WE WERE EDUCATED IN LANGUAGES, THE SCIENCES, MEDICINE, AND OTHER ACADEMIC DISCIPLINES...
AS WELL AS MILITARY STRATEGY, ENGINEERING, AND--SOMETIMES--ASSASSINATION TACTICS.
WE WERE ALSO GIVEN CAREFUL INSTRUCTION IN... PHILOSOPHY, SHALL WE SAY. TAUGHT HOW TO THINK.
HOW TO THINK...?
OF US ALL, AMADEUS IMMEDIATELY SHOWED EXCEPTIONAL PROMISE.
EVEN SURROUNDED BY OTHER BRILLIANT MINDS, HE RECEIVED SPECIAL HANDLING. HE WAS ALLOWED TO DO AS HE PLEASED.
SO... IT'S BASICALLY A SCHOOL, THEN?
A SCHOOL THAT TURNS OUT SECRET OPERATIVES, YES.

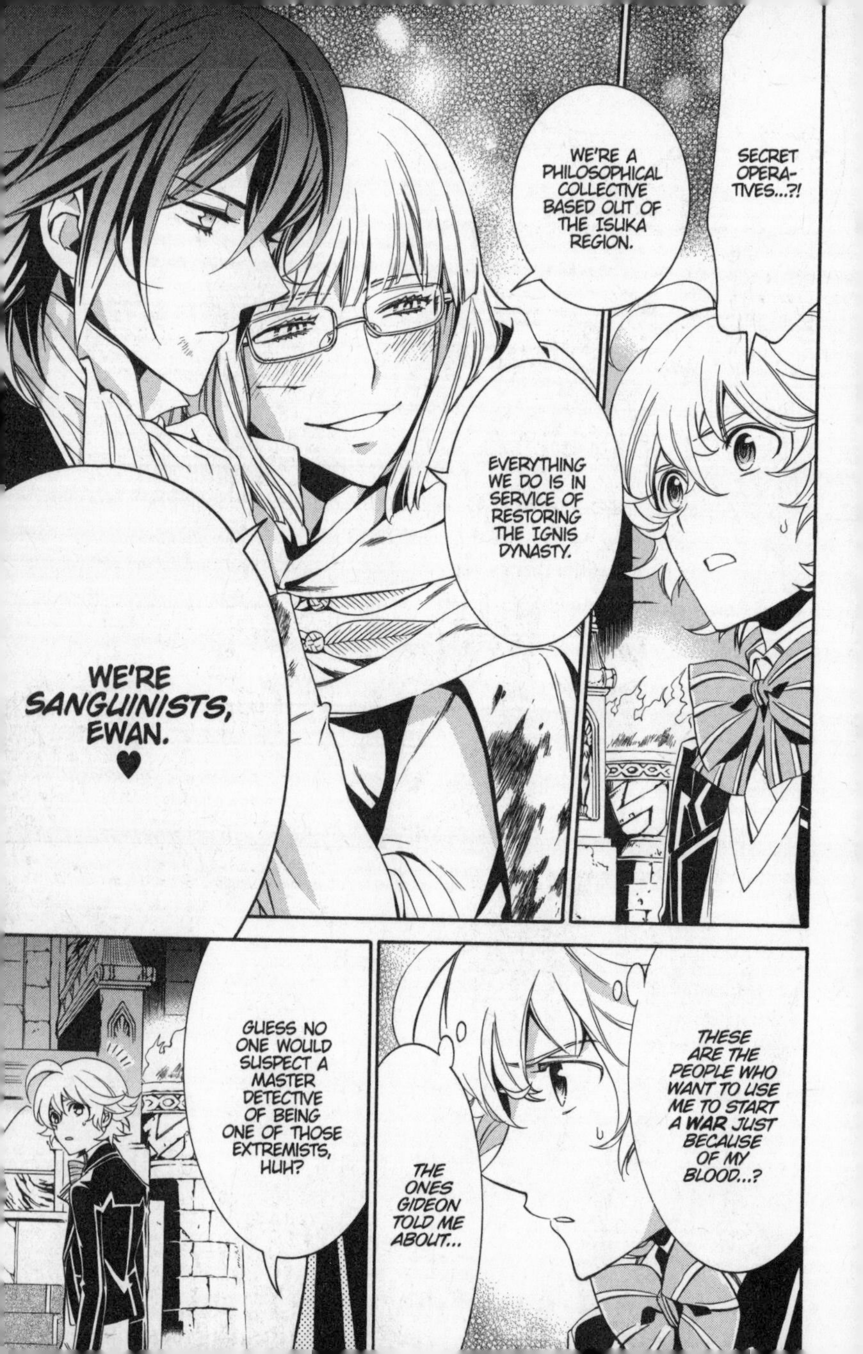
SECRET OPERATIVES...?!
WE'RE A PHILOSOPHICAL COLLECTIVE BASED OUT OF THE ISUKA REGION.
EVERYTHING WE DO IS IN SERVICE OF RESTORING THE IGNIS DYNASTY.
WE'RE SANGUINISTS, EWAN. ♥
THESE ARE THE PEOPLE WHO WANT TO USE ME TO START A WAR JUST BECAUSE OF MY BLOOD...?
THE ONES GIDEON TOLD ME ABOUT...
GUESS NO ONE WOULD SUSPECT A MASTER DETECTIVE OF BEING ONE OF THOSE EXTREMISTS, HUH?

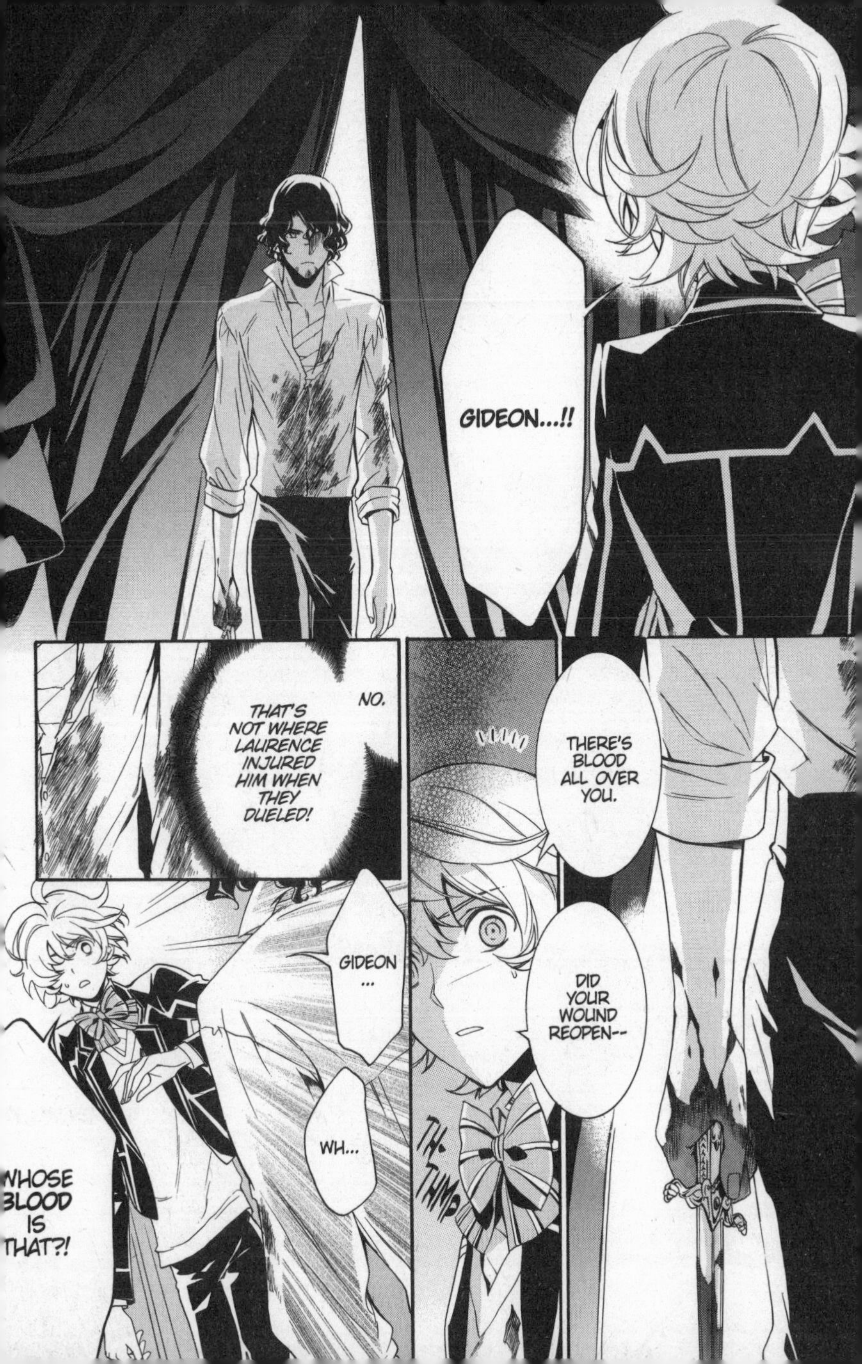
GIDEON...!!
THERE'S BLOOD ALL OVER YOU.
DID YOUR WOUND REOPEN--
THMP
NO.
THAT'S NOT WHERE LAURENCE INJURED HIM WHEN THEY DUELED!
GIDEON ...
WH...
WHOSE BLOOD IS THAT?!

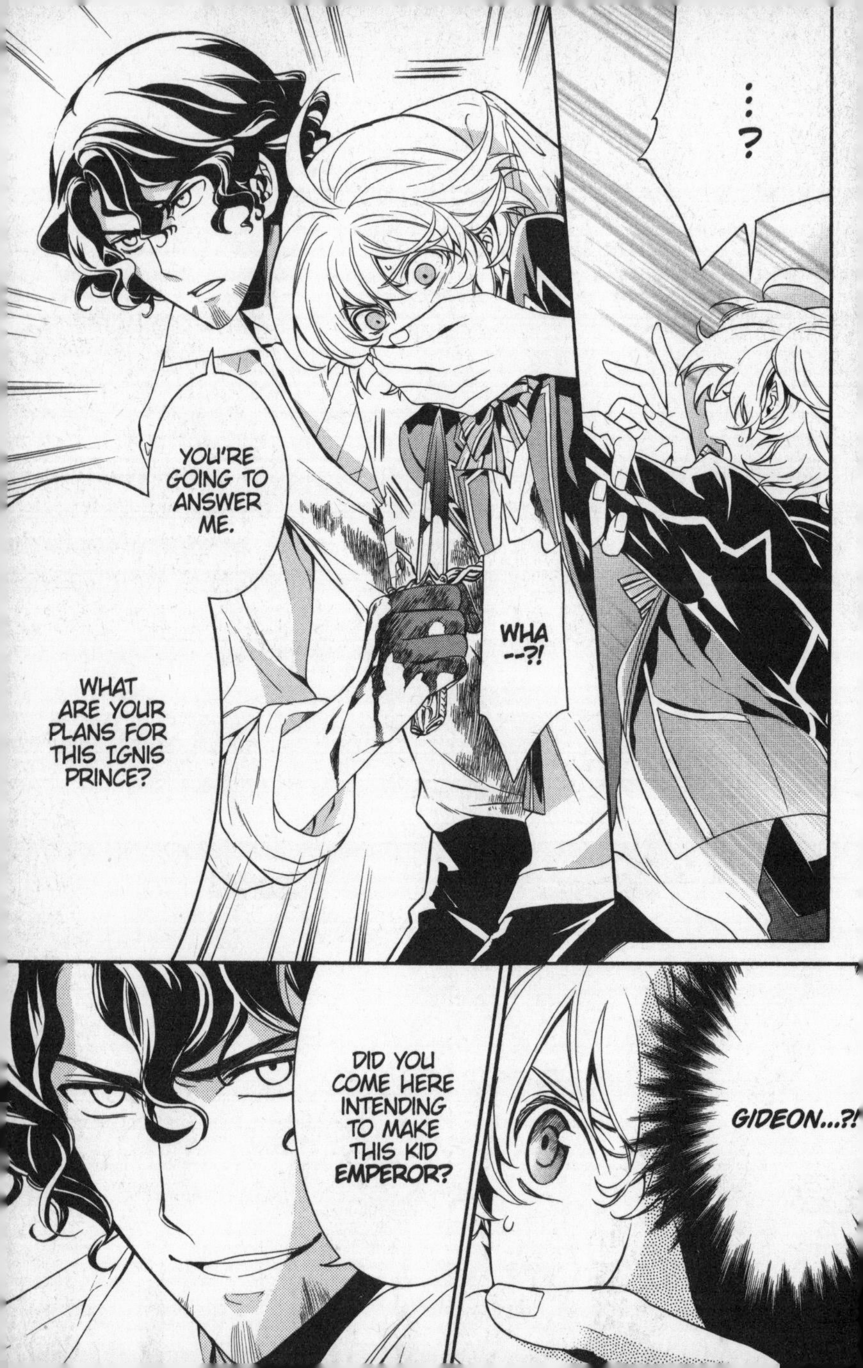
...?
WHA--?!
YOU'RE GOING TO ANSWER ME.
WHAT ARE YOUR PLANS FOR THIS IGNIS PRINCE?
GIDEON...?!
DID YOU COME HERE INTENDING TO MAKE THIS KID EMPEROR?

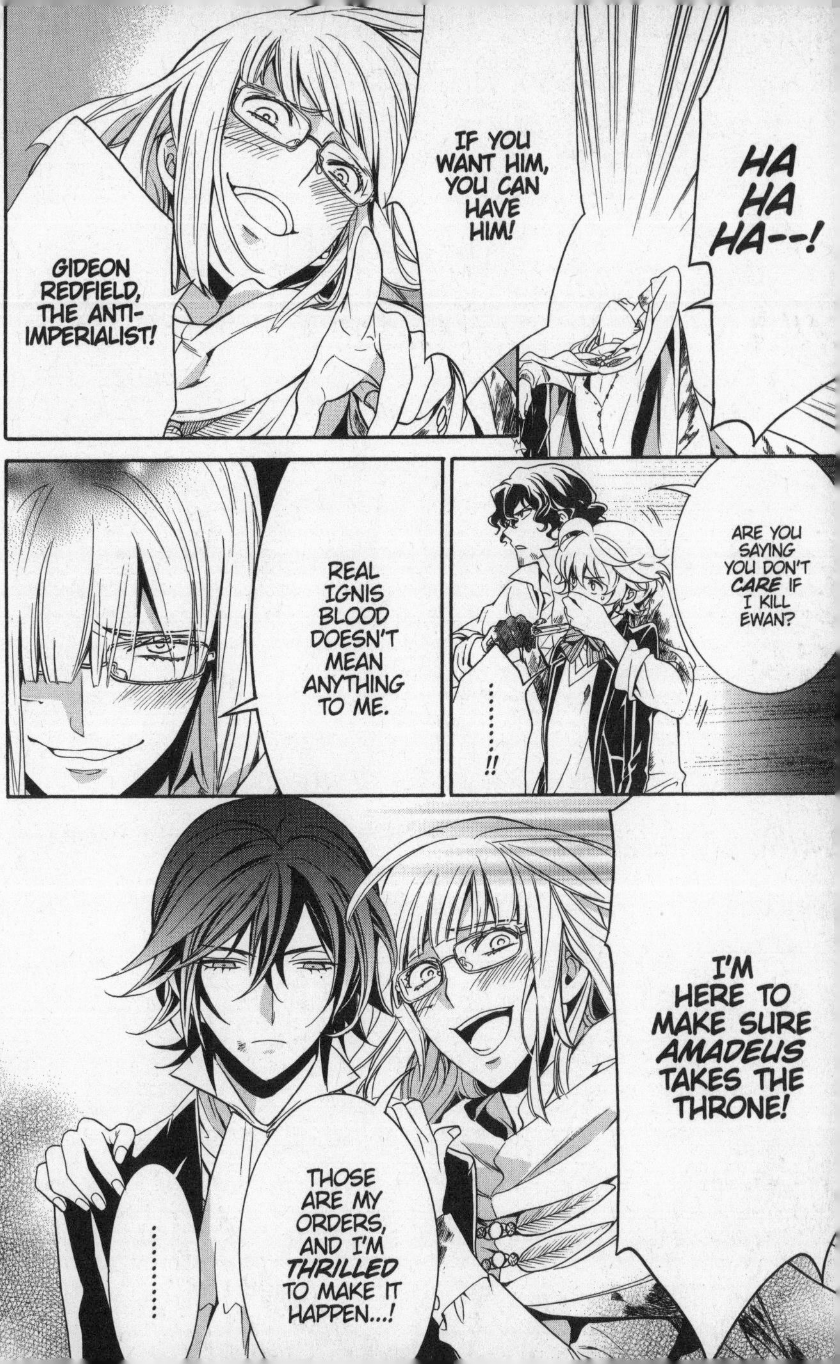
HA HA HA--!
IF YOU WANT HIM, YOU CAN HAVE HIM!
GIDEON REDFIELD, THE ANTI-IMPERIALIST!
ARE YOU SAYING YOU DON'T *CARE* IF I KILL EWAN?
......!!
REAL IGNIS BLOOD DOESN'T MEAN ANYTHING TO ME.
I'M HERE TO MAKE SURE *AMADEUS* TAKES THE THRONE!
THOSE ARE MY ORDERS, AND I'M *THRILLED* TO MAKE IT HAPPEN...!
......

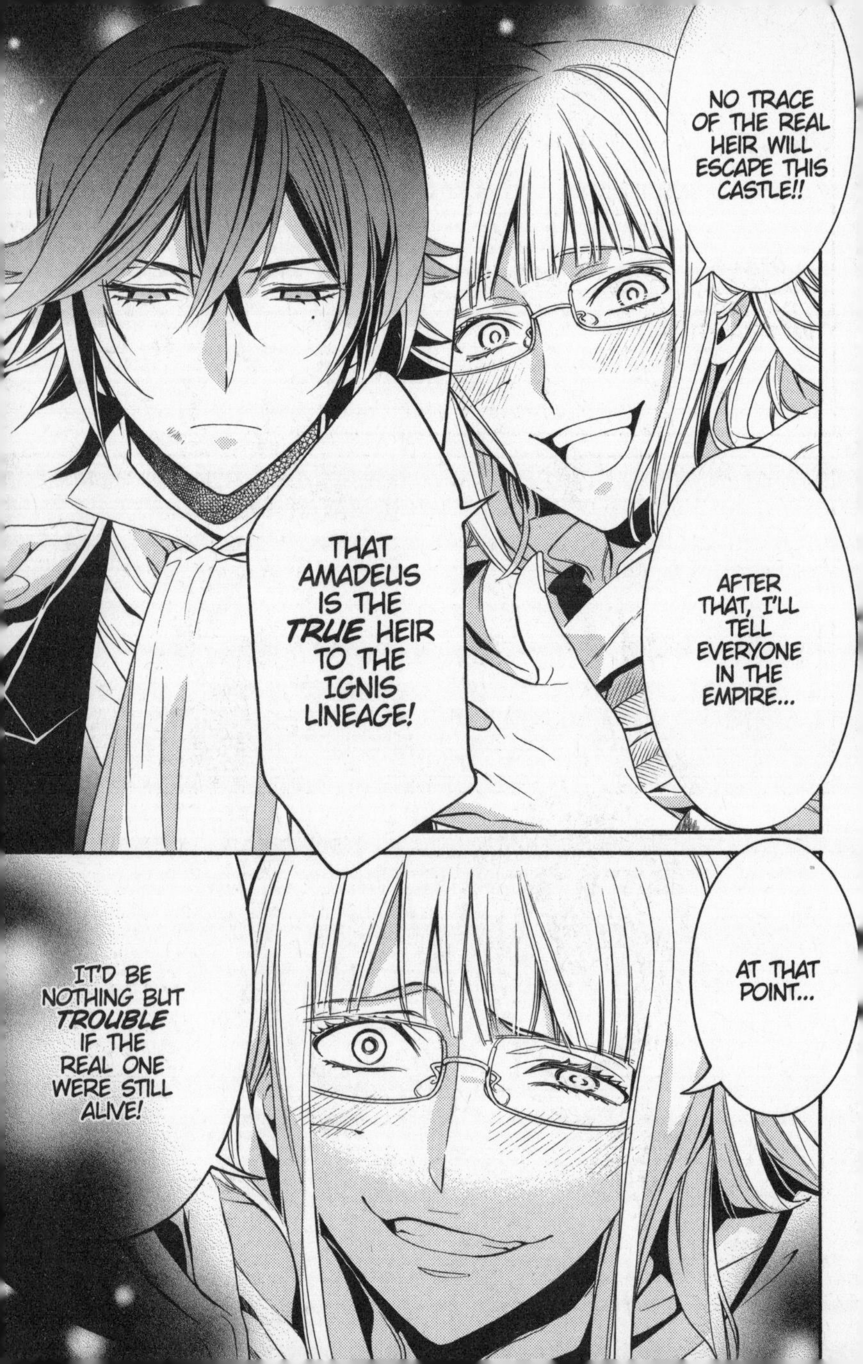
NO TRACE OF THE REAL HEIR WILL ESCAPE THIS CASTLE!!
AFTER THAT, I'LL TELL EVERYONE IN THE EMPIRE...
THAT AMADEUS IS THE *TRUE* HEIR TO THE IGNIS LINEAGE!
AT THAT POINT...
IT'D BE NOTHING BUT *TROUBLE* IF THE REAL ONE WERE STILL ALIVE!

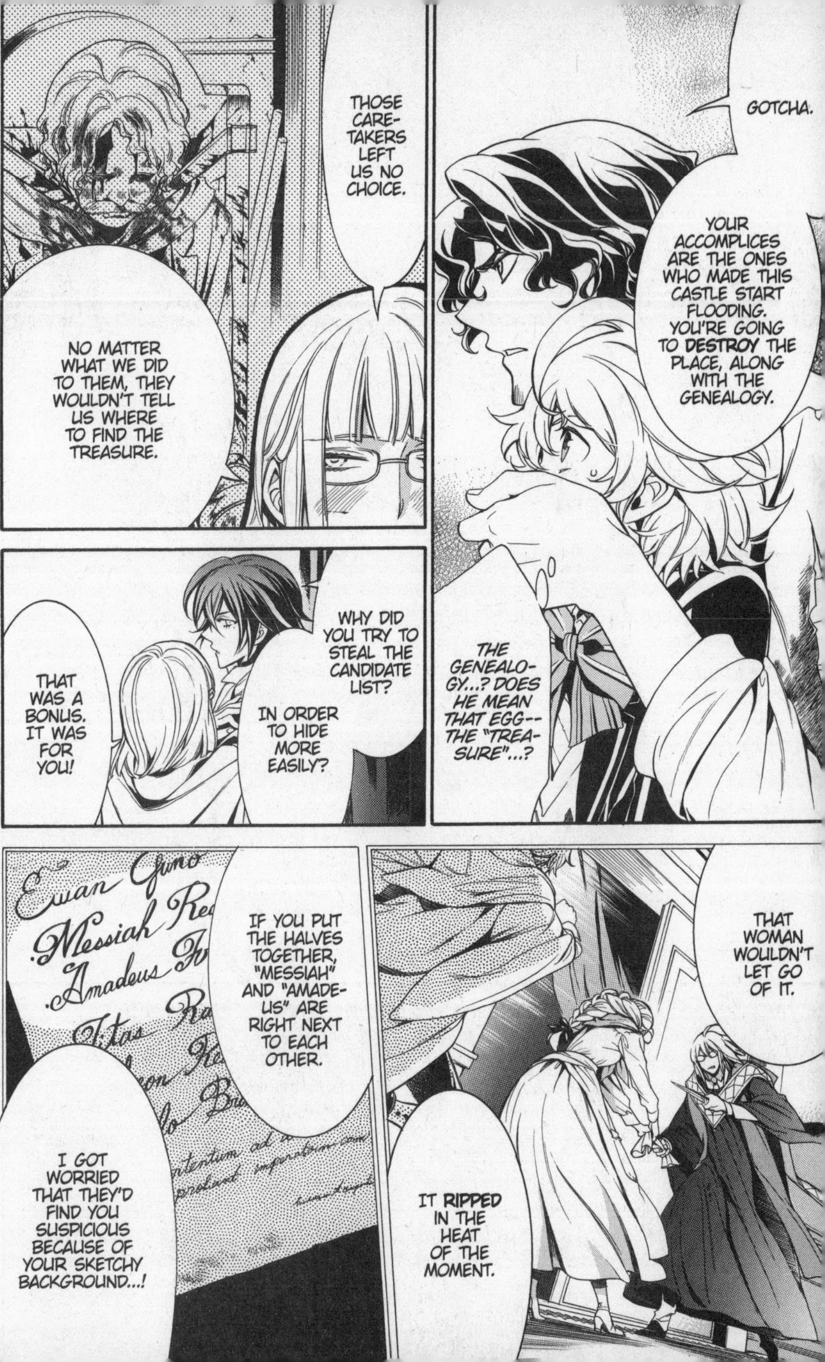
GOTCHA.
YOUR ACCOMPLICES ARE THE ONES WHO MADE THIS CASTLE START FLOODING. YOU'RE GOING TO **DESTROY** THE PLACE, ALONG WITH THE GENEALOGY.
THE GENEALOGY...? DOES HE MEAN THAT EGG--THE "TREASURE"...?
THOSE CARETAKERS LEFT US NO CHOICE.
NO MATTER WHAT WE DID TO THEM, THEY WOULDN'T TELL US WHERE TO FIND THE TREASURE.
WHY DID YOU TRY TO STEAL THE CANDIDATE LIST?
IN ORDER TO HIDE MORE EASILY?
THAT WAS A BONUS. IT WAS FOR YOU!
THAT WOMAN WOULDN'T LET GO OF IT.
IT **RIPPED** IN THE HEAT OF THE MOMENT.
IF YOU PUT THE HALVES TOGETHER, "MESSIAH" AND "AMADEUS" ARE RIGHT NEXT TO EACH OTHER.
I GOT WORRIED THAT THEY'D FIND YOU SUSPICIOUS BECAUSE OF YOUR SKETCHY BACKGROUND...!

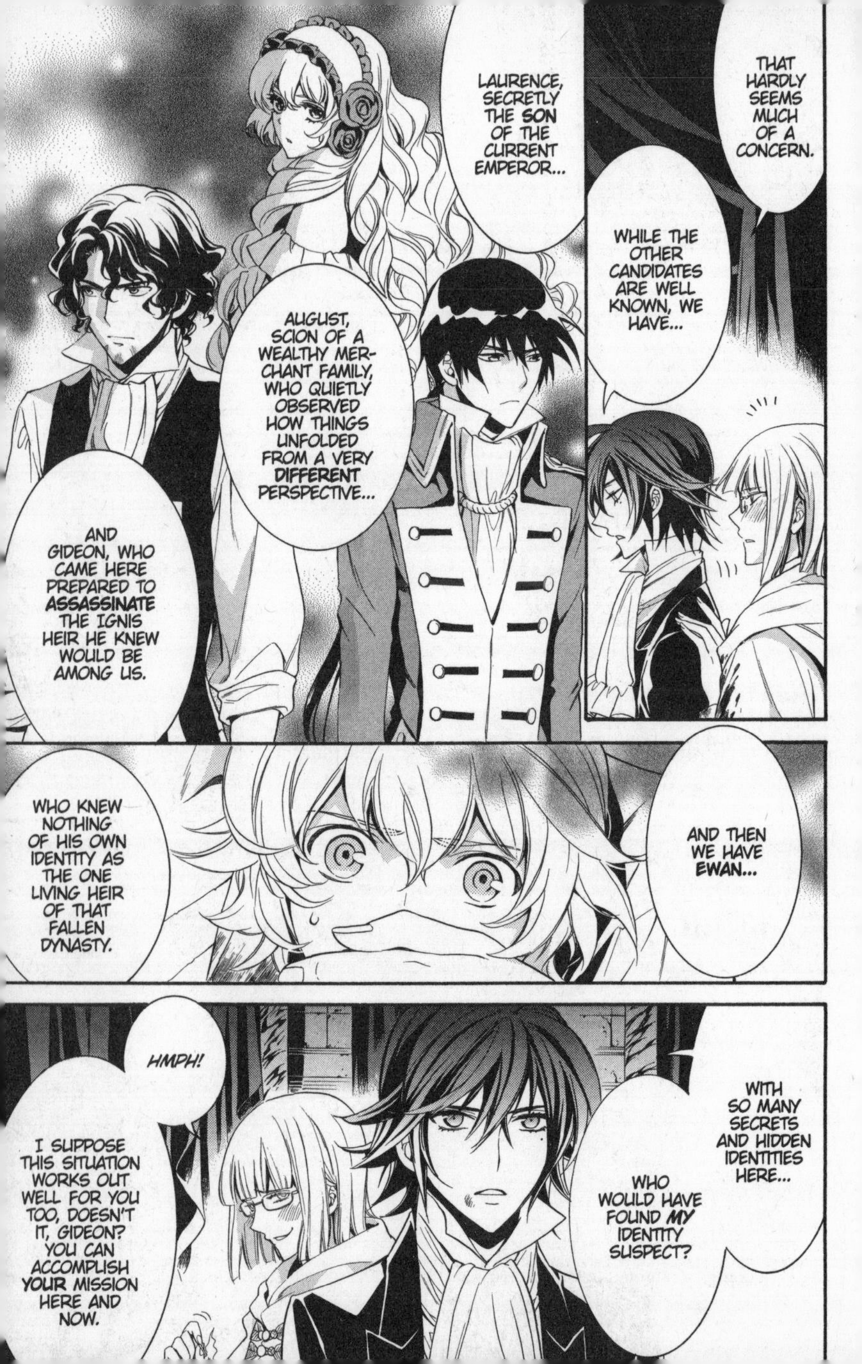
THAT HARDLY SEEMS MUCH OF A CONCERN.
WHILE THE OTHER CANDIDATES ARE WELL KNOWN, WE HAVE...
LAURENCE, SECRETLY THE **SON** OF THE CURRENT EMPEROR...
AUGUST, SCION OF A WEALTHY MER-CHANT FAMILY, WHO QUIETLY OBSERVED HOW THINGS UNFOLDED FROM A VERY **DIFFERENT** PERSPECTIVE...
AND GIDEON, WHO CAME HERE PREPARED TO **ASSASSINATE** THE IGNIS HEIR HE KNEW WOULD BE AMONG US.
AND THEN WE HAVE **EWAN**...
WHO KNEW NOTHING OF HIS OWN IDENTITY AS THE ONE LIVING HEIR OF THAT FALLEN DYNASTY.
WITH SO MANY SECRETS AND HIDDEN IDENTITIES HERE...
WHO WOULD HAVE FOUND *MY* IDENTITY SUSPECT?
HMPH!
I SUPPOSE THIS SITUATION WORKS OUT WELL FOR YOU TOO, DOESN'T IT, GIDEON? YOU CAN ACCOMPLISH **YOUR** MISSION HERE AND NOW.

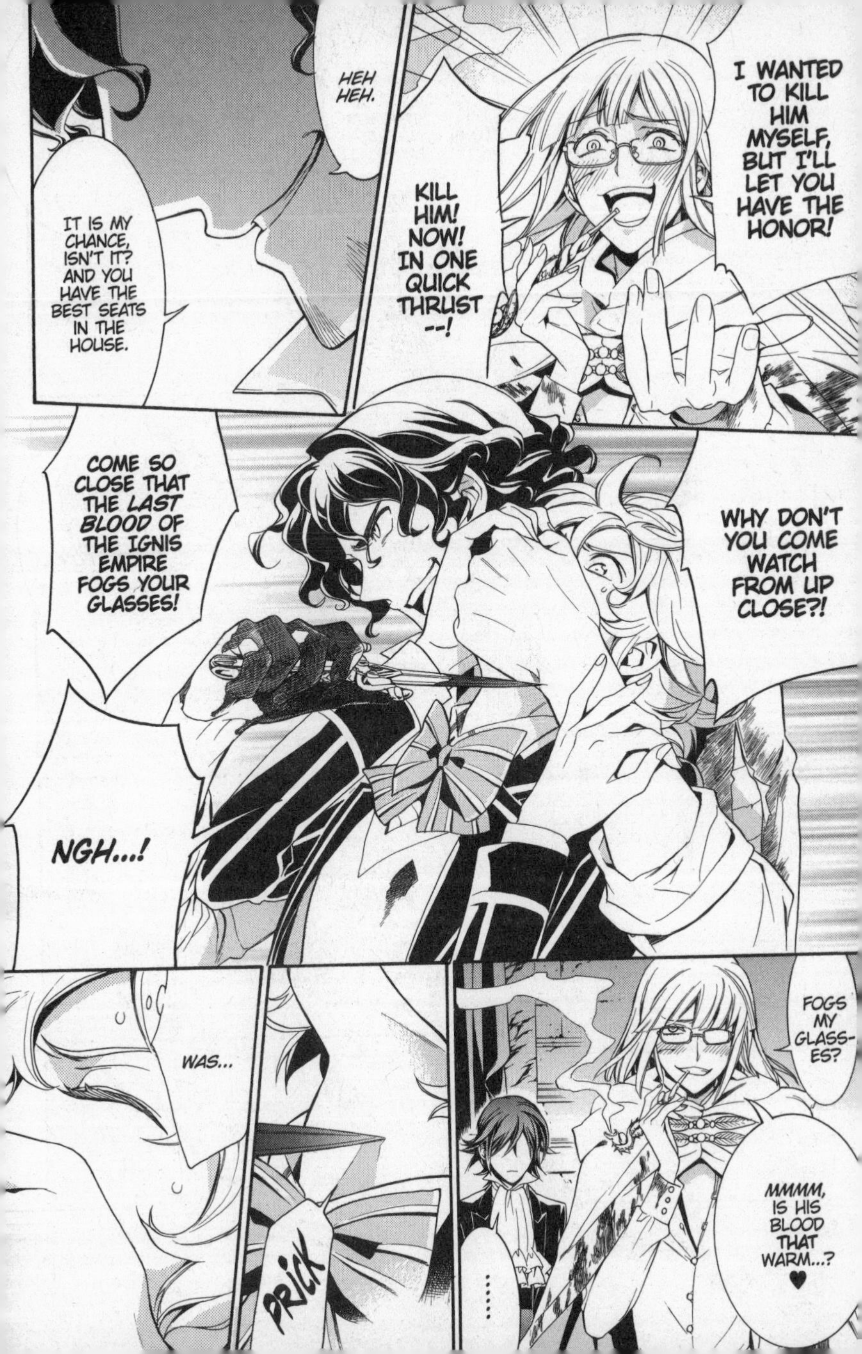
I WANTED TO KILL HIM MYSELF, BUT I'LL LET YOU HAVE THE HONOR!
KILL HIM! NOW! IN ONE QUICK THRUST --!
HEH HEH.
IT IS MY CHANCE, ISN'T IT? AND YOU HAVE THE BEST SEATS IN THE HOUSE.
WHY DON'T YOU COME WATCH FROM UP CLOSE?!
COME SO CLOSE THAT THE LAST BLOOD OF THE IGNIS EMPIRE FOGS YOUR GLASSES!
NGH...!
FOGS MY GLASS-ES?
MMMM, IS HIS BLOOD THAT WARM...? ♥
......
PRICK
WAS...

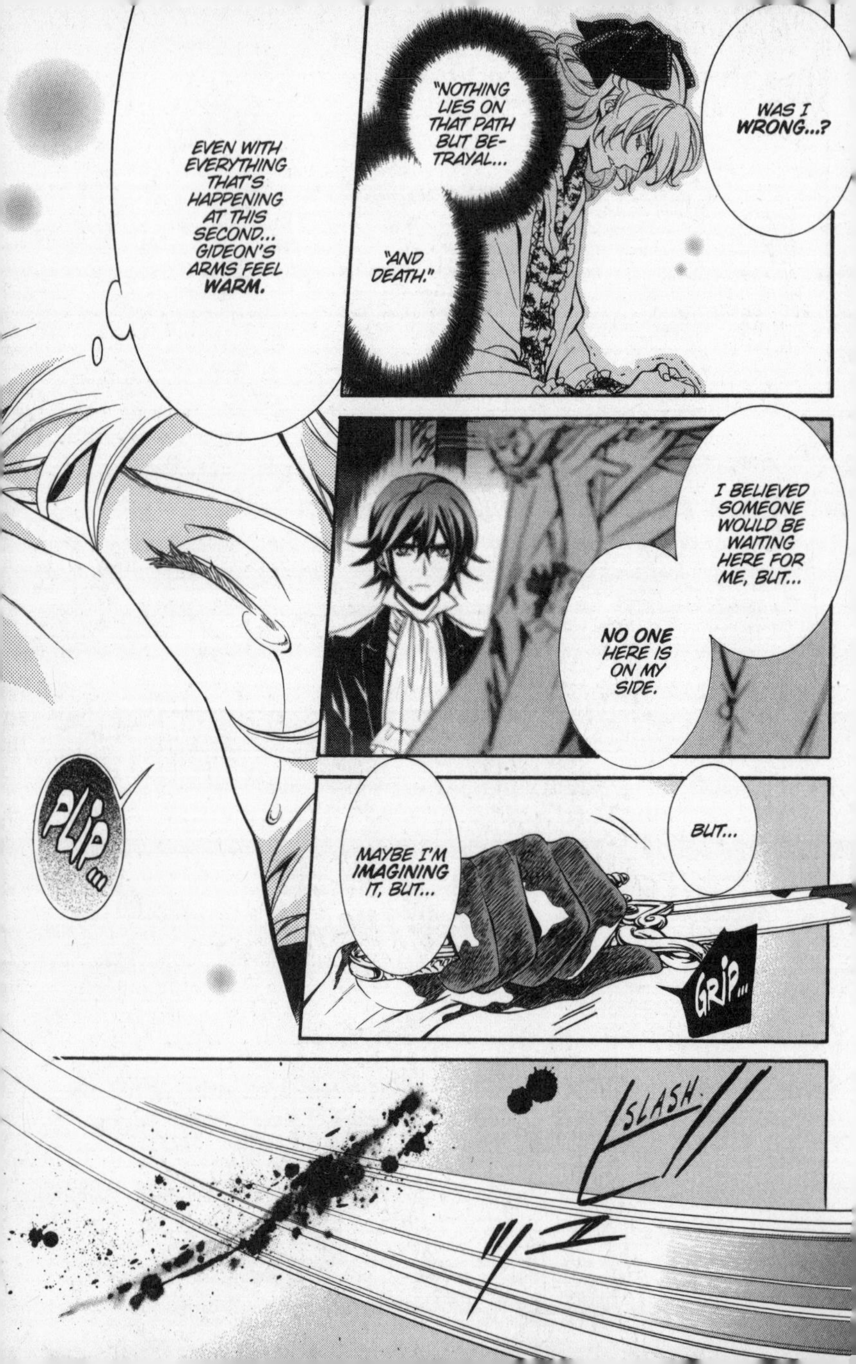
WAS I WRONG...?
"NOTHING LIES ON THAT PATH BUT BE-TRAYAL...
"AND DEATH."
I BELIEVED SOMEONE WOULD BE WAITING HERE FOR ME, BUT...
NO ONE HERE IS ON MY SIDE.
BUT...
MAYBE I'M IMAGINING IT, BUT...
GRIP...
EVEN WITH EVERYTHING THAT'S HAPPENING AT THIS SECOND... GIDEON'S ARMS FEEL WARM.
PLIP...
SLASH.

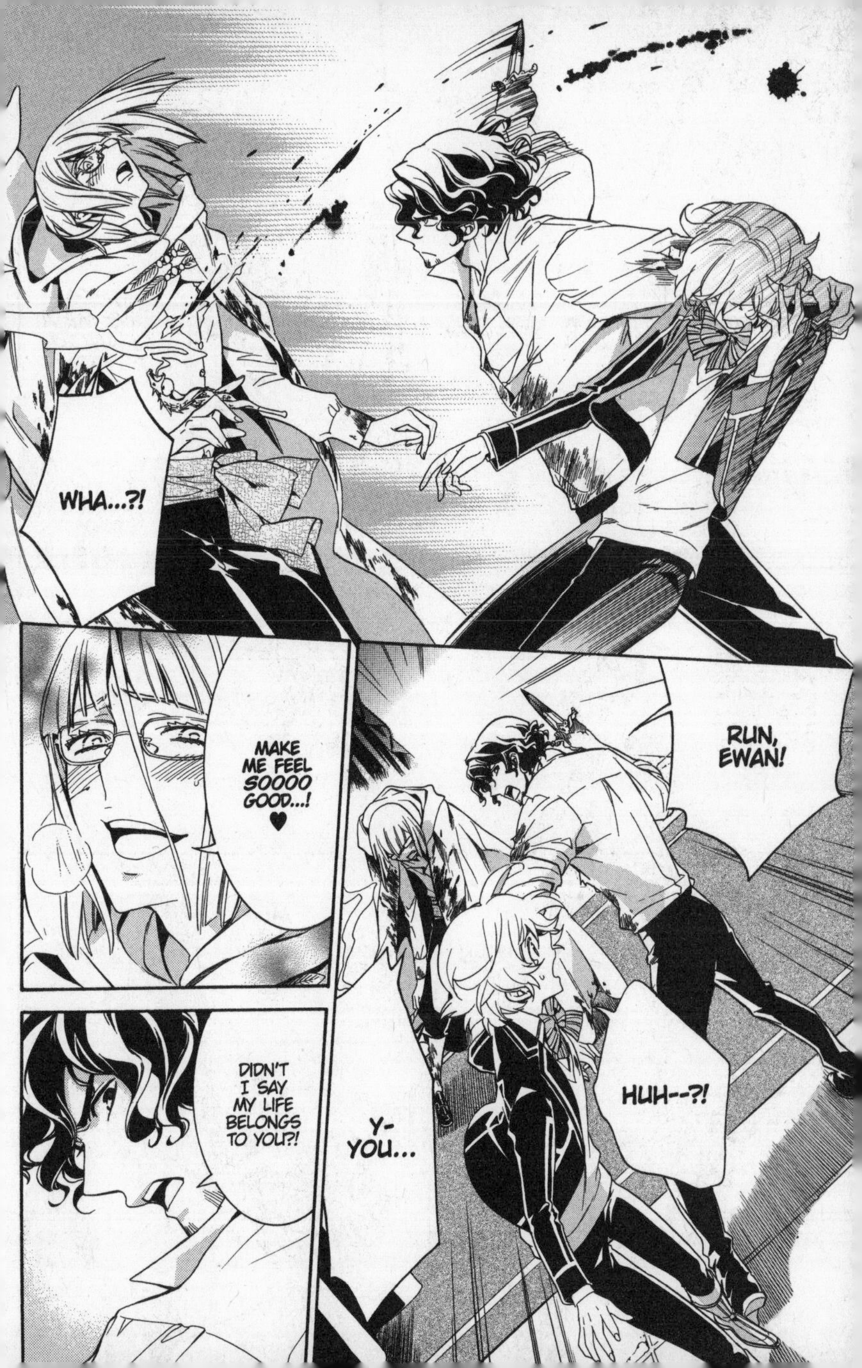
WHA...?!
RUN, EWAN!
HUH--?!
Y-YOU...
MAKE ME FEEL SOOOO GOOD...! ♥
DIDN'T I SAY MY LIFE BELONGS TO YOU?!

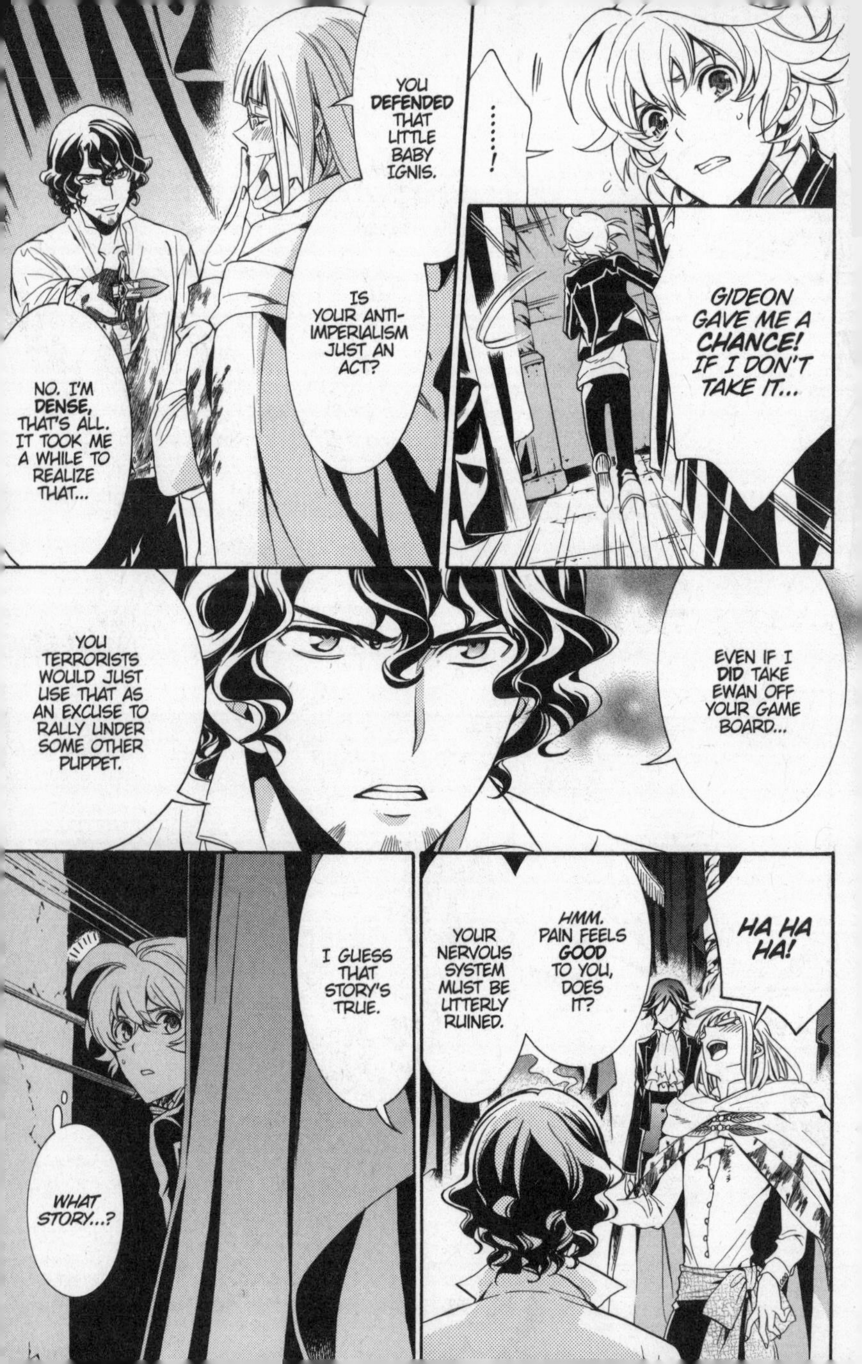
......!
GIDEON GAVE ME A CHANCE! IF I DON'T TAKE IT...
YOU DEFENDED THAT LITTLE BABY IGNIS.
IS YOUR ANTI-IMPERIALISM JUST AN ACT?
NO. I'M DENSE, THAT'S ALL. IT TOOK ME A WHILE TO REALIZE THAT...
EVEN IF I DID TAKE EWAN OFF YOUR GAME BOARD...
YOU TERRORISTS WOULD JUST USE THAT AS AN EXCUSE TO RALLY UNDER SOME OTHER PUPPET.
HA HA HA!
HMM. PAIN FEELS GOOD TO YOU, DOES IT?
YOUR NERVOUS SYSTEM MUST BE UTTERLY RUINED.
I GUESS THAT STORY'S TRUE.
WHAT STORY...?

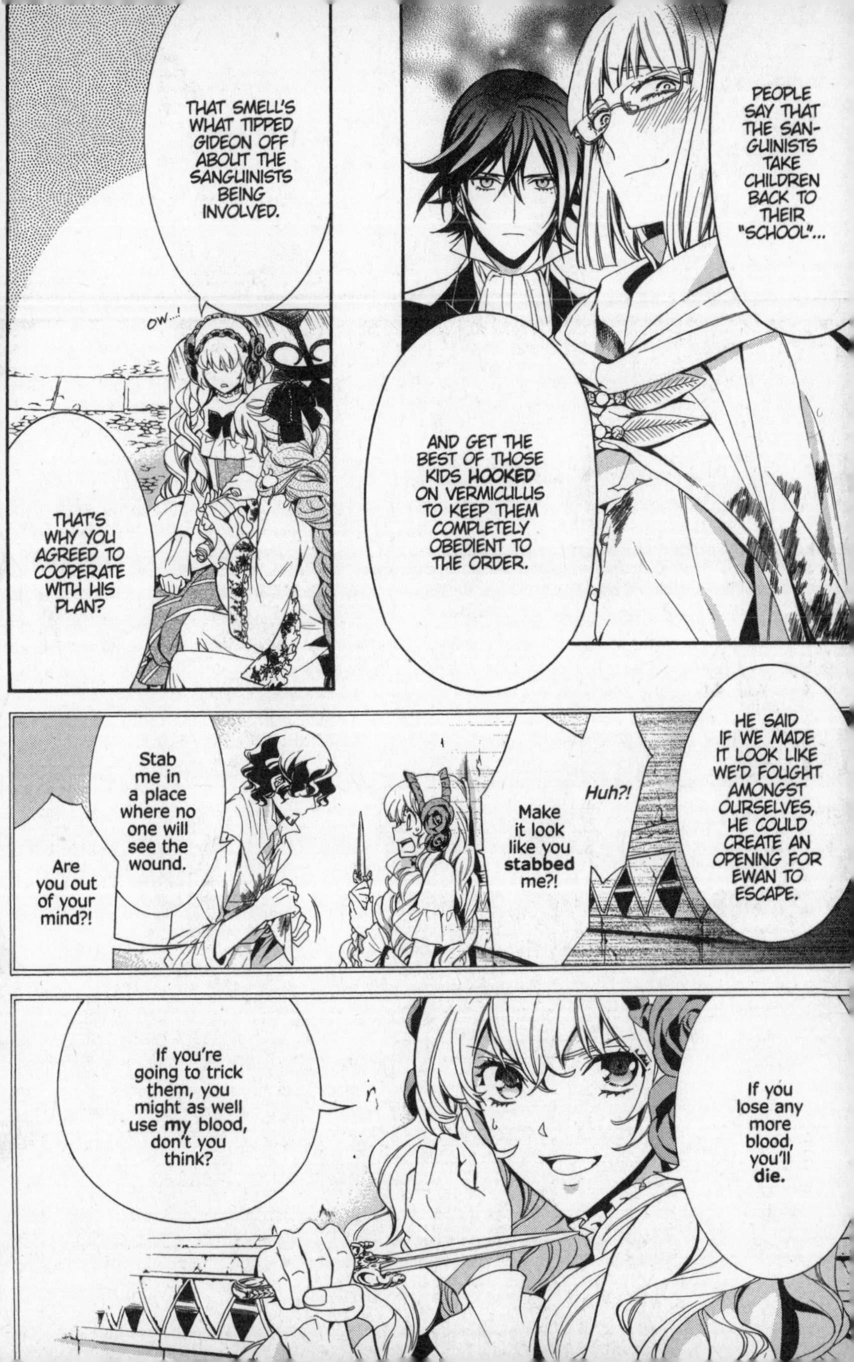
PEOPLE SAY THAT THE SAN-GUINISTS TAKE CHILDREN BACK TO THEIR "SCHOOL"...
AND GET THE BEST OF THOSE KIDS **HOOKED** ON VERMICULUS TO KEEP THEM COMPLETELY OBEDIENT TO THE ORDER.
THAT SMELL'S WHAT TIPPED GIDEON OFF ABOUT THE SANGUINISTS BEING INVOLVED.
OW...!
THAT'S WHY YOU AGREED TO COOPERATE WITH HIS PLAN?
HE SAID IF WE MADE IT LOOK LIKE WE'D FOUGHT AMONGST OURSELVES, HE COULD CREATE AN OPENING FOR EWAN TO ESCAPE.
Huh?!
Make it look like you **stabbed** me?!
Stab me in a place where no one will see the wound.
Are you out of your mind?!
If you lose any more blood, you'll **die**.
If you're going to trick them, you might as well use **my** blood, don't you think?

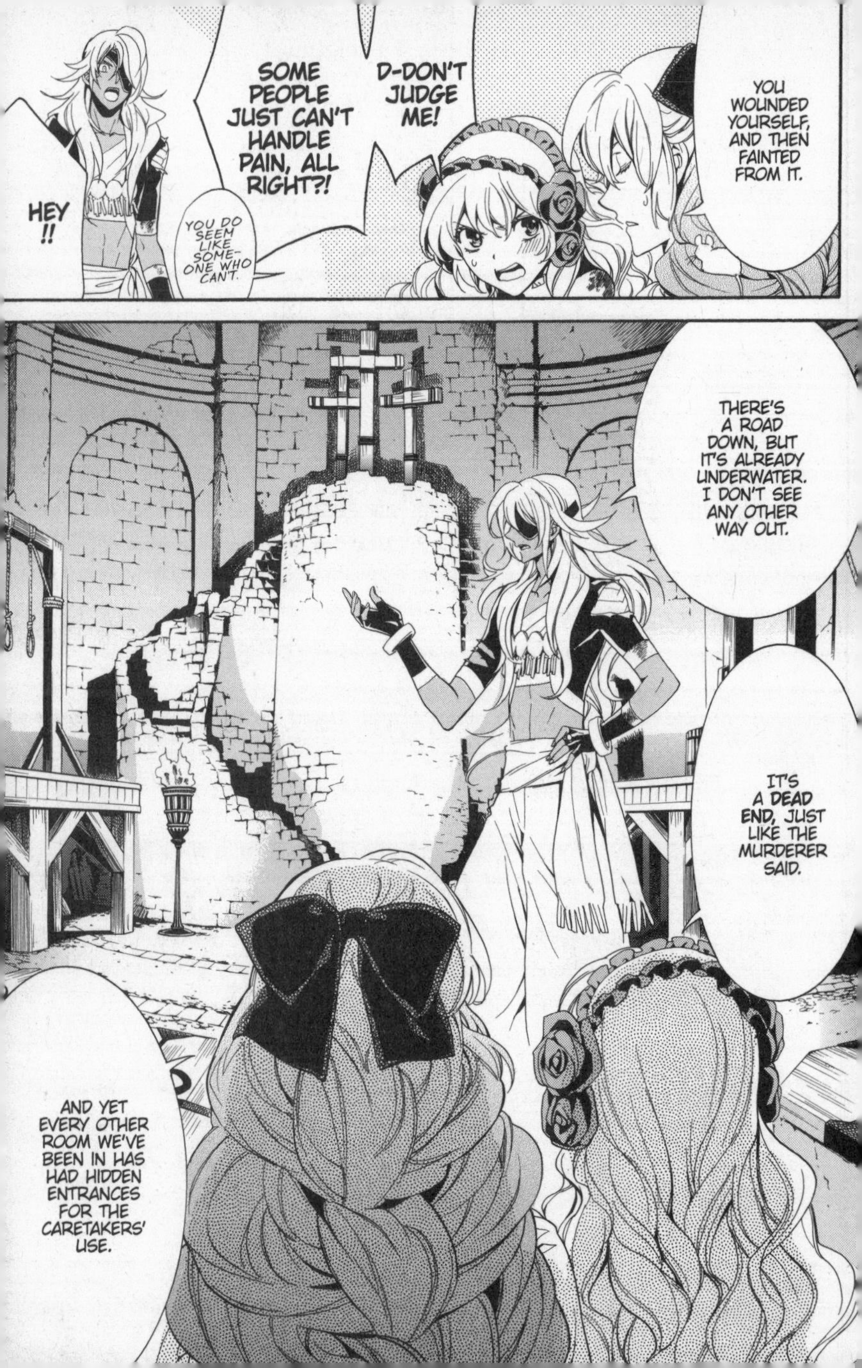
YOU WOUNDED YOURSELF, AND THEN FAINTED FROM IT.
D-DON'T JUDGE ME!
SOME PEOPLE JUST CAN'T HANDLE PAIN, ALL RIGHT?!
YOU DO SEEM LIKE SOME-ONE WHO CAN'T.
HEY!!
THERE'S A ROAD DOWN, BUT IT'S ALREADY UNDERWATER. I DON'T SEE ANY OTHER WAY OUT.
IT'S A DEAD END, JUST LIKE THE MURDERER SAID.
AND YET EVERY OTHER ROOM WE'VE BEEN IN HAS HAD HIDDEN ENTRANCES FOR THE CARETAKERS' USE.

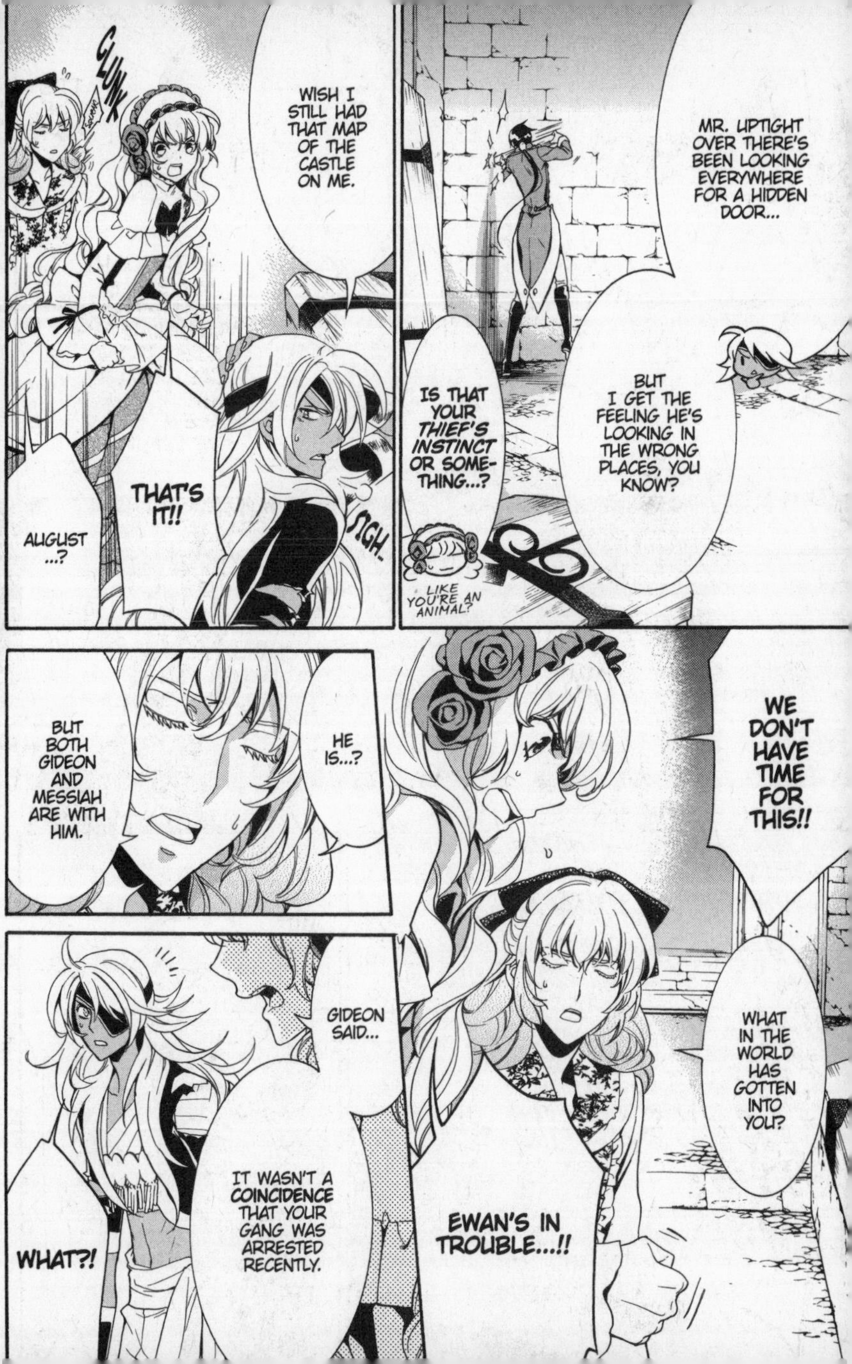
MR. UPTIGHT OVER THERE'S BEEN LOOKING EVERYWHERE FOR A HIDDEN DOOR...
BUT I GET THE FEELING HE'S LOOKING IN THE WRONG PLACES, YOU KNOW?
IS THAT YOUR *THIEF'S INSTINCT* OR SOMETHING...?
LIKE YOU'RE AN ANIMAL?
WISH I STILL HAD THAT MAP OF THE CASTLE ON ME.
CLUNK
SIGH...
THAT'S IT!!
AUGUST ...?
WE DON'T HAVE TIME FOR THIS!!
WHAT IN THE WORLD HAS GOTTEN INTO YOU?
EWAN'S IN TROUBLE...!!
HE IS...?
BUT BOTH GIDEON AND MESSIAH ARE WITH HIM.
GIDEON SAID...
IT WASN'T A COINCIDENCE THAT YOUR GANG WAS ARRESTED RECENTLY.
WHAT?!

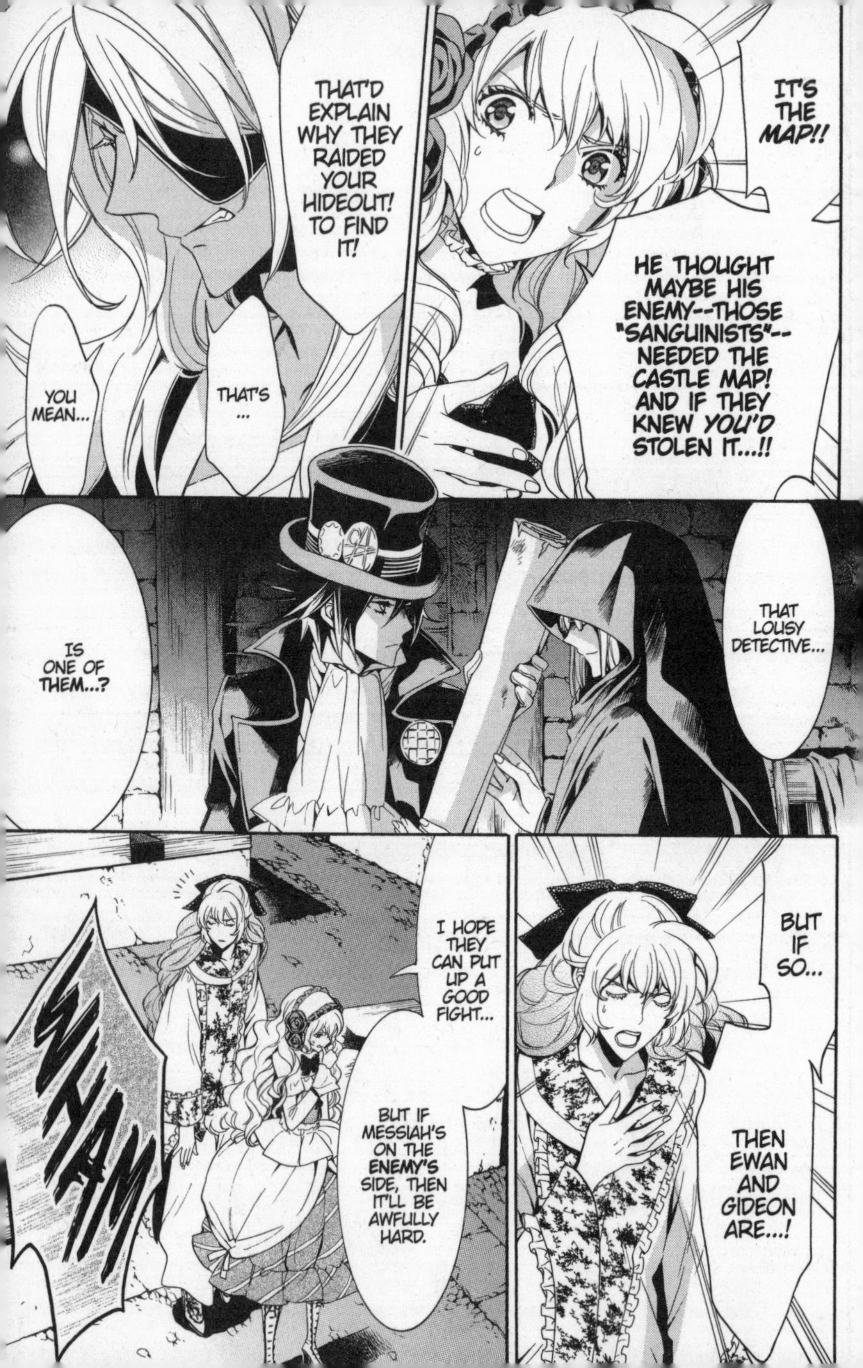
IT'S THE *MAP!!*
HE THOUGHT MAYBE HIS ENEMY--THOSE "SANGUINISTS"--NEEDED THE CASTLE MAP! AND IF THEY KNEW *YOU'D* STOLEN IT...!!
THAT'D EXPLAIN WHY THEY RAIDED YOUR HIDEOUT! TO FIND IT!
THAT'S ...
YOU MEAN...
THAT LOUSY DETECTIVE...
IS ONE OF THEM...?
BUT IF SO...
THEN EWAN AND GIDEON ARE...!
I HOPE THEY CAN PUT UP A GOOD FIGHT...
BUT IF MESSIAH'S ON THE ENEMY'S SIDE, THEN IT'LL BE AWFULLY HARD.
WHAM

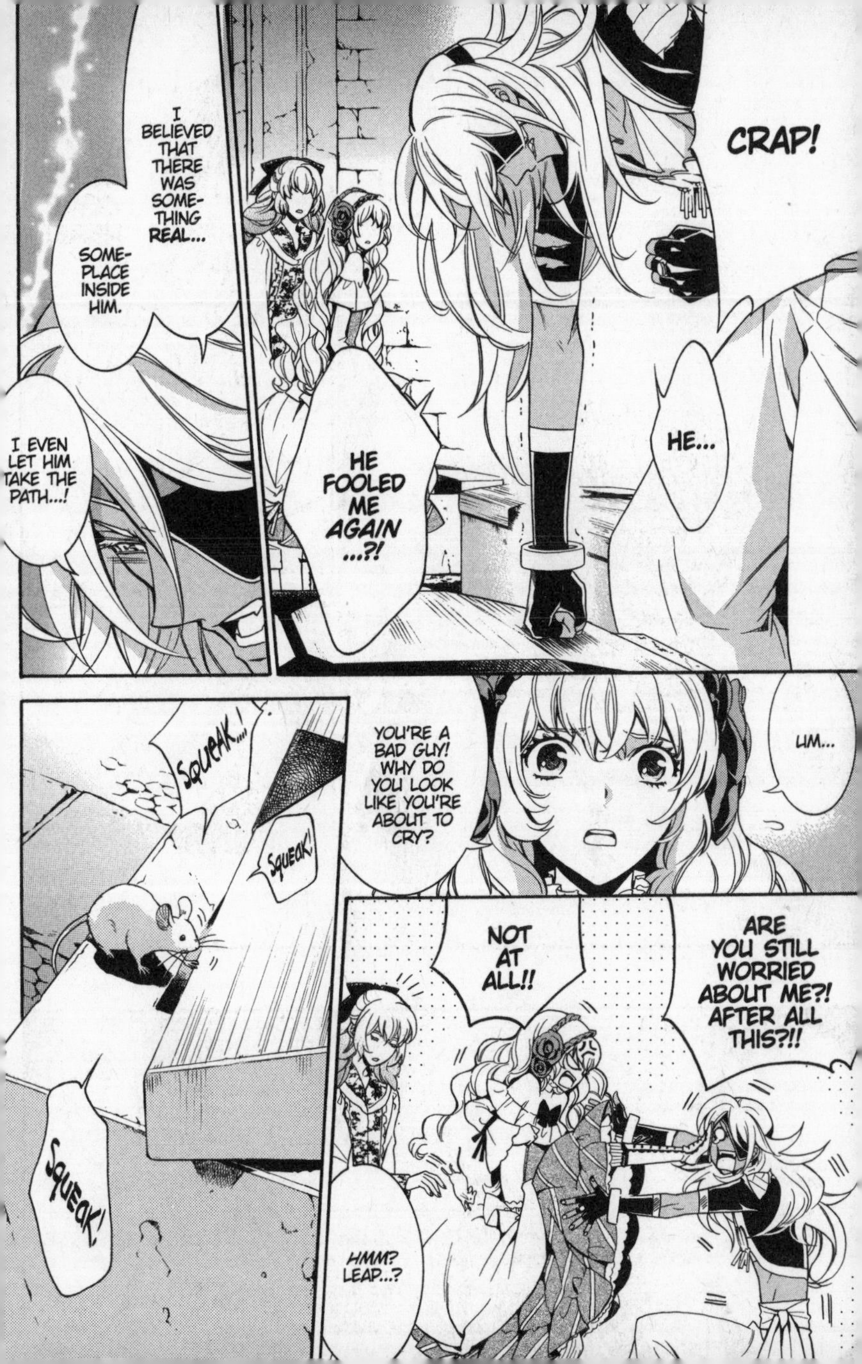
CRAP!
HE...
HE FOOLED ME AGAIN...?!
I BELIEVED THAT THERE WAS SOME-THING REAL...
SOME-PLACE INSIDE HIM.
I EVEN LET HIM TAKE THE PATH...!
UM...
YOU'RE A BAD GUY! WHY DO YOU LOOK LIKE YOU'RE ABOUT TO CRY?
ARE YOU STILL WORRIED ABOUT ME?! AFTER ALL THIS?!!
NOT AT ALL!!
HMM? LEAP...?
SQUEAK...!
SQUEAK!
SQUEAK!

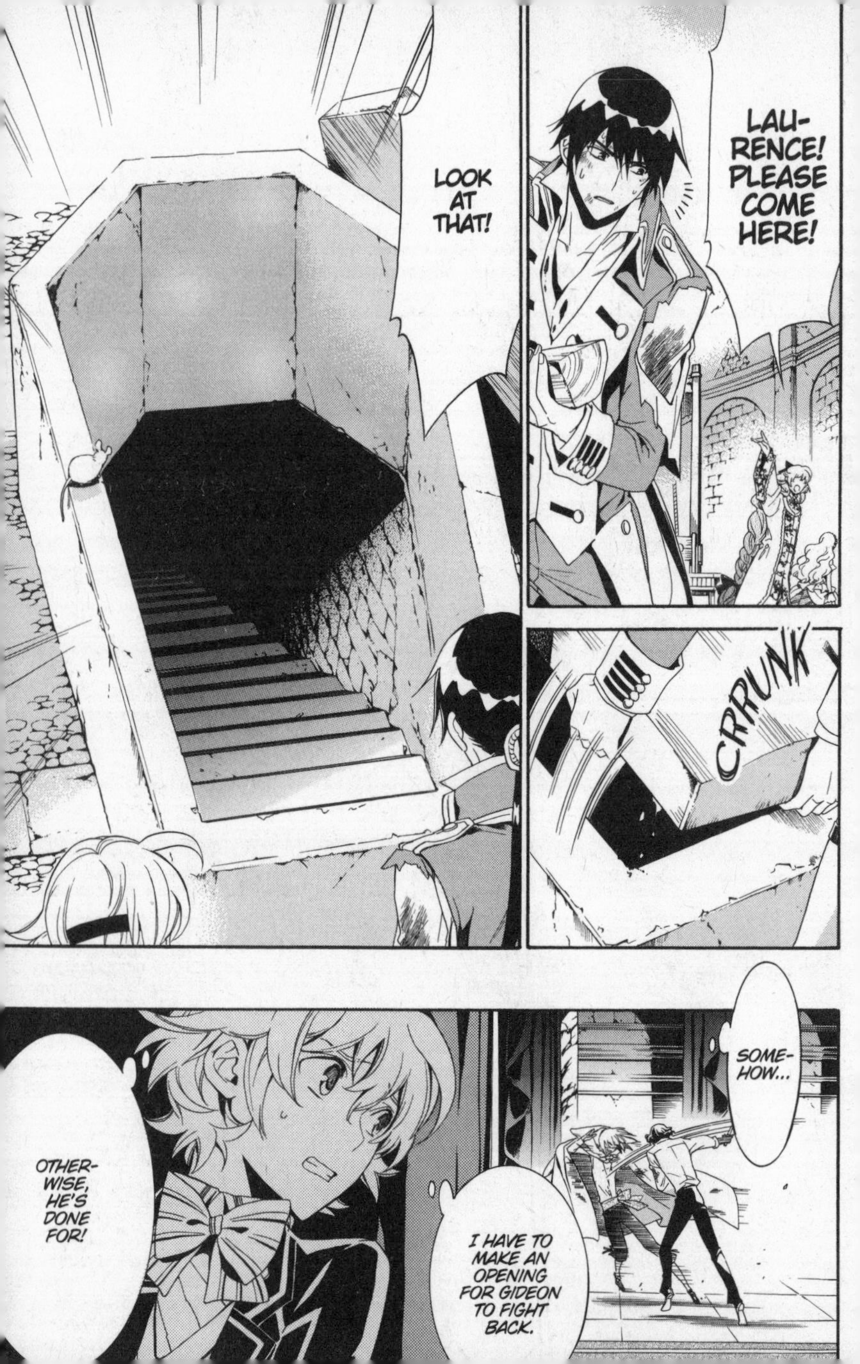
LAU-RENCE! PLEASE COME HERE!
CRRUNK
LOOK AT THAT!
SOME-HOW...
I HAVE TO MAKE AN OPENING FOR GIDEON TO FIGHT BACK.
OTHER-WISE, HE'S DONE FOR!

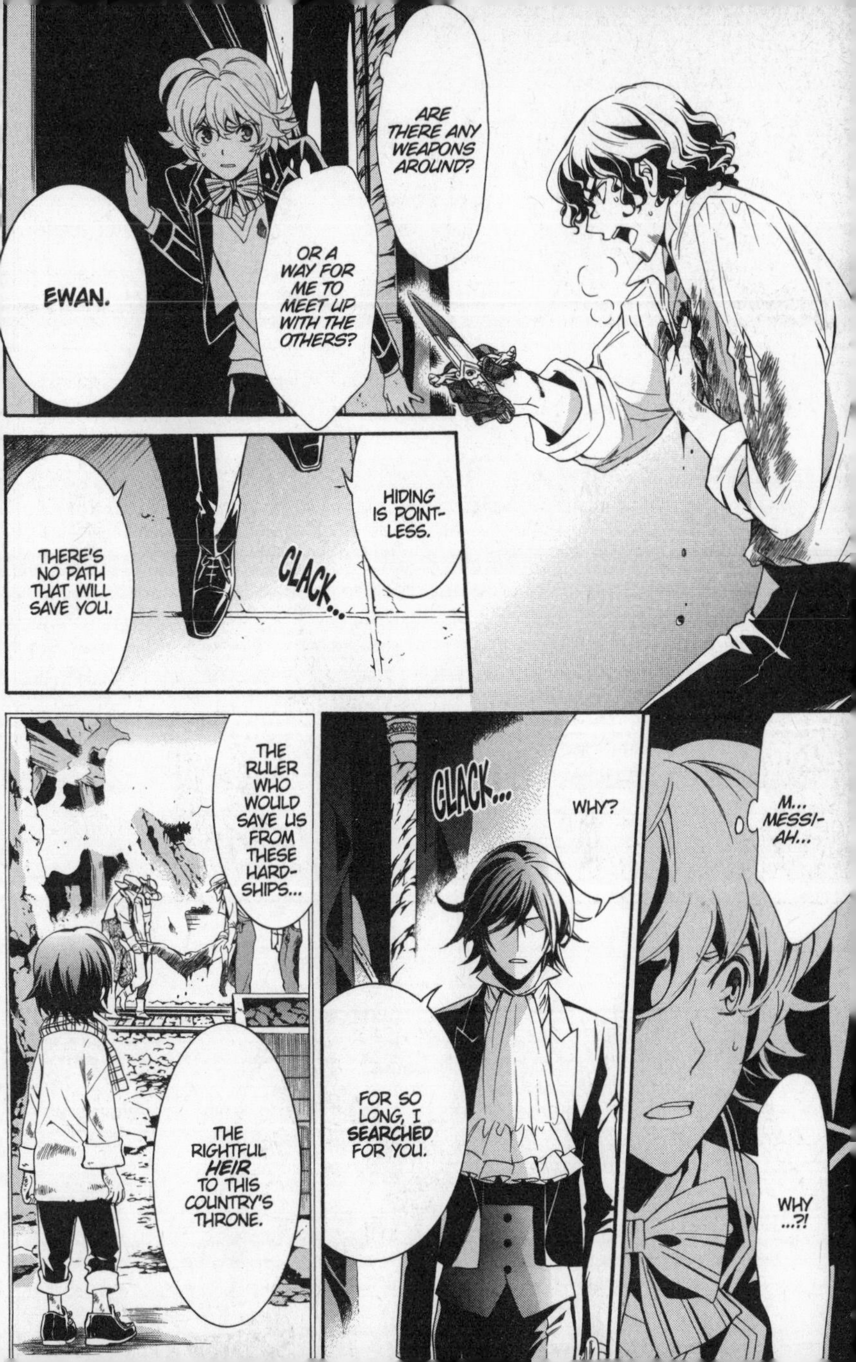
ARE THERE ANY WEAPONS AROUND?
OR A WAY FOR ME TO MEET UP WITH THE OTHERS?
EWAN.
HIDING IS POINT-LESS.
CLACK...
THERE'S NO PATH THAT WILL SAVE YOU.
M... MESSI-AH...
WHY ...?!
CLACK...
WHY?
FOR SO LONG, I SEARCHED FOR YOU.
THE RULER WHO WOULD SAVE US FROM THESE HARD-SHIPS...
THE RIGHTFUL HEIR TO THIS COUNTRY'S THRONE.

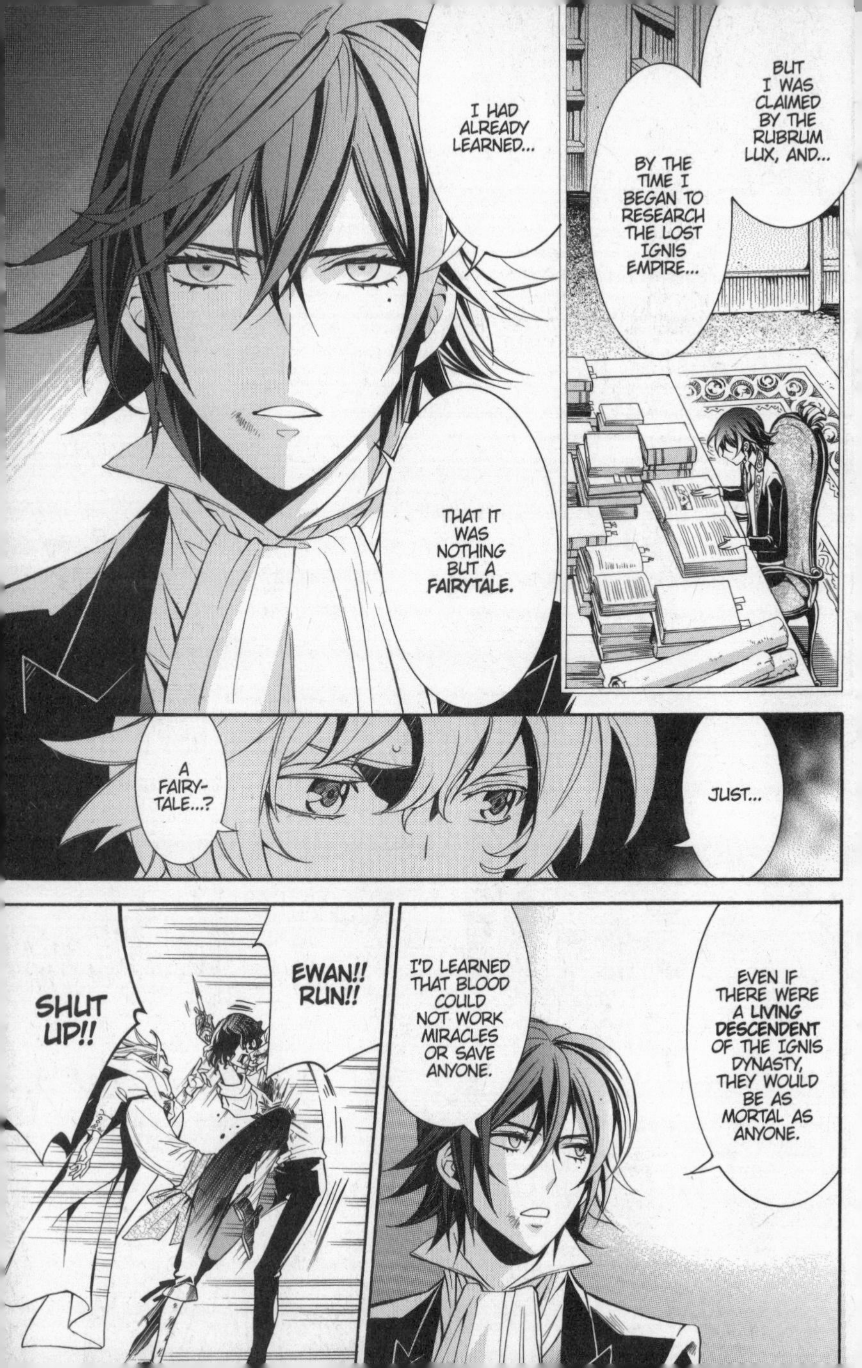
BUT I WAS CLAIMED BY THE RUBRUM LUX, AND...
BY THE TIME I BEGAN TO RESEARCH THE LOST IGNIS EMPIRE...
I HAD ALREADY LEARNED...
THAT IT WAS NOTHING BUT A FAIRYTALE.
JUST...
A FAIRY-TALE...?
EVEN IF THERE WERE A LIVING DESCENDENT OF THE IGNIS DYNASTY, THEY WOULD BE AS MORTAL AS ANYONE.
I'D LEARNED THAT BLOOD COULD NOT WORK MIRACLES OR SAVE ANYONE.
EWAN!! RUN!!
SHUT UP!!

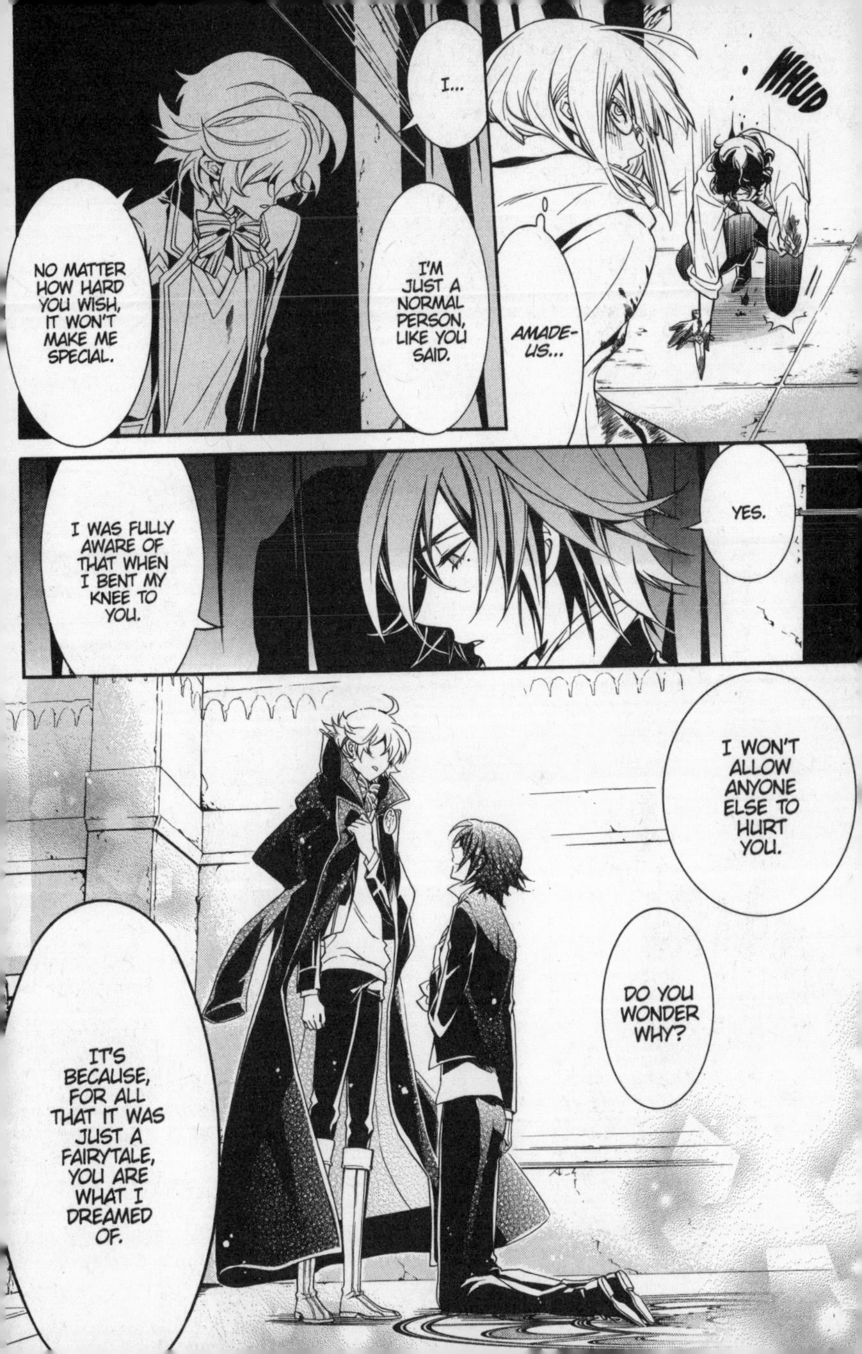
WHUD
AMADEUS...
I...
I'M JUST A NORMAL PERSON, LIKE YOU SAID.
NO MATTER HOW HARD YOU WISH, IT WON'T MAKE ME SPECIAL.
YES.
I WAS FULLY AWARE OF THAT WHEN I BENT MY KNEE TO YOU.
I WON'T ALLOW ANYONE ELSE TO HURT YOU.
DO YOU WONDER WHY?
IT'S BECAUSE, FOR ALL THAT IT WAS JUST A FAIRYTALE, YOU ARE WHAT I DREAMED OF.

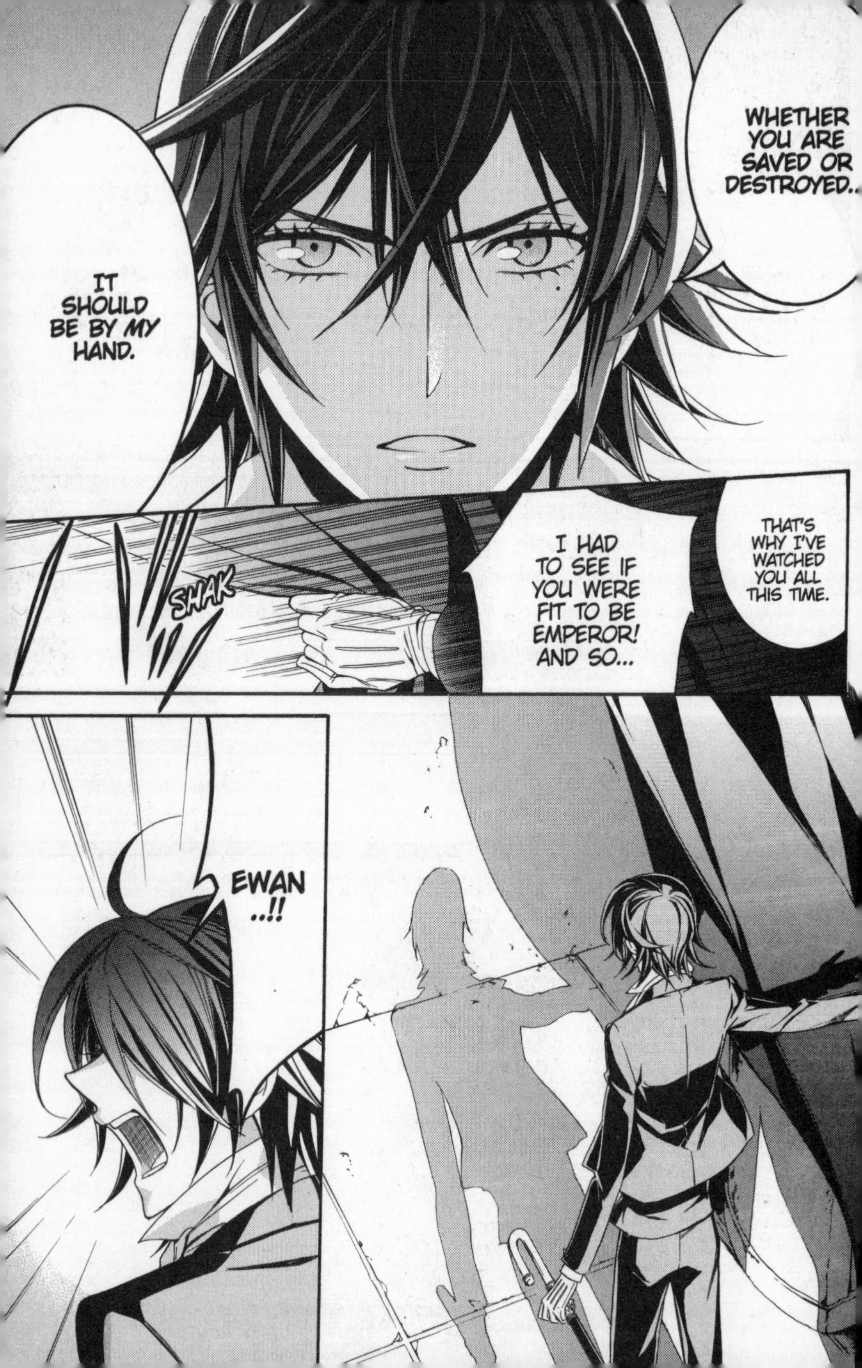
WHETHER YOU ARE SAVED OR DESTROYED..
IT SHOULD BE BY MY HAND.
THAT'S WHY I'VE WATCHED YOU ALL THIS TIME.
I HAD TO SEE IF YOU WERE FIT TO BE EMPEROR! AND SO...
SHAK
EWAN ..!!

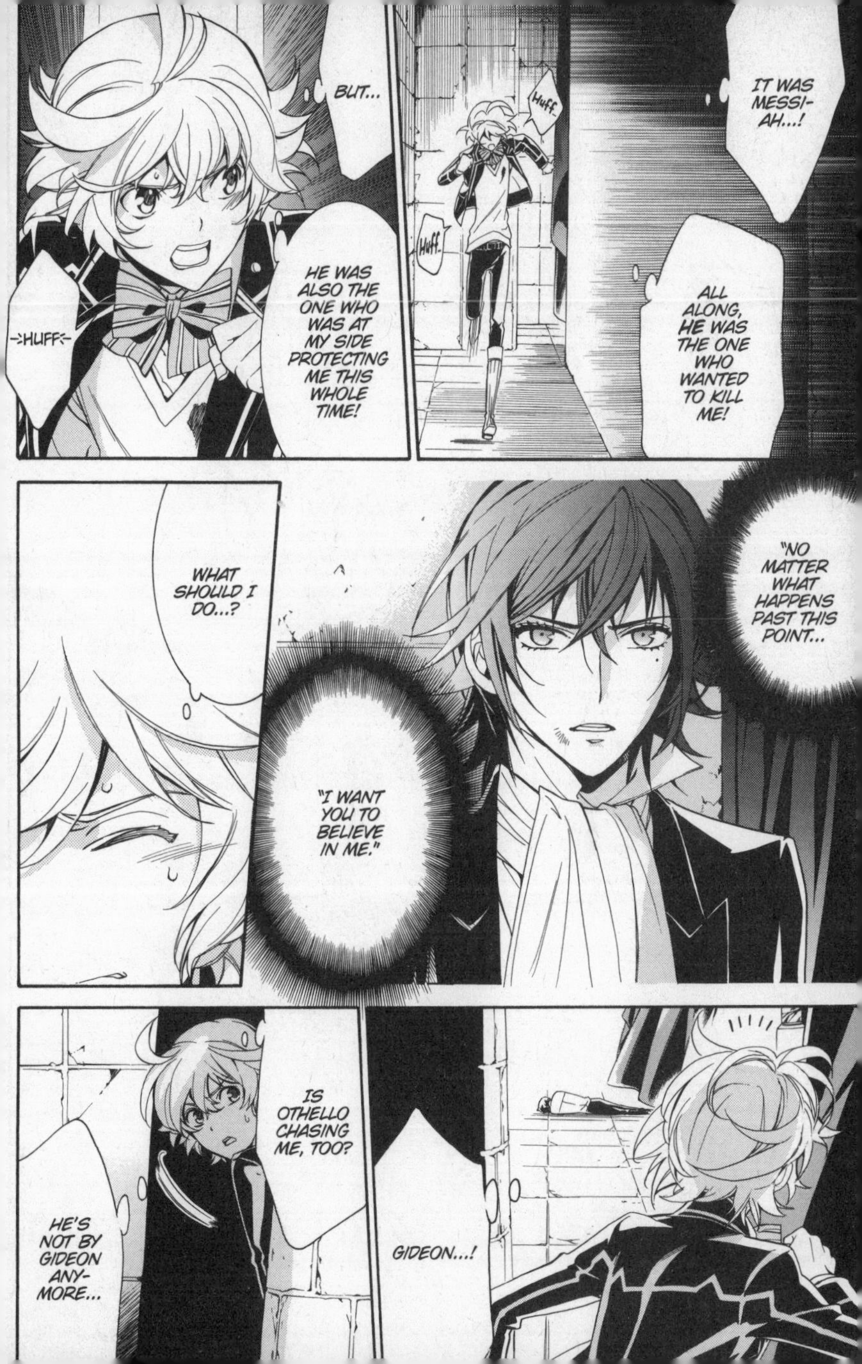
IT WAS MESSI-AH...!
Huff..
ALL ALONG, HE WAS THE ONE WHO WANTED TO KILL ME!
Huff..
BUT...
HE WAS ALSO THE ONE WHO WAS AT MY SIDE PROTECTING ME THIS WHOLE TIME!
HUFF
"NO MATTER WHAT HAPPENS PAST THIS POINT...
"I WANT YOU TO BELIEVE IN ME."
WHAT SHOULD I DO...?
GIDEON...!
IS OTHELLO CHASING ME, TOO?
HE'S NOT BY GIDEON ANY-MORE...

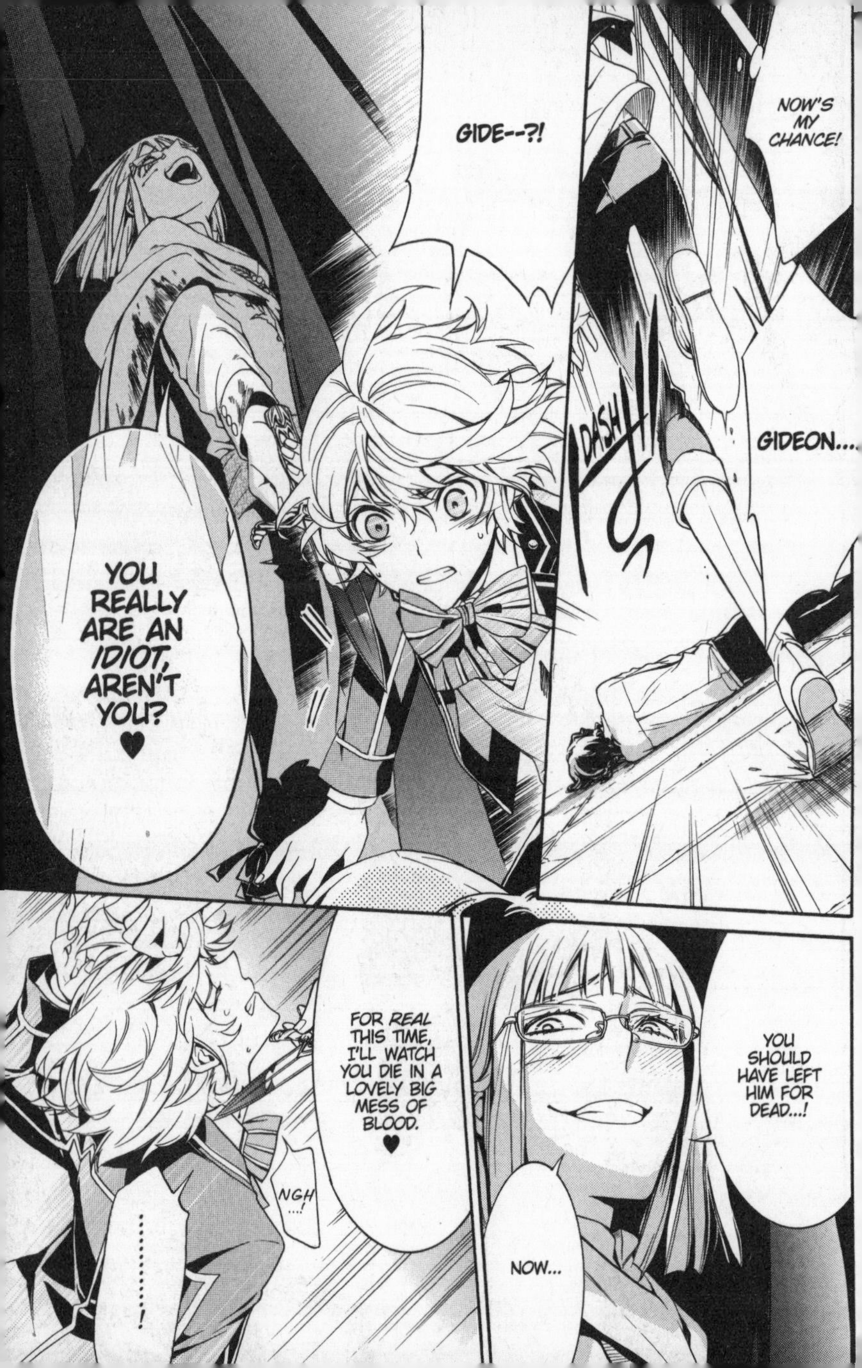
NOW'S MY CHANCE!
DASH
GIDEON....
GIDE--?!
YOU REALLY ARE AN *IDIOT*, AREN'T YOU? ♥
YOU SHOULD HAVE LEFT HIM FOR DEAD...!
NOW...
FOR *REAL* THIS TIME, I'LL WATCH YOU DIE IN A LOVELY BIG MESS OF BLOOD. ♥
NGH ....!
.........!

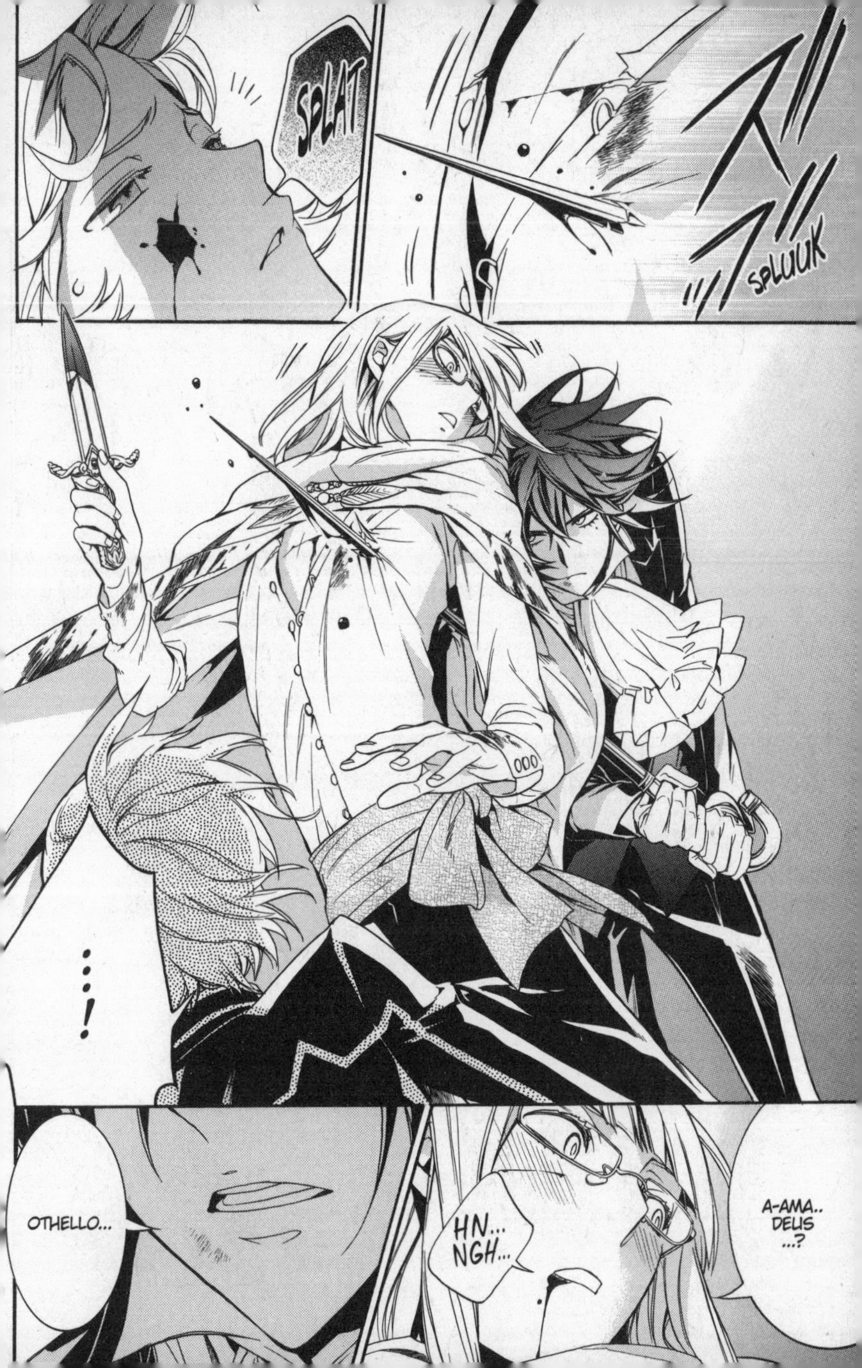

SPLUUK
SPLAT
...!
A-AMA.. DEUS ...?
HN... NGH...
OTHELLO...

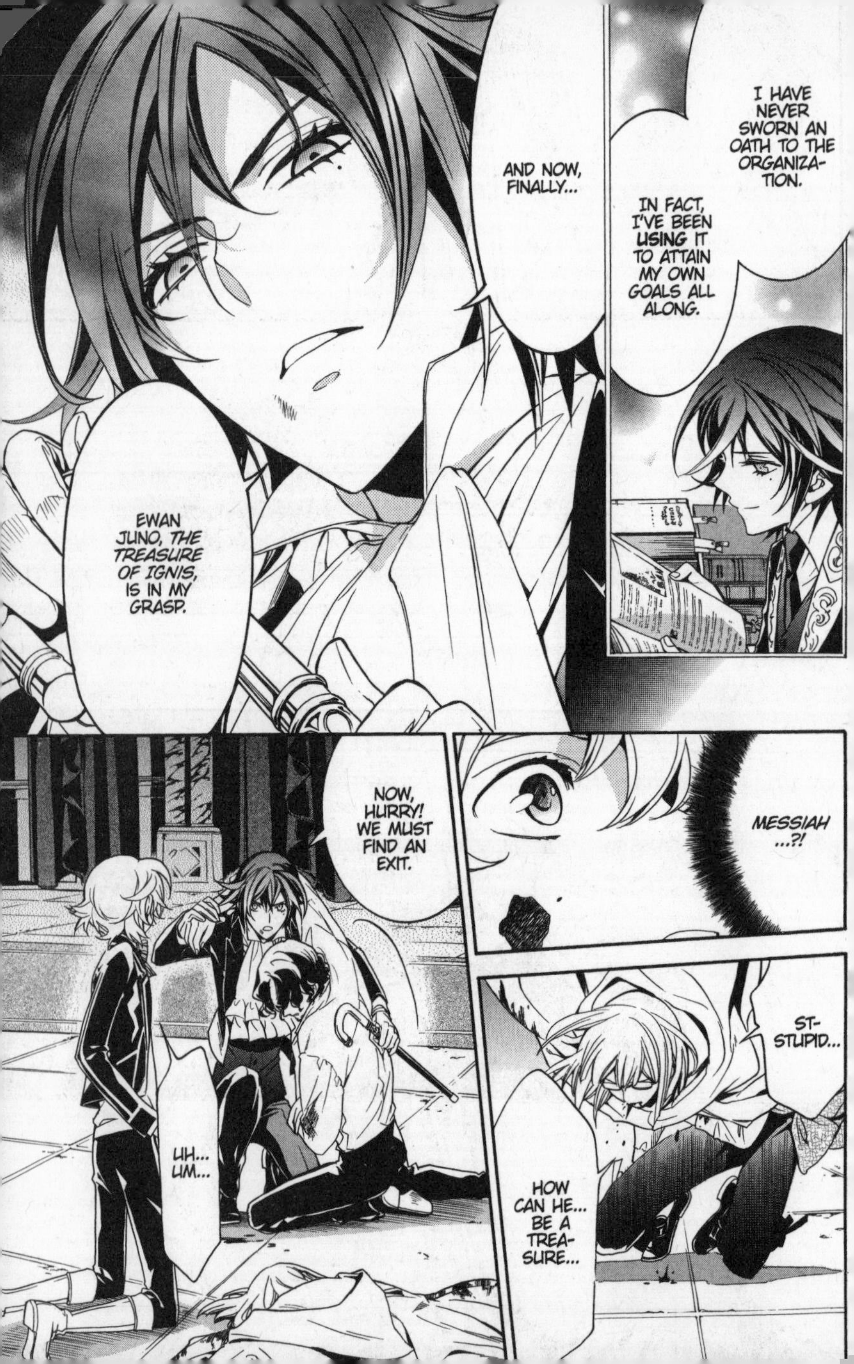
I HAVE NEVER SWORN AN OATH TO THE ORGANIZATION.
IN FACT, I'VE BEEN USING IT TO ATTAIN MY OWN GOALS ALL ALONG.
AND NOW, FINALLY...
EWAN JUNO, THE TREASURE OF IGNIS, IS IN MY GRASP.
MESSIAH ...?!
ST-STUPID...
HOW CAN HE... BE A TREASURE...
NOW, HURRY! WE MUST FIND AN EXIT.
UH... UM...

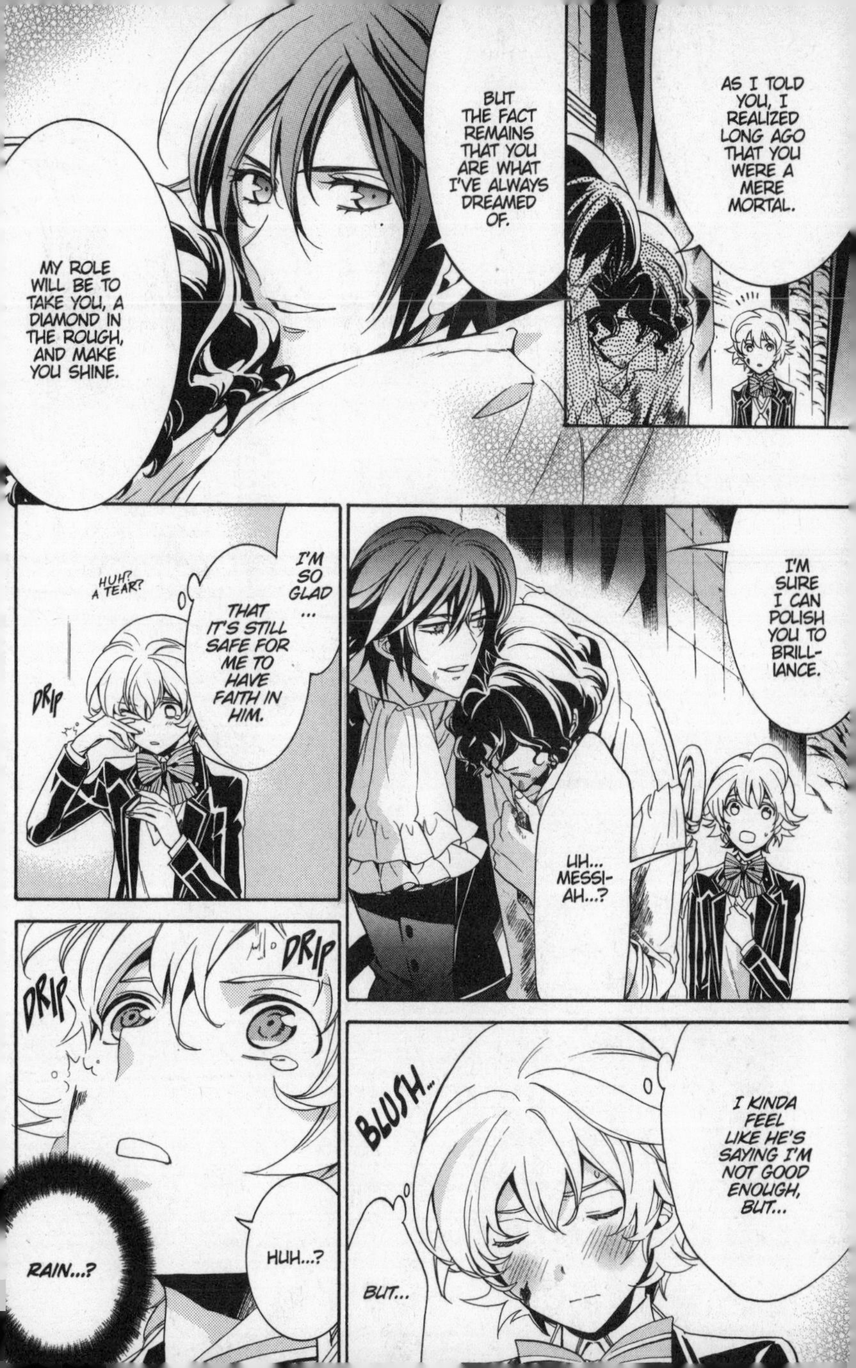
AS I TOLD YOU, I REALIZED LONG AGO THAT YOU WERE A MERE MORTAL.
BUT THE FACT REMAINS THAT YOU ARE WHAT I'VE ALWAYS DREAMED OF.
MY ROLE WILL BE TO TAKE YOU, A DIAMOND IN THE ROUGH, AND MAKE YOU SHINE.
I'M SURE I CAN POLISH YOU TO BRILL-IANCE.
UH... MESSI-AH...?
I'M SO GLAD...
THAT IT'S STILL SAFE FOR ME TO HAVE FAITH IN HIM.
HUH? A TEAR?
DRIP
I KINDA FEEL LIKE HE'S SAYING I'M NOT GOOD ENOUGH, BUT...
BLUSH...
BUT...
DRIP
DRIP
HUH...?
RAIN...?

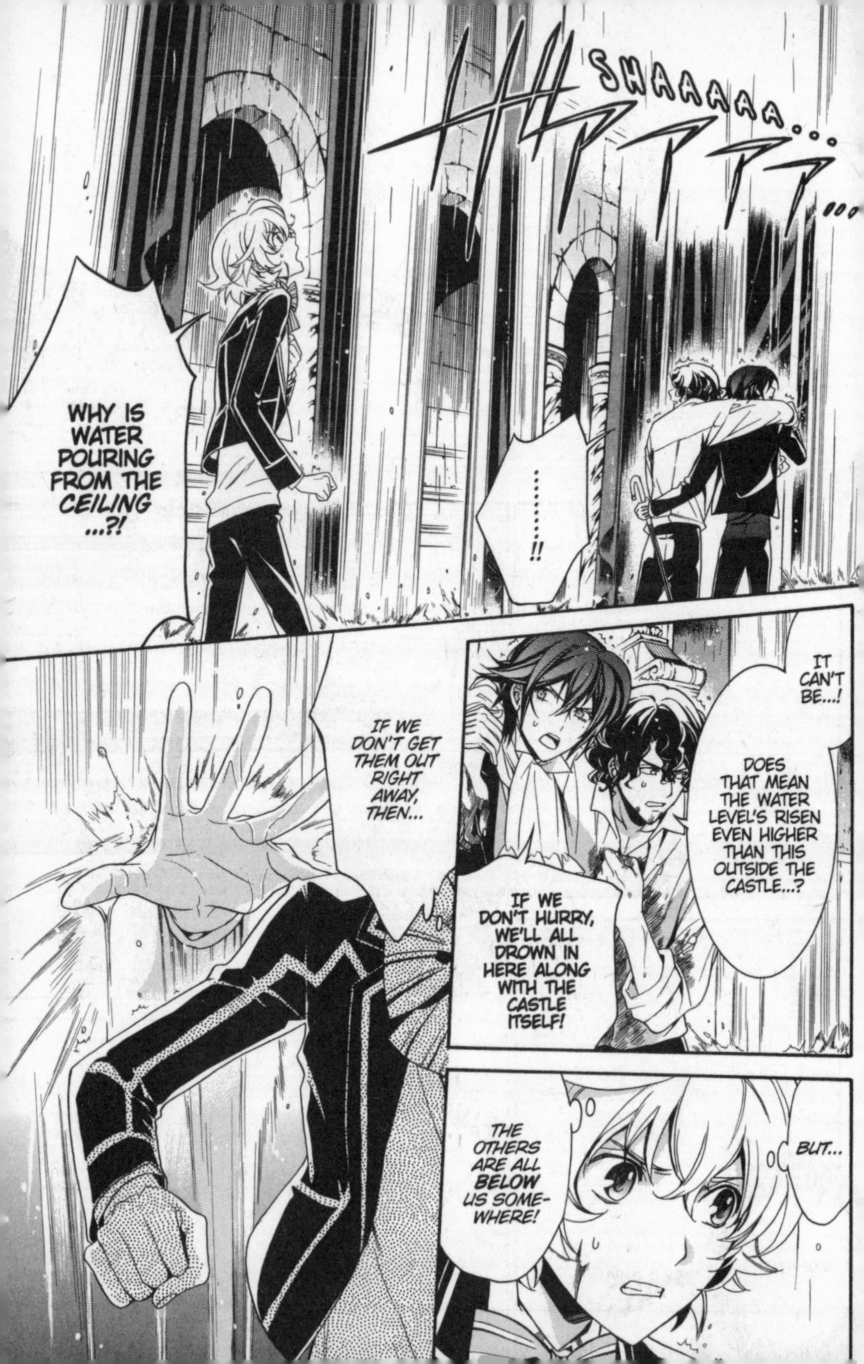
SHAAAAAA...
......!!
WHY IS WATER POURING FROM THE CEILING ...?!
IT CAN'T BE...!
DOES THAT MEAN THE WATER LEVEL'S RISEN EVEN HIGHER THAN THIS OUTSIDE THE CASTLE...?
IF WE DON'T HURRY, WE'LL ALL DROWN IN HERE ALONG WITH THE CASTLE ITSELF!
BUT...
THE OTHERS ARE ALL BELOW US SOME-WHERE!
IF WE DON'T GET THEM OUT RIGHT AWAY, THEN...

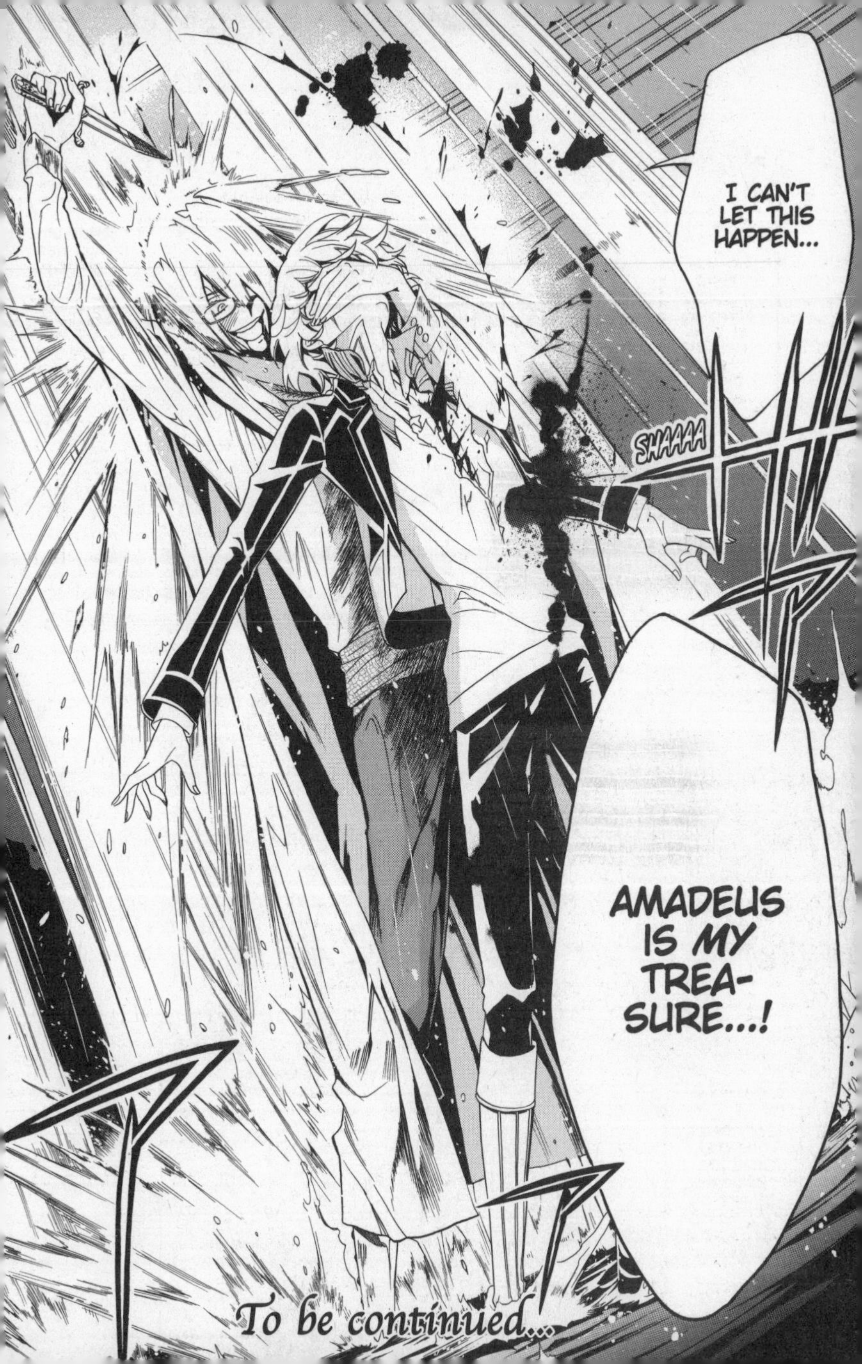
I CAN'T LET THIS HAPPEN...
SHAAAA
AMADEUS IS MY TREA-SURE...!
To be continued...

Bonus Manga!

The Dreamer of the Thousand-Year Labyrinth

Art: Atori
Story: Aikawa

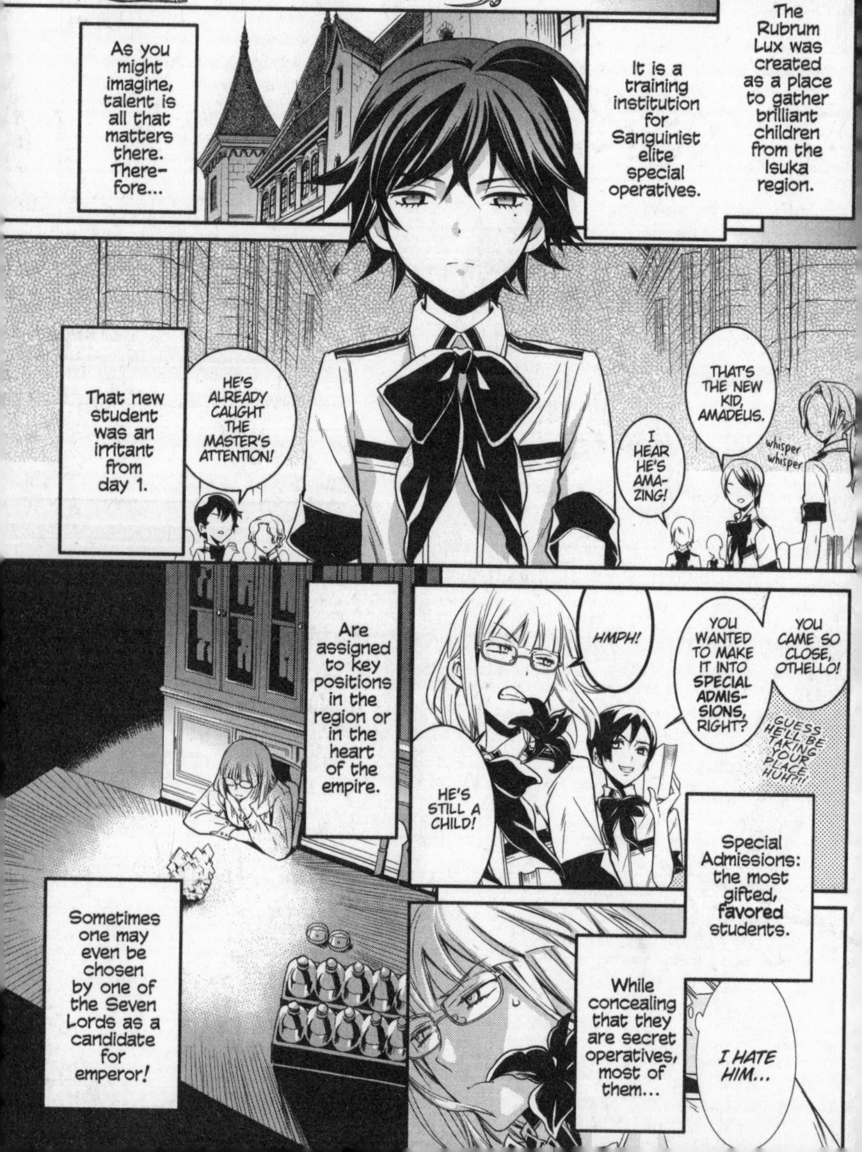

The Rubrum Lux was created as a place to gather brilliant children from the Isuka region.
It is a training institution for Sanguinist elite special operatives.
As you might imagine, talent is all that matters there. Therefore...
THAT'S THE NEW KID, AMADEUS.
whisper whisper
I HEAR HE'S AMAZING!
HE'S ALREADY CAUGHT THE MASTER'S ATTENTION!
That new student was an irritant from day 1.
YOU CAME SO CLOSE, OTHELLO!
GUESS HE'LL BE TAKING YOUR PLACE, HUH?!!
YOU WANTED TO MAKE IT INTO SPECIAL ADMISSIONS, RIGHT?
HMPH!
HE'S STILL A CHILD!
Special Admissions: the most gifted, favored students.
I HATE HIM...
While concealing that they are secret operatives, most of them...
Are assigned to key positions in the region or in the heart of the empire.
Sometimes one may even be chosen by one of the Seven Lords as a candidate for emperor!

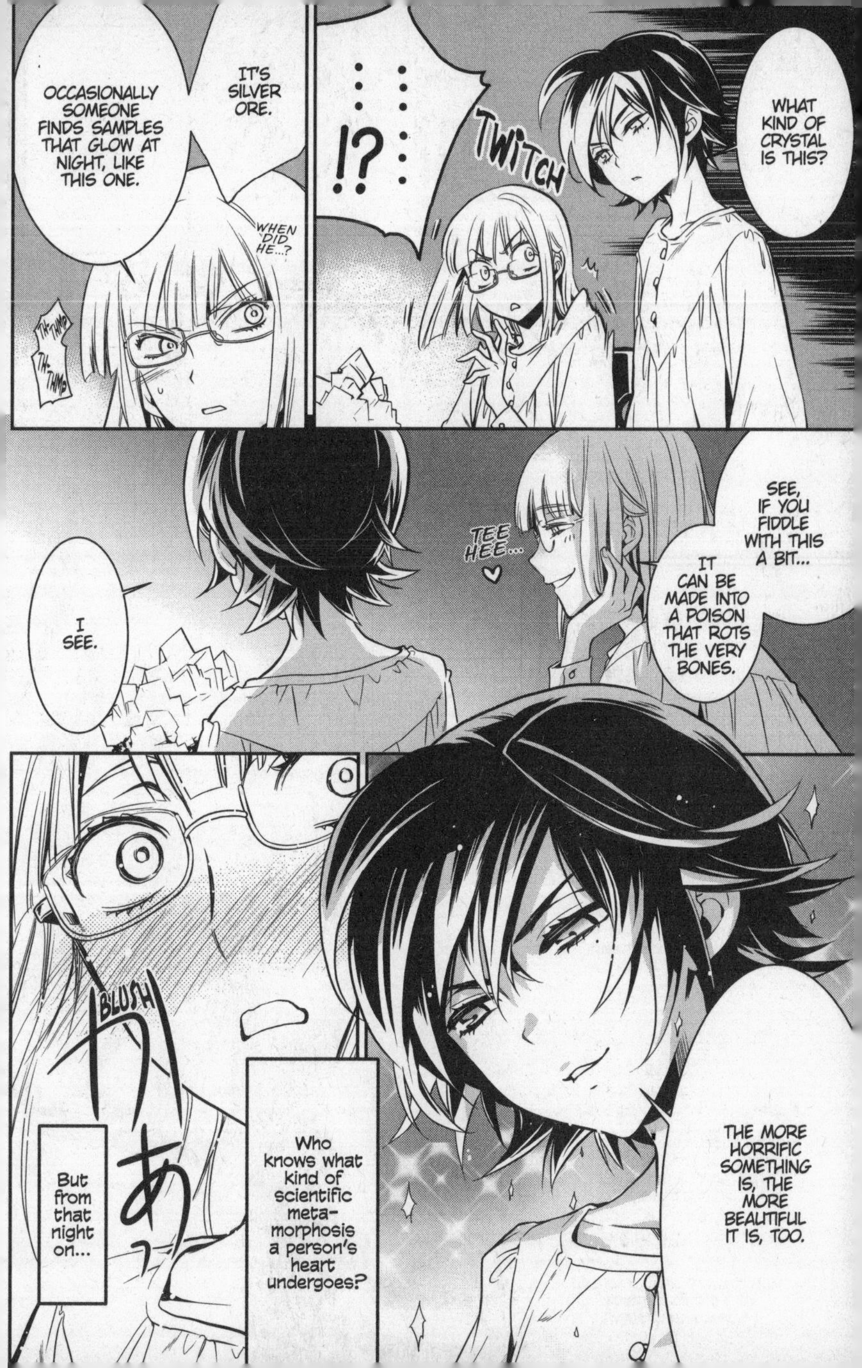
WHAT KIND OF CRYSTAL IS THIS?
TWITCH
!?
IT'S SILVER ORE.
OCCASIONALLY SOMEONE FINDS SAMPLES THAT GLOW AT NIGHT, LIKE THIS ONE.
WHEN DID HE...?
TH-THMP
TH-THMP
SEE, IF YOU FIDDLE WITH THIS A BIT...
IT CAN BE MADE INTO A POISON THAT ROTS THE VERY BONES.
TEE HEE...
I SEE.
THE MORE HORRIFIC SOMETHING IS, THE MORE BEAUTIFUL IT IS, TOO.
BLUSH
わあっ
Who knows what kind of scientific meta-morphosis a person's heart undergoes?
But from that night on...

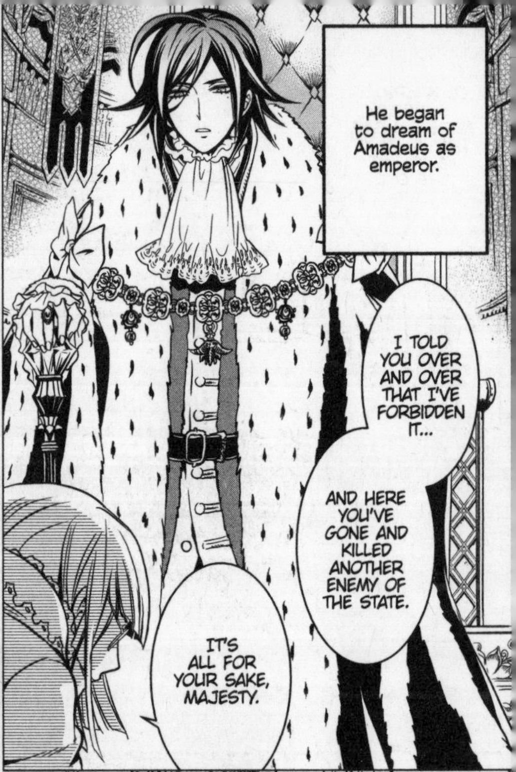
He began to dream of Amadeus as emperor.
I TOLD YOU OVER AND OVER THAT I'VE FORBIDDEN IT...
AND HERE YOU'VE GONE AND KILLED ANOTHER ENEMY OF THE STATE.
IT'S ALL FOR YOUR SAKE, MAJESTY.

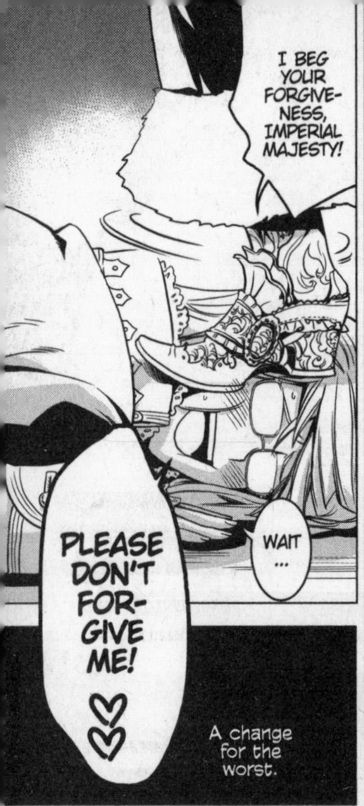
I BEG YOUR FORGIVENESS, IMPERIAL MAJESTY!
WAIT ...
PLEASE DON'T FORGIVE ME!
A change for the worst.

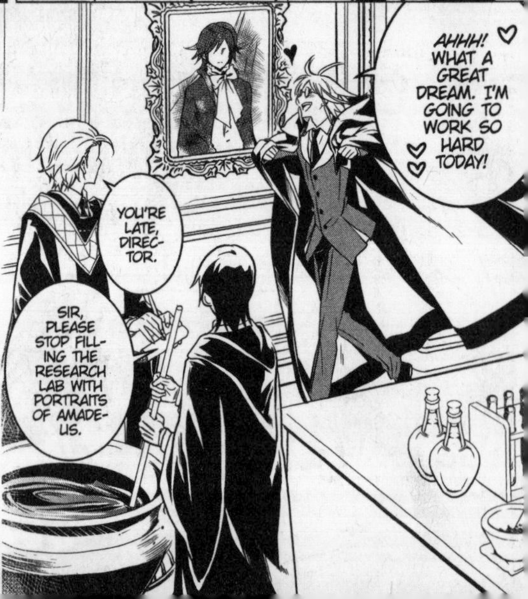
AHHH! WHAT A GREAT DREAM. I'M GOING TO WORK SO HARD TODAY!
YOU'RE LATE, DIRECTOR.
SIR, PLEASE STOP FILLING THE RESEARCH LAB WITH PORTRAITS OF AMADEUS.

Thank you for reading this far!
I'm cheering on the seven from behind the scenes!
(What's going to happen, hmm?) I have to work hard, too! I keep reminding myself of that.

Best wishes!!

花鶏ハル
Atori Haruno

Thank you for reading volume 3! It's weird, but I'm slowly starting to have a thing for characters with glasses. I hope you'll read the next installment!

Y. AIKAWA

(Twitter → @aikawayou)
↑ I do four-panel comics and stuff.

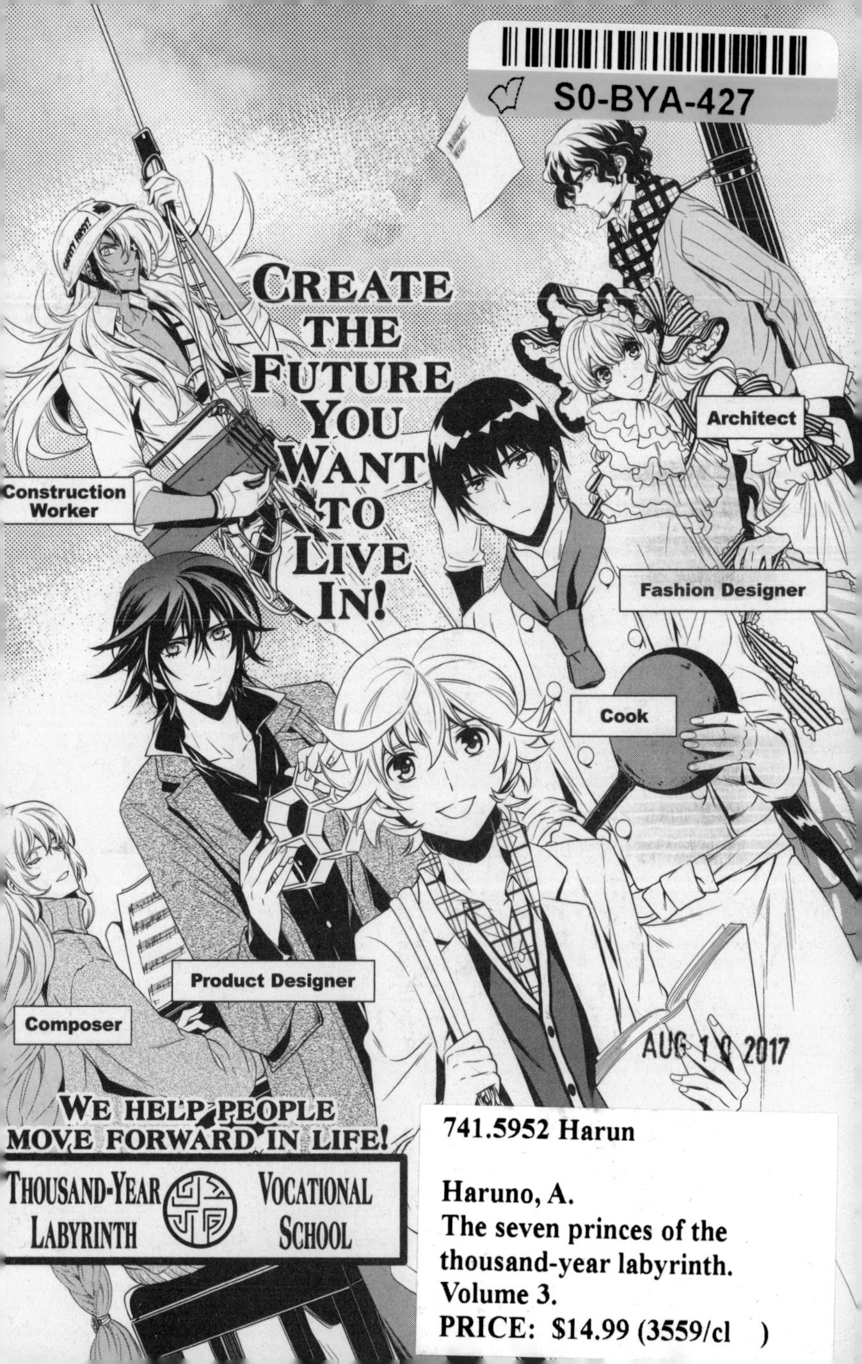
CREATE THE FUTURE YOU WANT TO LIVE IN!
Architect
Construction Worker
Fashion Designer
Cook
Product Designer
Composer
WE HELP PEOPLE MOVE FORWARD IN LIFE!
THOUSAND-YEAR LABYRINTH VOCATIONAL SCHOOL